THE CULTURAL
GUIDE
TO JEWISH
EUROPE

THE CULTURAL GUIDE
TO JEWISH EUROPE

SEUIL CHRONICLE

PUBLISHED WITH THE ASSISTANCE OF THE
JACQUES AND JACQUELINE LÉVY-WILLARD FOUNDATION.

JEAN-YVES CAMUS **Denmark**
Estonia
Finland
Latvia
Lithuania
Norway
Sweden
EMMANUEL HAYMANN **France**
FLORENCE LA BRUYÈRE **Hungary**
CHARLES LESSELBAUM **Spain**
Portugal
SANDRA LUMBROSO **Ireland**/Northern Ireland
KATINKA MEZEI **Austria**
ALAIN NAVARRO **Greece**
ELIE NICOLAS **France (Provence)**
EDGAR REICHMANN **Romania**
LUC ROSENZWEIG **Germany**
MARC SAGNOL **Belarus**
Poland
Russia
Ukraine
MARC SEMO **Italy**
The Czech Republic
Slovakia
Turkey
NICOLAS SHASHAHANI **Bosnia-Herzegovina**
Bulgaria
Croatia
Serbia and Montenegro
Slovenia
BRIGITTE SION **Switzerland**
CATHERINE TAYLOR **Belgium**
Great Britain
OLIVIA ZEMOR **The Netherlands**

WROTE THIS BOOK
WITH THE COLLABORATION OF DENIS AND ANNETTE LÉVY-WILLARD

Contents

Comment

F ROM GEOGRAPHICAL information to philosophical, social, and economic analyses or psychological
portraits, everything about this *Cultural Guide to
Jewish Europe* is superbly written and illustrated:
each place and its history, each community and its
destiny. Turning the pages, we go from one century
to the next, from one event to another, from history
ancient to contemporary. There are many shortcuts
but few omissions: Paris and the murder on the
Petit-Pont in 583; Amsterdam and the excommunication of Baruch Spinoza in 1656; the Jews of
Mainz and the Crusades; Abraham Senior the convert and Don Isaac Abravanel the exile in Catholic
Spain in 1492. This rich, useful book is packed
with dramatic tales and picturesque anecdotes.

This guide is not just for travelers.

ELIE WIESEL
New York, 2002

The terms in bold print are explained in the glossary on page 595.

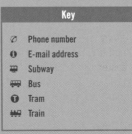

Key
⌀ Phone number
❶ E-mail address
🚇 Subway
🚌 Bus
🚋 Tram
🚂 Train

Introduction

VISITORS TO NOTRE-DAME CATHEDRAL IN PARIS are often unaware that the frieze on the Saint Anne portal, which relates the meeting between the future mother of the Virgin Mary and her husband-to-be, Saint Joachim, is also a moving image of Jewish life in Paris in the Middle Ages. The anonymous twelfth-century sculptor has in effect taken Jews with their long robes and pointed hats as his model to represent the inhabitants of the Holy Land prior to the coming of Christ.

Judaism has profoundly marked the history of the Old Continent. Representations of this culture are in evidence everywhere throughout Europe. It is a heritage that offers much to appreciate if one is prepared to make the effort. Jewish Europe remains forgotten, overlooked by tourist circuits, with the exception of only a few famous must-sees such as the old Jewish quarter of Prague, the synagogues of Venice's ghetto, or the old *judería* in Toledo. And yet there are many handsome old synagogues to be seen in the small towns of Piedmont, Provence, and Alsace, and eastern Europe—the Czech Republic, Poland (especially Kraków and surrounding areas), Romania, Ukraine, and Belarus—has some magnificent temples. Some of them are neglected, but more and more, they are being restored. The narrow streets of the Jewish quarters in small towns and villages—the old **shtetlach**—testify to life in this Yiddishland that was destroyed by the *Shoah*. Often little known, these places speak of a history that is the same and yet so different from the one recalled by the commemorative plaques on the sites of the death camps, the ghettos, or the transit areas: the systematic, planned extermination of six million Jews. This *Cultural Guide to Jewish Europe* sets out to fill the gap. And while it is intended for anyone who wants to find out more about that history and discover its traces, this book could never have given a voice to all those old stones without the strong ties linking it to the Jewish communities living in these towns and countries today.

"The greatest danger is not forgetting what happened in the past but forgetting the essential: how the past happened." These words, spoken by Yosif Hayim Yerushalmi, the author of a key work on Jewish history and memory entitled *Zakhor* (Remember), recall the great biblical imperative. This key obligation is as pertinent as ever. While this book was never meant to be a history of European Judaism, it was nonetheless vital to contextualize Jewish heritage in order to give eloquence to its testimony and to revive a memory that is innately shifting, vulnerable, and subjective.

This book would have been impossible to write ten years ago. Today, there is a marked renewal of interest in the Jewish past of Europe. Everywhere, books and guides are being published. In Italy, Paris, and Berlin new museums have opened, telling us about this world that was swept away by the *Shoah* just as its last survivors are leaving us. This praiseworthy effort, this rehabilitation and recreation of memory, has taken an especially remarkable form in the German capital. The synagogue on

Oranienburgerstrasse, which was spared during Kristallnacht but bombed in 1943, has been restored, and local initiatives are multiplying and plaques are going up on buildings recalling the names of the Jewish residents who were sent to the camps. The fall of the Wall has given fresh impetus to this process of rehabilitation, allowing memories stifled by fifty years of Communism to breathe again. Whereas researchers like the Czech Jiri Fiedler once had to work in semisecrecy in order to draw up the inventory of this endangered heritage, today their work is published and recognized. In Poland there is real debate about the past and about the horrors of anti-Semitism, a scourge that continued even after the war when virtually the entire Jewish population had been wiped out. The role of the Jews in the history and culture of European nations is now being given full consideration. From America, initiatives, aid, and rabbis themselves are helping to bring back a Jewish presence in towns and villages that were once important centers of **Hasidism.**

The Cultural Guide to Jewish Europe has of course drawn on this resurgence and on the many new publications. But in some cases, such as Ukraine, Russia, and the Baltic states, it is also a pathfinder. It is designed to accompany travelers as a supplement to more traditional publications, hence our determination to fit everything into one handy volume. This has meant making some drastic and sometimes heartrending choices. Since we could not include everything, we decided to give priority to places that were centers of Jewish culture and to those where there is still something to see.

We also had to delimit our geographical scope. How far does Europe extend? We have taken it in its basic, geographical sense: from the Atlantic to the Ural Mountains—in other words, including Russia and Ukraine, whose Jewish community of half a million men and women is second only to that of France. And Turkey, too, or at least its European part with Istanbul, has also been included because the history of the Jews in that country, most of whom came from Spain in the fifteenth century, is inseparable from that of their brothers and sisters in the Balkans, who, like them, prospered for centuries under the protection of the Ottoman sultans.

Another question concerned the mode of classification. Logical though it may seem, taking the countries in simple alphabetical order raised some problems. The centuries-old history of Jewish communities does not fit easily with the current frontiers of Europe's nation-states, especially those in the center and to the east, most of which came into being at the end of the nineteenth century or after World War I. Consequently, we decided to divide up the continent into broad geographical zones (northwest Europe, southwest Europe, central Europe, southeast Europe, eastern Europe, and northern Europe), which more or less correspond to the territories of the great empires.

In the course of this tormented history punctuated by shifting frontiers, the names of towns and villages have changed countless times. We use the present-day names, except where custom preserves an older one.

A guidebook is by definition open-ended, in permanent evolution. The phone numbers that we provide were updated just before going to press. Nevertheless, some of them have already changed. Many of the sites we refer to can be visited only after prior appointment, and security measures are likely to be reinforced in the coming years. In case of uncertainty about a phone number, address, or access for visitors, it is always advisable to contact the local Jewish community, which will be happy to give you needed information and share its historical heritage. These communities were of great help to us in writing this book, and for that we thank them once again.

MARC SEMO

Northwest Europe

France

THE HISTORY OF JEWISH COMMUNITIES IN FRANCE is characterized by a remarkable diversity, both historically and regionally. It would be futile to look for a coherent identity or shared experiences that would link the communities that were "taxed to the hilt" by the monarchy in the heartlands of the kingdom (Paris, Rouen) to the "rich hours" of the **Sephardim** in the Comtat Venaissin (Carpentras, Cavaillon), or the village communities of Alsace (Marmoutier, Bischheim). The distinctive destiny of Judaism in each of these major regions was the result of specific political events and historical circumstances.

In 70 C.E., after the destruction of the Temple in Jerusalem, the Roman emperor Vespasian II filled three boats with prisoners and abandoned them to the waves. The first one ran aground at Arles, the second at Bordeaux, and the third, which sailed up the Rhone, at Lyon. This is how, it is said, the kernels of Gaul's first Jewish communities came to be.

These communities had their golden age. In the eleventh century, Champagne was lit up by the presence and influence of Rashi in Troyes. A rabbi but also a judge and commentator on the Bible

Synagogue, Avignon.

Bible, Lorraine/Franche-Comté, 1286. Bibliothèque Nationale de France, Paris.

and the **Talmud,** he remains one of the great figures of Judaism, and his works are still the object of enthusiastic study today.

Under the reign of Charles VI, the population complained of crushing taxes. It vented its anger on the Jews, holding them responsible for every ill, and sacked many of their houses. Not long afterward, on 3 November 1394, the king put an end to the disorder by expelling the Jews from his lands. This decision sounded the death knell for any viable Jewish presence in the French kingdom, and so it remained until the Revolution.

In January 1790, the "Portuguese" Jews of southern France made representations to the Constituent Assembly. They were heard and granted French citizenship. The communities of Alsace-Lorraine did not gain this privilege until September

1791. In an effort to impose some kind of organization on this multifaceted community, Napoleon assembled the rabbis and lay leaders in a "Great Sanhedrin." One of the important tasks for this assembly was to "persuade Israelites to view military service as a sacred duty." At the same time, the emperor created a central Jewish consistory, which continues to preside over the religious life of French Jews to this day.

The Israelite religion was given official recognition in 1831, and from that date its ministers were paid out of the public purse, a situation that endured until the separation of church and state in 1905 but which has survived in the "concordatory departments" of eastern France (which were occupied by the Germans from 1870 to 1918). The movement for Jewish emancipation began to get

Synagogue on Rue Notre-Dame-de-Nazareth, *late nineteenth century. Private collection, Paris.*

under way in the mid-nineteenth century. Jews started to gain admission to the Institut de France, the Collège de France, and the Parliament. Communities built their synagogues in a neo-Romanesque style with a touch of orientalism. But the period also saw the rise of the political anti-Semitism championed by Édouard Dumont. This was at its most strident during the Dreyfus Affair, which divided the country from 1894 to 1906.

In the twentieth century, immigration from eastern Europe changed the face of French Judaism. During the dark years of the Nazi occupation, some 76,000 of the 300,000 Jews living in France were killed in the death camps. After the war, the arrival of Jews from North Africa instilled a new vitality in the community. In the absence of reliable statistics, the number of Jews in France today is estimated at between 600,000 and 700,000, half of whom live in and around Paris.

→ **To call France from the United States, dial 011 33** followed by the number of the person you are calling minus the initial 0 (used only for domestic calls).

Paris
and Surrounding Areas ■

Paris

In 1182, King Philippe Auguste decided to expel the Jews from the capital. Synagogues were converted into churches and buildings owned by Jews were sold, with proceeds going to the Crown. The sovereign used the sums thus amassed to build the keep of the castle at Vincennes and to put a wall around the nearby woods. Within Paris itself he built a market in the now deserted Champeaux quarter that became known as Les Halles. Thus the creation of the capital's famous old market (itself transferred to the suburbs in the 1970s) originated with the expulsion of the Jews.

Seventeen years later, however, those expelled Jews were called back to the capital. They settled in the Saint-Bont quarter (near today's Pompidou Center), on Rue des Roslers, and on the Left Bank between Rue de la Harpe and Boulevard Saint-Germain. Indeed, the latter zone constituted the biggest *juiverie* (Jewry) of the day, as evidenced by the large medieval Jewish cemetery brought to light in the last century during construction work in the area. In the

MURDER ON THE PETIT-PONT

One Saturday morning in the year 583, a Jew wearing his prayer shawl was crossing the Seine to go to the synagogue on the Île de la Cité. His name was Priscus, and he was the moneylender to the Merovingian king Chilperic I. As he was walking along the Petit-Pont, a renegade Jew, Phatir, threw himself on him and stabbed him to death. As related in Gregory of Tours's *History of the Franks,* this crime constitutes the first historically confirmed event in the history of Parisian Jewry.

thirteenth century, under the authority of Rabbi Yehiel, the Jewish School of Paris enjoyed great prestige. On 6 June 1242, after a theological disputation between the rabbi and Nicolas Donin, an apostate Jew, Saint Louis ordered that all the copies of the **Talmud** found in the city be burned at the Place de Grève (today's Place de l'Hôtel de Ville). Rabbi Yehiel left France for good and founded a new school at Acre (today's Akko). In 1394, Charles VI promulgated a decree prohibiting Jews from living in Paris. It was not until the Enlightenment, nearly four centuries later, that they were allowed back into the city.

King of Judah, *Gallery of Kings, Notre-Dame Cathedral. Musée national du Moyen Âge des Thermes de Cluny, Paris.*

THE ÎLE DE LA CITÉ

■ The sculptures on the Saint Anne portal of Notre-Dame Cathedral (Notre-Dame de Paris) offer one of the most moving testimonies we have to medieval Judaism. The frieze in question, just above the doorway, dates from the late twelfth century. It represents the Virgin's mother, Saint Anne, meeting her future husband, Saint Joachim. The unknown artist used Parisian Jews as his models in order to represent these early Christians. The men have the long robes and pointed hats worn by Jews in medieval times.

The left-hand side illustrates Anne and Joachim's wedding. Wrapped in his prayer shawl, the rabbi stands between the betrothed, whom he takes by the hand. All the details here

evoke the atmosphere of a Parisian synagogue. The artist has painstakingly sculpted the arks, the eternal lamp, and the piles of books that are so characteristic of Jewish life.

The iconography in the center is purely Christian: an angel announces the coming birth of Mary to the barren couple.

On the right, Anne and Joachim are taking their offerings to the synagogue. On the altar is a **Torah** scroll. The end of the frieze depicts two Jews in conversation. These stone figures convey images of Judaism from ancient times.

On the two central buttresses on the main facade, notice the niche on the right housing *The Vanquished Synagogue,* an allegorical statue by Fromanger depicting the eyes covered by a snake, a broken scepter, and crown trodden underfoot. The pendant statue on the left is *The Church Triumphant* by Geoffroy Dechaume. These sculptures were made during the restoration work undertaken by Viollet-le-Duc in the nineteenth century, replacing the original sculptures destroyed during the Revolution.

Just above them, the Gallery of Kings represents twenty-eight kings of Judah and Israel who, according to Christian tradition, were the ancestors of Jesus. In 1977, 364 fragments of sculptures from Notre-Dame that had been smashed during the Revolution were found during work on Rue de la Chaussée d'Antin. Although no traces of the Vanquished Synagogue were found, twenty-one of the twenty-eight heads of the kings of Judah and Israel were discovered. These are on display at the Cluny Museum (Musée national du Moyen Âge des Thermes de Cluny).

[Notre-Dame de Paris: 10, parvis Notre Dame, 75005 Paris. ✆ 0142345610. Crypt: Open Mon–Sat 9:30 A.M.–3:45 P.M., Sun 2:30–5:30 P.M. Closed some public holidays. Towers: ✆ 0153100700. Open Oct 1–Mar 31, daily 10 A.M.– 4:45 P.M.; Apr–Jun and Sep, daily 9:30 A.M.–6:45 P.M.; Jul–Aug, Mon–Fri 9 A.M.–6:45 P.M., Sat–Sun 9:00 A.M.–10:15 P.M. Closed Jan 1, May 1, Dec 1, Dec 25. 🚇 Cité.]

[Musée National du Moyen Âge des Thermes de Cluny: 6, place Paul Painlevé, 75005 Paris. ✆ 0153737800 or 0153737830 (group reservations). Open Wed–Mon 9:15 A.M.–5:45 P.M. 🚇 Cluny-Saint-Michel.]

THE MARAIS

In the eighteenth century, the area around the Place Saint-Paul was known as "the old Jewry." Until the first years of the twentieth century, the square itself bore the name Place des Juifs. The narrow streets here are best explored on a Sunday morning, when everyday Jewish life has resumed after the **Shabbat**.

■ Rue Pavée is a few yards from the Saint-Paul métro station. This is the *pletzel,* which is **Yiddish** for small square. In this street, which runs perpendicular to Rue des Rosiers, stands a surprising registered historical building in the "nouille" (noodle)

The synagogue on Rue Pavée, Paris.

style. This is the synagogue designed in 1913 by Hector Guimard, then the leading exponent of Art Nouveau, who is responsible for Paris's famous métro entrances.

[Agoudas Hakehilos Synagogue: 10, rue Pavée, 75004 Paris. ✆ 0148872154. Open Mon–Thu and occasionally Sun 10 A.M.–noon. Call for admission. 🚇 Saint-Paul.]

■ Jews have lived on Rue des Rosiers since the Middle Ages. When Charles VI expelled them from his kingdom, the street fell empty—or so it seemed. That the newly emancipated Jews came back to live in this same street after the French Revolution, some 400 years later, has led historians to suggest that Jewish families went on living here in secret during the intervening centuries. Thus, when the edict was revoked, it was natural for many of the returning Jews to join fellow believers.

🕎 ANOTHER WORLD

"You cross the bridge, turn right behind the Hôtel de Ville, and there you are in another world. The street is too narrow, the houses too tall, and all of them cracked. Between the shops you glimpse gloomy courtyards with gloomy lights at the back. There are Hebrew words on the posters, on the signs, and even on the labels of the bottles in the wine merchant's window. The secondhand man buys up old newspapers, rags, crusts of bread, metals, and tailors' and cap-makers' offcuts."
EDMOND FLEG, *L'ENFANT PROPHÈTE* (THE CHILD PROPHET) (PARIS: GALLIMARD, 1926)

In all likelihood an oratory was built on the upper floor at 17 Rue des Rosiers a few years before the French Revolution. Unfortunately, the relevant archives were destroyed during the Nazi occupation.

Today, in spite of its many luxury stores, Rue des Rosiers remains an important center of Parisian Jewish life with its bookstores, restaurants, and other typical emporia.

[Bibliophane Bookstore: 26 rue des Rosiers, 75004 Paris. ✆ 0148878220. Open Mon–Thu 10 A.M.–7 P.M., Fri 10 A.M.–4 P.M., Sun 10 A.M.–8 P.M.]
[Diasporama (Jewish art and music, religious articles, etc.): 29 rue des Rosiers, 75004 Paris. ✆ 0142783050. Open Sun–Thu 10:30 A.M.–7 P.M., Fri 10:30 A.M.–5 P.M., 🚇 Saint-Paul.]

■ Be sure to visit Jo Goldenberg, the legendary restaurant and delicatessen for Parisian **Ashkenazic** society. The menu features all the old classics such as goose leg, goulash, Russian-style raw sauerkraut, and other old-time specialties that will delight those who hanker after the **shtetl** experience.

[Jo Goldenberg: 7 rue des Rosiers, 75004 Paris. ✆ 0148872016. Open daily 8:30 A.M.–midnight (delicatessen: 8:30 A.M.–11 P.M.)]
[Le Café des Rosiers: 2 rue des Rosiers, 75004 Paris. ✆ 0148879409. Open Mon–Sat 8 A.M.–8 P.M.]

[Sacha Finkelsztajn: 27 rue des Rosiers, 75004 Paris. ✆ 0142727891.
Open Wed–Mon 10 A.M.–2 P.M. and 3–7 P.M.
🚇 Saint-Paul.]

■ Many Jewish moneylenders lived on Rue des Écouffes. In Old French, *escouffe* was the word for a bird of prey, the kite, which was the symbol for pawnbrokers. The street name thus recalls the financial professions to which Jews were limited by the authorities.

■ Until the beginning of the twentieth century, Rue Ferdinand-Duval was called "Rue des Juifs" (Street of the Jews). Realizing that this moniker might be offensive, City Hall renamed it "Ferdinand Duval," after a prefect of Paris.

[Suzanne (Jewish bazaar): 14 rue Ferdinand-Duval, 75004 Paris. ✆ 0148873484.
Open Mon–Sat 9:30 A.M.–7 P.M.]

■ The Hôtel de Saint-Aignan, a superb seventeenth-century mansion, now houses the Museum of Jewish Art and History (Musée d'Art et d'Histoire du Judaïsme) remarkable both for its collections and for its ambition. The museum is the fruit of a three-way cooperation between the City of Paris, the Culture Ministry, and community institutions.

Items amassed by the conductor Isaac Strauss in the nineteenth century form the basis of the museum's collection. Like his Viennese namesakes, the French Strauss composed waltzes that were popular with Second Empire society. His success soon reached beyond French Second Empire ballrooms and, on his travels

Édouard Moyse, The Great Sanhedrin, *1867. Musée d'Art et d'Histoire du Judaïsme, Paris*

around Europe, this keen student of Jewish history set out to acquire ritual objects from every period. In 1890 his remarkable collection was bought by Baroness Nathaniel de Rothschild, who donated it to the state. The museum also houses the objects formerly exhibited at the Musée d'art juif. Now closed, this museum was established in Montmartre at the end of World War II and contained wooden models of Polish synagogues made by students of the ORT trade school. In addition, the new museum has the collections of the Consistory of Paris (**Torah** crown, Galicia, 1810) and those of the Fondation du judaïsme français, plus its own acquisitions (*The Jewish Cemetery,* a painting by Samuel Hirszenberg from 1892).

The visit starts on the first floor with the fundamental texts and symbolic objects. The rooms that follow reveal the diverse facets of Judaism. The medieval Jewries are represented by tombstones discovered in the nineteenth century when Boulevard Saint-Germain was built. Italy and its ghettos are represented by liturgical furniture (a circumcision chair *[kisei shel Eliyahu]* from the early eighteenth century), silverware, and embroidery. Amsterdam, London, and Bordeaux are evoked by objects and prints (a painting by Jean Lubin Vauzelle of the synagogue at Bordeaux, 1812) that exemplify integration of the Jews cast out of Spain. Considerable space is

devoted as well to the celebrations that punctuate the Jewish year: **Purim** rolls, **Hanukkah** lamps, a nineteenth-century Austrian **sukkah** decorated with a view of Jerusalem.

Two sections, The Traditional **Ashkenazic** World and The Traditional **Sephardic** World, offer overall artistic and religious views of these two main ritual communities. A sequence entitled "Emancipation: The French model" offers a historical vision from the French Revolution onward (an 1867 painting by Edouard Moyse shows the Great Sanhedrin of Paris), highlighting key moments of integration. The Jewish presence in twentieth-century art presents works from the early decades of the last century. Underlying these runs the eternal question of Jewish expression in art through folklore, ornament, biblical sources, and calligraphy.

The *Shoah* is commemorated by a kind of memorial, a break in the sequence. Last, this impressive complex has temporary exhibition rooms for contemporary artists, an auditorium for concerts, talks, and film screenings, a library, a photo library, a video library, and a tearoom.

[Musée d'Art et d'Histoire du Judaïsme: 71 rue du Temple, 75003 Paris. ✆ 0153018653. ❶ info@www.mahj.org. Open Mon–Fri 11 A.M.–6 P.M., Sun 10 A.M.– 6 P.M. 🚇 Rambuteau.]

■ The Memorial to the Unknown Jewish Martyr (Mémorial du Martyr Juif Inconnu) was built in 1953 by international subscription on land made available by the municipality. The facade presents text in French, Hebrew, and **Yiddish** in remembrance of the victims of the *Shoah*. In front of the building, designed by the architects Georges Goldberg and Alexandre Persitz, there is a symbolic

basin inscribed with the names of the main Nazi camps and the Warsaw Ghetto. It serves as a light well for the underground crypt with its perpetual flame. The upper floor of the building has rooms for temporary exhibits on the war and its genocide.

The Center for Contemporary Jewish Documentation (CDJC) library

Memorial to the Unknown Jewish Martyr, Paris.

and archives are wholly dedicated to the Nazi period.

[Mémorial du Martyr Juif Inconnu: 17 rue Geoffroy-l'Asnier, 75004 Paris. Centre de Documentation Juive Contemporaine: 37 rue de Turenne, 75003 Paris. ✆ 0142774472. Open Mon–Wed 11 A.M.– 5:30 P.M., Thu 11 A.M.–8 P.M. 🚇 Pont-Marie.]

■ As you walk toward the Place des Vosges, there is a synagogue on Rue des Tournelles. The original building, from 1861, was burned down during the Paris Commune of 1871. It was rebuilt following a design by Marcellin Varcollier in a style close to that of the synagogue on Rue de la Victoire. The facade features the Tablets of the Law and the Paris city coat of arms. Consecrated in 1876, this synagogue has a visible metal inner structure built in the workshops of Gustave Eiffel more than ten years before his famous Tower. The two rows of galleries, made entirely of iron and cast iron, provide both support and ornament.

[Synagogue des Tournelles: 21 bis rue des Tournelles, 75004 Paris. ✆ 0142743265. Services daily at around 7:15 A.M. and 5 P.M. 🚇 Bastille.]

The synagogue on Rue des Tournelles, Paris.

MONTPARNASSE

At the beginning of the twentieth century, the legendary bohemia of Montparnasse included many Russian Jewish painters who had fled the anti-Semitic pogroms of the day. Among them were Soutine, Chagall, and Zadkine. Others, such as Modigliani, were simply attracted by the city's prestige and contributed to the tremendous creative effervescence of the day.

■ Division 22 of the Montparnasse cemetery (Cimetière de Montparnasse) is the resting place of the painter Jules Pascin, one of the "artistes maudits" who lived out his wild, nocturnal life in this quarter.

Born in Bulgaria in 1885, he committed suicide in Paris in 1930. A drawing engraved on his tombstone evokes his work, accompanied by the words: "A free man, hero of dreams and desire, opening the golden doors with his bleeding hands, flesh and blood, Pascin disdained to choose and, master of life, ordained his own death." A little further on, in Division 28, a white stone bears the name of the officer Alfred Dreyfus (1859–1935). Here lies the man who was wrongly accused of high treason, of betraying French military secrets to Germany.

[Cimetière de Montparnasse: 3, boulevard Edgar-Quinet, 75014 Paris. ✆ 0144108650. Open Mar 16–Nov 5, Mon–Fri 8 A.M.–6 P.M., Sat 8:30 A.M.–6 P.M., Sun and public holidays 9 A.M.–6 P.M.; Nov 6–Mar 15, Mon–Fri 8 A.M.–5:30 P.M., Sat 8:30 A.M.–5:30 P.M., Sun and public holidays 9 A.M.–5:30 P.M. 🚇 Raspail or Edgar-Quinet.]

■ *Homage to Captain Dreyfus (Hommage au capitaine Dreyfus)* is a sculpture by cartoonist Louis Mitelberg, best known as Tim. It functions on two levels: Captain Dreyfus is depicted presenting his arms, but his sword is broken—representing the degradation of his first trial.

[*Hommage au capitaine Dreyfus:* place Pierre-Lafue, 75006 Paris. 🚇 Notre-Dame-des-Champs.]

■ West of Montparnasse, near the avenue de Ségur, curious travelers will make a point of visiting what older Parisians consider to be the capital's most handsome and original synagogue. Consecrated on 29 September 1913, it was designed by the architect Bechmann. The square hall has sides fifteen yards long. The gallery is supported by wooden columns that rise all the way to the octagonal wooden dome of the roof.

[ACIP Synagogue: 14, rue Chasseloup-Laubat, 75015 Paris. ✆ 0142733629. 🚇 Ségur.]

THE OPERA QUARTER

■ In addition to its architecture and activities, the Opéra de Paris (or Palais Garnier) is notable for its extraordinary ceiling, painted by Marc Chagall in 1964.

The synagogue on Rue Chasseloup-Laubat, Paris.

[Opéra National de Paris: 8 rue Scribe, 75009 Paris. ✆ 0140011789. Visits 10 A.M.–4:30 P.M. except during matinees. 🚇 Opéra.]

■ Not far from here, in a room at the Hôtel de Castille (37, rue Cambon), Theodor Herzl wrote *The Jewish State*. This was the founding work of political Zionism, which bore fruit some fifty years later in the proclamation of the State of Israel.

■ The synagogue on Rue de la Victoire is the biggest in Paris. This is where the Jewish community's official ceremonies are held. Consecrated on 9 September 1874, it was, according to the original design, supposed to have an entrance on Rue Ollivier (today's Rue de Châteaudun). However, on the advice of her confessor, Mgr. Bernard Bauer, a Hungarian of Jewish origin, Empress Eugénie opposed this idea: the Grande Synagogue de Paris must not open onto a main thoroughfare!

The synagogue was built to plans by the head architect of the City of Paris, Aldrophe, who was himself a Jew. The overall conception is a rather florid Romanesque, with Moorish echoes. Outside, the main facade is forty-three yards high. On it, the Hebrew inscription under the two Tablets of the Law reads: "My house shall be called the house of prayer for all peoples." Inside, the large prayer hall and the five arches are flanked by two galleries. The upper gallery was designed purely for architectural effect. Nowadays, though, it can

THE *TSARPHAT*

During the early planning stage in 1850, the synagogue on Rue de la Victoire was intended to house a unique French rite, the *Tsarphat,* a single liturgy combining Portuguese chants and Alsatian pronunciation. This generous idea caused no end of debate. In 1866, a report by the consistory noted that "The construction of the temple on Rue de la Victoire will make it possible to fulfill the oft-expressed wishes of our coreligionists from the German rite and the Portuguese rite, namely to meet in a shared sanctuary, in a word to establish there a unified rite that is so desirable in every way."

The war with Prussia in 1870 delayed the project. Finally, on 16 May 1874, Zadoc Kahn, the grand rabbi of France, brought together 150 **Sephardic** notables, who, after a debate, firmly rejected the idea. The synagogue on Rue de la Victoire would thus become an **Ashkenazic** temple. However, prayers were still spoken "in the oriental manner" for another fifteen years; they had not given up all hope of fusion.

be used to hold worshippers during major celebrations, thus increasing the synagogue's capacity.

The building, which is thirty-four yards high to the keystone, is fifty two yards long and thirty-three wide. Its only decoration is twelve stained-glass windows by Lusson, Lefèvre, and Oudinot representing the symbols of the biblical Twelve Tribes.

[Synagogue de la Victoire: 44, rue de la Victoire, 75009 Paris. ✆ 0145269536. 🚇 Le Peletier.]

In 1874 the leaders of the Portuguese-Jewish community refused the fusion of **Sephardic** and **Ashkenazic** rites and, at the same time, decided to build their own temple. To this end, a non-trading stockholders' company was set up by Jews from Bayonne, Comtat Venaissin, and the Ottoman Empire with a view to buying land and financing construction. The architect

Stanislas Ferrand was entrusted with the design. The resulting synagogue, on Rue Buffault, was consecrated on 3 September 1877. The facade is twenty-eight yards high. On it, the following lines from Deuteronomy are written in Hebrew: "Blessed are you when you come in, and blessed are you when you go out." Inside, the gallery is supported by six marble columns. The arches around the keystone form the Tablets of the Law and have biblical names inscribed on them. At the center of the prayer hall, a large seven-branch candelabrum stands on the altar. To the rear, a large staircase with a wrought iron balustrade leads to the cupboard that houses the **Torah** scrolls. Above the cupboard, emerging from sculpted stone clouds, are the Tablets of the Law.

[Synagogue Buffault: 28–30, rue Buffault, 75009 Paris. ✆ 0140707000. 🚇 Cadet.]

LA VILLETTE

"Here is buried the body of Sieur Salomon de Perpignan, one of the founders of the Free Royal Drawing School established in the year 1767 of the glorious reign of Louis XV in the city of Paris . . . . Died 22 February 1781." These are the words on one of the oldest tombs in Paris's Jewish cemetery. They give an idea of the social importance acquired by the "Portuguese" Jews of Paris in the eighteenth century, even though they were only "tolerated" as an exception to the expulsion edict, which was still in force.

This small plot of land was bought on 3 March 1780 by Jacob Rodrigue Pereire, an "agent of the Portuguese-Jewish nation in Paris." The legality of the cemetery was recognized in an edict that allowed Jews to be buried there "at night, without noise, scandal, or ceremony, in the accustomed manner." The cemetery was closed in 1810, when Père-Lachaise opened a special area for Jewish sepulchers. It now lies hemmed in between the tall buildings of this modern quarter.

[Cimetière Juif Portugais: 44, avenue de Flandre, 75019 Paris. 🚇 Stalingrad. Ask for the key from the Hevra Kadisha service of the Consistoire Israélite de Paris: 17, rue Saint-Georges, 75009 Paris. ✆ 0140822690. 🚇 Notre-Dame-de-Lorette.]

Drancy

■ *The Deportation Monument* (Le Monument de la Déportation), a work by the sculptor Shlomo Selinger erected in 1976, serves as a reminder that the buildings in this northern suburb in Seine-Saint-Denis were used as a concentration camp during the occupation. Tens of thousands of French Jews who were sent to the extermination camps transited via Drancy. The last remaining building from this episode was put on the historical register in May 2001.

In the center of the piece, the block represents ten figures, the ten men needed to recite the **kaddish.** The wavelike pattern at the foot of the sculpture evokes the fire in which so many Jews died. Two stairs, each with seven steps, symbolize the seven degrees of suffering and the seven degrees of the elevation of the soul. On the right-hand side, the man's beard forms the letter *lamed* and the woman's hair a *vav*. These Hebrew letters have a numerical value of thirty-six and so recall the Thirty-Six Righteous Individuals who, according to Jewish tradition, support the world. Close by the monument, a cattle car used during the deportation houses photographs and documents pertaining to the conditions of internment and the history of the convoys to the death camps.

[Monument de la Déportation: square de la Libération, 93700 Drancy. Open Sat 2–4 P.M.]

Normandy ■

Rouen

In medieval times there was an intense intellectual life around the synagogue's Talmudic school in what was called "Le Clos aux Juifs" (the Jews' Enclosure). Contrary to what its name suggests, the enclosure in question was never a closed space. There were Jews living elsewhere in the town and Christians living in the Clos. All this disappeared in 1306, when the community was expelled. After that, only very few were able to identify Rouen as the brilliant and lively "Rodom" described in ancient texts.

■ In 1976, repaving work in the courtyard of the Palais de Justice brought to light an extraordinary archaeological find: the walls of an eleventh-century Jewish building, the oldest Jewish monument in Western Europe! Since then, it has been the object of endless debate between specialists. The home of a wealthy merchant, a Talmudic school, a synagogue—what exactly was it? The following fragment from the divine words spoken to Solomon (1 Kings 9:8) were clumsily engraved into the walls three times: "this house, which is high." No doubt they were hastily inscribed at the moment of the expulsion.

At their base two small columns, a stone dragon and, facing it, a wild beast, placed strangely back to front, with two bodies and only one head (a typical Roman sculpture), are probably an evocation of Psalm 91 (verse 13): "The young lion and the dragon shall thou trample under feet." A stone spiral staircase leads to a low room with narrow windows that may have been used to store manuscripts.

[Palais de Justice: rue aux Juifs, 76000 Rouen. ✆ 0232083240. Open by appointment through the tourist office: 25, place de la Cathédrale, 76000 Rouen. ✆ 0232083240.]

Caen and the rest of the region

Traveling rabbis served the small local communities, made up of several or more families (some ten at Evreux and Lisieux, around two hundred at Le Havre). The only sizable community structure, a small synagogue, was built by the Jews themselves after the liberation of France.

[Synagogue of the Hebrew Cultural Association: 46, avenue de la Libération, 14000 Caen. ✆ 0231436054.]

Alsace ■

■ Alsace is rich in Jewish history. In the village of Schirrhoffen, for example, in around 1850, the population of 650 included some 450 Jews. Today, there are over 200 specific sites (synagogues, ritual baths, cemeteries). Unfortunately, though, there are many that visitors cannot see because they are closed, abandoned, or located on private property. Thus, while the small town of Rouffach (in Haut-Rhin) may pride itself on the vestiges of a twelfth-century synagogue, all you will see is the refaced facade of a banal half-timbered house.

[Old Synagogue of Rouffach: 8, rue Ullin, 68250 Rouffach.]

■ Elsewhere, the nineteenth-century village synagogues offer a remarkable architectural panorama. The reality of Jewish emancipation can be read in stone: one need only compare the discreet facade of the synagogue in Hochfelden (Bas-Rhin), built in 1841, with that of the synagogue in Saint-Louis (Haut-Rhin), consecrated in 1904, whose two Rhenish-style domes rise proudly to the sky.

Misrach indicating the direction of Jerusalem. Musée des Arts et Traditions Populaires, Marmoutier, Alsace.

[Synagogue and Museum of Hochfelden:
place du Général-Koenig,
67270 Hochfelden.]

[Synagogue of Saint-Louis:
rue de la Synagogue, 68300 Saint-Louis.
✆ 0388154588.]

■ In recent years, tremendous efforts have been made to save Alsace's Jewish heritage. Restored synagogues and new museums now form a fascinating and unique Jewish itinerary.

The tourism development agency of Bas-Rhin, which is managing this program, publishes brochures and a calendar of events.

[Tourism Development Agency of
Bas-Rhin: 9, rue du Dôme, BP 53,
67061 Strasbourg Cedex.
✆ 0388154588, fax 0388756764.
ℹ catherine.lehmann@tourisme67.com.]

Pfaffenhoffen

■ The small village shul from 1791 with its modest facade is no doubt the most moving historical site in Alsace. There is no ostentatious gold or bright marble here, just a simple synagogue with white walls and, on the first floor, its *Kahlstube,* its kitchen and room for any visiting schnorrers. Note, at the entrance, a stone fountain that is even older than the synagogue itself. Its Hebrew date corresponds to the year 1744. On the upper floor, the prayer hall still has its wooden pews and handsome carving of the Holy Ark decorated with lions of Juda and vines of

Alsace. In the bull's eye, note the blue and white glass, which, according to the Talmud, indicated when it was time for morning prayer, i.e., at dawn, when one could clearly distinguish the two colors. This elementary way of marking time fell out of use in the nineteenth century with the advent of the fob watch.

[To visit, ask at the Musée de l'Image
Populaire: 24, rue du Docteur-Albert-
Schweitzer, 67350 Pfaffenhoffen.
✆ 0388078005.]

Bouxwiller

■ Housed in a synagogue built in 1842, the unique Judeo-Alsatian Museum (Musée Judéo-Alsacien) set out to present the life and history of Judaism in the countryside. There are no rich collections here, therefore, but a sequence of displays with re-creations and moving, ritual objects reflecting ordinary life and the major moments of Jewish life in Alsace. The building's empty interior—the Nazis converted it into a factory—allows for a unique architectural experience. It contains a sequence of ramps and platforms that permit visitors to share in the traditions of the Jewish hawkers and wholesale butchers of the countryside. Mannequins with heads in twisted iron and ceramic models also bring to life these lost communities.

[Musée Judéo-Alsacien: 62, Grand'rue,
67330 Bouxwiller. ✆ and fax 0388709717.

[Open mid-Mar–mid-Sep, Tue–Fri
10 A.M.–noon, 2–5 P.M., Sun 2–4 P.M.
Guided tours for groups year-round,
by appointment.]

Marmoutier

■ This small town lying in the shadow of an old abbey once had a very active community. You can still see the birthplaces of its two famous Jewish sons: the painter Albert Lévy, who was born here in 1843 and died in Algiers in 1918, and whose work bore witness to Alsace's rural communities; and Albert Kahn, born in 1860, who died in Boulogne-sur-Seine in 1940.

[House of Alphonse Lévy:
5, rue des Écoles, 67440 Marmoutier.]
[House of Albert Kahn:
8, rue du 22 Novembre (formerly
rue des Juifs), 67448 Marmoutier.]

■ The synagogue, built in 1822 and now unused, can still be seen. Take Rue Neuve out of the village. Once in the forest, you will come to a small cemetery built in 1799. Interestingly, though the engravings on the tombstones are in Hebrew, there are also brief annotations in the local language on the back. While these are sometimes in German on the oldest stones, they are all in French beginning from the annexation of Alsace by the Germans in 1870.

[Old Synagogue: 11, rue du Plan,
67440 Marmoutier.]

■ The Museum of Popular Arts and Traditions (Musée des Arts et des Traditions populaires) is housed in a fine timbered building dating from 1590 that was home to Jewish families without interruption from 1680 to 1922. Here you can see the mikvah from 1710 and, in the kitchen, a flat oven that may have been used to cook matzohs for Passover. The collection of Jewish cultural objects gives an idea of the size of the community in those days. Note in particular a remarkable curtain for the Holy Ark (1857) from the synagogue at Quatzenheim.

[Musée des Arts et des Traditions
populaires: 6, rue du Général-Leclerc,
67440 Marmoutier. Open May 1–Oct 31,
Sun and public holidays 10 A.M.–noon and
2–6 P.M. For groups, visits by appointment
through the tourist office: ✆ 0388714684.]

Synagogue, Strasbourg.

Strasbourg

■ Jewish history is evident throughout Strasbourg. Indeed, it is said that Rue de la Nuée-Bleue is named after the cloud *(nuée)* that went before the Jews expelled from the town in 1349, and that Rue Brûlée recalls the 2,000 Jews who were burned alive that same year when they refused to be baptized.

[French Hebrew Bookstore: 19, rue du Maréchal-Foch, 67000 Strasbourg, ✆ 0388363839.]

■ The monumental synagogue on the Quai Kléber was destroyed by

the Nazis in 1940 (commemorative plaque). The community's new place of worship was opened in 1958. Inside, note the admirable Holy Ark, whose bold forms set off a tapestry by the artist Jean Lurçat.

[Synagogue and Community:
1A, rue René-Hirschler, 67000 Strasbourg.
✆ 0388144650.]

■ Discovered during construction work on Rue des Juifs in 1984, a mikvah was built in about 1200. The central element is a ten-foot-square room built in gray sandstone and topped by red bricks. Romanesque-style corbels remain in each corner.

[Mikvah: 20, rue des Charpentiers,
67000 Strasbourg. Guided tours available for groups. Ask at the tourist office:
✆ 0388522820.]

■ The Alsatian Museum (Musée Alsacien) features a reconstruction of a small country oratory and its bookshelf, complete with Torah scroll and Shabbat lamp. There are two other rooms devoted to Judaism. Curiosities include a carved wooden Star of David with an imperial two-headed eagle from 1770, panels in Hebrew and French from the synagogue at Jungholtz calling down divine blessings on Emperor Napoleon III, and a painting commemorating the "unveiling of a Pentateuch in Reichshoffen on 7 November 1857"— a moving evocation of fervor and patriotism.

[Musée Alsacien: 23, quai Saint-Nicolas,
67000 Strasbourg. ✆ 0388525001.
Open Wed–Mon 10 A.M.–6 P.M.]

■ In the courtyard of the Musée de l'œuvre Notre-Dame, devoted to the arts in the Strasbourg region between the eleventh and seventeenth centuries, one can see Jewish headstones from the medieval cemetery located on the site of today's Place de la République.

[Musée de l'Œuvre Notre-Dame:
3, place du Château, 67000 Strasbourg.
✆ 0388525000.
Open Tue–Sun 10 A.M.–6 P.M.]

Bischheim

■ In this suburb of Strasbourg one can see a fine eighteenth-century mikvah. A room dedicated to Davis Sintzheim (the first Grand Rabbi of France and director of the Talmudic school in Bischheim between 1786 and 1792) retraces the history of the Jewish community and houses temporary exhibitions.

[Mikvah: cour des Boecklin,
17, rue Nationale, 67800 Bisscheim.
✆ 0388814947. Open by appointment:
Tue, Wed, Fri–Sun 2:30–6:30 P.M. during exhibitions; Jul–Aug, Tue 4–7 P.M.,
Wed 2–6 P.M., Fri 10 A.M.–1 P.M.,
Sat 10 A.M.–6 P.M.]

ALSACE

Rosenwiller

In 1727 the Jews, who had been burying their dead here for nearly four centuries, were granted permission to build a wooden fence around the cemetery and, twenty-two years later, a stone wall. With 6,470 tombs over twelve acres, Rosenwiller bears witness to a long history: the oldest tomb dates from 1657.

♔ PLACE DE L'ÉQUARRISSEUR

"When the Jews asked for a place to bury their dead (around 1350), they were shown a huge, arid square in Rosenwiller at one end of which the slaughterer buried dead horses. At the other end, they were allowed to bury their deceased coreligionists."

ÉLIE SCHEID, *HISTOIRE DES JUIFS D'ALSACE* (HISTORY OF THE JEWS OF ALSACE), 1887 (PARIS: LIBRAIRIE ARMAND DURLACHER. REPRINT WILLY-FISCHER, 1975.)

■ Here and there in the older part of the cemetery, visitors will come across short Hebrew poems in homage to the dead, as well as a number of recurrent symbols: broken columns for child mortalities or young women who died without offspring; **Shabbat** lamps for pious women; jugs for the **Levites**; blessing hands for the **kohanim** (according to tradition, the Levis and Cohens descend from tribes devoted to the priesthood).

[Walk through Rosenwiller and turn left into the road for Grendelbruch. Open summer Sun–Fri 7 A.M.–7 P.M., winter to 5 P.M. Closed on Jewish feast days.]

Obernai

Traces of the old Jewish community can still be seen in this charming tourist town.

On Ruelle des Juifs, an arched doorway with an engraving in Hebrew signals the entrance to the old synagogue, dating to 1454.

■ On Rue du Général-Gouraud the voussoir of an arch bears the Hebrew date 5456, corresponding to 1696 C.E. In the porch, note the two blessing hands carved in stone with the inscription "The master, Rabbi Samson, the Cohen."

■ Along the walls of the synagogue, you will observe the vestiges of a Jewish community house built circa 1750 with traces of the Holy Ark and altar. The hammered lilies recall that the French kings protected the Jews of Alsace (in the courtyard, an image reproduces the place of worship). When the old synagogue became too small, it was deconsecrated in 1876 and replaced by the neo-Romanesque one still in use today.

[Synagogue: 9, rue de Sélestat, 67210 Obernai. Inquire at the tourist office: ✆ 0388956413.]

49. COLMAR
Rue des Juifs
Maison Moll

Rue des Juifs, Colmar, 1919.

Colmar

■ The Bartholdi Museum pays homage to the sculptor of the Statue of Liberty. One room features an interesting collection of **Judaica**. Particularly admirable is a bowl used by the brotherhood charged with final duties *(Hevra Kadisha)*; it is in the form of a coffin with bearers (mid-nineteenth century). There are also precious examples of circumcision chairs and an ablution fountain from the cemetery at Herrlisheim.

> [Musée Bartholdi: rue des Marchands,
> 68000 Colmar. ✆ 0389419060.
> Open Wed–Mon 10 A.M.–noon and 2–6 P.M.
> Closed Jan and Feb]

Hegenheim

■ On the Franco-Swiss border, Hegenheim cemetery, which covers over five acres, has tombstones dating from its establishment in 1673. It is the only cemetery to have preserved a wooden funeral slab. The original is now on exhibit in the Jewish Museum in nearby Basel. This busy Swiss trading town was long a magnet for local inhabitants and, since they were refused the right to reside there, Jews settled in the nearby areas of Alsace and, for two centuries, the cemetery at Hegenheim was used by local communities, including those across the Swiss border. It is now a moving historical site where you can walk among more than 7,000 tombs and discover weathered stones overgrown with ivy or scattered among the undergrowth.

[The Jewish cemetery is on the left just after leaving the village by the D12 bis road.]

☙ ONCE IN AN ALSATIAN TOWN

"[On Rue des Juifs] All one could see were tall, decrepit buildings, furrowed with rusting gutters; and from the dormer windows the whole of Judaea hung its stockings, dirty old petticoats, patched underwear, and frayed linen. At all the basement windows could be seen doddering heads, toothless mouths, noses and chins like carnival masks; you would have thought that this people came from Nineveh, from Babylon, or that they had escaped from captivity in Egypt, so old did they look."

ÉMILE ERCKMANN AND ALEXANDRE CHATRIAN, *L'AMI FRITZ* (FRIEND FRITZ) (STRASBOURG: ÉDITO, 1966).

Rhône-Alpes ■

Jews lived in Roman Lugdunum but disappeared from Lyon because of the expulsions. It was only under the reign of Louis XV that a community was re-created with immigrants from Comtat Venaissin and Alsace. The region is associated primarily with World War II and the French Resistance. The notorious war criminal Klaus Barbie, who was tried in 1986, was head of the Lyon Gestapo.

notable sites surrounding the Grand Synagogue, built in 1864, as well as some excellent **kosher** restaurants. All in all, they make Lyon a very pleasant stop. Event information is available from the Chief Rabbinate.

[Chief Rabbinate of Lyon and Grand Synagogue: 13, quai Tilsitt, 69002 Lyon. ✆ 0478371343.]

[Restaurant Lippmann: 4, rue Tony-Tollet, 69002 Lyon. ✆ 0478424982.]

Lyon

■ The Jewish community in the historical capital of the Gauls and, for historians, capital of the French Resistance, has now regained an undeniable dynamism. There are many

Izieu

During the Nazi occupation, this village in the department of Ain was the scene of a raid ordered by Klaus Barbie on 6 April 1944. Forty-four Jewish refugee children and their seven teachers were arrested and deported. Only one survived.

The Memorial Museum of the Children of Izieu (Musée-Mémorial des enfants d'Izieu) exhibits letters and drawings in honor of these victims of Nazi barbarity, who lived in the village for nearly a year. An adjoining building has audiovisual displays that recall those dark years, exploring the concept of "crimes against humanity" and showing excerpts from the Barbie trial concerning the crime at Izieu.

[Musée-Mémorial: ✆ 0479872008. ✉ izieu@alma.fr. Open mid-Sep–mid-Jun, Mon–Fri 9 A.M.–5 P.M., Sat–Sun 10 A.M.–6 P.M; mid-Jun–mid-Sep, daily 10 A.M.–6:30 P.M. From Lyon or Chambéry, take the A43 expressway, then the Chimlin–Les Abrets exit and take the D952 in the direction of Belley.]

Provence

The term *Provintçia* in the Hebrew sources corresponds roughly to Provence and Languedoc. In the history of France's Jews, this region is notable for the outstanding figures and works that it produced in the Middle Ages and by the unbroken presence of Jews in Comtat Venaissin for 2,000 years.

A lamp dating from the first century C.E. found near the **oppidum** at Orgon and kept in the synagogue at Cavaillon, and a Hebrew epitaph at Narbonne ("Peace on Israel") accompanied by a **menorah**, probably seventh century, are the oldest relics of the Jewish presence in France. In the sixth and seventh centuries, Marseille was home to a large Jewish community. The Saracen invasions of the following century brought to the fore Jewish "patriotism": during the siege of Narbonne, Jews played an active part in defending the town. The emperor rewarded them with a grant of one of the town's three districts. The legend of the "Jewish king of Narbonne" dates from this period.

Historical studies of Provençal towns reveal a Jewish community integrated into its urban and rural environment. Its members were, among other things, tradesmen (plasterers) in Avignon, winemakers in Tarascon, merchants in Marseille and Toulouse, and shopkeepers, moneylenders, and doctors almost everywhere. However, it was in the cultural domain that the vitality and openness of Provence's Jewish communities was most remarkable. In the twelfth century the traveler Benjamin of Tudela related that, "In Lunel there lives a big Jewish

community that studies the **Torah** day and night. All those who wish to study are boarded. Posquières is a town that shelters more than 400 Jews as well as a Talmudic school directed by the grand rabbi Abraham, son of David (abbreviated as RABaD). People come from the most

A. Rousseau, The Northern Gate ot Jewry, Carpentras, *1838.* *Musée de Carpentras.*

distant lands to learn the **Torah**." There is not enough space here to list all the learned men who lived in Provence between the twelfth and fifteenth centuries. Among the most remarkable, though, were the Abraham ben David of Posquières (1125–98), as mentioned by Benjamin of Tudela; Menahem ben Solomon He-Meiri (1249–1316) and his father Solomon, both famous **Talmudists** who wrote important commentaries; the four generations of Tibbonides (1120–1307), who translated a number of philosophical, religious, and scientific works from Arabic into Hebrew, notably Maimonides' *Guide for the Perplexed (Dalalat al-Ha'irîn);* and, finally, Levi ben Gershom (1288–1344), or Gersonides, who spent most of his life in Orange and produced a vast and highly diverse body of work, much of which was translated into Latin at the time (commentaries on Aristotle and Averroës, on the Bible and the prophets, on the **Talmud,** works of arithmetic and geometry, a treatise on astronomy, etc.).

In 1306 Philippe le Bel expelled all the Jews from the Kingdom of France. They were called back in 1315 by Louis X. In 1320 the Crusade of the Pastoreaux caused massacres throughout southwest France. The expulsion of 1394 put an end to the Jewish presence in Languedoc. The communities of Provence, Comté de Nice, and the Principality of Orange, then still distinct from France, were not affected by these expulsions. However, they were hit hard by the Black Death of 1348. The Jews were accused of poisoning the wells in order to spread the epidemic. The communities of Provence and Comtat Venaissin were almost totally wiped out in riots.

The fifteenth century, too, brought its series of anti-Jewish riots: there was violence and killing in Manosque in 1425, in Aix-en-Provence and Pertuis in 1430, in Digne in 1475, and again in Manosque in 1495. The destiny of this region changed course on 11 December 1481 when, following the death of Count Charles III, Provence was bequeathed to the king of France, Louis XI. The latter committed himself to respecting the rights of the Jews but, after his death in 1483, Louis XII signed the edict expelling the Jews from Provence. He renewed it in 1510. Part of the community converted, the other part left. In 1505, the prince of Orange signed the Edict of Courthézon, expelling the Jews from the principality. Part of Provence's Jewish community emigrated to Italy, while others traveled to Barbary (North Africa), the Ottoman Empire, or Comtat Venaissin, the last area in this part of the continent to welcome the Jews.

Any peace enjoyed in Comtat Venaissin was short-lived. At the end of the fifteenth century, the Pope (to whom this region belonged) decided to group Jews together in *carrieres* (urban dwelling places for Jews). This compounded the discriminatory measures dating back to the Fourth Lateran Council (1215): strict separation from

Christians; the obligation to wear an identifying sign (a yellow patch, then a yellow hat); economic restrictions (a prohibition against owning property, apart from their dwelling); selling limited to secondhand items (clothes, objects); and disqualification from manual professions.

Following Cardinal Barberini's order in September 1624, the Jews in Comtat Venaissin had to congregate in three towns: Carpentras, Cavaillon, and L'Isle-sur-la-Sorgue. Most historians add Avignon to this list and speak of "Comtat's *four carrieres*," but this is clearly a misnomer since Avignon was never part of Comtat Venaissin.

At night the *carrieres* were closed off and the gate was watched by a Jewish porter who was paid by the community. As Armand Lunel notes, these *carrieres* were "small republics" where the Jewish population lived in isolation; they were administered by syndics who issued *escamots* (from the Hebrew *Haskama,* meaning "agreement").

Although the edict of 1394 had not been repealed, starting in the seventeenth century the Jews from Avignon and Comtat Venaissin took advantage of the ambiguous *regnicole* (rights-holding) status of the inhabitants of Comtat Venaissin and gradually began settling in the Kingdom of France. This window considerably increased their access to new markets and improved their economic situation.

In the eighteenth century, the financial situation of the region's Jewish community improved. While still restricted to their *carrieres* and obliged to wear the yellow hat, many were able to make a living from lending money for interest and from the authorized professions. Jews were active in numerous mercantile areas, such as horse dealing, buying and selling cotton, the silk trade, secondhand clothes, etc. The synagogues in the *carrieres* were rebuilt at great expense: Carpentras in 1740, L'Isle-sur-la-Sorgue and Avignon in 1760–1770, and Cavaillon between 1771 and 1774.

Despite these gains, the specific status of the Jews did not improve, and in fact restrictions increased. On 28 January 1790 the National Assembly passed a decree stipulating that "Portuguese, Spanish, and Avignonnais Jews shall continue to enjoy the rights settled in their favor by the letters patent; and, consequently, they will enjoy the rights of active citizens once they have met the conditions laid down by the decrees of this Assembly."

Avignon

The first attestation of a Jewish presence in Avignon dates from the fourth century. It is a seal representing a five-branch **menorah** and bearing the inscription *avinionensis*. Jewish commercial activity was intense under Avignon's popes. The tailor of Gregory XI was a Jew, as was his bookbinder. During the Black Death epidemic in 1348, the community in Avignon was spared popular wrath thanks to the energetic intervention of Clement VI. The edicts of 1558 included a description of the community's organization. Its members were divided into three categories according to wealth. The *baylons,* for example, were responsible for collecting taxes, charity, caring for the sick, and teaching. In the seventeenth century, Jews worked mainly in secondhand trade and horse dealing. When the city became part of the French Republic in 1791, the number of Jews in Avignon fell quickly. By 1892 there remained only fifty-four families. The arrival of **Sephardic** Jews in the 1960s revived the community.

Avignon was the birthplace and home of many important figures in Hebrew literature. Among the best known were Kalonymos ben Kalonymos, the author of *Even Bohan* (The Touchstone), a satire of Jewish life in Provence during the Middle Ages, and Levi ben Gershom (Gersonides).

The Jewish quarter was opposite the Palace of the Popes, as indicated today by Rue de la Vieille Juiverie. Around 1221 it was transferred to the Place de Jérusalem (now Place Victor-Basch). The *carriere* was Rue Jacob, where some of the old houses can still be seen. It was surrounded by a wall with three gates.

■ The old synagogue was destroyed by fire in 1845 and replaced by a new, circular one, which can be visited.

[Synagogue: 2, place Jérusalem, 84000 Avignon. ✆ 0490852124. Open Mon–Fri 10 A.M.–noon and 3–5 P.M.]

Carpentras

Carpentras had a Jewish population when it was yielded to the papacy by the king of France in 1274. In the fourteenth century, the Jewish quarter on Rue Fournaque, near the town walls, was home to ninety families. In 1459 it was sacked by rioters and sixty people were killed. The community was forced to move to Rue des Muses in the town center, which became Rue des Juifs, a *carriere* closed off at both ends by gates. During the fourteenth century Jews lived mainly from trading agricultural products and money lending. A census in 1473 revealed sixty-nine Jewish families living in Carpentras. In 1523 Jacopo Sadoleto, the bishop of Carpentras, imposed restrictions on their activities and the community shrank considerably. After the expulsions of 1570 and 1593, only a few families remained, but in 1669, when the small communities of Comtat Venaissin were put in the four *carrieres,* the number rose to eighty-three families, or 298 persons.

New restrictions were imposed throughout the eighteenth century. There was, notably, a long, drawn-out conflict over the construction of the synagogue. Begun in 1741 in answer to the growing number of believers, the construction proceeded swiftly until, in 1757, the bishop obtained authorization from Rome to reduce the building to its medieval dimensions. He himself set about the demolition with the help of masons. The Jews protested, and the conflict dragged on until 1784, when a compromise was reached as to the acceptable dimensions. At the end of the eighteenth century, the community numbered some 2,000 members. Most of them lived modestly, or even in poverty. Some, though, were rich, such as Jacob de la Roque and Abraham Crémieux. During the Revolution, the synagogue was a Jacobin meeting place. It returned to being a place of worship in 1800.

The community in Carpentras produced few renowned intellectuals. Most were doctors and poets. Mardochée Astruc, from Carpentras, wrote the play *La Reine Esther* with Jacob de Lunel in the eighteenth century. It inspired *Esther de Carpentras,* a comic opera with a libretto by Armand Lunel that was presented in Paris in 1938.

■ The synagogue was registered as a historical monument in 1924.

A monumental staircase leads to the place of worship, which is organized on two levels: the meeting room with the tabernacle, and the gallery/tribune with the *tevah.* The interior decoration is remarkable.

Synagogue, Carpentras.

Note the blue ceiling spangled with stars, the wooden paneling, the gilding on the tabernacle, the columns supporting the *tevah,* the Chair of Elijah, and the chandeliers and candlesticks. In the basement, elements from the medieval construction are still in place: the matzoh oven, the mikvah, and the women's prayer room, where a specially chosen rabbi led the prayers in Judeo-Provençal (Judeo-Comtadin).

[Synagogue: place Maurice-Charretier, BP 90, 84200 Carpentras. ✆ 0490633997. Open Mon–Thu 10 A.M.–noon and 3–5 P.M., Fri 10 A.M.–noon and 3–4 P.M. Closed public holidays. For more information, contact the tourist office: 170, allée Jean-Jaurès, 84200 Carpentras. ✆ 0490635788.]

■ The *carriere* and the Place de la Juiverie were destroyed in the nineteenth century.

■ The Lapidary Museum (Musée lapidaire) houses a number of funerary inscriptions.

[For safety reasons, the museum is closed until further notice.]

Pernes-les-Fontaines

Pernes-les-Fontaines remained the capital of Comtat Venaissin until Pope John XXII bought back the rights over Carpentras from its bishop. Two elements reveal the Jewish presence in this town: the name Place de la Juiverie and the traditional identification of the large house standing in that square as the old "Jewish baths."

L'Isle-sur-la-Sorgue

Regrettably, this town, which had one of Comtat Venaissin's four *carrieres,* preserves no vestiges of its Jewish past—apart, that is, from the name Place de la Juiverie and the cemetery outside the town.

[For more information, contact the tourist office: place de l'Église, 84800 L'Isle-sur-la-Sorgue. ✆ 0490380478.]

Cavaillon

The Jewish presence in Cavaillon goes back to at least the thirteenth century. The Jews lived on Rue Hébraïque, which became their obligatory residence in 1453 and has changed very little since. Permission to build a synagogue was granted in 1494, and it was probably on the vestiges of this older building that the new place of worship was built in 1772. On the second floor is the men's school; the bread oven and the women's school, which also served as a bakery, were on the first floor. The arrangement is unusual in having preserved its original plan, which consists of two distinct elements: the synagogue, which forms a covered passage above Rue Hébraïque, and the mikvah, located in the basement of the courtyard and reached by a stairway with seventeen steps. The synagogue is laid out on the same model as that in Carpentras, with wood and ironwork, fluted columns, the Chair of Elijah, the tabernacle set into the wall, and the *tevah* above supported by four wooden columns. But unlike the

Carpentras synagogue, the bakery/women's school has no direct access to the upper part of the structure (the men's school and synagogue). In this room there is a domed stone oven, a kneading table, and the Judeo-Comtadin museum, which has one of the oldest archaeological relics of the Jewish presence in France: an oil lamp found in an *oppidum* near Orgon. The lamp dates from the first century C.E.

[For information or to visit, contact the Conservation des Musées: ✆0490760034. Museum open Oct 1–Mar 31, Mon, Wed–Fri 9 A.M.–noon and 2–5 P.M.; Apr 1 to Sep 30, Wed–Mon 9:30 A.M.–12:30 P.M. and 1:30 P.M.–6:30 P.M.]

Synagogue, Cavaillon. Museon Arlaten, Arles.

Saint-Rémy-de-Provence

■ The Jewish cemetery is not far from the Saint-Paul-de-Mausol monastery. Most of the tombstones date from the nineteenth century, although this was also the site of the medieval cemetery.

[For more information, contact the tourist office: place Jean-Jaurès, 13210 Saint-Rémy-de-Provence. ✆ 0490920522.]

Tarascon
and surrounding areas

■ The only remaining trace of Tarascon's Jewish community, which was large in the Middle Ages, is Rue des Juifs with its gray-fronted houses. Some of the houses have been restored.

■ Not far from the town, near Font-vieille, there is a fine Romanesque chapel, Saint-Gabriel, sheltered by a ruined tower with graffiti in Hebrew characters: T(av) T(av) Q(of) N(un) V(av) [4]956, which correspond to the date 1195–96 C.E.

[Tourist office: 58, rue des Halles, 13150 Tarascon. ✆ 0490910352.]

Nîmes

■ The Archaeological Museum (Musée Archéologique) possesses a funerary inscription stating "This is the sepulcher of the venerated sage Isaac."

■ The Municipal Library (Biblio-thèque Municipale) has copies of three funerary inscriptions (the orig-inals have been lost): "This is the sepulcher of Dame Dolcena, daugh-ter of . . . "; "This is the sepulcher of Rabbi Isaac, son of Haviv and of Meir"; and "Sepulcher of the vener-ated sage Rabbi . . ."

[Musée Archéologique:
13, boulevard de l'Amiral-Courbet, 30000 Nîmes. ✆ 0466767480.
Open Mar 15–Oct 14, Tue–Sun 10 A.M.–6 P.M.; Oct 15–Mar 14 11 A.M.–6 P.M.]
[Bibliothèque Municipale:
place Maison-Carrée, 30000 Nîmes.
✆ 0466763503. Open Tue and Thu 10:30 A.M.–7 P.M., Wed, Fri, and Sat 10:30 A.M.–6 P.M.]

Arles

■ The medieval Rue des Juifs is the present-day Rue du Docteur-Fanton. As in Aix-en-Provence, the Jewish quarter was totally transformed and integrated into the town after the expulsion of the Jews from Arles in 1493. This prefigured the expul-sion of all the Provençal Jews in 1500–1501.

■ The Museum of Old Arles (Musée de l'Arles Antique) holds two funer-ary inscriptions. On the first we read: "This is the burial place of Juda, the young son of Rabbi Mardochée. May the spirit of he who never sinned rest. May he abide in Eden." The second indicates that "This is the sepulcher of our master Meir."

The Museon Arlaten, a museum devoted to folk art and traditions, has a number of Jewish objects from the Provence region.

[Musée de l'Arles Antique:
avenue de la Iʳᵉ-Division-France-Libre, 13200 Arles. ✆ 0490188888.
Open Mar 1–Oct 31, daily 9 A.M.–7 P.M.; Nov 2–Feb 28, daily 10 A.M.–5 P.M.]
[Museon Arlaten:
29, rue de la République, 13200 Arles.
✆0490935811.
Open Jun 1–Aug 31, daily 9:30 A.M.–1 P.M. and 2–6:30 P.M.; Apr, May, and Sep, daily 9:30 A.M.–12:30 P.M. and 2–6 P.M.; Oct 1–Mar 31, daily 9:30 A.M.–12:30 P.M. and 2–5 P.M. Closed Jan 1, May 1, Nov 1, Dec 25, and Mon Oct 1–Jun 30.]

Complete transcription of the Song of Songs in Hebrew. Museon Arlaten, Arles.

Marseille

There are no remaining traces of Marseille's old Jewish communities. ■ However, visitors can admire the Grand Synagogue, which dates from the nineteenth century.

[Grand Synagogue: 117, rue de Breteuil, 13000 Marseille. Open Mon–Thu 2–6 P.M., Fri 2–3 P.M.]

Les Milles

When war was declared in September 1939, the authorities opened an assembly camp in a tile works in the village of Les Milles. Here they assembled foreign nationals from the hostile powers: anti-Nazi Germans and Austrians, Jews, and refugees. Among them were members of the émigré intelligentsia: Max Ernst, Hans Bellmer, Max Lingner. After the defeat of the French army and the armistice, the camp was turned into a "transit camp" for possible emigrants. Even before the Germans occupied the "Free Zone" in August–September 1942, the Vichy authorities ordered that some 2,000 Jews be deported to Drancy, and from there to the death camps. The camp was closed in March 1943.

[For more information, contact the Direction Départementale des Anciens Combattants et Victimes de Guerre: 11, rue Lafon, 13006 Marseille. ✆] 0491047500.]

Aix-en-Provence

The census ordered in 1341 by Robert, count of Provence, gave the Jewish population of Aix at the time as 1,205, representing the 203 families grouped together in the Jewish quarter.
■ The present-day Rue de la Verrerie corresponds to part of the old Jewish quarter.
■ Rue Vivaut was the site of the community buildings, including the synagogue, the butcher shop, the hospital, and the alms house. Nothing of these buildings remains.
■ The Granet Museum (Musée Granet) houses a cast of a funerary inscription stating "Rabbi Salomon, son of Rabbi David up above in the year [500]2."

The Jewish year 5002 corresponds to 1241–42 C.E.

[Musée Granet: 13, rue Cardinale, 13100 Aix-en-Provence. ✆ 0442381470. Open daily 10 A.M.–6 P.M. Note: the museum is closed for renovation until 2006.]

Trets

An important village in the Middle Ages—it had a *studium papale*— Trets had a Jewish community that lived in the present-day Rue Paul-Bert, known in those days as the *carriera judaica* or *judea*. The Jewish quarter in Trets is not unlike that in Gerona, Catalonia. Sadly, there has been no restoration so far. The medieval facade on Rue Paul-Bert could be a vestige of the synagogue.

[For more information, contact the tourist office at the Mairie de Trets, 13530 Trets. ✆ 0442615490.]

Antibes

■ The Picasso Museum (Musée Picasso) has the mold and a cast of an original inscription, now lost, in Greek characters (in ancient times, Antibes was called Antipolis): "Justus son of Sials, he lived seventy-two . . ."

[Musée Picasso: place Mariejol, 06600 Antibes. ✆ 0492905420. Open Oct 1–May 31, daily 10 A.M.–noon and 2–6 P.M.; Jun 1–Sep 30, Tue–Sun 10 A.M.–6 P.M.]

Languedoc ■

Montpellier

■ The present-day Rue de la Barra-lerie is the old Jewish *carrière.* The religious buildings include the synagogue, the House of Charity, and the medieval **mikvah,** which was rediscovered and restored. There is an entrance for visitors at number 1. One can see the ground water, the bath itself, and the room where the women undressed.

[To visit contact the tourist office:
Esplanade Comédie,
30, allée Jean de Lattre de Tassigny,
34000 Montpellier. ✆ 0467606060.]

Pézenas

■ The Jewish *carrière* in Pézenas is located below the castle walls, between the Faugères and Biaise gates. It is reached via a vaulted passage that gives onto Rue de la Juiverie.

[For more information and to visit, contact the tourist office: 1, place Gambetta,
34120 Pézenas. ✆ 0467983640.]

Béziers

■ The cloister of Saint-Nazaire cathedral has a synagogal inscription dated 1224 that can be compared to the one at Olot in Catalonia. The inscription

is on the wall to the right of the entrance on a stone set about six feet above the ground. Just beside it one can read the funerary inscription of Daniel, son of the rabbi Paregores.

Narbonne

■ The Museum of Art and History (Musée d'Art et d'Histoire) in Narbonne has the oldest known inscription relating to the Jewish presence in France. It is an epitaph for the three children of Paragorus: Justus, aged thirty; Matrona, twenty; and Dulciorella, nine. Absolute proof of the Jewishness of the inscription is given by a seven-branch candelabrum and a short text in Hebrew: "Peace on Israel." The museum also has a funerary inscription.

[Musée d'Art et d'Histoire: place de l'Hôtel de Ville (inside the city hall),
11100 Narbonne. ✆ 0468903030. Open Apr 1–Sep 30, Tue–Sun 9:30 A.M.–12:15 P.M. and 2–6 P.M.; Oct 1–Mar 31, Tue–Sun 10 A.M.–noon and 2–5 P.M.]

■ The Lapidary Museum (Musée Lapidaire) has a synagogal inscription dating from 1240 and a funerary inscription.

[Musée Lapidaire: place Lamourguier,
11100 Narbonne ✆ 0468655358.
Open Wed P.M. for guided tours at 2:30 P.M. and 3:30 P.M.]

The Southwest ■

After many years of English domination, the southwest was returned to France in the fifteenth century, at the end of the Hundred Years War. In an effort to stimulate growth in this ravaged region, Louis XI offered special privileges to foreigners wishing to settle there. This largesse attracted Portuguese and Spanish Jews oppressed by the Inquisition and religious intolerance in their home countries.

Bayonne

On the day of tishah b'ab—the commemoration of the destruction of the Temple in Jerusalem—the old synagogue resounds to these words in Spanish: "Hemos perdido Sion pero tambien hemos perdido. España tierra de consolacion" (We have lost Zion, but we have also lost Spain, land of consolation).

■ Bayonne's synagogue was built in 1837, but its Holy Ark, kept from the earlier place of worship, dates back to the reign of Louis XVI. It is said that even some of the **Torah** scrolls are of Spanish origin, from before the expulsion of 1492. They are said to have been brought by Marranos fleeing persecution.

[Synagogue: 35, rue Maubec, 64100 Bayonne. ✆ 0559550395.]

Synagogue, Bayonne.

Synagogue, Bordeaux.

■ Located at the corner of the avenue des Foix and avenue du 14-Avril, the cemetery was created in 1660. It contains the tombs of the community leaders and, surprisingly, those of eighteenth-century Jewish corsairs.

Bordeaux

For three centuries, the cellars of tumbledown houses in the old town were home to a hidden Jewish community, that of the *conversos* who came here from Spain after 1474. Used to hiding their faith in Spain, these "new Chris-tians" continued to practice their old religion in secret when they came to France. Bordeaux's Jewish community began to emerge from the shadows only in the mid-eighteenth century.

■ The synagogue was built in 1882 and designed by the architect Charles Durand. It has an impressive Ark bearing symbols of the twelve Biblical tribes and twelve colored stones that represent the breastplate worn by the high priest in the Temple at Jerusalem.

[Synagogue: 8, rue du Grand-Rabbin-Joseph-Cohen, 33800 Bordeaux. ✆ 0556917939.]

CHOCOLATE AT SAINT-ESPRIT-LES-ISRAÉLITES

In the seventeenth century the Jewish immigrants from Spain were cast out of central Bayonne and settled in Saint-Esprit. This quarter became known in popular parlance as Saint-Esprit-les-Israélites because Jews constituted the majority of its population—which was extremely rare in France. It was a Jew of Spanish origin, Gaspar Dacosta, who introduced the art of chocolate-making to Saint-Esprit, and indeed to France.

זֶה הַיָּם גָּדוֹל וּרְחַב יָדָיִם שָׁם רֶמֶשׂ

Great Britain

🕎 LONDON 🕎 OTHER CITIES IN ENGLAND |
🕎 SCOTLAND |

T HERE IS NO HISTORICAL RECORD of organized
Jewish communities in the British Isles before the
Norman invasion of 1066, when King William
encouraged Jews—mainly merchants and craftsmen—to follow him. Those who did came mainly
from France (Rouen) but also from Germany, Italy,
and Spain. They settled in London, York, Bristol
and Canterbury. Well regarded by the Norman
kings, the Jews' main role was financial; as moneylenders, they kept the kingdom's finances, and the
heavy taxes they paid represented a not inconsider-
able source of revenue.

Anti-Semitic feelings first surfaced in 1144,
when Jews were accused of making human sacri-
fices, and culminated with the massacre at York in
1190. A new stage was reached when Jews were
forced to wear a distinctive yellow sign in 1217.
The trend eventually led to the decree of expulsion
by Edward I in 1290. But if England was the first
country to expel the Jews, they were never completely absent. In London a *domus conversorum,* or
"house of converted Jews," standing on the site of
today's Chancery Lane Library, was home to Jews,

The Creation of the Fish, *twentieth century.*
Saint John's Wood Synagogue, London.

mostly Marranos, who continued to practice their religion in secret.

Foundations for a real return were laid after 1649 under Cromwell's Commonwealth as a result of intercession by Menasseh ben Israel, a rabbi of Portuguese origin living in the community at Amsterdam. The period of William of Orange (1650–1702) saw the arrival of numerous descendants of Jews who had been expelled from Spain and Portugal by the Catholic Monarchs, Ferdinand and Isabelle, in 1492. At the end of the seventeenth century,

Tom Merry, Queen Victoria with Benjamin Disraeli at Hughenden, *1887.*

Judaism was made legal by the Act for Suppressing Blasphemy. One of the results of this legalization, was the construction of the Bevis Marks Synagogue in London. A jewel of the city's Jewish heritage, the building is still in use today.

From 1750, most new immigrants came from Central Europe, and they tended to settle further to the north than their predecessors, attracted by the burgeoning cotton and wool industries in Birmingham, Manchester, and Liverpool.

A new wave of Jewish immigrants reached the shores of the British Isles after 1881, driven this time by Russian anti-Semitism. By 1882 there were 46,000 Jews living in England.

This presence is highlighted by the figure of Moses Montefiore (1784–1885), who was knighted by Queen Victoria in the first year of her reign; the launch in 1841 of the *Jewish Chronicle,* which remains one of the more lively Jewish newspapers even today; and, above all, the career of Benjamin Disraeli, who twice held the position of prime minister (1868, 1874–1880). From such evidence we can conclude that by 1890 Jewish emancipation in the United Kingdom was complete. Certainly, this would explain the strong attraction of the country for immigrants. There were no fewer than 120,000 new arrivals between 1880 and 1914 and, on the eve of World War I, the community numbered over 250,000.

One result of the First World War, was a new anti-Semitic feeling, which led to a marked slowdown in immigration. Immigration however, resurged in the 1930s with the arrival of some 100,000 German and Central European Jews, who brought economic and cultural knowledge.

The British government declared itself favorable to "the establishment in Palestine of a national home for the Jewish people" (Balfour Declaration, 2 November 1917). Placed under British mandate in 1922, Palestine suffered frequent clashes between the autochthonous and Jewish populations. In an effort to safeguard good relations with the Arab states, the British government published a white paper limiting Jewish immigration into Palestine to 15,000 persons a year for the five years from its promulgation. This was in May 1939, just as Nazism was beginning to threaten all of Europe. The situation was further complicated in 1945 when the survivors of Nazism were stopped on their way to the Promised Land and kept in camps on Cyprus—British camps, this time. In Great Britain itself, which escaped occupation by the Axis powers, deportations were virtually non-existent.

The Jewish community in Britain reached its apogee in the late 1960s, when the population exceeded 400,000. Today there are only 350,000, with two-thirds living in London; nonetheless, this represents one of the world's biggest Jewish communities.

→ **To call Great Britain from the United States, dial 011 44**
followed by the number of the person you are calling minus the initial 0 (used only for domestic calls).

London ■

The Jewish communities of London are highly diverse, in terms both of their rites and origins and of their geographical distribution. The Orthodox and **Hasidic** communities are found mainly in the north (Stamford Hill). For information on services, contact (preferably by phone) the very congenial Board of Deputies of British Jews.

[Board of Deputies of British Jews:
6 Bloomsbury Square, London WC1A 2LP.
✆ 02075435400, fax 02075430010.]

■ One introduction to Jewish life in London is to take a Stepping Out walking tour with professional City of London or Blue Badge guides. The Jewish Museum also offers numerous tours of the East End, including visits to synagogues that are usually closed to the public.

[Stepping Out Walking Tours:
✆ 02088812933 (answering machine giving list of times and meeting places).]
[Jewish Museum, Raymond Burton House:
129–131 Albert Street, London NW1 7NB.
✆ 02072861007.

Open Mon–Thu 10 A.M.–4 P.M. and
Sun 10 A.M.–5 P.M. 🚇 Camden Town.]

■ The British Museum is a must. Here, the British Library's Hebrew Collection is one of the biggest in the world, with some 3,000 manuscripts including Bibles, **Talmuds, kabbalah,** and **Haggadoth,** many of them illuminated. These come from all over Europe and some are over 1,000 years old. The collection also has the original Balfour Declaration of 1917.

[British Museum: Great Russell Street,
London WC1B 3DG. ✆ 02073238000.
Open Sat–Wed 10 A.M.–5:30 P.M.,
Thu and Fri 10 A.M.–8:30 P.M.
🚇 Tottenham Court Road.]

■ Finally, there are many documents on Jewish settlement in the British capital at the Guildhall Library, which specializes in history.

[Guildhall Library: Aldermanbury,
London EC2P 2EL. ✆ 02073321868.
Open Mon–Sat 9:30 A.M.–5:30 P.M.
🚇 Saint Paul's or Moorgate.]

CENTRAL LONDON (THE CITY, THE EAST END, AND THE WEST END)

■ Of the Jewish presence in the City during the Middle Ages there remains little more than memories, but it is a pleasure to walk around here. The three streets around the Bank of England—Poultry, Cheapside, and Old Jewry—were home to a community before the expulsion of 1290. Jewry Street, near Aldgate Underground station, is where the Jews took refuge during the riots that broke out at the coronation of King Richard I in 1189. And in Creechurch Lane the Cunard building marks the spot where the first synagogue was built in London after Cromwell's decision to allow Jews back onto English soil.

■ Still close to Aldgate Underground station, up Duke's Place, we come to Bevis Marks Synagogue, which was built in 1701 by the Portuguese and Spanish Jews after the return of the Jews from 1655 onward. The synagogue was located within the city walls, and its site was chosen so that it would not be visible from the street because the community wanted to remain discreet. Extremely well preserved, it is one of the oldest and most handsome synagogues still in use in Great Britain today. It also has a rich history, having been frequented by Sir Moses Montefiore and Benjamin Disraeli and because of its links with the Rothschild family. In addition, it houses one of the finest sets of pews from the Cromwellian and Queen Anne periods. The interior was strongly influenced by the mother synagogue in Amsterdam, which indeed donated one of the candelabras.

[Bevis Marks Synagogue: Bevis Marks, London EC3A 7JB.✆ 02076261274. Open Sun–Wed 11:30 A.M.–1 P.M. 🚇 Aldgate.]

■ The East End has a long tradition of immigration. Located close to London's docklands, it welcomed Huguenots and Irish immigrants and, after them, Jews. Today, its population is mainly made up of immigrants from India, Pakistan, and Bangladesh. This evolution is amusingly embodied in the history of the gloomy building on the corner of Fournier Street and Brick Lane: originally a Huguenot church, it later became a synagogue and is now a mosque. Before World War II, some 100,000 Jews lived here. There are now only 6,000. To get an idea of the old days, read Israel Zangwill (1864–1926), called the "Jewish Dickens." Zangwill paints a highly enjoyable and marvelously vivid picture of Jewish daily life here during the late nineteenth and early twentieth centuries.

■ The synagogue on Princelet Street is a real treasure. Built in 1870 on the foundation of an old Huguenot house dating from 1709, it is well worth a visit. Be sure to phone to make sure that it is open. The same goes for the Dutch Synagogue on Sandy's Row, installed in a Huguenot chapel of 1766.

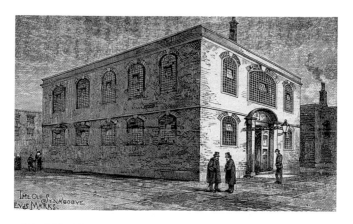

Bevis Marks Synagogue, London, 1891.
Musée d'Art et d'Histoire du Judaïsme, Paris.

[Princelet Street Synagogue:
19 Princelet Street, London E1.
✆ 02072475352. 🚇 Shoreditch.]

[Sandy's Row Synagogue:
Middlesex Street, London E1 7HW.
✆ 02073775854, or contact Mr. Wilder:
✆ 02072538311. 🚇 Liverpool Street.]

■ The West End of London also has plenty to satisfy visitors' curiosity. The history of British Zionism reminds us that Chaim Weitzman and other Zionists used to meet at 17 Piccadilly, which is also where Lord Rothschild received Lord Balfour's famous letter on 2 November 1917. Hyde Park has a small garden laid out in 1983 in memory of the *Shoah*.

[17 Piccadilly is closed to the public.
🚇 Hyde Park Corner or Green Park.]

■ The New West End Synagogue is one of London's finest. The first stone was laid on 7 June 1877 by Leopold de Rothschild, and the synagogue opened on 30 March 1879. It is similar in appearance to the Princes Road Synagogue in Liverpool. Both were built at around the same time by the same architect, George Audsley. There are fine stained-glass windows, as well as twenty **Sifrei Torah**, embroidery, and silverware from the early eighteenth century.

[New West End Synagogue:
St Petersburg Place, London W2 4LB.
✆ 02072292631. 🚇 Bayswater,
Queensway, or Notting Hill Gate.]

■ The synagogue on Great Portland Street, also known as the Central Synagogue, was built on the site of London's first **Ashkenazic** synagogue, consecrated in 1870. It was destroyed by a German bomb on 10 May 1941 and rebuilt in 1958. This modern structure has twenty-six stained-glass windows illustrating the Jewish festivals.

[Central Synagogue: 36–40 Hallam Street,
London W1N 6NN. ✆ 02075801355.
🚇 Regent's Park or Great Portland Street.]

■ The very handsome Westminster Synagogue, close to Harrods, has a unique collection of 1,000 **Torah** scrolls. Confiscated by the Nazis in Bohemia and Moravia, the scrolls were transported to London in 1964. They can be viewed on request.

[Westminster Synagogue: Rutland Gardens, London SW7 1BX. ✆ 02075843953. ⛟ Knightsbridge.]

■ On the other side of the Thames, the Holocaust Museum is housed in the Imperial War Museum. Among the surprising objects on display here are a cart from the Warsaw Ghetto that was used to carry corpses and a railway car used in the deportation (a donation from the Belgian railways authority). Also worth a mention for its originality is the exhibit showing how Jews have contributed to Her Majesty's Army from the Crimea through to the present.

[Imperial War Museum: Lambeth Road, London SE1 6HZ. ✆ 02074165000. ⛟ Lambeth North or Waterloo.]

NORTH LONDON

Saint John's Wood, Hampstead, and, above all, Golders Green and Stamford Hill are at the heart of London's Jewish life and have large numbers of shops. Amusingly enough, most of the shops selling **kosher** products are now run by Indians.

■ The Jewish Museum has two buildings, one in Camden and the other in Finchley. Founded in 1932, the museum in Camden houses the world's finest collection of religious and other objects, many of them brought by immigrants from the Norman Conquest to more recent times. Particularly notable are the eighteenth-century portraits, an interactive map showing population movements in Great Britain, an Italian *aron* from the sixteenth century, the oldest **Hanukkah** lamp in England, and illuminated marriage contracts.

In Finchley, the other part of the museum is a cultural center with pedagogical activities (Leo Baeck College trains Reform rabbis). The second floor presentation depicts the life of a person who escaped the *Shoah* and focuses on the history of World War II. With its 400 recorded testimonies and photographic archives, this museum specializes in social history, and also features temporary exhibitions.

[Camden: Raymond Burton House, 129–131 Albert Street, London NW1 7NB. ✆ 02072841997. Open Mon–Thu 10 A.M.–4 P.M., Sun 10 A.M.–5 P.M. ⛟ Camden Town.]
[Finchley: The Sternberg Centre, 80 East End Road, London N3 2SY. ✆ 02083491143. Open Mon–Thu 10:30 A.M.–5 P.M., Sun 10:30 A.M.–4:30 P.M. Closed Sun in Aug and Jewish holidays. ⛟ Finchley Central.]

■ Finally, the most picturesque but little-known and least accessible district is Stamford Hill. It can be reached only by car or by train from Liverpool Street station. It has some sixty synagogues and prayer halls representing a wide range of religious tendencies, especially Orthodox and **Hasidic**.

Other Cities in England ■

Oxford

Oxford's oldest synagogue was transformed into a tavern, then incorporated into one of the university's oldest colleges, Christchurch. There is, however, a new synagogue. It was built in 1974 on the site of an older one from 1880, of which only a wall remains.

[Oxford Synagogue: 21 Richmond Road, Oxford, OX1 2JL. ✆ 01865514356.]

Manchester

With 30,000 Jews, Manchester has the highest Jewish population in Great Britain after London. Ashkenazic and Sephardic immigrants came here between 1883 and 1905. Many of the Oriental Jews were drawn by the cotton industry, which processed the raw material from North Africa. The city still has about forty synagogues.

[For more information, contact the Jewish Representative Council of Greater Manchester: Bury Old Road, Manchester N8 GFY. ✆ and fax 01617208721.]

■ The Jewish Museum is housed in a Spanish and Portuguese–rite synagogue dating from 1874 that was saved from destruction and transformed into a museum in 1985. It is a magnificent structure with a splendid collection of **Judaica.**

[Jewish Museum: 190 Cheetham Hill Road, Manchester M8 8LW. ✆ 01618349879.]

Liverpool

The Merseyside city of Liverpool can proudly claim to have been home to northern England's largest Jewish community in the nineteenth century. Today, the community centers around Dunbabin Road, location of the city's Jewish cultural center at Harold House.

[For more information, contact the Jewish Youth and Community Centre at Harold House: Dunbabin Road, Liverpool L15 6XL. ✆ 01514755671.]

■ Liverpool boasts one of Britain's finest synagogues. Consecrated on 3 September 1874, the building on Princes Road is particularly admirable for its late Victorian interior. Be sure to call ahead before attempting to visit.

[Synagogue: Princes Road, Liverpool L8 1TG. ✆ 01517093431.]

Leeds

There are still 10,000 Jews living in the Yorkshire town of Leeds. They began arriving around 1840 and, in

Jewish Museum, Manchester.

increasing numbers, between 1881 and 1905 as a result of persecution in Russia. The town had a flourishing wool industry and, in 1885, was the scene of the first spontaneous strike by Jewish workers. The inhabitants of the Chapeltown and Leylands quarters have since moved to more spacious districts like Moortown, in the northern part of the city. The area has several synagogues, the most frequented one being the Beth Hamedrash, as well as restaurants, butcher shops, and a few specialty bookstores.

[For more information, contact the community center: Shadwell Lane, Leeds LS17 8DW. ✆ 01132697520.]

[Beth Hamedrash Synagogue: 399 Street Lane Gardens, Leeds LS17 6HQ. ✆ 01132692181.]

York

York's Jewish community was the victim of the bloodiest outbreaks of anti-Semitism in the twelfth century. In those days the Jews were well established alongside the merchant classes, to whom they provided financial services. However, following the death of Henry II, the protector of the Jews, and the coronation of Richard I, "the Lionheart," anti-Jewish riots struck. On 16 March 1190, while the king was away on a crusade, the barons in debt to the Jewish moneylenders attacked Clifford's Tower, where the moneylenders had taken refuge. The Jews were trapped: some committed suicide; the rest were slaughtered.

Scotland

The first mention of a Jew in Scotland is in the minutes of a meeting by the Edinburgh Council dated 1 September 1665, and it relates to his request to be converted so that he can work in the city. Jewish communities in Scotland date from 1717 in Edinburgh and 1823 in Glasgow.

Glasgow

Most of Glasgow's synagogues are in the suburbs, where the majority of the city's 6,500 Jews now live. The oldest of them, dating from 1879, is in Garnethill.

[Garnethill Synagogue: 127 Hill Street, Glasgow G3 6UB. ✆ 01413324911.]

Edinburgh

Edinburgh's community of about 1,000 Jews has a synagogue built in the 1930s and designed by the Glaswegian architect James Miller. It is in the modern style with a red brick facade.

[Edinburgh Synagogue: 4 Salisbury Road, EH16 5EB. ✆ 01316673144.]

Republic of Ireland and Northern Ireland

☙ DUBLIN ☙ CORK ☙ LIMERICK ☙ BELFAST ▮

W HILE IRELAND IS NOT AN OBVIOUS DESTI-NATION for those interested in Jewish culture, the island does offer a few surprises. Ireland's Jewish population has never been higher than 8,000, and that was in the late 1940s. Today, it is down to under 2,000, of which 1,500 are in the Republic of Ireland. The last **kosher** butcher closed shop in May 2001.

The first trace of a Jewish presence is found in the *Annals of Innisfallen,* which relates the arrival of five Jews, probably from Rouen, in Limerick harbor. But it was not until 1290, and the expulsion of the Jews from England, that a real community took shape. The expulsion of the Jews from the Iberian Peninsula in the fifteenth century sent a second wave of emigrants to Irish shores, mainly the southern coast. A century later, in 1656 or 1660, depending on the source, a group of Marranos opened the first prayer hall, opposite Dublin Castle. The cemetery at Ballybough (County Dublin) has allowed Jewish burials since the beginning of the eighteenth century.

The Dublin home of Leopold Bloom, a character in James Joyce's Ulysses.

Between the end of the Napoleonic Wars and the start of the twentieth century, pogroms drove Jews to Ireland from Central Europe, especially Lithuania. Some of those who did not continue on to the Americas settled in Irish towns, built synagogues, opened **kosher** butcher shops, and created close-knit communities. The most important of them was located around Dublin's South Circular Road.

Jews also became prominent in public life. Those from czarist Russia played a leading part in the establishment of the Tailors' Union in 1909. Jews were involved in the independence movement, which triumphed in 1921. Robert Briscoe is the best remembered of these: a colorful figure and, as he claimed, the only Jewish member of the IRA, he was twice mayor of Dublin, in 1956–57 and 1961–62. His son Benjamin occupied the same position in 1988–89.

Another memorable name is that of the Herzog family. After occupying the highest religious positions in Ireland, Rabbi Isaac Herzog became the first chief rabbi of the fledgling state of Israel. His son Chaim, who was born in Belfast and raised in Dublin, became the sixth president of the Jewish state. Today, the Dublin rabbinate's offices are still at Herzog House, on Zion Road.

→ **To call the Republic of Ireland from the United States, dial 011 353**

→ **To call Northern Ireland from the United States, dial 011 44**
followed by the number of the person you are calling, minus the initial 0 (used only for domestic calls).

Dublin

Dublin's Jewish community reached its apogee at the end of the nineteenth century. It centered around South Circular Road. Indeed, Dubliners nicknamed Warren Street, Martin Street, and Saint Kevin's Parade "Little Jerusalem."

■ The Irish Jewish Museum is housed in the old synagogue on Walworth Road. This place of worship was the center of Jewish life in the capital until the movement out to the suburbs and a gradual shrinking of the population led to its closure in the 1970s. In 1985 Chaim Herzog, former president of Israel, gave a speech inaugurating the new museum. It houses archives and objects and depicts the distinctive characteristics of the community. On the first floor, visitors can admire a kitchen ready for a typical **Shabbat** at the turn of the twentieth century. On the second floor, one can admire the well-preserved synagogue.

[Irish Jewish Museum: 3/4 Walworth Road, South Circular Road, Dublin 8. ✆ 14901857 or 14531797. Open May 1–Sep 30, Tue, Thu, and Sun 11 A.M.–3:30 P.M.; Oct 1–Apr 30, Sun only 10:30 A.M.–2:30 P.M.]

■ 52 Upper Clanbrassil Street (Dublin 8) is the birthplace of Leopold Bloom, one of the two protagonists of *Ulysses,* the 1922 masterpiece by James Joyce (1880–1941). Bloom was the son of a Hungarian Jew who emigrated to Dublin and changed his name. A plaque on the wall recalls his presence here. *Ulysses* also mentions Emorville Square, Lombard Street West, and Saint Kevin's Parade. Bloom has become such a popular character that Ireland's main literary festival is named after him: Bloomsday is held every year on 16 June.

[For more information, contact the James Joyce Centre: 35 North Great George's Street, Dublin 1. ✆ 18788547.]

The synagogue on Adelaide Road, Dublin.

♈ ULYSSES

"I, Rudolph Virag, now resident at no 52 Clanbrassil Street, Dublin, formerly of Szombathely in the kingdom of Hungary, hereby give notice that I have assumed and intend henceforth upon all occasions and at all times to be known by the name of Rudolph Bloom."

JAMES JOYCE, *ULYSSES*
(PARIS: SHAKESPEARE & CO., 1922.)

DUBLIN'S SYNAGOGUES

■ The synagogue on Adelaide Road, which was consecrated in 1892, closed in June 1999. Another, Greenville Hall, built in 1920, is now home to a high-tech company. The Greek columns and Stars of David that decorate the exterior can still be admired.

[Adelaide Road Synagogue:
Adelaide Road, Dublin 2.]
[Greenville Hall: Mason Technology,
228 South Circular Road, Dublin 8.]

■ Three active synagogues remain; the times of services can be obtained from the Jewish Community Centre.

[Jewish Community Centre: Herzog House, Zion Road, Rathgar, Dublin 6. ✆ 14923751, fax 14924680. Open Mon–Fri 9 A.M.–2 P.M.]

[Dublin Hebrew & Terenure Congregation: contact Michael Coleman, 33 Rathfarnham Road, Terenure, Dublin 6. ✆ 14923751, fax 14924680.]

[Machzikei ha-Das: Rathmore Villas, Rear 11, Terenure Road North, Dublin 6. ✆ 14923751.]

[Orthodox Synagogue: 7 Leicester Avenue, Rathgar, Dublin 6. ✆ 14923751.]

CEMETERIES

■ The last burial at Ballybough cemetery was in 1908, but the Jewish community has continuously employed a guardian to take care of the site since then. An inscription on the guardian's lodge, at the entrance to the cemetery, reads: "Built in the year 5618."

■ Dublin's Jews are buried at Dolphins Barn cemetery, not far from the Donore Avenue bridge over the Grand Canal.

[To visit, contact Mr. and Mrs. C. O'Neill: ✆ 18336956.]

Cork

Shalom Park opened in 1989 on the site of the old "Jewstown." This was the quarter where James Joyce's father was born.

Limerick

Limerick's small Jewish community (170 people) disappeared in 1904 after the only pogrom in Irish history— a pogrom with zero victims.

■ The small Jewish cemetery of Kilmurray at Newcastle, County Limerick, has been restored and its six tombstones are perfectly preserved.

Belfast

■ Belfast Synagogue holds regular Friday evening services.

[Belfast Synagogue: 49 Somerton Road, Belfast BT15 3LH. ✆ 02890775013.]

■ The cemetery on Falls Road, a few miles north of Belfast, has one of the oldest Jewish tombs in Northern Ireland, a big granite obelisk in memory of Daniel Joseph Jaffe. Sadly, the monument has been neglected and is covered with graffiti.

The Netherlands

HOLLAND HAS ALWAYS WELCOMED political and religious refugees. The first great wave of Jews immigrated to the Netherlands from Spain and Portugal at the end of the sixteenth century. Although nominally present since the twelfth century, the Jews in Holland were able to openly practice their religion for the first time beginning in this later period. The **Sephardic** Jews were the first to make a mark on Holland. In the turbulent context of the Dutch struggle for independence from Spain, they preferred to identify themselves as Portuguese rather than Spanish, even when they had immigrated from Castile or Andalusia. The Spaniards were attempting to impose their Catholic faith on the Calvinist Dutch as well as their centralized system of government and unpopular taxes, and so given their common distrust of Hapsburg Spain, the provinces of the Low Countries constituted an unexpected refuge for the Jews.

The first nucleus of a Jewish community arose on the banks of the Amstel River. It would take some fifteen years for this community to be recognized, since the Jews used Dutch names for managing

Man dressed in a tallith bearing a scroll of the Torah, seventeenth century. Musée d'Art et d'Histoire du Judaïsme, Paris.

their commercial affairs until 1616. Little by little they openly declared their identity, practiced circumcision, and reconnected to a Jewish tradition that a segment of the community did not even know. Although tolerated in Holland, Jews could not yet hold a civil or military office, nor could they become Christians or proselytize. Guild membership and engaging in retail trade were likewise prohibited, but not a single Jewish ghetto existed.

The first synagogue was constructed in Amsterdam in 1612. In 1619, a law stipulated that each city of the United Provinces was free to determine its own policies regarding the Jews, but that the towns could under no circumstances require Jews to bear any distinguishing sign. In 1657, Holland officially recognized Jews as citizens of the country. The Dutch authorities asked them not only to declare their religion but also to behave as "good Jews," in other words, to practice in an orthodox manner. This demand, applied equally to various Protestant sects, went beyond the promise of religious freedom, and left a majority of the exiles perplexed. The Jews of Portuguese descent, having largely modified their rituals in order to practice them in secret, no longer knew exactly the correct form of their rituals and had to summon rabbis from other countries for help. The first among these was a Spanish-speaking rabbi from Thessaloníki. This situation gave significant power to the leaders of Jewish religious communities, who then issued strict regulations. These leaders (parnassim) were responsible to the Dutch authorities for maintaining order within their groups. To be a member of the Jewish community in good standing it was necessary to pay a tax and comply with its rules. The community founded its first synagogue, created educational and charitable institutions, and even

Megillah of the Scroll of Esther, seventeenth century. Musée d'Art et d'Histoire du Judaïsme, Paris.

established a trade tribunal for settling disputes between Jews. Among the first students at one of Amsterdam's early Talmudic schools was a young boy of five years old who later became the famous philosopher Baruch Spinoza. Because the magistrates of Amsterdam recognized only religious communities, not belonging to such a group risked serious trouble. A failure to obey Jewish law brought the threat of excommunication (**herem**), which not only isolated the individual but also threw him into a legal no-man's-land. Those who were excommunicated were forbidden even to speak to family members. Records show cases of **herem**, which lasted anywhere from a day to eleven years.

A HEREM FOR LIFE

A lifelong **herem** was pronounced only on two occasions, notably in 1656 against Baruch Spinoza. This descendant of Portuguese converts was banned from the community for having doubted the value of biblical writings. His views knit together notions of the immortality of the soul, the supernatural, the existence of miracles, and the possibility of a God outside philosophy. According to this disciple of Descartes, religion was entirely invented by mankind in order to impose a moral order upon society and to obtain obedience.

Attributed to Jan ten Compe, Houtegracht *(Jonas Daniel Meijerplein), eighteenth century. Private collection, Amsterdam.*

Beginning in 1635 Jews from eastern Europe began settling in Holland, first from Germany and then, after 1648, from Poland and Lithuania. In general, the immigrants arrived impoverished and were forced to live in the slums. By the middle of the seventeenth century, however, 20 percent of the

ASHKENAZIM VERSUS SEPHARDIM

As new arrivals, the **Ashkenazim** were initially shunned by **Sephardic** society to the point that it was even forbidden to give them alms at the entrance to the synagogue. Intermarriage between the two communities was not permitted, nor was the burial of **Ashkenazim** in the Ouderkerk (Old Church) cemetery (located in the suburbs of Amsterdam). Unable to find better employment, the **Ashkenazim** were relegated to domestic labor for the **Sephardim**. At the time, the word *tudesca* (literally "German woman") was synonymous with "household servant." Later the wealthier Polish-Lithuanians would adopt the same elitist attitude and attempt to get rid of the poor among them. . . .
In 1674, the **Ashkenazim** joined the **Sephardic** community in large numbers for the first time. Of a total population of 180,000 Jewish inhabitants in Amsterdam, the **Sephardic** community numbered around 2,500 members. The **Ashkenazim** had become the clear majority, with the **Sephardim** representing only 10 percent of Amsterdam's Jewish population (down to 6 percent at the beginning of the twentieth century).

Ornamented handle of a Torah scroll, Amsterdam, seventeenth/ eighteenth century. Musée d'Art et d'Histoire du Judaïsme, Paris).

stockbrokers registered with the Amsterdam Stock Exchange were Jewish. They had a recognized expertise owing largely to their knowledge of languages and connections developed during their Diaspora experiences. These same qualities permitted the Jews to act as intermediaries in diplomatic affairs. Jews held visible positions in the silk industry, sugar refineries, and diamond cutting, as well as becoming printers, librarians (primarily of religious books), and doctors. They also pursued careers in banking and commerce. Some of these became successful in commerce with the Antilles and Dutch East Indies to the point of owning a quarter of the shares in the Dutch East India Company. By the mid-eighteenth century, Amsterdam possessed the largest Jewish community in Europe.

Levi Phoebus ha-Levi, illustrations from the Book of Customs *depicting Passover, Hanukkah, and Shabbat, Amsterdam, 1662. Musée d'Art et d'Histoire du Judaïsme, Paris.*

With the French Revolution and the creation of the Batavian Republic in 1796, the National Assembly granted civil rights to the 23,400 Jews in Holland. The Netherlands was the first country to accept Jews in Parliament and to grant them access to government posts. Napoleon Bonaparte's occupation of Holland led to the promulgation of an agreement regulating relations between "German" and "Portuguese" Jews, and to the establishment of a mutual organization under the direction of a Jewish assembly. King William I (1815–40) likewise advanced the welfare and education of the Jewish community. In 1857, Jews were permitted to attend public schools and obliged to reserve religious education for Sundays and evenings. Jewish schools were reopened In Amsterdam only in the twentieth century.

The first half of the twentieth century was marked by an increasing number of mixed marriages and

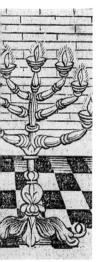

thus a decline in the traditional structure of the Jewish community. The new captains of industry such as Samuel Van den Bergh, whose margarine factory gave birth to the giant Unilever, or those who headed the large department store chains were perfectly integrated into non-Jewish society. Jewish newspapers (four weeklies and numerous monthly newspapers and magazines) are still in existence from before the outbreak of the Second World War, but from that period on have been published in Dutch.

In May 1940 German troops occupied the Netherlands. The Jews of Holland suffered greatly under Nazi domination: Of a total population of 140,000, 104,000 were killed. A Dutch minority actively opposed to the Nazis helped 22,000 Jews go into hiding. Sadly 8,000 of those Jews were caught. After the war, between 20,000 and 30,000 Jews resettled in their Dutch homeland. At the dawn of the new millennium, Jews numbered around 27,000 of a total population in the Netherlands of 15.5 million inhabitants. Of the hundred synagogues that existed before World War War II, some thirty remain. Regular services take place in only a few of the surviving synagogues.

→ **To call the Netherlands from the United States, dial 011 31** followed by the number of the person you are calling minus the initial 0 (used only for domestic calls).

Northern Holland

Amsterdam

Despite the devastations of the Second World War and the aesthetic short-comings of post-war reconstruction, Amsterdam offers the visitor a Jewish patrimony of extraordinary richness that is concentrated, for the most part, in its memorials. The former Jewish quarter, the Jodenbuurt, is yours to discover along the streets and canals in the southeast of the city. It is easy to imagine the period when the area was home to a population that had grown from several hundred inhabitants at the end of the sixteenth century to some 100,000 in 1940. Among the attractions are exceptional museums, synagogues, and period homes of famous residents (Rembrandt, de Pinto) preserved in their original state. Diamond-cutting workshops, guild houses, and religious monuments are also among the numerous traces of 350 years of Jewish presence.

If Amsterdam has brought a lot to the Jews, the reverse also holds true. The city has absorbed many typically Jewish characteristics into its language, cuisine, and sense of humor. Hence, *mazel* (good luck) and *meshuga* (crazy) can still be heard in the local dialect; likewise, the Netherlands adopted pickled herring and onions, sausages, and fromage blanc.

THE JEWISH HISTORICAL MUSEUM

■ The Jewish Historical Museum alone requires nearly a half day. Since 1987, the museum has been the heart of a cultural complex made up of four synagogues active until 1943 and subsequently sold to the municipality in 1955. The museum depicts Jewish customs, the fundamentals of the Jewish religion and Zionism, as well as the way of life of Dutch **Sephardim** and **Ashkenazim** in past centuries.

In 1943 the collection of the synagogue complex was taken to Offenbach in Germany. Less than 20 percent of the stolen goods were recovered by the Dutch government after the war. With the aid of glass and metal installations, the displays of these four synagogues recall the massacre of the majority of Amsterdam's Jewish inhabitants, a tragedy not only for the Jews but for the city as well. The Grand Synagogue was consecrated in March 1671 by the **Ashkenazic** community, which had renounced the claims of the false Messiah Sabbataï Zevi. Today display cases containing silver ritual objects occupy the former location of the **bimah.** The Ark of the Covenant, made completely of marble, has been restored, as have the galleries

reserved for men and women and the **mikvah.** Space demands led to the construction of three other synagogues nearby: Obbene Sjoel (1685), Dritt Sjoel (1700), and the New Synagogue (1752). In addition to religious objects and works of art, the museum also displays documents retracing the history of the two Jewish communities and the people who influenced them. One such figure gives the square its name: Jonas Daniel Meijer (1780–1834), a lawyer and highly-ranking civil servant who attempted to improve the welfare of underprivileged Jews in Amsterdam.

[Jewish Historical Museum:
Jonas Daniel Meijerplein 2-4,
Postbus 16737, 1001 RE Amsterdam.
℃ 0206269945 or 0206254229 (information),
fax 0206241721. ❶ info@jhm.nl.

Pieter Schenck, Ashkenazic Synagogue, *Amsterdam, seventeenth/eighteenth century. Musée d'Art et d'Histoire du Judaïsme, Paris).*

NORTHERN HOLLAND

Open 11 A.M.–5 P.M. Closed Yom Kippur.
🚇 Waterlooplein (exit Nieuw Amstelstraat).
🚌 9, 14, or 20 (bus stop Waterlooplein).]
■ After your visit to the museum, explore the ancient Jewish quarter as you read what follows, much of which has been mentioned in connection with the museum.

President of the High Court in 1939, Lluis Ernest Visser actively defended the Jews during the Nazi occupation. After you cross the square that bears his name, Mr. Visserplein, you come upon the Moses and Aaron Catholic Church. The tiny statues that once decorated the facade and gave the church its name are presently found on the back wall. On your left, enter Jodenbreestraat. From the eighteenth century to the Second World War, this street was the principal artery in the Jewish quarter. In 1965, the northern part was destroyed and the street rerouted.

THE REMBRANDT MUSEUM

■ At numbers 4–6 Jodenbreestraat stands the house where the famous painter Rembrandt lived and worked from 1639 until 1658. Although not a Jew, he lived in the Jewish quarter. He occupied the first floor of the house with his first wife, Saskia van Uylenburgh, who died young, and then with Hendrickje Stoffels, his second wife. Rembrandt created the majority of his paintings in the second-floor workshop and gave lessons in the attic. Restored between 1907 and 1911 and decorated with furniture and housewares from the seventeenth century, Rembrandt's house displays numerous drawings and nearly the entire oeuvre of the artist's etchings (250 of the 300 that he executed). Among these works are self-portraits, nude studies, beggars, and scenes of domestic life.

The influence of Rembrandt's Jewish environment is visible in his work. Several wealthy Jews commissioned their portraits from the artist, including Menasseh ben Israel, whose likeness is on display in the museum. The rabbi and author lived for many years across the street from Rembrandt and even commissioned him to illustrate several of his books. Likewise, Rembrandt often asked his neighbors to pose for his biblical scenes. Among this group of images on display are engravings such as *The Sacrifice of Abraham* (1635), *Jacob and Benjamin* (1637), *The Triumph of Mordecai* (1641), *Abraham and Isaac* (1645), and *David and Goliath* (1655).

[Rembrandt Museum:
Jodenbreestraat 4–6, 1011 NK Amsterdam.
✆ 0206384668, fax 0205200400.
Open Mon–Sat 10 A.M.–5 P.M.,
Sun and public holidays 1–5 P.M.
Closed New Year's Day.]
■ The Rijksmuseum (located in another area of the city) displays many of Rembrandt's paintings. Besides the famous *Nightwatch,* a number of significant works from the artist's Jewish period are to be found here,

Rembrandt, The Jewish Synagogue, *seventeenth century. Rothschild Collection, Musée du Louvre, Paris.*

including *The Jewish Bride* and *The Lamentations of Jeremiah.* One also finds at the Rijksmuseum *The Portuguese Synagogue* by Emmanuel de Witte and the *Jewish Wedding* by Kosf Israels.

[Rijksmuseum: Stadhouderskade 42, 1070 DN Amsterdam. ✆ 0206747047. Open daily 10 A.M.–5 P.M.]

■ Upon leaving the Rembrandt Museum, cross the Saint Antoniebrug, a small bridge accessing Saint Antonie-breestraat and offering a nice view of Amsterdam. You will notice further down the street the ornately carved wooden belfry of Montelbaan Tower. It is said this is where the first Jews coming from Spain and Portugal disembarked.

THE ISAAC DE PINTO HOUSE

The house of the wealthy Portuguese Jew Isaac de Pinto, at 69 Antonie-breestraat, was purchased in 1651 for the considerable sum of 30,000 florins. De Pinto had the house remodeled in 1680 following the

plans of Elias Bourseman. The cream-colored Italian Renaissance-style facade is undeniably one of the loveliest in the neighborhood. With six imposing pilasters crowned by a blind balustrade concealing the roof, the facade gave rise to the expression "as rich as de Pinto." Partly destroyed during the Nazi occupation, the majority of the home's occupants perished in the *Shoah*. The building was saved from demolition thanks to a preservation campaign that led to its restoration in 1975 and that, in the end, facilitated the revival of the entire district. Still

located in a residential neighborhood, the building now houses a public library. Be sure to go inside to see the birds and cupids that adorn the original paintings on the ceiling.

[Isaac de Pinto House:

St. Antoniebreestraat 69,

1011 HB Amsterdam. Open Mon and Wed

2–8 P.M., Fri 2–5 P.M., and Sat 11 A.M.–2 P.M.]

WATERLOOPLEIN

■ Returning across the Saint Antoniebrug and turning right just before the Rembrandt Museum will bring you to the Waterlooplein, where a flea market used to take place every day except Saturday (now it is closed on Sunday). This location has served as the marketplace for the Jewish quarter since 1886. The filling of two canals created this large square in the heart of the Jodenbuurt, which occupies the site of an ancient artificial island between the current city hall and the opera house. Because originally Jews did not have the right to own retail businesses, they bought and sold goods in the streets. Much less picturesque today than in the past, the market now attracts primarily people selling used clothes, African batiks, and Indonesian jewelry.

[Waterlooplein Flea Market: Located

behind the new theater. Waterlooplein 1,

1011 NV Amsterdam. ✆ 0205512512.

Open Mon–Sat 9 A.M.–5 P.M. 🚇 The subway

runs directly to Waterlooplein from

Centraal Station.]

■ Continuing straight ahead, with the canal on your right-hand side, you will come to a black marble memorial erected in 1988 that commemorates the Jewish resistance during the Second World War.

■ Turn to your left and follow the Amstel River for 656 ft. Just before the Blauwbrug bridge, a glance to the left reveals the outline of a house in front of the Muziektheater. Before World War II, this house was an **Ashkenazic** orphanage for boys established by Megadlei Yetomim in 1738. In March of 1943 the children living in the orphanage were deported to the Sobibór concentration camp.

■ Cross the street at this point and continue along the river to your right. Turn to the left just before the wooden bridge (Walter Süsskindbrug) to reach Nieuwe Herengracht Street. During the war Walter Süsskind made use of his position as a member of the Jewish Council and saved many Jewish children from deportation. A plaque on the other side of the bridge commemorates Süsskind's courage.

■ Walk to the end of Nieuwe Herengracht, inhabited since the nineteenth century by wealthy Jews. Turn to the right and cross the Vaz Diasbrug bridge, which commemorates a Jewish journalist of Portuguese origin. You should now be on Weesperstraat. Some 150 feet ahead there is a small square with a monument to the memory of "those who protected Dutch Jews during the years of occupation."

The memorial, created by the sculptor J. Wertheim, was erected in 1947.

■ Turning right at the following bridge brings you to Nieuwe Keizersgracht. During the war the Jews named the waterway "the new martyrs' canal," since at the time 58 Nieuwe Keizersgracht housed the Jewish Council. As in other occupied countries, highly placed Jews who accepted a role in this organization imposed by the Nazis believed that their participation would slow the process of the realization of the Final Solution. Unfortunately, this was rarely the case.

■ Return to Weesperstraat, turn right, follow this street to Nieuwe Kerkstraat, and turn left. At one time inhabited by Portuguese Jews, Nieuwe Kerkstraat was also known as "Jewish Churchstreet." Number 127 Nieuwe Kerkstraat, now occupied by a wine and soft drink company, was once the morgue *(Metaarhuis)* attached to the hospital on the Nieuwe Keizesgracht. Bodies were washed and prepared there following Jewish ritual. It was said at the time, "One enters by the Keizersgracht and leaves by the Kerkstraat." A little further down the street, at number 149, is a synagogue founded by Russian Jews, the Russian **shul**. On the facade of the building you can make out a round, stained-glass window with a Star of David. Just beside this building is the Sailors' Synagogue, no doubt so named because of the considerable number of Dutch

Jews who had to work at sea during the economic recession at the end of the eighteenth century.

■ Cross the bridge at the end of the Nieuwe Kerkstraat (on the left), which will bring you to the Lau Marzirelbrug bridge, named after a lawyer who opposed the registration of Jews during the war and participated in an attack on the offices where the records containing the names of Jews were held.

■ You now enter the Plantage quarter, which was a detention area outside the city limits. Cafés, tearooms, and theaters proliferated in this area that was home to numerous wealthy Jews. In 1924, nearly half the inhabitants of the quarter were Jewish.

Walk down Plantage Kerklaan until you come to the traffic light and turn left into the Plantage Middenlaan. Immediately to your left is the former Dutch Theater, one of the most important memorials consecrated to the victims of the Second World War in Holland.

DUTCH THEATER
(HOLLANDSCHE SCHOUWBURG)

■ This theater, which before the war produced such renowned Dutch actors as Esther de Boer van Rijk, Louis de Vries and his troupe, and even Herman Heyermans, was requisitioned in 1942 by the Germans. The Jews were detained here before they were taken to the Westerbork transit camp and then transferred to concentration camps. Since 1962 this building has served as a memorial. Engraved here are the names of 7,600 families whose relatives are among the 104,000 Jews who never returned from the concentration camps. Inside the memorial, documents, photographs, and films testify to the gradual isolation of the Jews during the occupation. Policies of discrimination were adopted slowly in an attempt to "gently" lead the Dutch toward considering the Jews as different beings. Such measures went from forbidding Jews to ride bicycles (a typically Dutch means of conveyance) or go fishing to prohibiting them from entering any public space. The Dutch were forced to declare they were pure Aryan, and when such was not the case, were fired from their jobs and forced to send their children to Jewish schools. The first deportations occurred in May 1942 and were masked as departures for "work camps" in eastern Europe. The Jews who had acquiesced to Nazi-enforced registration were summoned alphabetically and assembled in the Dutch Theater. The Germans also raided areas with a high concentration of Jews in order to round up other members of the community. In the span of a year, more than 60,000 Jews were held in this theater, whose seats had been removed to accommodate them. That, at the beginning of the occupation, the theater had been reserved for a Jewish public who came to watch

Jewish actors forbidden to act on any other stage reveals a tragic irony.

[Hollandsche Schouwburg: Plantage Middenlaan 24, 1001 IE Amsterdam. Open daily 10 A.M.–4 P.M., closed Yom Kippur. Free entrance. For more information about the theater, direct inquiries to the Jewish Historical Museum.]

■ As you exit the theater, head back toward the traffic light and turn left onto Plantage Kerklaan. The building at number 36 was the location of the city's population records during the war. The plaque commemorates the attack on the office of 27 March 1943 by a Resistance group attempting to destroy the records. The attack failed because the files were too thick and well bound to burn rapidly. Twelve members of the group, including several Jews, were captured and executed.

■ A little further along on the same street is one of the oldest zoos in the world, the Artis. For 125 years it has delighted the inhabitants of the quarter, notably on the days of **Shabbat**, because visitors only had to pay the following day if they did not have a membership card. Continuing to number 61, you will find the decorative facade of Plancius, a building dating from 1876 that housed groups of musicians and theater companies. It was established on the initiative of a Jewish choral society, called Oefening Baart Kunst ("from practice art is born"). A Star of David on the pediment recalls the cultural origins of this edifice. At the end of the nineteenth century, when socialism gained popularity among the Jews, the building also functioned as a meeting hall. This was where the great Jewish leader Henri Polak, founder of the diamond workers' union, spoke. Since 1999, the first floor of the building has housed the Resistance Museum, a must-see attraction in Amsterdam.

Megillah of the Scroll of Esther, Holland, eighteenth century. Musée d'Art et d'Histoire du Judaïsme, Paris.

NORTHERN HOLLAND

THE RESISTANCE MUSEUM

The Resistance Museum (Verzets-museum) offers a rich permanent collection as well as temporary exhibitions. The displays permit the visitor to consciously analyze the choices and dilemmas that Dutch citizens confronted during Nazi occupation. What did the Resistance really do and how? The exhibition runs the gamut of the era's history, from telling the stories of strikes and the clandestine circulation of pamphlets and newspapers to all manner of protest actions, from spying to sabotage. Photos on the walls and objects dating from World War II such as bicycles, radio broadcasts, telephones, and a printing press recreate the atmosphere of the period. Authentic letters and films allow the visitor to follow the daily life of those who were sent to the Westerbork camp. Recorded testimonies give voice to the Dutch men and women who helped the Jews hide themselves, but also to those who didn't have the courage to do so. A short film from 1942 depicts life inside the Westerbork transit camp and is particularly chilling since it captures how the camp was administered by the Jews themselves (work, sports, administration). It shows the departures from the camp en route to Auschwitz, with the prisoners enclosed in train cars on which one can read in large letters "Westerbork-Auschwitz," as if it were a train line

providing "regular" service. The museum displays some of these macabre train signs.

[Verzetsmuseum: Gebouw Plancius, Plantage Kerklaan 61, 1018 CX Amsterdam. ✆ 0206202535. ❶ info@verzetsmuseum.org. Open Tue–Fri 10 A.M.–5 P.M., Sat–Mon and public holidays noon–5 P.M. Closed Dec 25, Jan 1, and Apr 30.]

■ Retrace your steps now and turn right on Henri Polaklaan. This street bears the name of the founder of the General Union of Dutch Diamond Workers (ANDB). Across from the ANDB at numbers 6–12 is the former Portuguese-Jewish hospital. Today the only distinguishing sign of the building's previous function is the small pelican that one can see on the facade nourishing her young, a symbol of the Portuguese-Jewish community.

■ Take a right at the end of Henri Polaklaan, cross Plantage Parklaan, and follow the path on the left to Anne Frankstraat. Cross Nieuwe Herengracht and turn left onto Rapenburgerstraat. Number 109 Rapenburgerstraat was the location of the **beth hamidrash** Etz-Haïm, an institution founded, according to an inscription on the facade, in 1883 for the study of the **Torah**. The building today houses the offices of the Dutch Jewish weekly the *NIW*.

Before the war, the café De Vlooiemarkt at 169–171 Rapenburgerstraat was an orphanage for young girls looked after by the **Ashkenazic** community. Nearby at number 173 there

At 9 Henri Polaklaan (at the end of the street) is the former union hall. It was constructed in 1900 and designed by the famous pioneer of Dutch modern architecture and ardent socialist Hendrik Petrus Berlage. The building is now the home of the National Museum of Trade Unionism. Founded in 1894, the ANDB was the first workers' union in the modern Netherlands. In the past, there were associations of diamond workers, but each unit (cutters, polishers, etc.) had been independent and no group numbered more than 200 members; Jews and non-Jews belonged to separate organizations. In 1894 a large strike erupted in the diamond industry, and the leaders of the trade unions, Henri Polak and Jan Van Zutphen, won an impressive victory in obtaining a 35 percent salary increase for union members. From that date, a single union came into being that united the various groups of workers. In 1910, the trade union obtained a week of unpaid vacation; two years later it won paid vacation. In 1911, the ANDB was the first trade union in the world to secure an eight-hour workday. After World War II an inscription was engraved on the right side of the hall: "Remember, visitor, the two million of our members who were deported during the occupation, never to return."

was a synagogue that later became the offices of the chief rabbi of Holland. You will notice the imprint of the **mezuzah** at the entrance to this former **shul**.

THE PORTUGUESE SYNAGOGUE

■ At the end of Rapenburgerstraat cross Mr. Visserplein Square. The Portuguese Synagogue is on the left. When it was completed in 1675 by Elias Bouman, this synagogue was the largest in the world. On the portico, by adding the value of the letters starred in the text of Psalm 5:8, the date 1672 can be deciphered—the date originally set for the building's completion. One can also make out the word *Aboab* (formed by the last

two words of the Psalm), the name of the rabbi who initiated the building's construction. Inside and out, the synagogue's appearance remains almost unchanged since the time of Spinoza, who lived nearby. The edifice rests on submerged pylons that are regularly checked by boat to verify the level of the water. The surrounding buildings—the secretariat, the archives, the living quarters of the administrators, the office of the rabbi, the morgue, and the world-renowned library Etz-Haïm—shelter the synagogue from the elements in winter.

Inspired by the plan of the Temple of Jerusalem, this enormous brick building was miraculously spared from damage by the Nazis and bombing during the war. The eight wooden ceiling vaults of the synagogue's interior are supported by four monumental ionic columns and illuminated by seventy-two windows. For important ceremonies, 1,000 candles in copper chandeliers bring flickering light to the cavernous space. The Ark with its gilt leather interior occupies the southeast corner and is oriented toward Jerusalem, while the *tevah* faces it. One can contemplate the monumental *heikhal* here, as well as a volume of the *Holy History* by Menasseh ben Israel and illustrated by Rembrandt. One of the Scrolls of the Law was brought here from Emden, Germany, by the Jewish printer Uri Halevi Phoebus in 1602. The synagogue furniture dates from 1639.

A video tells the history of the synagogue and that of the three **Sephardic** communities of the Netherlands, each of which had its own synagogue before uniting in the **Talmud Torah** in 1639. Today there are no more than 600 Jews of **Sephardic** origin living in the Netherlands. A handful still attend services at this synagogue on important religious holidays, but the majority live outside the city center (as do most **Ashkenazic** Jews).

[Portuguese Synagogue: Mr. Visserplein 3, 1011 RD Amsterdam. ✆ 0206245351. Open Sun–Fri 10 A.M.–4 P.M.]

■ At the exit of the Portuguese Synagogue on Jonas Daniel Meijerplein is the statue of a robust dockworker. It commemorates the strike led by Amsterdam port workers in February 1941 to oppose the anti-Jewish measures of the Germans. Without equal in the rest of the world, this protest was harshly suppressed by the occupying forces. Every year on 25 February, a memorial service takes place here in honor of the strikers.

THE GASSAN DIAMOND-CUTTING WORKSHOP

■ Cross Mr. Visserplein Square and once again take Jodenbreestraat. From Jodenbreestraat, turn right onto Uilenburgersteeg and walk until you come to Nieuwe Uilenburgerstraat. In an immense brick building at 173–75 Nieuwe Uilenburgerstraat is the superb diamond-cutting workshop of Samuel Gassan. The building dates to 1879, at which time the workshop was the largest producer of diamonds in Europe. In 1812 the patriarch of the family, Marcus Abraham Boas, lived on the Rapenburgerstraat and sold used clothing. His son, Juda Boas, became a cobbler and had seven children. Three of Juda Boas's children went into business together to establish the workshop after having studied the diamond business in Paris. During the war, the Nazis requisitioned the building, forcing Marcus Boas and his family to flee to the United States just in time to escape persecution. Bertha Boas left with her son for England, while Bernard emigrated to Switzerland. Martha, Julius, and Elisabeth Boas died in concentration camps.

Having learned the diamond-cutting trade as a worker in the Boas factory, in October 1945, Samuel Gassan founded Gassan Diamonds. Today the company is run by two of Gassan's grandsons. It includes several factories in Amsterdam and has numerous salesrooms all over the world. The four-story building you see before you has large windows that permitted the workers to labor using daylight alone, as did the students of the diamond-cutting school, who were housed in the same building. The back of the building faces a canal, making it easy for the tour boats, which make the workshop one of the stops on their itinerary, to access the building directly. Inside you can see how craftsmen cut and polish the diamonds, learn to recognize the various types and grades of stones, and even buy diamonds that can be set and certified within the hour at factory prices.

[Gassan Diamond Cutting Workshop: Nieuwe Uilenburgerstraat 173–175, 1011 LN Amsterdam. ✆ 0206225333. ❶ info@gassandiamonds.nl. Open daily 9 A.M.–5 P.M. Free admission for guided tours of groups of at least ten. Tour lasts 45 minutes.]

■ Before heading back to the Waterlooplein subway station or walking the short distance to the city center on foot, be sure to notice the lovely facade of the former synagogue of Uilenburg built in 1724 (on the same side of the street as the Gassen workshop, at number 91). If the metal grille of the door is open, you can enter the sanctuary to admire its completely restored interior.

[Uilenburg Synagogue: Nieuwe Uilenburgerstraat 91, 1011 LN Amsterdam. ✆ 0206237791. Visit by appointment if the metal outer door is closed.]

THE ANNE FRANK HOUSE

The Anne Frank House is not in the Jewish quarter but in Jordaan, in northwest Amsterdam not far from Centraal Station. Anne Frank and her family hid in this house from July 1942 until August 1944, when they were discovered and taken away by the Nazis. After the invasion of the German army in May 1940, Otto Frank had the back of his office altered to accommodate a secret annex where his family and Jewish employees (a total of eight people) could live hidden away. Thirteen-year-old Anne Frank recorded the details of life in the annex until the day of the group's discovery. In the ensuing search and seizure, the journal was dropped, its pages left scattered about as the Germans looted the house and deported its inhabitants. Anne and Margot were sent to Bergen-Belsen, while the rest of the family was sent to Auschwitz.

Portuguese Synagogue, Amsterdam.

Anne Frank.

begins on the third floor with a video and then leads you to the annex, which was hidden behind a door disguised as a bookshelf. In the various empty rooms, one can still see the map of Normandy on the wall that was used to chart the Allied advance, the pencil lines marking the children's growth, and the magazine clippings of movie stars Anne had pasted to her bedroom wall for decoration. Each year the museum welcomes some 500,000 visitors. Proceeds from the sale of the book benefit the Anne Frank Foundation and are used to fight racism.

Only Otto Frank survived the concentration camps. Upon his return to Amsterdam, his assistant gave him the journal written by his daughter Anne. The visit to the museum

[Anne Frank House: Prinsengracht 267, 1016 DW Amsterdam. ✆ 0205567100. Open Apr–Aug, daily 9 A.M.–9 P.M.; Sep–Mar, Mon–Sat 9 A.M.–7 P.M., Sun 10 A.M.–9 P.M. Closed Yom Kippur.]

Southern Holland ■

The Hague

The monumental **Ashkenazic** Synagogue in The Hague was sold to the municipality, which put it at the disposal of a congregation of Turkish Muslims. It has since become the Al-Aqsa Mosque. The **Ashkenazic** community in The Hague then acquired a former Protestant church in the Bezuidenhout quarter and transformed it into a synagogue and community center. Because the maintenance costs were too expensive, however, the synagogue was turned into an apartment building. Today only the first floor serves as a synagogue and community center.

[Synagogue and Community Center: Cornelis Houtmanstraat 11, 2593 RD The Hague. ✆ 0104669765.]

■ The first Jewish burials in the recently restored Scheveningseweg cemetery occurred around 1700.

[Scheveningseweg Cemetery:
Begraafplaats, Scheveningseweg 21a,
2117 KS The Hague.]

■ There is a statue of Baruch Spinoza in front of the house where he spent the latter part of his life and where he wrote his most important philosophical works after being banished from the Jewish community for his "heretical opinions." In 1763, he was offered the chair of philosophy at the University of Heidelberg on the condition that he cease his attacks on organized religion, but he declined the offer, preferring to continue to study in his retirement.

[The only house officially recognized as
inhabited by Spinoza is in Rijnsburg
and belongs to the Spinoza House
Association: Paganinidreef 66,
2253 SK Voorschoten. ✆ 0715612759.
✱ ivspinoza@xs4all.nl.]

Drente-Westerbork

■ A memorial was erected in 1983 in the former transit and deportation camp in the northeastern Netherlands. It depicts two broken railway tracks, a symbol of the death trains. The monument was designed by the Jewish artist Ralph Prins, who was deported from this camp as an infant.

■ In addition to the monument, the Dutch government added in 1992 a paving of 104,000 bricks (corresponding to the number of Dutch Jews assassinated) in the shape of a map of the Netherlands. Each brick bears a Star of David. In the museum, which opened in 1983, there is a list of the Dutch casualties who were buried in unmarked graves during the war.

[Camp Westerbork Museum: Oosthalem 8,
9414 TG Hooghalen. ✆ 0593592600.
Open Sep–Jun, Mon–Fri 10 A.M.–5 P.M.,
Sat and Sun 1–5 P.M.; Jul–Aug, Mon–Fri
10 A.M.–5 P.M., Sat and Sun 11 A.M.–5 P.M.]

Belgium

T HE HISTORY OF THE BELGIAN JEWS is similar to that of the Jews of western Europe generally, involving migrations and internal changes as the old communities came under the influence of other traditions.

The Jews came to what is now Belgium in the thirteenth century, settling at Arlon (Aarlen), Brussels, Hasselt, Jodoigne (Geldenaken), Zoutleeuw (Léau), Leuven (Louvain), Mechelen (Malines), Sint-Truiden (Saint-Trond), and Tienen (Tirlemont). A Jewish tombstone from 1255 found in Tienen bears a Hebrew text mentioning the name Rebecca. It is now exhibited at the Musée royal d'art et d'histoire du cinquantenaire.

From 1348 to 1350 the Black Death swept through western Europe; the Jews were accused of poisoning fountains and, as a result, were persecuted. In the sixteenth century a new era began. Portuguese and Spanish Marranos arrived in Antwerp and made a major contribution to the town's prosperity. Charles V ordered the expulsion of the "new Christians" on several occasions but was opposed by the town.

Flemish Jew and craftsman's wife in Ghent, fifteenth century

By the eighteenth century the Jews were engaged in economic activities very different from those of their brothers in eastern Europe. They put themselves at the service of the monarchy, went into trade, and thus made an important contribution to economic development.

In 1808 the 800-odd Belgian Jews were integrated into the Israelite consistory of Créfeld, recognized by the French state. In 1831, after long negotiations with the new Parliament, an independent Israelite consistory was set up in Brussels, which welcomed the growing migrant population from eastern Europe.

In 1914, at the beginning of World War I, the Jews of Antwerp sought refuge over the border in the Netherlands, which remained neutral until the armistice in 1918. They congregated in Amsterdam, The Hague, and Scheveningen. In 1939 a large part of Antwerp's Jewish population fled to Cuba. Some returned years later; others went on to the United States. On the eve of World War II, Belgium's Jewish population was estimated at 90,000. Some 28,000 Jews were deported to Auschwitz from the Dossin barracks in Mechelen. Half never came back.

Today, the Jewish population of 50,000 lives mainly in Brussels and Antwerp (but also in Liège and Charleroi). Their political and religious positions divide up geographically: Antwerp is religious, Brussels secular. Still, these communities do have a number of shared positions, notably their strong attachment to and solidarity with Israel.

→ **To call Belgium from the United States, dial 011 32** followed by the number of the person you are calling minus the initial 0 (used only for domestic calls).

Flanders ■

Brussels

The Belgian capital, Brussels, is a cosmopolitan city: a quarter of its population is foreigners. Its Jewish population is similarly diverse. Before the war, the Jewish quarter was located in the borough of Anderlecht and Schaerbeek, close to the two main railway stations. This demographic concentration unfortunately facilitated the work of the Nazis during their roundups. At the intersection of Rue Émile-Carpentier and Rue des Goujons, you will find the National Monument to the Jewish Martyrs of Belgium. The names of 23,838 victims are engraved in the stone. The square on which it stands has been renamed Square des Martyrs Juifs (Square of the Jewish Martyrs).

■ Brussels is the seat of the Central Israelite Consistory of Belgium, which represents Belgian Judaism. Contact by phone, fax, or e-mail for information on Jewish life in Belgium.

[Central Israelite Consistory of Belgium: 2, rue Joseph-Dupont, 1000 Brussels. ℘ 025122190, fax 025123578. ✆ consis@tufcalinet.be.]

■ There are no longer any **kosher** shops in Brussels, but travelers will find three delightful restaurants: Chez Gilles has a wide choice of **Ashkenazic** and Sephardic dishes and more exotic cuisine. The pastries are particularly fine. The Athénée Maïmonide is a school whose canteen is open to the public, with carefully prepared dishes at reasonable prices.

[Chez Gilles: 21, rue de la Clinique, 1070 Brussels. ℘ 025221828. Open daily 10 A.M.–4 P.M. 🚇 Clemenceau.]

[Athénée Maïmonide: 67, boulevard Poincaré, 1070 Brussels. ℘ 025236336. Open daily noon–1 P.M. 🚇 Lemonnier.]

[El Assado: 154, avenue Rosendael, 1190 Brussels. ℘ 023463487. Open Sun from 12:30 P.M., Mon–Thu from 7:30 P.M.]

THE SYNAGOGUES

■ The Grande Synagogue de la Régence, built circa 1878, stands next to the Royal Conservatory and not far from the law courts. The rather conventional facade gives no idea of the dazzling majesty of the interior nor the size of the organ. This traditional community meets on Saturdays and for the main festivals. The male choir and the **cantor** are renowned. Note that none of Belgium's synagogues have permanent wardens, but they can be visited by appointment (phone numbers supplied).

[Grande Synagogue de la Régence:
32, rue de la Régence, 1000 Brussels.
℘ 025124334. 🚇 Place-Louise.]

■ English-speaking Jews, most of them working in the city's European institutions, form a fifth of Belgium's Jewish community. They attend **Shabbat** services with Liberal French-speaking Jews. The Beth Hillel Synagogue is strongly attended during Jewish festivals.

[Synagogue of the Liberal Israelite
Community of Belgium:
96, avenue de Karsbeek, 1190 Brussels.
℘ 023322528. 🚌 50. 🚆 18 or 52.]

■ Egyptians, Moroccans, Syrians, and Iraqis meet at the Sephardic Synagogue, which is small but very congenial.

[Sephardic Synagogue: 47, rue Pavillon,
1030 Brussels. ℘ 022150525.
🚆 55, 56, or 90.]

National Monument to the Jewish Martyrs of Belgium. Anderlecht, Brussels.

FLANDERS

MUSEUMS

■ Directed by Michel Dratwa, a learned authority on the Jewish world, the Jewish Museum of Belgium has a large collection of ancient and modern documents illustrating Jewish life. The objects exhibited come from Europe, Africa, and Asia. This permanent exhibition is designed to be educational and follows the chronology of the Hebrew calendar. The rites of passage—birth, marriage, and death—are clearly illustrated. In order to provide the Belgian capital with a fitting site for Jewish memory and history, the museum has been given a prestigious annex, a building housing a major Center of Belgian and European Jewish Art and History.

[Jewish Museum of Belgium:
74, avenue de Stalingrad, 1000 Brussels.
✆ 025121963. Open Mon–Thu noon–5 P.M.,
Sunday 10 A.M.–1 P.M. 🚇 Lemonnier.]

■ The Nazis used barracks as assembly camps for the Belgian Jews. Between 1942 and 1944, 25,267 Jews were imprisoned in the camps before being sent to Auschwitz. The Jewish Museum of the Deportation and Resistance is presented as a kind of antechamber to death—which in effect it was. It presents the history of the Final Solution and the deportation of the Belgian Jews, half of whom never came back. It pays tribute to those Belgians who saved thousands of Jews, including 4,000 children

[Jewish Museum of the Deportation and Resistance: Caserne Dossin, Goswin de Stassurstraat 153, 2800 Mechelen.
✆ 015290660. ❶ infos@cieb.be.
Open Sun–Thu 10 A.M.–5 P.M.,
Fri 10 A.M.–1 P.M. From Brussels take 🚆 to Mechelen then 🚌 5 or 7.]

Antwerp

The last real **shtetl** in western Europe, Antwerp is known for its Orthodox Jews and its diamond industry. Approximately 80 percent of Antwerp's Jewish population makes a living from the diamond industry. More than half the world production of diamonds passes through these few streets near Centraal Station. The diamond centers, which can be visited, also serve as meeting places where ongoing debate takes place over the social, cultural, and political issues affecting the Jewish community.

THE SYNAGOGUES

■ There are six **Ashkenazic** rite synagogues in Antwerp. The biggest is Romi Goldmunz, whose world-famous **cantor** is Benjamin Muller. The Shromei ha-Das (Guardians of the Law) Synagogue, with over 6,000 members, and the Israelitische Gemeente van Antwerpen, founded in 1904, represent the city's Jewish community.

[Romi Goldmunz Synagogue:
Oostenstraat 2, 2018 Antwerp,

✆ 032301364. To visit, call at the
Israelitische Gemeente van Antwerpen
(administration): Terlistraat 35, 2018
Antwerp. ✆ 032320187.]

The Ghetto, Antwerp, 1935.

■ Next come the more Orthodox communities, united under the Makhzikia
organization. This includes all the
currents in the **Hasidic** movement,
such as the Satmaer, the Gourer, and
the Sanzer. In Europe, only London's
Stamford Hill can offer comparable
diversity.

[Makhzikei ha-Das: Jacob Jacobstraat 22,
2018 Antwerp. ✆ 032335567.]

[For information on Antwerp's Hasidic
community, contact the Centrale, whose
social service will provide much useful
information: Jacob Jacobstraat 2,
2018 Antwerp. ✆ 032323890.]

■ The **Sephardim** meet in their synagogue opposite the Diamond Exchange. Antwerp's Portuguese-rite
Israelite Synagogue (Beth Haknesset
Portugeese) includes some 300 families and has been swollen by the
arrival of numerous Israelis. A plaque
on an outside wall commemorates
the victims of the 1987 terrorist
attack, which was claimed by a
Palestinian group.

[Beth Haknesset Portugeese:
Hoveniersstraat 32, 2018 Antwerp.]

FLANDERS

THE KOSHER PLEASURES OF YIDDISH TOWN

Yiddish Town, also known as "Pelikan," from the name of one of its main streets, is located around Centraal Station. Here, at the back of the houses or in arcades, you can find various restaurants and delicatessens usually bearing the name of the family owners. Apart from USA Pizza on the Isabellalei, none of them have views onto the street, but all offer prayer books.

■ Malka, located in the Diamond Exchange, is exclusively for employees and clients of the Diamantkring (Diamond Circle). The cooking is *glat* **kosher**—dairy products only. Breakfast is served until 10:30 A.M. Throughout the day, you can enjoy drinks and pastries in the diamond merchants' hall outside the restaurant.

[Malka: Diamantkring, Hoveniersstraat 2, 2018 Antwerp. ✆ 032269121. Open Mon–Thu 8 A.M.–6 P.M., Fri 8 A.M.–3:30 P.M.]

■ Walking around here, one would not guess that access to the Dresdner is through the butcher shop. This leads to a galleried yard at the back of which stands a small modern restaurant. The cloakroom, where long traditional coats, black hats, and prayer books are left by the tables, gives an idea of the place's great orthodoxy.

[Dresdner: Simonsstraat 10, 2018 Antwerp. ✆ 032316042. Open daily 9 A.M.–6:30 P.M. Restaurant open noon–3:00 P.M.]

■ A stone's throw from the station, Geldkop is located in a family mansion. This restaurant's kitchen is slightly above first-floor level and overlooks the street. Four rooms were recently made available to tourists, who will find here a family atmosphere. The establishment is strictly **kosher**.

[Geldkop: Van Leriusstraat 28, 2018 Antwerp. ✆ 032330753. Open Fri evening and Sat. Reservations necessary (Thu at the latest for Sat).]

■ Also worth noting is the excellent Blue Lagoon. Located in the Diamond District, this is Benelux's one and only **kosher** Chinese restaurant.

[Blue Lagoon: Lange Herentalsestraat 70, 2000 Antwerp. ✆ 032260114. Open daily noon–2:30 P.M. and 6 P.M.–10:30 P.M.]

■ Antwerp has a large number of butcher shops, bakeries, and stores specializing in typical Jewish products. Be sure to stock up on cakes and pastries at Kleinblatt and Steinmetz.

[Kleinblatt: Provinciestraat 206, 2018 Antwerp. ✆ 032337513. Open Sun–Thu 6 A.M.–6:30 P.M., Fri 10 A.M.–4 P.M.]

[Steinmetz: Lange Kievitsstraat 64, 2018 Antwerp. ✆ 032340947. Open Sun–Thu 6:30 A.M.–8 P.M., Fri 6:30 A.M.–4 P.M.]

Ghent

The first communities were established in Ghent in the thirteenth century. After the Jews' expulsion, there was no trace of a Jewish presence until the eighteenth century. The reputation of Ghent's university attracted many Romanian and Russian Jews, who formed the famous "generation of engineers." During World War II, the solidarity of their non-Jewish fellow citizens helped save 125 of the city's 200 Jews. Today's Jewish community comprises some twenty families. The municipal authorities have granted their request to name a street after Michaël Lustig, the local rabbi who died during the war.

[Synagogue: Koolsteeg 11, 9000 Ghent. ✆ 092257085.]

[Mrs. Sperling, Belgian vice president of the International Council of Jewish Women and member of the Ghent community, is a very helpful source of information. ✆ 092223112 or 092223116.]

Ostende

■ The synagogue of the handsome coastal town of Ostende becomes busy in the summer. It was built partly with the help of rich financiers. At one time as many as 300 families came to pray here. Among the famous Jewish figures who stayed in Ostende were Marc Chagall and Albert Einstein.

This synagogue is unusual in that it is little frequented by Jews. Its beauty and harmonious proportions have made it a popular tourist attraction. Indeed, it is supported by contributions from non-Jews. It is the only synagogue in west Flanders to have a facade giving onto the street.

[Synagogue: Maastrichtplein 10, 8400 Ostend. ✆ 059802405.]

Wallonia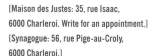

Charleroi

As many as 600 families lived in Charleroi before the war. Jewish life was active, with schools, butcher shops, and a famous hotel, the International, used by all the new arrivals from the east. The Jews of Charleroi have since emigrated yet again, this time to the Belgian capital. Only some forty families remain in the town.

■ Note, however, a small museum, the Maison des Justes.

[Maison des Justes: 35, rue Isaac, 6000 Charleroi. Write for an appointment.]
[Synagogue: 56, rue Pige-au-Croly, 6000 Charleroi.]

Liège

There is no trace of a Jewish presence in Liège before Belgian independence in 1830. Prior to that, Liège was still a principality directed by a prince-bishop. In 1914 the community, comprising Dutch and Alsatian Jews, was swollen by Russian Jews who had been taken prisoner by the Germans. Some of them settled in Liège from 1917. The international reputation of the École des Mines drew Jews from eastern Europe between the two world wars. Many of the city's Jews have emigrated to Israel, and now only 200 traditionalist families remain.

[Synagogue: 19, rue Léon-Frédéricq, 4020 Liège. ✆ 043433651.]

Synagogue, Liège.

מאזנים

לראש בחר באומרל תראש כבכורה בתאינה בראש ביטה
נהדרוש מכל אום לפרוש לנשאה על בל ראש גו עלה תשיה
יד ראש והיאתרים ראש בכסא כבוד מראש

Germany

AT THE END OF THE NINETEENTH CENTURY, an international conference took place sponsored by the Zionist Organization that was dedicated to the problem of the future national language of the Jewish state. A heated debate was held and the question put to a vote: Hebrew won out only by several votes over German to become the national language. As absurd as it might seem, the language of Goethe nearly became the official spoken tongue of Israel. Between the end of the nineteenth century and the present day, there is a distinct "before" and "after," a period the Jews call *Shoah* and the Germans the Holocaust. Why was this tragedy conceived, organized, and put into action in Germany of all places? The very country known for its high level of civilized culture, fatherland of poets and thinkers? Between 1870 and 1914, Germany served as a refuge (France had come under suspicion because of the Dreyfus Affair) for a considerable number of Jews expelled from Russia, Poland, and Ukraine by the miserable conditions and pogroms that regularly bloodied the shtetlach. Born in Russia in 1885, Nahum Goldmann, the founding father of the World Jewish Congress, came to

Mahzor, *Worms, 1272, Jewish National and University Library, Jerusalem.*

Frankfurt am Main at the age of five. He explained in his memoirs that it was natural for him, a Jew and Zionist, to enter into the services of the propaganda machine of Kaiser Wilhelm II. At the time he thought, "The great power of anti-Semitism was in the hands of czarist Russia, and the victory of Germany seemed to me a good thing for the emancipation of Jews oppressed in the east in Poland, Lithuania, and other territories arbitrarily forced to submit to Russian governance."[1] A half century later the same Nahum Goldmann would negotiate with Konrad Adenauer the sum of reparations to be paid to the survivors of Hitler's genocide and to the new state of Israel by a Germany in ruins after the war.

The synagogue of Worms in the Palatinate alone can serve as a symbol of the history of Germany and its Jews. Founded in 1034, the synagogue of Worms is one of the oldest in Europe. It was built by the same architects and craftsmen as the Romanesque cathedral of the city. Seven times destroyed and rebuilt, it was dynamited and razed during the violence of Kristallnacht on 9 November 1938, unleashing the anti-Semitic violence of Hitler's regime. Reconstructed after the war, it now serves as a place of worship for Jewish soldiers from the neighboring American military base because there are no longer enough Jews in Worms to make up a **minyan.**

ORIGIN AND LEGENDS

According to certain tales, the Jewish presence in Worms dates back to the first destruction of the Temple of Jerusalem in 587 B.C.E. and the Jews' refusal to respond to the call of the prophet Ezra to return to their land at the end of the Babylonian exile. Other stories suggest the first Jews landed on the banks of the Rhine with Marcellinus, a Roman officer who participated in the conquest of

George Grosz, Kristallnacht, *1938. New Walk Museum, Leicester.*

Jerusalem in 70 C.E. Hence, in the Middle Ages the Duisberg family simultaneously claimed to have directly descended from Marcellinus and demanded from the city the right to protect Jews and thus enjoy the comfortable revenues this privilege garnered.

As in all of Christian Europe, the Jews of Germany have known alternating periods of tolerance and more or less harmonious existence with Christians (tolerance most often in periods of relative economic prosperity) and oppression, persecution, and expulsion. Yet the Jews had always seen this country as the **Ashkenazi**, or the Promised Land (Genesis 10), from which comes the general name for Jews of Central and Eastern Europe, **Ashkenazim**. The arrival of the first Jews in Germany was made the subject of several legendary tales. Leo Trepp, the honorary rabbi of Mainz and the author of *A History of the German Jews,* notes with sagacity that "certainly, legend can not replace history, but history should not be in total contradiction with legend, lest history itself be rejected. Insofar as we are concerned, it means that we firmly believe in the settling of Jews in Germany dating back to ancient times." The first written mention of a Jewish presence in present-day Germany is contained in an edict signed by Emperor Constantine dating from 321 C.E. that requests the Jews of Cologne (Colonia Agrippina) to send "two or three members" of their community to the city's curia (government). This was not really the "privilege" that it might seem to be: the magistrates were responsible for Roman tax collection and often had to pay the emperor themselves when the populace was too poor or rebellious to be taxed. This edict indicates that by this period the community of Rhenish Jews had acquired a certain level of economic comfort. This situation continued after the fall of the Roman Empire. The new masters of the country, the lords and bishops coming from the Germanic tribes, maintained cordial relations with the Jews. But there was some tension, since the papacy saw in Judaism a rival with Christianity. The emperor, claiming the heritage of his Roman predecessors, saw himself as the protector of the Jews and the guarantor of a prosperity from which he could take his share. This situation irritated a portion of the clergy. Agobard, bishop of Lyon in the ninth century, complained bitterly that the Jews in his diocese had acquired too much influence under imperial protection: the nobles more often sought the blessings of the rabbis than of the bishop, and Jewish merchants had succeeded in moving the weekly market from Saturday to Sunday.

In the cities, Jews increasingly confronted hostility from Christian artisans' guilds. Excluded from membership in most guilds, Jews devoted themselves to commerce and trade, notably with the Muslim Orient, taking advantage of their relations with Jewish communities settled in those regions. The scarcity of currency in the west and the ban on Christians lending money with interest pushed Jews toward this activity. In the course of the ninth century, the prosperous Jewish communities of Speyer, Mainz, and Worms maintained excellent relations with the local (notably ecclesiastical) authorities. For example, in 1096 the archbishop of Speyer invited Jews persecuted elsewhere to settle in his city because their presence, he affirmed, "considerably increases the prestige of the city." The religious and cultural life of these communities flourished: numerous synagogues were erected, "sages" such as Gershom ben Yehuda and Salomon ben Isaac, known as Rashi, moved there to give teachings on religion and law that still have authority today.

The beginning of the Crusades in 1096 and the gradual hardening of the Church toward the Jews during the Third and Fourth Lateran Councils (1179 and 1215) finally put an end to peaceful coexistence. In the wake of the first Crusades, non-Christians encountered on the way were put to the sword by bands of religious fanatics, landless peasants, and adventurers en route to Jerusalem. Despite the warnings given by Jews in France who had already experienced murderous assaults from

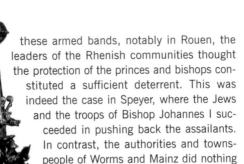

these armed bands, notably in Rouen, the leaders of the Rhenish communities thought the protection of the princes and bishops constituted a sufficient deterrent. This was indeed the case in Speyer, where the Jews and the troops of Bishop Johannes I succeeded in pushing back the assailants. In contrast, the authorities and townspeople of Worms and Mainz did nothing to stop the massacres.

Pursued or contained in ghettos as a result of increasingly severe discriminatory practices imposed by the Pope, the German Jews generally did not escape the destinies of fellow Jews meted out by Christians in the rest of Europe. At regular intervals in history, accusations that Jews performed ritual murders provoked pogroms and expulsions that conveniently settled outstanding debts owed to Jewish lenders. These persecutions drove numerous German Jews east toward Poland, where the sovereigns were more kindly disposed toward them and likely to welcome Jews in order to take advantage of their skills as merchants and bankers. Thus **Yiddish**, a mixture of Middle High German dialect and Hebrew syntax, was preserved in eastern Europe until these communities disappeared, victims of the *Shoah*.

The annals of Jewish history from the Roman Empire to the Wars of Religion reveal periods of relative tolerance alternating with episodes of extreme anti-Jewish violence. On the whole tolerance for the Jewish faith was

Spice container, Berlin, early eighteenth century. Jewish Museum, London.

scattered and disparate, occurring wherever a local prince declared himself "protector of the Jews" out of what was essentially self-interest. These periods of calm were preferred, however, to the acts of violence that sometimes broke out. In 1298, for example, 140 Jewish communities in Franconia and Saxony were annihilated in the space of six months by the hordes under the command of Chevalier Rindfleisch. Led by Martin Luther, the Reformation provoked upheaval in the Holy Roman Empire that did nothing to improve the well-being of the Jews there. Luther had first hoped to convert them by treating them with kindness and understanding. He thus protested in 1523 against the unfair treatment inflicted on them and noted that, "if the Apostles, who were Jews themselves, had behaved this way toward other pagans, not a single one among them would have become Christians." Twenty years later, profoundly disappointed with the minimal impact he had in converting the Jews to the reformed faith, Luther gave free rein to his anti-Jewish hatred.

"WITH REGARD TO JEWS AND THEIR LIES: THE REFORMATION AND THE JEWS"

In this infamous writing, Luther suggests a policy of "tough love" toward the Jews: "burn their schools and synagogues . . . , destroy their homes and make them understand that, like the Gypsies, they are not in their own land . . . , destroy all their books, [forbid] their rabbis to preach their heresies, so that we follow the sensible example of other nations like France, Spain, and Bohemia, which have always excluded Jews from their territories." For four centuries these imprecations justified popular anti-Semitism in Germany, despite efforts by numerous Protestant theologians and pastors to distance themselves from this interpretation of the great reformer's text.

In this precarious situation, the Jewish communities of Germany owed their survival to the presence and ability of "courtly Jews" whom German princes, ever lacking in funds, needed in order to maintain their standard of living or to finance military campaigns. It was thus in this capacity that Samuel Oppenheimer gathered the means necessary to defend Vienna against the Turks, and how Joseph Süsskind Oppenheimer (1692–1738), known as "the Jewish Süss," became the chief adviser of Duke Charles Alexander of Württemberg. The favor of princes permitted Jews of the courts to obtain dispensations for their fellow believers, privileges often quickly reconsidered as soon as dynastic succession was at issue. At the end of the seventeenth century, the Jews living in the Hapsburg Empire numbered approximately 60,000 of a total 40 million inhabitants. The largest Jewish community, with a population of 3,000, was in Frankfurt.

The process that granted German Jews citizenship and enabled them to leave the ghettos was a long one, begun at the end of the seventeenth century and reaching its apogee after 1871, under Wilhelm I. The dawning of the *Aufklärung,* the German equivalent of the French Enlightenment, contributed to the secularization of the Jewish community. Despite the restrictions of Jews' civil rights in effect in the majority of German states, under Frederick Wilhelm I, and especially Frederick the Great (Frederick II), Prussia welcomed rich Jewish families banished from Austria in the same way that it had opened its doors to the French Huguenots ejected from their country after the revocation of the Edict of Nantes.

Moses Mendelssohn (1729–86) emerged in Berlin as a great figure in German Judaism. The founder of **Haskalah,** a contemporary method of practicing the faith, Mendelssohn helped Jews leave both the literal and spiritual confinement of the ghettos. Ignoring the criticism of Orthodox rabbis, he translated the **Torah** into German and encouraged Jews to use this language in their intellectual exchanges with scholars of other religions in order to dissipate misunderstandings of Judaism in caricatures and in Judeo-phobic polemics. This current of thought opened the way to the massive secularization of German Jews, often manifesting itself as conversion to Christianity, the "admission ticket" required for entry into the ruling class.

Moses Mendelssohn.

The victory of the armies of the French Republic, and then the Napoleonic Empire, brought the Jews of Germany the legal emancipation established in France by the laws of 1791 and 1807. In a vanquished Prussia, Chancellor Hardenberg, busy preparing his revenge, thought it an opportune moment to rally the Jews to his cause by granting them full citizenship in 1812. In return, the vast majority of German Jews made a show of their patriotism in the exalted Wars of Liberation of 1813–15.

HEINE AND MARX, TWO JEWISH CONVERTS FROM THE RHINELAND

Heinrich Heine (1797–1856), born in Düsseldorf, and Karl Marx, born in Trier, are the two most famous representatives of the wave of more or less sincere Jewish conversion to Christianity among members of the Jewish bourgeoisie for whom baptism constituted the "admission ticket" into high society. Their respective attitudes toward the religion of their forefathers are, however, completely opposite. For Heine, conversion changed nothing. The great German poet originally explained this in French, noting, "One doesn't change religions. One leaves one of them that one no longer has for another that one will never have. I am baptized, but I am not converted." In contrast Marx, baptized at the age of six, declared: "The earthly foundation of Judaism which conditions the Jew's life here on earth is egotism. His religion is merely lip service, and his god money."

The childhood homes of Heine in Düsseldorf and Marx in Trier have been turned into museums.

[Heinrich Heine Institute: Bilkerstrasse 10, 40213 Düsseldorf. ✆ 02118995574. Open Tue–Fri 11 A.M.–5 P.M., Sat 1–5 P.M.]

[The Karl Marx House: Brückenstrasse 10, 54290 Trier. ✆ 0651970680. Open Nov to Mar, Tue–Sun 10 A.M.–1 P.M. and 2–5 P.M., Mon 2–5 P.M.; Apr to Oct, Tue–Sun 10 A.M.–6 P.M., Mon 1–6 P.M.]

Despite the persistent anti-Semitism across all strata of society, the Jews persisted in their undivided loyalty toward their German homeland until it became evident that, with Hitler's rise to power, the Jewish-German symbiosis was destined to come to a tragic end. In 1871, Germany counted 512,153 Jews among its citizens (1.25 percent of the population); in 1933 they numbered a similar 502,773 (0.76 percent of the population) and represented the third largest Jewish community in Europe after Poland and Russia. Their economic, intellectual, and cultural influence on German society was relative to their demographic presence. Figuring in the ranks of legendary businessmen are great bankers such as the Rothschilds, the Warburgs, the Bleichröders, and others; industrialists like the chemist Heinrich Caro, cofounder of IGFarben; and weapons contractors such as Alfred Ballin, president of HAPAG, the most important maritime company in Germany. German Jews are among the founders of department stores (Hermann Tietze, Wertheim) that have left their mark on retail and whose signs are still to be found in German cities. Likewise, many significant contributions to the sciences and culture were made by celebrated Jews: Albert Einstein, Robert Oppenheimer, Hermann Cohen, Hannah Arendt, Alfred Döblin, Lion Feuchtwanger, Arnold Schönberg, Max Reinhardt, Fritz Lang, Billy Wilder—among many others who came from the cultural world of German Jews, a spirit that lives on in many other places, brought there by those who could escape Hitler's extermination plans.

1938, A YEAR OF DEVASTATION

1 January: Jews are excluded from the Red Cross.

25 July: Jewish doctors are no longer allowed to practice medicine.

17 August: Jews are required to add the name "Israel" or "Sara" to their official papers.

27 September: Jewish lawyers are labeled "forbidden professionals."

8 October: Jewish passports are required to be stamped with the letter "J."

9 and 10 October: Kristallnacht. At the instigation of the Gestapo, armed bands plunder and damage Jewish synagogues, institutions, and shops.

15 November: Jewish children are excluded from public schools.

3 December: Jews are forbidden to go to cinemas, theaters, museums, and sporting events; driver's licenses belonging to Jews are cancelled.

8 December: Jews are excluded from universities.

Today, the Jewish community in Germany numbers some 100,000 members. For many years this population has comprised Jews who survived the concentration camps and had nowhere else to go, or Jews who fled into exile but returned to Germany out of nostalgia. With the arrival of Jews from the former Communist countries in the last decade, however, the population has abruptly grown. In welcoming them, the new and reunified Germany wishes to demonstrate that the country assumes full responsibility for its history. This same concern pushed the country's authorities to preserve what remained of the Jewish heritage after the destruction wrought by the Nazis. In that regard, Germany is paradoxically the European country where one finds the largest number of Jewish memorials, safeguarded at the initiative of officials in the larger cities and thanks to the action of persons or associations that have wrestled with the tendency to forget the Jewish heritage in towns and villages. The scope of the present guidebook does not permit an exhaustive listing of these sites. In general, municipalities with tourist information offices will willingly furnish all the information necessary to visit them.

→ **To call Germany from the United States, dial 011 49** followed by the number of the person you are calling minus the initial 0 (used only for domestic calls).

Northern Germany

Berlin

Once again the capital of a unified Germany, Berlin today has the largest Jewish community in the country (11,000 people). This is nonetheless far fewer than the some 170,000 Jews who lived here just before Hitler's rise to power in 1933. One can well imagine that the ghosts of history will wander Berlin for a long time to come, a city that, like Vienna, was a major economic, intellectual, and religious center for German Jews. Some monuments and cemeteries (notably the Weissensee, the largest Jewish cemetery in Europe) escaped Nazi destruction and the Allied bombings of 1945. The willingness of the new Germany to accept the totality of its heritage, including its most somber and shameful episodes, and to deliver its mea culpa for the horrors committed in the name of the German people, is the source of the efforts to build or rebuild synagogues, community centers, schools, and memorials in all areas of the city today.

THE DUTY OF REMEMBRANCE

■ The fall of the Berlin Wall in 1989 permitted the reconstruction of part of the old Jewish quarter of Oranienburgerstrasse. The Jewish Museum of Berlin, designed by architect Daniel Libeskind, was opened in 1999.

■ On a more modest scale, in the "Bavarian quarter" of Schöneberg, eighty panels have been applied to the lampposts that recall the successive steps the Nazis took in their persecution of the Jews. Mingled with these chilling historical facts are extracts of letters written by inhabitants of the neighborhood who were deported. Throughout the city as a whole, commemorative plaques attest to a vanished Jewish lifestyle: in Steglitz, for example, the names of the 3,186 Jews living in the area in 1933 are engraved on a mirrored panel measuring approximately 12.5 ft. wide x 40 ft. long.

■ After long debate, on 25 June 1999 the German Bundestag accepted a motion to erect a monument in memory of the *Shoah* near the Brandenburg Gate. The realization of this project was entrusted to the American architect Eisenman. It will be composed of 2,700 concrete pillars of varying heights and contain at its center information about the persecution of the Jews under Nazism.

■ In contrast to the contemporary initiatives to preserve the pre–World War II Jewish cultural heritage, the most ancient evidence of a Jewish presence in Berlin has been erased. Whether by the fires that ravaged the large village in its early days, the periodic attacks on the Jewish population, or finally the torments of the Second World War, the oldest traces of the Jews that had been proven to date from 1295 (only sixty years after the founding of the city) have disappeared.

■ The Topography of Terror Foundation has been installed in the primary locations where the Nazi terror machine (the Gestapo, Reichsführung SS, Sicherheitsdienst) formerly had its headquarters. This institution, federally financed and supported by the State of Berlin, allows visitors to familiarize themselves in situ with how the Nazi state functioned. Awaiting its permanent home designed by the Swiss architect Peter Zumthor, the foundation organizes outdoor exhibitions and guided visits to the quarter.

[Topography of Terror Foundation:
Budapesterstrasse 40,
10787 Berlin. ✆ 0302545090.
Open Oct–Apr, 10 A.M.–6 P.M.;
May–Sep, 10 A.M.–8 P.M.
🚇 Potsdamerplatz.]

■ The Anne Frank Center pursues the same educational aims as the Anne Frank House in Amsterdam (see page 94), but with a vision oriented more toward adolescents, high school students, and college-age visitors.

[Anne Frank Center: Rosenthalesstrasse 39,
10178 Berlin. ✆ 03030872988.
Open Mon–Thu noon–8 P.M., Fri 11 A.M.–8 P.M.
🚇 Hakerschermarkt.]
[Guided walks on the theme "Jewish Berlin" are offered by StattReisen: ✆ 0304553028.
🅸 StattReisen@berlin.snafu.de
and by Iris Weiss: ✆ 0304535304.
🅸 iris.weiss@berlin.snafu.de.
These two organizations can arrange tours in English by request.]

CENTRAL BERLIN

Until 1989 the historic center of Berlin was situated in the former German Democratic Republic, (GDR) separated by a wall from the western part of the city since 1961. Central Berlin was the site of the palace of Frederick II (the Great) and Prussian political and economic activity. The first synagogue in Berlin was erected in this quarter in 1714 (on Heidereuterstrasse, today called

Rosenstrasse). Although spared the ravages of Kristallnacht because it had been requisitioned by the German postal service, it was completely destroyed by the bombings of 1945.

■ Oranienburgerstrasse was not properly a "Jewish quarter" since the number of Jews who lived here never grew beyond 10 percent of the Jewish population in the city overall. During the Prussian Empire and the Weimar Republic, this centrally located Berlin street and neighboring arteries were a gathering point for Jewish immigrants from the east. These Jews, with their caftans, long beards, and earlocks, were thus more visible than their assimilated German counterparts. The restoration of this quarter, and notably of the Grand Synagogue, is almost complete.

Grand Synagogue, Berlin.

■ Opened in 1866, the Grand Synagogue was designed by the architect Edward Knoblauch in the Moorish style so fashionable at the time. With its 164 foot gilt dome and its capacity to serve 1,800 faithful, the Grand Synagogue gave the opulent Jewish population in Berlin a reason to be proud. The synagogue escaped damage in the violence of Kristallnacht on 9 November 1938 thanks to the courageous action of a brigadier police officer, William Krütfeld, who, with several other men, managed to make the hordes of SA withdraw by pretending that the synagogue had been placed under police protection due to the riches it contained. Closed by the Nazis in 1940, the synagogue was transformed into a warehouse. It was seriously damaged by a bombing in 1943.

In an effort to change its image in the eyes of Israeli Jews, the GDR began the renovation of the synagogue and construction of a Jewish community center nearby in the late 1980s. While not all of them are kosher, the cafés and restaurants surrounding the synagogue offer drinks and traditional dishes typical of the Eastern European Jewish kitchen mingled with highlights from Israeli cuisine. At the Jewish Gallery, paintings are displayed by Jewish artists hailing mostly from the former Soviet Union, as well as religious objects, both old and new.

[🚇 Oranienburgerstrasse or Oranienburger Tor.]

[Grand Synagogue: Oranienburgerstrasse 29, 10117 Berlin.]
[Jewish Gallery: Oranienburgerstrasse 31, 10117 Berlin. ✆ 0302828623.]
[Beth Café (kosher): Tucholskystrasse 40, 10117 Berlin. ✆ 0302813135.
Open Mon–Thu noon–8 P.M.]
[Café Oren: Oranienburgerstrasse 28, 10117 Berlin. ✆ 0302828228.
Open Mon–Fri noon–1 A.M.,
Sat and Sun 10 A.M.–1 A.M.]

■ Completed in 1765, the Ephraim Palace belonged to financier Veitel Heine Ephraim (1703–75), the banker of Frederick the Great. Demolished during the major urban renewal efforts of 1935, the rococo facade was nevertheless saved and later protected from the bombings. In 1987, the facade was reassembled during the renovations of central Berlin undertaken by the GDR. The palace today houses an annex of the Museum of Fine Arts that contains, most notably, a collection of ancient coins.

[Ephraim Palace: Poststrasse 16, 10178 Berlin. ✆ 03024002121.
🚇 Alexanderplatz (U-Bahn 2 or 8).]

CHARLOTTENBURG-WILMERSDORF

■ Charlottenburg-Wilmersdorf is the heart of the former West Berlin, whose principal thoroughfare is the Kurfürstendamm. The administrative center for the Jewish community in Berlin is located here with its social and cultural institutions.

KLEZMER IN BERLIN

In East Berlin, before the fall of the Wall, a few young musicians began, in a provocative effort, to play **klezmer** music, a mixture of Jewish music from Central Europe and American jazz originating from the encounter between these two musical styles in the Jewish neighborhoods in New York. This music, underground during the Communist era, has become very popular in Berlin. The Theater in den Hackeschen Höfen offers **klezmer** concerts almost every Monday evening and Saturday evening.

[Theater in den Hackeschen Höfen: Rosentahlerstrasse 40–41, 10100 Berlin. ✆ 0302832587.]

[Administrative Center for the Berlin Community: Fasanenstrasse 13, 10179 Berlin. ✆ 030880280.]

■ The synagogue on the Pestalozzistrasse was built in 1912 at the initiative of Betty Sophie Jacobson, a wealthy businesswoman in the neighborhood. On the night of 9 November 1938, the synagogue was set afire and might have burned to the ground, had firemen not quickly extinguished the flames fearing that they would spread to nearby buildings. The interior of the synagogue thus suffered only minor damage and could be reopened as early as 1946. The services there are celebrated according to the liberal liturgy with a mixed choir and organ music. Contact Mr. Goldman at the administrative center for information ✆ 030880169.

[Synagogue: Pestalozzistrasse 14, 10625 Berlin.
✆ 0303138411, fax 030318411.
🚇 Wilmesdorferstrasse (U-Bahn 7).]

■ The synagogue on Joachimstalerstrasse is a former meeting hall of the B'nai Brith. Now Orthodox services are celebrated here.

[Synagogue: Joachimstalerstrasse 13, 10625 Berlin. ✆ 03088028110.
🚇 Kurfürstendamm (U-Bahn 9 or 15).]

■ The Jewish Museum of Berlin contains a permanent exhibition on the history of Berlin's Jews and houses the collection of objects, religious and secular, that were contained in the former Jewish Museum, a private institution in existence until 1938. This museum is remarkable above all

Pestalozzistrasse Synagogue, Berlin, 1949.

for its metaphorical architecture, designed by Daniel Libeskind. The metal facades, torn in shreds, powerfully evoke the abuse and victimization the museum has suffered.

[Jewish Museum of Berlin:
Lindenstrasse 9–14, 10969 Berlin.
✆ 03025993300 9 A.M.–3 P.M. for
information. Open Tue–Sun 10 A.M.–8 P.M.,
Mon 10 A.M.–10 P.M. 🚇 Hallesches Tor
(U-Bahn 1 and 6).]

■ The cemetery on Schönhauserallee, established in 1827, contains the graves of the personalities who animated the cultural and economic life of Berlin at the end of the nineteenth and beginning of the twentieth centuries, personalities such as the bankers Gerson von Bleichröder and Joseph Mendelssohn, the musician Giacomo Meyerbeer, and the painter Max Liebermann.

[Cemetery: Schönhauserallee 23–25,
10435 Berlin. ✆ 0304419824. Open
Mon–Thu 10 A.M.–4 P.M., Fri 10 A.M.–1 P.M.
🚇 Senefelderplatz (U-Bahn 2).]

■ With its ninety-nine acres of land, Weissensee is one of the largest Jewish cemeteries in Europe. Established in 1880 and devastated during the Second World War, it was renovated little by little by the authorities of the GDR and the reunification accelerated this rehabilitation. One finds here the graves of eminent Jewish personalities from prewar Berlin: the philosopher Hermann Cohen, the theologian Leo Baeck, the editor Samuel Fischer,

and the heads of the press Theodor Wolff and Rudolf Mosse.

[Weisesensee Heerstrasse 141, Berlin.
✆ 0303043234. Open daily 7 A.M.–4 P.M.
🚇 Greifswalderstrasse, then 🚊 2, 3, or
4 to Antonplatz.]

■ The Literaturhandlung is the most important Jewish bookstore in the whole of the German-speaking community (with satellite stores in Munich and Vienna). You can find items for religious worship here (mezuzoth, candelabra, prayer shawls, etc.), as well as greeting cards for the Jewish holidays.

[Literaturhandlung:
Joachimstalerstrasse 13, 10719 Berlin.
✆ 0308824250. Open Mon–Fri
9:30 A.M.–6:30 P.M., Sat 9:30 A.M.–2 P.M.
🚇 Joachimstalerstrasse.]

■ Cafes and restaurants certainly are not lacking in this area. Noah's Ark is located in the community center. It is the oldest postwar kosher restaurant in Berlin, where you can taste authentic cholent, gefilte fish, Pickelfleisch, and other specialities. Salomon's Bagels is a miniscule shop devoted to bagels, or according to the owner of the place, Andreas Pfeffer, "edible wisdom." He has opened another, larger shop in the new center of Berlin.

[Noah's Ark: Fasanenstrasse 79–80,
10625 Berlin. ✆ 0308826138.]
[Salomon's Bagels:
Joachimstalerstrasse 55, 10963 Berlin.
✆ 0308210404. 🚇 Kurfürstendamm.]
[Salomon's Bagels: Potsdamerplatzarkaden,
10625 Berlin. ✆ 03025297626.
🚊 Potsdamerplatz.]

Jewish Museum, Berlin.

128

The concentration camps situated in the territory of the former GDR (Sachsenhausen, Buchenwald) have been transformed into memorials. The transformation was a way for the Communist regime to tell its own version of the story of Nazi resistance. The victims of the camp are gathered together under the rubric "antifascists," and emphasis is on the role of deported Communists in the underground Resistance and that of the Red Army in the liberation of the camps. Since Germany's reunification in 1990, Western revisionist historiography has been introduced, although not without difficulty, as attested by the numerous manifestations of anti-Semitism and xenophobia in this part of the country.

Sachsenhausen

Sachsenhausen concentration camp was opened in 1933 to imprison Hitler's German opponents: Communists, social democrats, and union leaders. Erich Honecker, the future leader of the GDR from 1971 to 1989, was detained here for ten years. Half of the 200,000 detainees who passed through this camp from all over Europe died of starvation, sickness, and abuse.

[Memorial and Museum: Strasse der Nationen 22, 16515 Sachsenhausen. ✆ 033012000.]

Ravensbrück

Ravensbrück was the largest of the camps reserved for women. More than 130,000 Resistance fighters, Jews, and Gypsies were imprisoned here, often with their children, in horrifying conditions. The minister Simone Veil was detained here before being transferred to Auschwitz.

■ Transformed after 1945 into barracks for Soviet occupation troops, this camp was refurbished in 1992 and turned into a museum that, notably, contains commemorative prison cells where each country can honor its own prisoners.

[Memorial: Strasse der Nationen, 16798 Fürstenberg/Havel. ✆ 0330936080. Open Tue–Sun 9:30 A.M.–5 P.M.]

Neuengamme

■ Of the 106,000 detainees in Neuengamme, 55,000 perished. SS doctors performed criminal medical experiments in this camp, primarily on Jewish children.

■ A monument in memory of the victims and an archive can be visited.

[Memorial: Jean-Dolidier-Weg 33, 21039 Hamburg. ✆ 04042896517 for information. Open Apr to Sep, Tue–Fri 10 A.M.–5 P.M., Sat–Sun 10 A.M.–6 P.M.; Oct–Mar, Tue–Sun 10 A.M.–5 P.M.]

THE RHINELAND AND BAVARIA

Buchenwald

■ Opened in 1937, Buchenwald camp was intended for Hitler's political opponents. After the outbreak of the war, it "welcomed" Nazi adversaries from occupied countries, among them such eminent French personalities as Léon Blum and Marcel Dassault, and numerous Resistance fighters (constituting more than a third of the 250,000 prisoners). Buchenwald was liberated after a revolt organized by the clandestine Resistance within the camp itself.

■ On its former location a monument was erected for all the victims of Nazi terror.

[Memorial: 99427 Weimar Buchenwald. ✆ 036434300, fax 03643430100. Open May–Sep, Tue–Sun 9:45 A.M.–6 P.M.; Oct–Apr, Tue–Sun 8:45 A.M.–5 P.M. Access by car: take Highway A4 and the B7, direction Ettersberg. 🚌 6 leaving from the Weimar Station.]

Bergen-Belsen

More than 50,000 Soviet prisoners of war died in Bergen-Belsen. Beginning in 1944, Bergen-Belsen served as an overflow camp for prisoners of other camps situated further east who were brought here by SS executioners fleeing the Russian advance. As many as 50,000 prisoners, among them the young Anne Frank, did not survive this forced march or died after arrival at the camp.

[Camp and Archive: ✆ 0505147590, fax 05051475981. Open daily 9 A.M.–6 P.M.

The Rhineland and Bavaria ■

The oldest vestiges of a Jewish presence in Germany are found in the Rhineland. For a long time the river constituted the western border of the Roman Empire. In the fortified cities of the frontier such as Colonia Agrippina (Cologne), the Diaspora Jews found favorable conditions in which to exercise their industrial and commercial talents. Later, in the Middle Ages, in cities such as Worms and Frankfurt, which were under the direct authority of the emperor, the Jews benefited from the sovereign's protection. Some prince-bishops, such as those of Speyer and Mainz, made a show of their autonomy from Rome by according the Jews the right to engage in trade. Seeing the Jews as heretics and rivals, the papacy in contrast preached a policy of separation. In the tenth and eleventh centuries, the vitality of Rhenish Judaism rivaled that of Andalusia before the

Mikvah, Friedberg.

Friedberg

Inquisition in its religious and intellectual prosperity. Rhenish Judaism
owed its survival in the face of persecution to the ability of the Jews at
court. Centuries later, this community
fostered the modern enlightened think-
ing of such figures as Meyer Amschel
Rothschild in Frankfurt, Karl Marx in
Trier, Heinrich Heine in Düsseldorf,
and Jacques Offenbach in Cologne.

■ The small city of Friedberg possesses the deepest **mikvah** in Germany: seventy-two steps carved into
the basalt lead the visitor to a natural
spring situated eighty-two feet below
the surface. At the bottom of the staircase, a stone tablet dedicated to the
builder of this bath displays the date
of its origin in 1260. An octagonal
opening in the dome above is the sole

source of light and gives the illusion of the moon's constantly shining in the somber depths of the water.

[Mikvah: Judengasse 20, 61191 Friedberg. Open Tue–Fri 9 A.M.–noon and 2 A.M.–5 P.M., Sat 9 A.M.–noon, and Sun 10 A.M.–noon. More information available at the tourist office: ✆ 0603188261.]

Frankfurt am Main

The independent city of Frankfurt has welcomed Jews since 1150. However, from 1460 until their emancipation at the end of the seventeenth century, the Jews were confined to Judengasse (Street of the Jews), a ghetto that became quickly overcrowded. In 1720, moneylender Meyer Amschel Rothschild, his wife, Gütele, and their eighteen children moved into one of the houses in the area. Meyer's success and the dispersion of his large family across Europe gave rise to the powerful financial network of this celebrated family. Unfortunately, the bombings of 1945 and the reconstruction of the city center after the war have wiped away all traces of this former Jewish quarter.

■ At the beginning of the 1960s, the municipality of Frankfurt decided to consecrate a museum to the history of the city's Jewish population. It was installed in the Rothschild Palace on the banks of the Main River, a classical building erected in 1821 and designed by the Paris-trained architect Johann Friederich Christian Hess.

The palace was acquired in 1846 by Baron Meyer Carl von Rothschild, head of the German branch of Rothschild banking. He had it renovated and redecorated to house his prestigious collection of furniture, paintings, and gold objets d'art. The Jewish Museum contains the objects from this collection that escaped Nazi pillage as well as a permanent exhibition about the Jewish community in Frankfurt. Facilities at the museum include an archive, a library, and a café. Theater performances and concerts of Jewish music are also frequently held here.

Family home of the Rothschilds, Frankfurt, 1880.

132

[Jewish Museum: Untermainkai 14–15, 60311 Frankfurt. ✆ 06921235000. ✉ info@juedischesmuseum.de. Open Tue and Thu–Sun 10 A.M.–5 P.M., Wed 10 A.M.–8 P.M.]

Mainz

At the height of the Middle Ages, the Jewish community in Mainz rivaled the communities of Worms and Speyer. Few traces of this community remain.

■ Among several stone tombs preserved in the Jewish cemetery is that of Rabbi Gershom ben Yehuda (c. 960–1028), called Meor ha-Golah (Light of the Exile).

[Jewish Cemetery: Mombacherstrasse 8, 55001 Mainz. To visit the grounds, ask for the key at the community center.]
[Jewish Community Center: Forsterstrasse 2, 55116 Mainz. ✆ 06131613990. Open Mon–Thu 8 A.M.–2 P.M.]

■ In 1938, the Nazis sacked the Jewish Museum. Certain rooms, notably a collection of religious objects from the eighteenth and nineteenth centuries, were saved and are currently on display at the Regional Museum.

[Regional Museum (Landesmuseum): Grosse Bleiche 49–51, 55116 Mainz. Open Wed–Sun 10 A.M.–5 P.M., Tue 10 A.M.–8 P.M.]

Worms

In Worms, directly administered by Emperor Henry IV, the Jewish community obtained the right to trade by public edict of the emperor as early as 1074. The synagogue of Worms was founded in 1034. Not only the location of worship but also a center for study, the synagogue made Worms the spiritual and cultural center of Judaism during the Middle Ages. A native of Troyes, the rabbi-scholar Salomon ben Isaac settled in Worms in around 1060 to study and edit commentaries of the **Torah** under the pen name Rashi. His commentaries and writings still have great authority today.

■ With 2,000 graves, the Jewish cemetery of Worms is the oldest preserved in Europe. Numerous small scrolls of paper slipped between the bars of Rabbi Meir of Rothenburg's

Jewish cemetery, Worms.

THE RHINELAND AND BAVARIA

RABBI MEIR OF ROTHENBURG

An expert in the study of the **Torah,** Rabbi Meir of Rothenburg attracted students to the **yeshiva** from all over Europe. He preached returning to the Jewish ancestral lands in order to escape the persecutions rife at that time. He himself left for Jerusalem but was stopped in Lombardy by the troops of Rudolph of Hapsburg, who did not want to see his "charges" flee to the Orient, because of their considerable value as taxpayers. The rabbi refused to let his friends pay the enormous ransom for his freedom and died in prison in 1286. It was only fourteen years later that the emperor consented to give his remains back to his community. They were brought by Alexander Süsskind Wimpfen, a wealthy Jew from Frankfurt who sacrificed his entire fortune to the Jewish community for the privilege of being buried next to the rabbi when he died.

tomb attest to the number of Jewish pilgrims from the world over who regularly come to honor his burial place. ■ In 1961, the city of Worms reconstructed the synagogue destroyed for the last time during Kristallnacht.

Located in the former Jewish quarter (the Judenhof), the synagogue is composed of a *Männerschul* (hall of prayer for men) and a *Frauenschul* (hall of prayer for women). The former **yeshiva,** a study hall known as the "chapel of Rashi," is located behind the synagogue. Beyond the study hall, underground, is one of the oldest *mikva'ot* in Europe, dating from the twelfth century.

[Synagogue: Judenhof, 67501 Worms.]

■ The Rashi House (Raschi-Haus) located near the synagogue on the Hintere Judengasse contains the collections of the Jewish Museum (Jüdisches Museum). The restoration completed in 1982 took special care to preserve the original vaults of the cellars, which date from the fourteenth century. This museum is dedicated to the history of the Jewish community in Worms from its origins to its annihilation by the Nazis. It also retraces the Jewish way of life in the city in its full splendor, displaying objects of

Rashi's seat, Worms, beginning of the tenth century.

worship, items taken from daily life, paintings, and historic documents.

[Jüdisches Museum im Raschi-Haus: Hintere Judengasse 6, 67547 Worms. ✆ 062418534701. ➊ stadtarchiv@worms.de. Open Tue–Sun 10 A.M.–12:30 P.M. and 1:30–4:30 P.M. (Open until 5 P.M. from Apr to the end of Oct).]

Heidelberg

■ The library in this university town of Heidelberg on the banks of the Neckar River contains a collection of Hebrew manuscripts dating back to the twelfth, thirteenth, and fourteenth centuries. Among the manuscripts are the songs of the Jewish troubadour Süsskind von Trimberg decorated with 137 illuminated miniatures.

[Library: Plöck 107–109, 69117 Heidelberg. ✆ 06221542380. ➊ ub@ub.uni-heidelberg.de.]

Speyer

The Jews of Speyer were invited by Archbishop Rüdiger Huzmann to settle in the city in 1090. They erected a synagogue at the same time as the construction of the prelate's cathedral that still dominates the city today.

■ Vestiges of the eastern wall are all that remain of the original synagogue. In contrast, the mikvah dating from the same period is preserved in excellent condition. Perhaps the oldest mikvah in western Europe, this structure is a classic example of the Romanesque architecture of the period.

[Synagogue: Kleine Pfaffengasse, 67346 Speyer. ✆ 06232291971. Open Apr–Oct, Mon–Fri 10 A.M.–noon and 2–5 P.M., Sat and Sun 10 A.M.–5 P.M.]

Dachau

Dachau was the first large concentration camp opened by the Nazis upon their rise to power in 1933. Their registers record 200,000 people entering the camp and 30,000 deaths, a tally that far from corresponds to the true number of victims, many of whom were brought here and executed without any kind of trial.

THE RHINELAND AND BAVARIA

■ A museum, archive, two churches, and a synagogue have been erected on the land once occupied by the camp.

[Memorial: Alte Römerstrasse 75, 85221 Dachau. ☎ 08131669970. Open Tue–Sun 9 A.M.–5 P.M.]

Entrance to Dachau concentration camp.

Switzerland

JEWISH CRAFTSMEN AND MERCHANTS settled in Switzerland's Roman cities between the third and fourth centuries, but the first documents that mention them date only from the thirteenth century. Throughout the following two centuries, Jews were regularly accused of ritualistic crimes on Christian children and poisoning wells. They were expelled from the cities during the period 1384–1491. Certain families, however, benefited from the tolerance of local authorities. Communities began to reform only in the early nineteenth century on the initiative of Alsatian Jews.

The Jews of Switzerland were among the last in Europe to gain political equality, under foreign pressure in 1866. A popular vote in 1893 forbade ritualistic slaughter in Switzerland. This ban is still in effect, and **kosher** meat must be imported.

Switzerland's supposedly neutral stance during the Second World War gave rise to an immense debate that began in 1995: substantial historical research showed that the Swiss government had adopted an anti-Semitic asylum policy during the war, driving back thousands of refugees by requiring

Süsskind von Trimberg sporting a Jewish hat, with a dignitary from the city of Constance, sixteenth century. University of Heidelberg Library.

that Germany issue a "J" stamp on the passports of its Jewish nationals. Swiss banks finally admitted having wrongfully confiscated accounts belonging to victims of the *Shoah*, while insurance companies were accused of failing to pay premiums to the appropriate parties after the war. This profound reevaluation of Swiss history, previously shrouded in the myth of neutrality, resistance, and humanitarian intervention, gave rise to a strong tide of anti-Semitism, stirred up by declarations from high political officials relayed in the media. Used to a low profile, Switzerland's small Jewish community (18,000 people) suddenly found itself on the front lines, squeezed between the demands of Jewish organizations and the reluctance of Swiss institutions. Several years of dialogue will be needed for anti-Semitism to abate in Switzerland.

[For all information concerning Swiss Judaism, make an appointment with the Swiss Federation of Hebrew Communities (SIG-FSCI), Gotthardstrasse 65, 8002 Zurich. ✆ 012015583.]

→ **To call Switzerland from the United States, dial 011 41** followed by the number of the person you are calling minus the initial 0 (used only for domestic calls).

French-Speaking Switzerland

Geneva

Established in 1852 by Alsatian Jews, the Jewish community of Geneva was offered a plot of land by the city to build a synagogue as a sign of tolerance toward non-Protestant minorities.

■ Located at the Place de la Synagogue and combining eastern style with Polish characteristics, the Beth Yaakov Synagogue was returned to its original colors in 1997: designed in 1857 by Jean-Henri Bachofen, it features a gray- and pink-striped facade, four crenellated turrets crowned by domes, and a central dome

Beth Yaakov Synagogue, Geneva.

topped with the Tablets of the Law. The interior (arches and dome) is predominantly light blue, while the stained-glass windows and paneling add to the vividness of the colors.

> [Beth Yaakov Synagogue:
> place de la Synagogue, 1204 Geneva.
> ✆ 0223178900. For visiting times, contact the Jewish Community of Geneva that oversees Synagogue Hekhal Haness as well: ✆ 0227369632.]

■ The Heikhal Haness Synagogue, serving the Sephardic Jewish community, was built in 1970. This marble construction was needed in answer to changes in Geneva's community, as Mediterranean Jews have now become the majority.

> [Synagogue Hekhal Haness,
> 54 ter, route de Malagnou, 1208 Geneva.
> ✆ 0227369632.]

■ The Community Center houses the Jewish main library, rich in several high quality scientific and artistic collections, as well as the Jardin Rose (Rose Garden) **kosher** restaurant.

> [Community Center (Jewish House):
> 10, rue Saint-Léger, 1205 Geneva.
> ✆ 0223178900.
> Open Mon–Thu 9 A.M.–noon and 2–3:30 P.M., Fri 9 A.M.–noon, or by appointment.
> The restaurant is open daily for lunch.]

♛ WHY AM I JEWISH?

Edmond Fleg, whose real name was Flegheimer, was a novelist, poet, and thinker born in Geneva in 1874. Until his death in 1963, he fought for the Jewish cause within the context of the Jewish Scouts of France, the Universal Jewish Alliance, and the Judeo-Christian Friendship. "I am Jewish because wherever suffering weeps, the Jew weeps. / I am Jewish because whenever despair cries out, the Jew hopes. / I am Jewish, because the word of Israel is the oldest and the newest. / I am Jewish, because the promise of Israel is a universal promise."

EDMOND FLEG, *POURQUOI JE SUIS JUIF* (WHY I AM JEWISH). PARIS: LES BELLES LETTRES, 1995.

Carouge

Before Jews were able to settle in Geneva, the neighboring city of Carouge (at the time part of the Kingdom of Sardinia) opened its doors to them around 1779.

■ The sole remaining Jewish vestige is the old cemetery, which was restored in 1996.

> [Jewish Cemetery: rue de la Fontenette, 1227 Carouge. For visiting times, contact the caretaker: ✆ 0792023370.]

■ The new cemetery, in the Franco-Swiss border town of Veyrier, contains the graves of numerous luminaries, such as the writer Albert Cohen.

> [New Jewish Cemetery:
> 16, chemin de l'Arvaz, 1255 Veyrier.
> ✆ 0792023370.
> Open Sun–Thu 8 A.M.–6 P.M. (8 A.M.–5 P.M. in winter), Fri 8 A.M.–2 P.M. Closed Sat and Jewish holidays.]

Synagogue, Lausanne.

Lausanne

■ Lausanne's synagogue, built in 1910 in a fairly remote neighborhood at the time, can be found today right near the train station in the heart of the city. Its Romano-Byzantine style is reminiscent of the synagogue located on Rue Buffault in Paris: Tablets of the Law dominate its facade, which contains a rose window shaped like a Star of David; it also features semicircular window arches, Romanesque apses, and two towers. The interior is neo-Byzantine. The Community Center is adorned with stained-glass windows by Jean Prahin.

[Synagogue: 1, avenue Juste-Olivier, 1003 Lausanne. For visiting times, contact the community center.]

[Community Center: 3, avenue Georgette, 1003 Lausanne. ✆ 0213417240. Open Mon–Thu 8 A.M.–8 P.M., Fri 8 A.M.–4 P.M. A kosher restaurant is open for lunch Mon–Fri.]

La Chaux-de-Fonds

■ Founded in 1833, Chaux-de-Fonds's Jewish community opened its first synagogue in 1896. Architect Kuder was inspired by the synagogue in Strasbourg, which was later destroyed by the Nazis. In Romanesque style and constructed in freestone, the building contains a 105-foot-high octagonal dome with twenty-four windows and covered in polychromatic tiles. The facade includes the Tablets of the Law and two turrets. Inside,

142

Synagogue, La Chaux-de-Fonds.

the central dome and four smaller domes at each corner are multi-colored, in harmony with the stained-glass windows. The principal motif is a Star of David, from which rays extend that bear the names of biblical characters upon a starry sky.

[Synagogue: 63, rue du Parc, 2300 La Chaux-de-Fonds.
☎ 0329130477.]

German-Speaking Switzerland ■

Endingen and Lengnau

Until the end of the eighteenth century, the two villages of Endingen and Lengnau were the only ones that authorized the permanent establishment of Jews. Beginning in 1622, they resided here under the rubric of "protected foreigners," and their communities were able to practice religion and conduct internal administrative affairs in total independence. In 1750, the two communities purchased a plot of land midway between the towns for a cemetery.

■ The first synagogues date from 1750 (Lengnau) and 1764 (Endingen) and were renovated in 1848 and 1852 respectively. They resemble churches, with a clock on their pediments and steeples, elements required by the authorities.

In Endingen, a churchless village, it was the synagogue on the central square that struck the hours. The building was renovated in 1998. The town's policy of tolerance must not overshadow the discrimination that was still current around 1910: all houses had two front doors, one reserved for Christians and the other for Jews.

[Endingen's synagogue, the cemetery, and Lengnau's inactive synagogue are all open to the public. Call ahead for key. ✆ 0562421546.]

Yahrzeit *(commemorative calendar)*.
Jüdisches Museum der Schweiz, Basel.

Basel

"In Basel, I created the Jewish State," wrote Theodor Herzl in his diary after attending the First Zionist Congress, held from 29 to 30 August 1897. Nine more congresses would take place in Basel. A street in his name and a plaque in the casino serve as a reminder of the Zionist adventure's origins in Basel.

■ First opened in 1868, the synagogue is the work of the architect Hermann Gauss, who took the one in Stuttgart, with its neo-Byzantine, Moorish, and Romanesque styles, as his model. It was enlarged twenty years later, and a second dome was

added. During a further renovation in 1947, someone decided to cover the synagogue's brightly colored walls in uniform gray. This gray corresponded better to the austerity of the era and local taste. Forty years later, the colors of yesteryear resuscitated the refinished building. Modernizing the motifs has nonetheless dampened the eastern style. Inside, yellowish beige dominates, with blue and red decorations. A multitude of golden stars stand out against the dome. The polychromatic facades are red and white.

[Synagogue: Leimenstrasse 24, 4051 Basel.]

■ The only Jewish museum in Switzerland (Jüdisches Museum der Schweiz) is found in Basel. Its collection reflects the region's Jewish heritage and features books in Hebrew printed in Basel, gravestones, and documents on Jewish history and the Zionist congresses.

[Jüdisches Museum der Schweiz: Kornhausgasse 8, 4051 Basel. ✆ 0612619514. Open Sun 11 A.M.–5 P.M., Mon and Wed 2–5 P.M.]

■ The Community Center houses as well the **kosher** restaurant Topas.

[Community Center: Leimenstrasse 24, 4051 Basel. ✆ 0612069500.]

Zurich

■ Zurich contains the headquarters of the Swiss Federation of Hebrew Communities, founded in 1904 and whose archives were recently entrusted to the Zurich Federal Polytechnic School for better preservation there. The collection includes the documents from JUNA, the FSCI press office, the Union of Jewish Mutual Aid Societies, the Swiss Refugee Council, the Union of Jewish Students, and the Action Group for Jews in the Soviet Union, along with extensive private archives.

[Swiss Federation of Hebrew Communities: Gotthardstrasse 65, 8002 Zurich. ✆ 012015583.]

[Archiv für Zeitgeschichte: Ethzentrum, 8092 Zurich. ✆ 016324003, fax 016321392. ❶ ganz@history.gess.ethz.ch.]

■ The former ghetto in the Brunnengassen was the site of a 1349 pogrom against the Jews, who were accused of having spread the plague. A commemorative plaque was unveiled 650 years later at 4 Froschausgasse, where the former synagogue stood. The narrow, nameless alley that leads to the Neumarkt was renamed Synagogengasse.

■ Today, the Israelitische Cultusgemeinde Zurich (ICZ), founded in 1862, represents the most important Jewish community in Switzerland. The ICZ's synagogue, at the corner of the Löwenstrasse and Nuschelerstrasse, was built in 1884 in Moorish style; it features a beige- and red-striped facade, two towers topped by domes, and traditional windows. Its Community Center houses as well the **kosher** restaurant Shalom. It also benefits from the presence of Morascha bookstore, only a short distance away.

[Israelitische Cultusgemeinde Zurich: Lavaterstrasse 33, 8027 Zurich. ✆ 012832222.]

[Shalom: same address. ✆ 012832233.]

[Schein und Fein: Schöntalstrasse 14, 8004 Zurich. ✆ 012413040.]

[Morascha Bookstore: Seestrasse 11, 8002 Zurich. ✆ 012011120. Open Mon–Thu 9 A.M.–noon and 2–6:30 P.M., Fri 9 A.M. to noon.]

■ In addition, three distinct Jewish communities inhabit the city, each centered upon its own synagogue: the Orthodox Israelitische Religionsgesellschaft; the Reform Or Chadasch community; and finally, the sizable **Hasidic** community around the Agudas Achim Synagogue, which gives off a truly **shtetl** ambiance.

[Synagogue of the Israelitische Religionsgesellschaft: Freigutstrasse 37, 8002 Zurich. For information, contact the office: Manessestrasse 10, 8003 Zurich. ✆ 012418057.]

[Or Chadasch: Hallwystrasse 78, 8004 Zurich. ✆ 0433220314.]

[Synagogue Agudas Achim: Erikastrasse 8, 8003 Zurich. ✆ 014635798.]

Bern

■ In the fourteenth century, the Jewish ghetto extended into the federal government's current site: the Insel-gasse, seat of the Department of the Interior, was called the Judengasse; the Federal Palace took over the spot of the Jewish cemetery. The current Community Center and its Moorish synagogue are not far away, on the Kapellenstrasse.

[Community Center and Synagogue: Kapellenstrasse 2, 3011 Bern. ✆ 0313814992.]

■ An unusual feature of the Korn-hausplatz is Ogre Fountain, which dates from 1544. For some, the statue of the ogre in the act of devouring children represents merely a carnival image. For others, it is a Middle Age representation of the Jew accused of killing Christian children. The ogre is wearing a pointed yellow hat, identical to the one imposed on the Jews to make them easily distinguishable.

Biel/Bienne

It was the clock-making industry that attracted Alsatian Jews to the Jura beginning in 1835.

■ They opened their Moorish synagogue in 1884. Its most recent interior renovation, in 1995, stressed the contrast between sober walls and the twelve multicolored stained-glass windows featuring biblical subjects, the work of Israeli artist Robert Nechin. The 1999 exterior renovation brought back four small domes shaped like bells that had been removed in 1956. The facades are light beige, discreetly decorated with red motifs on the friezes and around the windows.

[Synagogue: Ruschlistrasse 3, 2502 Biel/Bienne. Open for religious festivities only.]

Southwest Europe

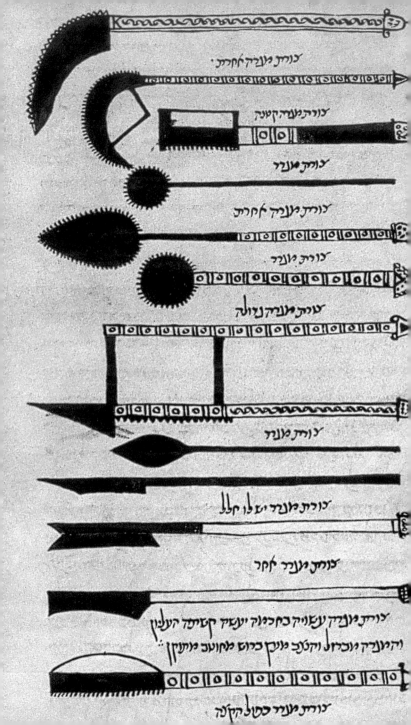

צורת מעבריה אחרת ·

צורת מעבריה קטנה

צורת מעבד

צורת מעבריה אחרת

צורת מעבד

צורת מעבריה גדולה

צורת מעבד

צורת מעבד יצא לו חלל

צורת מעבד אחר

צורת מעבריה עשויה כחכמיה יעשה קטיבה העליון
והמעבריה מבדיל והכתב מעק כרום מחועב מיתקן ··

צורת מעבד כטול הקנה

T HERE ARE NUMEROUS LEGENDS surrounding the arrival of the Jews in Spain. They were propagated by Jewish and Christian chroniclers, especially in the sixteenth century. Some say they came in the time of King Solomon, following in the wake of the Phoenician sailors; others that the event was one consequence of their exile from Judaea, as ordered by Nebuchadrezzar.

Historians, for their part, specify that the first Jews came here in a relatively organized way after the destruction of the Temple in Jerusalem, in 70 C.E. They settled first on the Mediterranean coast, then spread throughout most of the Iberian Peninsula. The oldest physical evidence of the Jewish presence in Spain is a trilingual inscription (in Hebrew, Latin, and Greek) on a child's sarcophagus found in Tarragona and dating from the Roman period (now displayed at the Sephardic Museum in Toledo). Further, there is no doubt that the mosaic at Elche (first century) originally decorated the floor of a synagogue. This is attested by the Greek inscriptions and the nature of its geometrical drawings. Finally, texts reveal a Jewish presence in Spain during the same period: examples are *The War of*

D'Albucasis, Book of Practice, *first half of the fifteenth century.*
Bibliothèque Nationale de France, Paris.

the Jews by Flavius Josephus (VII, 3, 3) and the *Mishna* (Baba Batra, III, 2).

SEPHARAD: JEWISH SPAIN

The term "Sepharad" appears in the Bible (Obadiah 20, King James version):

". . . And the captivity of this host of the children of Israel shall possess that of the Canaanites, even unto Zarephath; and the captivity of Jerusalem, which is in Sepharad, shall possess the cities of the south."

Since the eighth century, "Sepharad" has traditionally referred to Spain and the Spanish Jews, and, by extension, has been applied to all the Jews in the communities around the Mediterranean.

Little is known of the Spanish-Jewish communities before the eighth century. Under the Romans, the Jews had the same status as elsewhere in the empire. Under the reign of the Visigoth kings, who were Aryans, the Jews were tolerated and many lived from farming. From 586, when King Recaredo converted to Christianity, the Jews endured nearly a century of persecution and forced conversions (making them the ancestors of the Marranos). King Egica even considered making them slaves.

When the Arabs came in 711, the Jews cooperated with them. The Arabs were few in number and in need of faithful allies. It was in the interest of both communities to get along, especially since large numbers of Jews from the Maghreb soon

Seal of Joseph, son of Judah, president of the community, Spain or France, fourteenth century. Musée National du Moyen Âge des Thermes de Cluny, Paris.

swelled the ranks of the Moors and the Jews of the Sepharad. The importance of the Jewish minority is reflected in the appellation "Jewish cities" some Arab geographers gave to Granada, Tarragona, and Lucena. The development of urban life called for shopkeepers and administrators, functions Arabs and Berbers were loath to take on.

The institution of the caliphate of Córdoba in 926 ushered in a golden age for Judaism in the Islamic lands. Abderrahman III (912–971) took as his doctor Hasday ibn Saprut, a Jew from Jaén, entrusting him not only with his personal health but also with diplomatic missions such as contacts with the abbot of Gorze and negotiations with the emerging kingdoms of León and Navarre. Hasday became a rich courtier and his life was sung by the poets Menahem ben Saruc and Dunas ben Labrat. He organized the translation of numerous works of science from Greek into Arabic and contributed greatly to the cultural prosperity of his community. The example of Arabic poetry inspired Jews to write superb poems and to study grammar. All this intellectual ferment favored the growth of a rich Hebrew culture.

In the eleventh century Granada was the capital of Arab Spain. Samuel ha-Nagid, known as Nagid (993–1056), was the key figure in this period. This tradesman from Malaga quickly rose to become the vizier charged with conducting Granada's policy and leading its Arab army, notably against Seville and Almería. Nagid was also a poet and learned rabbi and did much for the arts, especially poetry. The same was true of his son Yosef, who succeeded him at his death.

These poets give us an idea of the degree of development of the Jewish communities in the Islamic lands and of the way of life of courtiers there, divided between their love of pleasure, literature and the arts, and their traditional religion. They would later serve as a model for Jews in Castile and Aragón.

♕ SALOMON IBN GABIROL

The great poet Salomon ibn Gabirol (1022–54), the protégé of Nagid and his son, wrote the 400-line Kingdom's Crown, *a contemplative hymn to God and His creation, which* **Sephardic** *communities used as part of the liturgy for* **Yom Kippur**. *He also wrote* The Source of Life, *a philosophical work in Arabic examining the principles of Neoplatonism, which the Muslims were then reintroducing. He is also credited with* Adon Olam, *the prayer recited several times during daily services in the week and at the* **Shabbat** *by Jewish communities all over the world:*

"Reigned the Universe's Master,
Ere were earthly things begun;
When His mandate all created,
Ruler was the name He won.
And alone He'll rule tremendous
When all things are past and gone,
He no equal has, nor consort,
He, the singular and lone,
Has no end and no beginning;
His the scepter, might and throne.
He's my God and living Savior,
Rock to Whom I in need run;
He's my banner and my refuge,
Fount of weal when call'd upon.
In His hand I place my spirit,
At nightfall and at rise of sun,
And therewith my body also;
God's my God—I fear no one."

THE NEW ENCYCLOPEDIA OF JUDAISM, ED. GEOFFREY WISODER (NEW YORK: NEW YORK UNIVERSITY PRESS, 2002).

However, with conflict between Arabic kingdoms and pressure from the Christians, especially after the reconquest of Toledo in 1080, the Spanish Arabs were driven to appeal to the Almoravids of North Africa for help. When the latter invaded southern Spain, the Jews only just avoided forced conversion. But the Almohads of Morocco, who invaded in 1146, were more intransigent: they prohibited the practice of Judaism, forcing Jews to either convert or hide their religion. Others chose exile in the neighboring Christian lands. Apart from Granada, the last Moorish kingdom, Islamic Spain began at this time to lose its Jews.

In all, Christian Spain took seven centuries to win back the Islamic territories. The recovery was completed with the capture of Granada in 1492, an event that deeply marked Jewish-Christian relations. In parallel to the victories won by the kingdoms of León, Navarre, Aragón, and Catalonia, the old Jewish communities of Catalonia and Aragón began to grow, and small groups settled along the road to Santiago de Compostela. The Jews colonized the reconquered territories and played an active part in trade and the textile industry.

In 1085 Alfonso VI took Toledo, establishing the new frontier between the Cross and the Crescent. The Jews were protected by the Christian monarchs, for they made useful administrators of the new territories as well as tax collectors and facilitated contacts in Arabic. The Jews grew wealthy. As the finance ministers of Castile and Aragón, it was they who advanced the tax revenues to the king.

By the twelfth century, the whole of Spain apart from Granada was Christian. A new golden age began for the Spanish Jews, but in the Christian lands now. This was especially true under Alfonso X ("the Wise") in Castile and Jaime I in Aragón. Toledo became a new Jerusalem, the capital of Jewish life. It was home to scholars, **Talmudists,** chief rabbis, and financiers. Catalonia, too, had a period of splendor with Nahmanides at Gerona and Salomon ben Adret at Barcelona. The Jews kept out of political life and were no threat to relations between Christendom and Islam. In legal terms, they belonged to the king, a status that gave them protection but also put them at his mercy.

As elsewhere in Europe, the power of the church grew as the reconquest spread. Although the Fourth Lateran Council (1215) decreed a number of anti-Jewish measures, they were implemented with a certain flexibility for reasons of political necessity and in the interests of the struggle against the remaining Moorish kingdoms. Nonetheless, in Aragón, Jews were excluded from public service, and in Castile, the Cortes made numerous propositions to limit Jewish freedom.

The Black Death, the influence of anti-Jewish polemical literature, and the effect of Jewish participation in the civil war between Peter the Cruel and his bastard brother, Henry of Trastamare, all contributed to a rejection of Judaism.

This was compounded by a decline in faith and slackening of moral and religious practice among the better off. The Jewish-Christian dialogue entered a new phase, and the Christian world began to consider conversion as the solution to the presence of the Jewish minority. This is the time of the famous Barcelona Controversy (1256), when Nahmanides's victory over the converted Jew Pablo Christiani was only partial.

The ground had thus been prepared for the explosion of violence orchestrated by the archdeacon of Ecija, Ferran Martinez. The anti-Jewish campaign that he launched in 1378 intensified when he was made archbishop in 1390. Taking advantage of the death of Juan I on 4 June 1391, he fomented a riot culminating in the destruction of the *judería* in Seville. Many Jews were forced to convert to save their lives. The violence spread from one *judería* to another across Andalusia and Castile. The most flourishing Jewish quarters, in Toledo and Córdoba, were hit extremely hard. In July 1391 the wave reached Valencia, Majorca, Barcelona, and Gerona, wiping out Jewish life there.

These massacres greatly altered the Jewish community. A new figure appeared, the *converso* (convert). The *conversos'* motives and hopes were highly diverse. Those forced to convert continued to practice Judaism in secret; these were the

Bible, Perpignan, 1299. Bibliothèque Nationale de France, Paris.

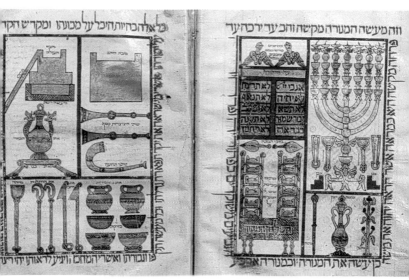

crypto-Jews, or Marranos. Others used the opportunity to become full participants in Christian society and gain access to positions closed to Jews. Still others sincerely wished to become Christians, even if their baptism was forced upon them. The disputation at Tortosa in 1413–14, when Zerahia Halevi and Joseph Albo debated with the Christian convert Jeronimo de Santa Fé (José Halorqui) on the usual themes of Jewish-Christian polemic, was perhaps the last attempt to persuade the Jews by means of reason. Christian society was uncertain as to what attitude it should take toward the Jews and *conversos.* The decision was made to separate Jews and converts in order to ensure that the latter became good and sincere Christians and to prevent them from returning to Judaism. This was the mission entrusted to the Inquisition in 1480. Thomas Torquemada, who was appointed Grand Inquisitor, turned this into a redoubtably effective institution, relentlessly tracking down both "sympathizers" of Judaism and *conversos,* in Spain and Latin America, dragging them before tribunals, sentencing them to death in autos-da-fé, or condemning them in other ways.

After the conquest of Granada, Isabella of Castile and Fernando of Aragón signed the expulsion decree of 31 March 1492. This set out to resolve the thorny question posed by the Jewish presence by either conversion or exile.

☙ THE DECREE OF EXPULSION

"Considering that every day it is manifest and patent that the aforesaid Jews continue to pursue their maleficent and pernicious objectives where they live and communicate with Christians, and so that in the future the faithful should be spared all opportunity to offend our holy faith, whom God has thus far kept from this sin, as should

*those who have committed it but have mended
their ways and have come back to our Holy
Mother Church; and this could easily happen
because of the weakness of our human nature
and the malignity of the power of the demon, who
is constantly assailing us, unless we do away
with the main cause of this peril, that it so say
unless we banish the Jews from our kingdoms."*

In spite of pressure from Abraham Senior and
Isaac Abravanel, two ministers of the Catholic monarchs, the Jews left their Spanish homeland on the
ninth day of the month of Av, the date of the
destruction of the Temple in Jerusalem. Abraham
Senior agreed to convert while Isaac Abravanel
joined others on the paths of exile to North Africa,
the Ottoman Empire, Portugal, and elsewhere in
Europe (Italy, France, England, the Netherlands).
This was the **Sephardic** diaspora, which retained its
customs and languages, Castilian and Catalan. The
number who went into exile is hard to determine.
Some 70,000 to 100,000 preferred exile to baptism—between a third and half of Spain's Jewish
population at the time.

By the seventeenth century, there were no Jews
left in Spain (except those in the tiny enclave on the
African coast, where their interpreting skills were
essential to the survival of the garrison; they were not
expelled until 1699). The Inquisition watched over
the *conversos* with all its notorious severity.

💮 RESISTANCE

*Some, like Isaac (Fernando) Cardoso, managed
to escape the Inquisition. Born in Portugal in
1604, he was a doctor at the court of Philip IV.
A respected intellectual, he knew all the great
figures of the age, including Lope de Vega, and*

was treated by them as one of their own. The son of forced conversos, *Cardoso lived ostensibly as a Christian and covertly as a Jew. In 1648, at the height of his fame, he suddenly left Spain and took refuge in Italy. There he publicly professed his Judaism in Venice and Verona and, under the name Isaac Cardoso, published one of the finest Jewish apologias,* Las Excelencias de los hebreos.

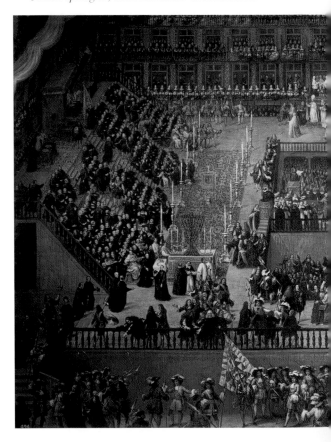

The memory of Spain's Jewish presence did not completely vanish, however. Count Duque Olivares had the idea of re-creating a Jewish community in Madrid in order to stimulate Spanish economic development. He must have known about the lucrative activity of the community in Amsterdam,

Francisco Rizi de Guevara, Auto-da-fé, 1683, Museo del Prado, Madrid.

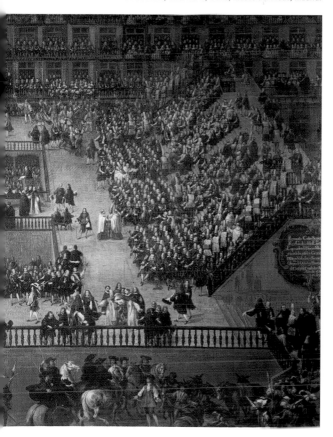

which still spoke Spanish. However, he was forced to abandon his plans. In the eighteenth century, a few thinkers became aware of the losses occasioned by the departure of the Jews, arguing that they represented an important part of the Spanish heritage. Joseph Rodriguez de Castro, for example, published an essay on Spanish writers and rabbis from the eleventh century onward. King Charles VI also thought of bringing Dutch Jews to Spain and canceling the expulsion edict. But the Inquisition remained vigilant. The Holy Office was not abolished until 1813, during the War of Independence and the Liberal movement at the Cortes in Cadiz. Although reestablished during the Restoration, it was abrogated for good in 1834.

In the nineteenth century Jewish merchants came to northern Spain for the textile trade. They were of Spanish or Portuguese origin but had French nationality and were based in Bordeaux or Bayonne. These were isolated cases, however, and never led to the creation of organized communities. This century was also marked by war in Africa and the occupation of Tétouan between 1859 and 1862. In 1858 Ceuta, one of the Spanish enclaves in Morocco, was attacked by Moroccan Montagnards. Spain demanded reparation from the sultan, which was slow in coming. Queen Isabella then sent an expedition commanded by Prim and O'Donnell. The Spanish troops occupied Tétouan, where they were met by a population speaking a mixture of Arabic and Hebrew. These were the descendants of the Jews expelled in 1492, who had almost miraculously kept going in that little town ever since. Until 1862, the occupation allowed the Jewish population to participate in the management of the town and to rise in society. It is appropriate to consider this a reunion of Spain and its Jews, for the event was made known to the general public by the newspapers and numerous accounts given by officers, and historians and philologists were fascinated to discover their language as it had been spoken four centuries earlier.

A visit by King Alfonso XIII to Seville in 1904 highlighted the existence of a small Jewish community there, most from North Africa. They welcomed the king to their street (Calle de la Feria) with a banner in Hebrew and Spanish. In the early 1900s, Doctor Angel Pulido (1852–1932) who, when traveling along the Danube came across eastern European Jews speaking an archaic Spanish, launched several press campaigns and petitions to persuade Spain to recognize the communities in Serbia, Bulgaria, Romania, and Turkey, whose customs were still close to those of the Sepharad. He published two important works on the recent history of the Spanish Jews: *Los Israelitas españoles y el idioma castellano* (1904) and *Españoles sin patria, y la raza sefardi* (1905). Pulido obtained authorization to open a synagogue in Madrid (1917) for about 150 families and one in Barcelona (1914) for 250 people. He also created the Hispano-Hebrea Association in 1910 and in 1913 invited Professor Abraham Shalom Yehuda to teach Hebrew at the university in Madrid.

In 1914, the Zionist leader Max Nordau was forced to leave France because of his Austrian nationality. He came to Spain. King Alfonso XIII personally interceded with the kaiser to moderate the persecution and violence against the Jews in Palestine. After World War I, this process of rapprochement with the Jews gained momentum as major political figures such as the count of Romanones, Melquiades Alvarez, Alejandro Lerroux, Juan de la Cierva, Niceto Alcalà Zamora, and several army generals publicly supported this effort of recognition.

After the 1923 Treaty of Lausanne had created a legal void around certain protected Jews by putting an end to the system of capitulations in the Ottoman Empire, the Spanish government under General Primo de Rivera published the decree of 24 December 1924, which granted Spanish nationality to **Sephardim** who met certain conditions. Although the decree was little used during the six-year period of its validity, it would prove highly useful during World War II.

Under the Second Republic (1931–36), whose constitution guaranteed religious liberty and affirmed the secular character of the state, Spain aroused considerable interest among Jews in Europe and the Orient, who saw these guarantees as tantamount to an abrogation of the expulsion decree. In 1935, the lavish celebrations in Córdoba for the 800th anniversary of the birth of the doctor and philosopher Maimonides were like a public demonstration of Spain's renewed interest in its Jewish past.

During the civil war, the communities of Seville and Ceuta and Tétouan in Morocco had to pay heavy taxes to support the nationalist troops of General Franco. Nazi influence revived anti-Semitic propaganda. Some 7,000 to 10,000 Jews from Europe, America, and Palestine came to fight in the international brigades, and even produced their own little **Yiddish** newsletter. At the end of the war, the victory of Franco's troops was followed by the closing of the synagogues in Madrid and Barcelona. Marriages and circumcisions were prohibited and Jewish cemeteries were closed. Jewish children were compelled to attend Catholic schools.

During World War II, neutral Spain became the only refuge in southern Europe from the lightning advance of the Nazi troops. Initially, transit visas were fairly easy to obtain. After the armistice of

1940, however, Spain and France took measures to regulate requests, especially through the Spanish consulate in Marseille. After July 1942 it was illegal for Jews to leave France, and so the crossings were made in secret, albeit with a degree of Spanish sympathy. Nevertheless, there were arrests, and a camp was established at Miranda de Ebro, where prisoners received psychological and material help from American Jewish organizations based in Madrid. These prisoners were gradually evacuated, most of them to Lisbon and the United States.

Spain still had to deal with the problem of the Jews in eastern Europe (Romania, Greece, Bulgaria, and Hungary) and France who were of Spanish origin or who, by virtue of the decree of 1924, had Spanish nationality. Jews in these areas called on Spain to help and protect them when their own governments abandoned them to the Nazis. Thanks to the actions of several Spanish ambassadors and consuls who knew about the fate of the deportees and put pressure on their minister in Madrid, notably Sebastian Romero, Julio Palencia, Romero Radigales, Bernardo Rolland, and Angel Briz, individual visas were issued, allowing several thousand people to escape. In some cases, in France and Greece, the property of these Spanish Jews was protected by the consular authorities and then returned after the war.

Alms box, Spain, fifteenth century.
Musée d'Art et d'Histoire du Judaïsme, Paris.

Although not favorable to the Jews, the policy of Franco and his ministers was not anti-Semitic. For Franco's authorities, the **Sephardic** Jews were living testimony to a glittering period of their country's history. Still, given Spain's position of pro-German neutrality, political prudence and consideration of the balance of power between the Allies and the Axis were vital.

In 1941, the government paradoxically decided to set up the Instituto Arias Montano, which, with its journal *Sefarad,* became one of the most renowned centers for the study of Spanish Judaism and its diaspora. In 1949 a small synagogue opened discreetly in a Madrid apartment. The same happened in Barcelona in 1952. Although Catholicism was now the state religion, these small communities were tolerated. In 1967 a synagogue was built in Madrid, the first one since 1492. In 1978 Spain's new constitution guaranteed religious freedom to all citizens. Today there are some 12,000 Jews in Spain, with communities established in Madrid, Barcelona, Valencia, Seville, Malaga, and the Moroccan enclaves of Ceuta and Melilla.

→ **To call Spain from the United States, dial 011 34**
followed by the number of the person you are calling.

Castile-La Mancha/ Castile-León ∎

The presence of Jews in Castile and León is attested as far back as the tenth century. Over the centuries that followed the rulers granted the Jews the same rights and duties as of the Christians. The rulers considered the Jews their personal property and, throughout the period of reconquest, the community helped with the administrative and commercial organization of the conquered territories. In the twelfth century, royal legislation sought to protect the Jews from the growing risk of violence by grouping them in special quarters around the king's or archbishop's palace, or within the shelter of its walls. Unfortunately, war between Christian kingdoms was rife in this period and the Jews often suffered the consequences.

In the thirteenth century Toledo became the capital of Castilian Judaism. The so-called "Huete census" of 1290 provides a reasonably faithful map of Jewish communities in Castile and León.

The wave of violence of 1391 hit nearly all these *juderías* and marked the beginning of their decline, notwithstanding efforts to revive them at the meeting in Vallodolid in 1432. In 1492 the Jews expelled from these regions headed mainly for Portugal. Whatever material traces they left behind have, with only one or two exceptions, been destroyed.

Madrid

We know that from the tenth century onward there was a small Jewish community in Muslim-ruled Madrid. This grew considerably after the reconquest. Though hit hard by the pogroms of 1391, it was slowly built

166

up again. It is also known that Jewish doctors such as Rabbi Jacob were, under the king's protections, allowed to live outside the Jewish quarter, the better to tend to the sick. In 1492 the Jews of Madrid left for Fès (Morocco) and Tlemcen (Algeria). The city's six Jewish doctors went with them, leaving it without medical assistance. However, they resumed their positions in 1493 after converting to Christianity.

■ Thanks to research by Madrid historians it is possible to locate the city's two Jewish quarters with considerable precision, although sadly few tangible traces remain. They formed around the Plaza Isabella (Calle Independencia and Vergara) and the Almudena cathedral, near the old Alcázar in the Cuesta de la Vega.

■ The Jews came back to Madrid only in the 1850s, sporadically and in an unorganized way. These were shopkeepers and bankers who, among other activities, were involved in the creation of the railroads. The best known of these families were the Bauers, who represented the Rothschild Bank. Since they did not have their own cemetery, they created a special section in the English cemetery in the first years of the twentieth century. A monument inspired by ancient Egypt houses the remains of Gustave Bauer (1867–1916), Manolin Bauer (1898–1906), and Ida Luisa Bauer (1906–08). Another thirty-odd tombs remind us of the existence and origins of this small community in the early twentieth century.

[English Cemetery Foundation: calle Comandante Fontanes, 28000 Madrid. Visits by appointment. Contact the secretary of the foundation at the British consulate: Pasco de Recoletos 7–9, 5th floor, 28004 Madrid. ✆ 913085201.]

■ A community of several thousand formed here during the Second Republic but disappeared during the civil war. In 1964 work was begun on the synagogue in the Calle Balmes, which also houses the community center. It was opened in 1968. The prayer hall is decorated with copies of the Hebrew inscriptions in the Tránsito Synagogue in Toledo. The community has a mikvah, a kosher butcher shop, and a school.

[Beth Yaakov Synagogue: calle Balmes 3, 28000 Madrid.]
[Community Center: same address. ✆ 915913131.]

■ Madrid is also the headquarters of the journal *Sepharad,* a publication of the CSIC (Higher Council of Scientific Investigation), which, since its foundation in 1941, has published most of the Spanish and international research on Sephardic Judaism.

[CSIC Bookstore: calle Medinacelli 6, 28000 Madrid. ✆ 914290626. Open Mon–Fri 9:30 A.M.–1:30 P.M. and 5–7 P.M.]

Tránsito Synagogue, Toledo.

Toledo

The "**Sephardic** Jerusalem" is known around the world for the beauty of its synagogues and its Jewish quarter. The memory of the community has remained vivid in Toledo; historians have from the thirteenth and four- teenth century onward been able to supply fairly precise information about the location and history of the city's Jewish community. Toledo is a city of great historical and artistic importance and is listed here as a World Heritage Site.

At the time of its greatest splendor, just before 1391, Toledo had ten syn- agogues and five to seven *yeshivoth*. In 1492 there were five grand syna- gogues, two of which survive: the

Tránsito, now the Sephardic Museum, and Santa María la Blanca.

THE TRÁNSITO SYNAGOGUE

The Tránsito Synagogue was built in 1357 at the order of Samuel Levi, treasurer to King Pedro I. Archaeological finds suggest this imposing edifice was erected on the site of an older synagogue. In 1492 the Catholic monarchs donated it to the Calatrava military order, which transformed it into a priory. During the Napoleonic Wars it served as a barracks. In 1877 it was declared a national monument. When Spain's Jewish community revived, the outbuildings became the Sephardic Museum.

As is often the case, the brick facade is austere, without decoration, but the interior is very beautiful. This is probably one of the finest examples of the Mudejar style in Spain. Harmonious in proportion (approximately 76 x 30 feet, 56 feet high) it has an ornate coffered larch-wood ceiling. The women's gallery has its own entrance and is well lit by five large windows. The synagogue is famed for its interior decoration. The wall with the niche made for the Sepher Torah is covered with panels and a plaster frieze sculpted in the oriental tradition. Numerous inscriptions along the wall commemorate Samuel Levi and Pedro I. Verses from the Psalms complete this decoration lit by windows with fine ornamental columns and lace-like *mashrabiyahs.*

In the outbuildings the museum exhibits gifts and articles collected from all over Spain, taking visitors through the history of Spanish Judaism. There are some very fine tombstones from León, and the oldest object is the sarcophagus of a child with inscriptions in Hebrew, Greek, and Latin and decorated with royal peacocks, a tree of life, a shofar, and a menorah. Seminars, courses, and talks are organized throughout the year on themes relating to Spanish Judaism. The synagogue is not used for worship.

[Tránsito Synagogue and Sephardic Museum (Museo Sefardi): calle Samuel Leví, 45000 Toledo. ✆ 925223665. They are currently being restored and will reopen in 2004.]

SANTA MARÍA LA BLANCA

The second synagogue, Santa María la Blanca, now bears its later name as a Christian church. Built in the early thirteenth century, it was consecrated as a church in 1411 by the preacher San Vicente Ferrer, the man behind the wave of conversions in 1391. From 1600 to 1791 it was an oratory, and after that a barracks. It was restored in 1851 and declared a national monument. It is in the Mudejar style, but less rich than the Tránsito. Its twenty-five horseshoe arches and thirty-two columns create an impression of considerable space. Note the variety and quality of the capitals and the building's similarity to Andalusian mosques.

CASTILE-LA MANCHA/CASTILE-LEÓN

Be sure to see the many streets of the old *judería* around the Calle Santo Tomé. In spite of much rebuilding, the area still has a certain charm.

[Santa María la Blanca Synagogue: calle de los Reyes Católicos 12, 45000 Toledo. ✆ 925227257. Open Tue–Sun 10 A.M.–2 P.M. and 3:30–6 P.M., Fri 10 A.M.–7 P.M.]

🕎 THE "HOLY INNOCENT CHILD"

Jews in the two small villages of Tembleque and La Guardia near Toledo were accused of the ritual murder of a child, who immediately became a figure of popular legend under the name of the "Holy Innocent Child." The accused were dragged before the Inquisition at Ávila in 1490 and 1491 and condemned. This story had such an impact that during the golden age, the great Spanish playwright Lope de Vega wrote the tragedy The Holy Innocent Child *and Bayeu, Goya's grandfather, painted a picture on the theme (it still hangs in the Toledo cathedral). Popular fervor bore fruit in the construction of a chapel on the road to Madrid, which still stands. Of course, historians have since shown that the accusation, although frequently repeated, was unfounded.*

Santa María la Blanca Synagogue, Toledo.

Segovia

Segovia was home to one of the biggest communities in the Kingdom of Castile. It produced important figures like Abraham Senior and his son-in-law Meyer Melamed, who served the Catholic monarchs up to 1492. Segovia also saw a violent anti-Jewish movement under the influence of the Santa Cruz convent and subsequently as a result of the "Holy Innocent Child" affair at La Guardia. ■ It is easy to find the old Jewish quarter, even if many of the buildings are more recent in origin. In particular, explore the streets of La Judería Vieja y Nueva. The synagogue has been transformed into the church of the Corpus Christi convent. It was in all probability built in 1410. In the nineteenth century, fire followed by negligent restoration destroyed the specifically Jewish part of the structure, apart from the original plan and a few pieces of stucco now in the local museum (Museo Provincial). In the Calle de la Vieja Judería, the Franciscan convent was built on a set of sixteenth- and seventeenth-century Jewish houses, including the home of Abraham Senior.

Synagogue, Segovia.

[Museo Provincial: "Casa del Sol,"
Socorro 11, 4003 Segovia. ✆ 921460613.
Open Tue–Sun 10 A.M.–1:30 P.M. and
3:30–6 P.M. Closed public holidays.]

Amusco

The village of Amusco is known to
have had a community of some 300
Jews in the fifteenth century.

■ The old synagogue is still here,
surprisingly positioned on the village
square next to the church and village
hall; it is now the Synagogue Café
(Café de la Sinagoga). The medieval
synagogue was at basement level. Its
powerful vaults are supported by six
arches. Its design is not surprising
since in those days synagogues were
not allowed to be too high or luxurious. Today it is a banquet hall.

[Café de la Sinagoga:
plaza Obispo German Vega 2,
34420 Amusco. ✆ 979802220.
Hotel/restaurant open daily.]

Puente Castro (León)

A small Jewish community lived in
Puente Castro until the twelfth century. It disappeared during the wars
between Castile and León.

■ The cemetery has yielded more
than a dozen magnificent tombstones. Three of them have been
on permanent loan at Toledo's
Sephardic Museum since 1969, and
a fourth can be seen at the diocesan

museum in León. A fifth one, at the
Archaeological Museum of Leon
(Museo Arceologico de León), was
discovered in fragments in 1983 and
probably dates from 1100. Its ele-
gantly written inscription reads:
"Cientos the Saint may he be blessed
and absolved, take him in Your
mercy and resurrect him to the life of
the future world, amen."

[Museo Arceologico de León:
plaza de San Marcos, 24001 León.
✆ 987245061.
Open Oct–Apr, Tue–Sat 10 A.M.–2 P.M.
and 4:30–8 P.M., Sun and public holidays
10 A.M.–2 P.M.; May–Sep, Tue–Sat 10 P.M.–
2 P.M. and 5–8 P.M.; Sun and public holidays
10 A.M.–2 P.M.]

Aguilar de Campó

The earliest mention of Jewish shopkeepers in Aguilar de Campó, situated along the trading route toward
the ports of Cantabria, is from 1188.

■ A Hebrew inscription can still be
seen under the town's coat of arms
on the old door of the Reinosa. It tells
that on 1 June 1380 work on building the door began, paid for by Don
Caq (Isaac) ben Malak and his wife
Bellida. The text is in Hebrew and
Castilian, with Hebrew characters
(aljamiado).

Northern Spain ■
(Galicia, Basque Country, and Navarre)

The historical province of Navarre, straddling the Spanish-French border, was violently disputed by the Castilians and counts of Champagne. It was also where Jews from Arab Spain came together with those of Castile and France to take advantage of the famous pilgrimage route to Santiago de Compostela and thus contribute to its commercial prosperity. The important center of Nájera gave its name to the eleventh-century charter in which the king allowed the Jews the same rights as Christians and, most important, gave them liberty to organize themselves in accordance with rabbinic laws. In 1492 the Jews of Navarre, along with refugees from neighboring provinces, obtained respite from the ultimatum to convert or leave, but in 1498 the king of Navarre bowed to the pressure of the Catholic monarchs. Most of the community preferred conversion to exile.

Yehuda ha-Levi, Abraham ibn Esra, and Benjamin of Tudela are some of this region's Jews who made an important contribution to the arts.

Ribadavia

Probably the most interesting *judería* in Galicia, Ribadavia has kept its old Jewish quarter despite later urban developments. Although it is known Jews were here as far back as the tenth century, few documents about the life of their community remain.

■ The old synagogue is the building with crests on its facade in the Calle Merelles, which runs between the Plaza Mayor and Plaza de la Magdalena. In September the locals organize a Festival of the Jews with a costumed parade.

Vitoria

The town of Vitoria had 300 Jews in 1290 and 900 on the eve of the expulsion—the equivalent of 6 or 7 percent of the total population. Their main activities were tax collecting and medicine. In 1492 they took refuge in Bayonne across the French border, where, even today, the Jews think of themselves as the descendants of those in Vitoria.

■ The most surprising vestige of the Jewish presence is the old cemetery, or Judizmendi (Jews' Mountain). On 27 June 1492, the town council signed an agreement with the community, undertaking to respect and maintain the cemetery. This accord was observed until 1952, when the town government obtained authorization from the Jewish community in Bayonne to transform it into a public garden. A monolith recalls this unusual piece of history.

[The Judizmendi public garden is on Calle de Olaguibel.]

Tudela

In the fifteenth century some 15 percent of Tudela's population were Jews. There were two quarters, one around the Zaragoza gate, the other within the castle walls, but nothing remains of these sizable communities.

■ Visitors can, however, go to the Ribotas landing stage at the confluence of the Ebro and Merdancho, where Benjamin de Tudela set off on his long journey.

♛ BENJAMIN OF TUDELA

In the twelfth century the tireless explorer Benjamin of Tudela spent some ten years traveling the world and filling his notebooks with impressions. He visited Zaragoza, Tortosa, Tarragona, Barcelona, and Gerona, journeyed through Roussillon and Provence to Marseille and from there sailed to Italy (Genoa, Pisa, Lucca, Rome, and Salerno) before going on to Corfu in the Aegean and then Constantinople. Reaching this gateway to Asia Minor, he hastened on to the Holy Land, then controlled by the Crusaders, and traveled to Jerusalem and Nablus before going to Damascus and Aleppo. He continued along the valley of the Tigris to Baghdad, then went to Cairo and from there via the Sinai back west to Sicily and Rome. Back in Europe, he felt the compulsion to head for Verdun and Paris, where he ended his journey. In addition to his own observations, Benjamin of Tudela also fleshed out his account with summaries of conversations with his fellow travelers about more remote lands such as Russia, Bohemia, and China.

Catalonia ■

The Jews settled in Catalonia in Roman times and communities began to take shape in Barcelona and Gerona in the tenth century. By the twelfth century, there were five major Jewish centers: Barcelona, Gerona, Lerida, Tortosa, and Perpignan (French Catalonia). The Jews are mentioned in Catalonia's first legal code, *Els Usatges de la Cort de Barcelona*. They distinguished themselves in agriculture, trade, administration, medicine, and the sciences. They also hosted Jews expelled from France, Germany, and Provence, which explains their influence on the ideas of the **kabbalah.** The Black Death of 1348 and the massacres of 1391 almost wiped out Jewish life, which was indeed annihilated by the events of 1492. In the first half of the thirteenth century, the Jewish community is estimated to have numbered between 10,000 and 12,000, or 4 to 7 percent of the total population.

Castelló d'Empúries

In the fourteenth century, and up to 1492, there was a large community in Castelló d'Empúries living around the Plaza Llana, in the calles de la Judería, del San Padre, and Peixetiries Velles.

■ There are two known cemetery sites. A tombstone found in one of them can be seen in the local museum (Museo Parroquial), while seven others have been reused in various constructions.

[Museo Parroquial:
plaza Mosén Cinto Verdaguer,
17486 Castelló d'Empúries.
Museum is currently closed.
For information, contact rabbinate:
✆ 972250519.]

Gerona

Gerona was the second most important community in Catalonia, both for its size (1,000 men and women in the twelfth and thirteenth centuries, but only 100 or so in the fifteenth) and for the quality of its scholars. Gerona was the home of Nahmanides, Johan ben Abraham Gerondi, Azriel of Gerona, Bonastruc da Porta, and Isaac the Blind.

■ Jewish Gerona has been famous since 1980, when the discovery of the Sant Llorenç, a forgotten lane in the *call* (the Catalan equivalent of a *judería*), brought to light a vivid image of Jewish life in the old town. Up to the thirteenth century, the

Judería, Gerona.

Jews lived in houses that belonged to the cathedral chapter, around today's Plaça dels Apostols. They gradually extended the quarter around the Carrer de la Força. The area is best toured on foot.

Gerona had three synagogues in quick succession. The first stood near the cathedral and was demolished in 1312 during construction work. The second was in the Carrer de la Força, probably at numbers 21–25, but it was closed in 1415 after the bull of Pope Benedict XII. The third synagogue was in use at the time of the expulsion and stood at 10 Carrer de la Força, where the municipality has set up the Bonastruc de Porta Center for Jewish studies (Centro Bonastruc de Porta). It is possible this building also housed the **kosher** butcher shop. The first phase of restoration work has revealed the handsome brick architecture. A second phase will include the establishment of a museum of Jewish art. A little further down the road, on the corner of the Carrer Cundaro, stands the house inhabited by Nahmanides.

[Centro Bonastruc de Porta:
carrer de la Força 8, 17004 Gerona.
☎ 972216761.
Open Nov–May, Mon–Fri 10 A.M.–6 P.M.;
Jun–Oct, Mon–Fri 10 A.M.–8 P.M.;
Sun and public holidays year-round
10 A.M.–3 P.M.]

■ The cemetery was located on a hill still called Montjuic (Jews' Mountain). In 1492 the Jews donated it to the knight Joan de Sarriera, who had helped the community during the anti-Jewish riots. Subsequent owners used the tombstones as building materials. Many of them have been retrieved and studied and are now superbly displayed in the Archaeological Museum (Museu Arqueologic), located in the cloister of Sant Pere de Galligants. Others are in the historical museum of Gerona (Museu Historia de la Civtat). These moving vestiges are notable for the quality of their sculpture and their texts.

[Museu Arqueologic:
church Sant Pere de Galligants,
carrer Santa Lucia 1, 17007 Gerona.
☎ 972202632. Open Tue–Sun 10 A.M.–1 P.M.
and 4:30–7 P.M.]
[Museu Historia de la Civtat:
carrer de la Força 27, 17004 Gerona.
☎ 972222229. Open Tue–Sun 10 A.M.–2 P.M.
and 5–7 P.M.]

■ Note also the jambs at the entrances to the old Jewish houses. At 5 Carrer de la Força, for example, the niche made for the **mezuzah** can still be seen. The Seminary Biblical Museum has a fifteenth-century one found at 15 Carrer de la Força in 1886.

The municipal archives (Arxiu Municipal) displays some notable documents and contracts written in Hebrew and Judeo-Catalan as well as old book bindings made from Hebrew parchments.

[Arxiu Municipal: placeta del Institut Vell 1,
17000 Gerona. ☎ 972221545.
Visits by appointment.]

Besalú

■ The presence of Jews in Besalú is attested in a document from 1229 in which Jaume I the Conqueror reserves to them the function of moneylender. In 1342 the community, hitherto linked to the one in Barcelona, became independent. In those days it numbered 200, a quarter of the total population, and lived side by side with the Christians. We have no information about 1391 and its pogroms. Not until the bull issued by the antipope Benedict XIII was a *call* created around the synagogue and the Plaça Mayor (Portal Belloch, Capellada, Carrer del Pont, Carrer del Forni i Rocafort). In 1435 the Jews abandoned Besalú for Granollers and Castelló d'Empúries.

■ A mikvah was discovered in 1964 on the site of an old dye manufacture. Since 1977, development and restoration work have made it accessible to visitors. It dates probably from the thirteenth century and is the only Romanesque mikvah in Spain. Thirty-six steps lead down to a small rectangular room in the basement. In keeping with tradition, the bath has a fine vault overhead and is lit by a window in the eastern wall. This mikvah probably belonged to a synagogue that stood in the site of the garden on today's Plaça dels Jueus (Jews' Square). From here there is a fine view of the Fluvia River and its Roman bridge.

[To visit the mikvah, contact the town hall or the tourist office: plaça de la Libertat 1, 17850 Besalú. Tourist office: on the first floor. ✆ 972591240. Open daily 10 A.M.–2 P.M. and 4 7 P.M.]

Barcelona

■ The *call major,* which was active between the twelfth century and the riots of 1391, is Spain's best-preserved Jewish quarter and the easiest to visit. It comprises a small zone between the Palau de la Generalitat and the calles Banys Nous, Sant Domenec del Call, Sant Honorat, Arc de Sant Ramon del Call, Sant Sever, la Fruita, Marlet, and del Call. The synagogue was at 7 Calle de Sant Domenec del Call, next to the houses of the rabbis Nissim Gerundi and Isaac bar Seset Perfet. At 1 Calle Marlet there is a cast of a Hebrew inscription (the original is at the City Historical Museum [Museu Història de la Civtat]) paying homage to Samuel ha-Sardi for setting up a "pious foundation."

[Museu Història de la Civtat: plaça del Rei 1, 08002 Barcelona. ✆ 933190222. Open Tue–Sat 10 A.M.–2 P.M. and 4–8 P.M., Sun 10 A.M.–3 P.M.]

■ The *call menor* was established in 1257 outside the city walls along the present-day Carrer Ferran. In 1595 its synagogue was replaced by the Saint Jaume church. This district underwent major changes in the nineteenth century and today there are no traces of its Jewish past.

■ Records of the cemetery on Montjuic, a name of uncertain origin (possibly "Jews' Mountain") go back to 1091. Today, the site is occupied by the Olympic stadium. In 1945, excavation brought to light some thirty headstones, now exhibited in the Military Museum (Museo Militar) housed in the old castle, as well as four rings and earrings that can be seen in the city's Historical Museum.

[Museo Militar: Montjuic Park,
paseo de Montjuic 66,
08000 Barcelona. ✆ 933298613.
Open Tue–Fri 9:30 A.M.–5 P.M.,
Sat and Sun 9:30 A.M.–8 P.M.]

■ Fragments of Hebrew inscriptions are visible on the houses in the Carrer Montacada and Condes de Barcelona.

In the Plaça del Rei, where the Inquisition held its first auto-da-fé in 1488, the Palau Reial Major was the scene of the famous controversy between Nahmanides and Pau Cristiani in 1263, as witnessed by King Jaume I. On the other side of the square, the Royal Archives of Aragón (Archivo de la Corona d'Aragón) contains many important documents about the history and life of Catalonia's Jews. The remains of a headstone found at Montjuic are also on display.

[Archivo de la Corona d'Aragón:
carrer Almogavares 77,
08018 Barcelona. ✆ 934854318.
Open Mon–Sat 9 A.M.–1 P.M.]

[Synagogue and Community Center:
carrer Porvenir 24, 08000 Barcelona.
✆ 932093147.]

Valls

Standing on the trading route between Lérida and Tarragona, Valls had a thriving little community that was, however, annihilated in the pogroms of 1391.

■ One can nonetheless visit the *call*, which has kept almost entirely intact its original structure and some of the old names of its streets (Carrer dels Jueus and Carrer du Call). At number 18A on the Carrer dels Jueus the patio could well have belonged to the old synagogue.

Tortosa

Tortosa was home to one of the peninsula's oldest communities, as attested by a seventh-century headstone discovered in the nineteenth century and now on display in the cathedral cloister. Its inscription is in Hebrew, Latin, and Greek and features two Stars of David and a candelabra. The community thrived under Arab rule, its illustrious sons including the grammarian Menahem ben Saruq and the poet Levi ben Ishaq ibn Mar. After the town's reconquest by Berenguer IV in 1148, the Jews obtained fiscal privileges and were granted land to build houses. The community flourished during this century thanks to the trade from the port, and its population rose to 300.

■ Tortosa was the setting of a debate between Jeronimo of Santa Fé and various rabbis. It was ordered by the antipope Benedict XIII, who hoped to persuade the Jews to convert to Christianity. Visitors can imagine the scene by going to the room where it took place, the chapter house of the Aula Mayor.

[Aula Mayor: carrer de las Taules Verdes, 43500 Tortosa. Located close to the cathedral cloister. ✆ 97741752. Open Tue–Sun 10 A.M.–2 P.M.]

■ The narrow streets around the *parador* and calles Mayor de Romlins, Jerusalem, Vilanova, Gentildones, and Figuereta still evoke the old *call*.

Aragón

In the Middle Ages the powerful kingdom of Aragón comprised not only Aragón itself but also Catalonia, Valencia, and the Balearic Islands. It was home to numerous Jewish communities, especially after the union with Catalonia in 1150. They had links with the Muslims, who lived here until around 1500.

Teruel

Teruel became important as the supply center for Catalan-Aragónese troops sent out to conquer Valencia. The Jews here became specialized in weaving wool. The Lonja, or produce exchange, was open to both Jewish and Muslim traders.

■ The local museum (Museo Provincial) has an interesting **Hanukkah** lamp made in the local green ceramic. Discovered in 1977 during an excavation in the old Jewish quarter near Ambeles castle, it has the traditional form, with eight holders for the candles synonymous with this festival commemorating the purification of the temple in Jerusalem in 165 C.E. Note the geometrical drawings and the alternating colors, showing the Jewish community's adaptation to the region's artistic techniques and contribution to the town's prosperity.

[Museo Provincial: plaza Fray Anselmo Polanco 3, 44171 Teruel. ✆ 978600150. Open Tue–Fri 10 A.M.–2 P.M. and 4–7 P.M., Sat and Sun 10 A.M.–2 P.M.]

The Balearic Islands ■

There have been Jews in the Balearic Islands since the Roman occupation. After Jaume I won the islands from the Arabs, many Jews arrived from Catalonia but also the south of France and North Africa to settle the new land. After 1343, when Pedro IV of Aragón seized the islands, the Balearic Jews began to enjoy a real golden age. The leading families traded throughout the Mediterranean and with North Africa, where they set up a highly efficient network of commercial agents. They also specialized in silver and gold and jewelry, as well as moneylending. They owned fine houses in the *call* at Palma de Mallorca and kept slaves. The community had its own laws and was directed by six secretaries and a council of thirty notables. Among its best-known men of learning were the rabbi Simon ben Zemah Duran, a great **Talmudist** who went into exile in Algiers, and the cartographers Abraham Cresques and his son Jafuda Cresques.

In 1391 the *call* was besieged. Many died and forced conversions followed. Some chose exile and left for Algiers. In 1435, after an accusation of ritual crime, the shrunken remainder of the community underwent forced conversion almost to a person. From this date onward, there were officially no more Jews. Jewish life continued only in a very diffuse form, among the chuetas, or crypto-Jews. They formed an extremely closed society of silver- and goldsmiths and jewelers whose integration into Majorcan society has remained problematic even in recent times.

Palma de Mallorca

■ The *call* is clearly defined by a small square and the Carrer de la Call. It is one of Spain's most important for the quality and richness of its houses, even if urban development work has done away with the smaller streets and blind alleys. The location of its four gates is known, but not that of its many synagogues.

■ The church of Santa Eulàlia is traditionally the preserve of the chuetas, a community of silver and gold workers who by custom marry endogamously. Historians have recently taken a keen interest in this particular case of marranism.

[Church of Santa Eulàlia:
plaza Santa Eulàlia 2,
07001 Palma de Mallorca.
✆ 971714625. Open during services,
or by request for groups.]

Moorish attribution, Defense Against the Siege of the Balearic Islands by King Jacob I of Aragon, *fresco. Museu Nacional d'Art de Catalunya, Barcelona.*

■ The Royal Archives of Majorca has two rare parchment **ketuboth,** and there is a compass at the harbor front recalling the cartographers of the Cresques family.

[Royal Archives of Majorca: calle Ramon Llull 3, 07001 Palma de Mallorca. ✆ 971725999.]

■ Documents tell us that there were also Jews at Inca, Felanitx, and Minorca, but all trace of them has disappeared.

Andalusia ■

It is possible to date the presence of Jews in Andalusia to the Council of Elvira (303–09), when references were made to the need to separate Jews and Christians.

Granada

Granada's splendor was at its apogee in the eleventh century, when Samuel ha-Nagid and his son Joseph were in charge of the kingdom. The large Jewish population exceeded 5,000 and reached 20,000 by the eve of the expulsion. Sadly, the *Judería* was destroyed by order of the Catholic monarchs.

■ In Granada's center (Calle Pavaneras), the modern statues of Yehuda ibn Tibbon and the **Talmudist** and poet Samuel ibn Negrella remind us of the city's Jewish past. When visiting the Alhambra, it is worth remembering that the Ambassadors' Room was where the Catholic monarchs signed the edict expelling Spain's Jews on 31 March 1492.

Lucena

Famed in the eleventh century for the influence of **Talmudists** such as Isaac ibn Gayata, Isaac Alfasi, and Joseph ibn Migas, who founded the so-called "Lucena School," Lucena preserves few material signs of its Jewish past. While the site of the *Judería* is reasonably well established, that of the synagogues is uncertain. However, two popular customs recall the Jewish heritage: the first is giving the house a general clean-up on Saturdays, and the second is whitewashing houses a few days before Holy Week. These probably derive from the old tradition of cleaning at **Passover**.

Córdoba

The home of Maimonides, Córdoba under the caliphate of Abderahman, had the biggest *Judería* in Andalusia.

■ The Jewish quarter spread out near the mosque and the Episcopal palace. It can be entered via the Moorish Almodovar Gate. The names of the squares and streets, chosen in the nineteenth century, allude to this past: Calle Maimonides, Plaza de Judá Levi, Plaza de Tiberiades.

■ The most important monument is the synagogue, which has been miraculously preserved. According to inscriptions on the walls, it was built, or rebuilt, in 1315. After the expulsion it was transformed into a hospital, and in 1588 it became the headquarters of the city's guild of cobblers. Rediscovered by an archaeologist in 1884, it was declared a historical monument and restored. It is reached via a small patio and a modest door crowned by a brick arch. The Mudejar-style interior is square in proportion (approximately 20 x 20 feet) and richly decorated with plant motifs. There are inscriptions, particularly around the *aron kodesh,* with quotations from Isaac Moheb ben Efraim, recording completion of the temple in 1315, and excerpts from the Book of Psalms, written in red on a blue background. The synagogue is the most spectacular symbol of the Jewish presence in Spain after Toledo.

[Synagogue. calle Judius 20,
14004 Córdoba. ✆ 957202928.
Open Tue–Sat 10 A.M.–1 P.M. and
3:30–5:30 P.M., Sun 10 A.M.–1 P.M.]

Seville

Seville's Santa Cruz quarter, protected by the Alcazar, was formerly the city's famous *judería.* The maze of streets and their evocative names give a good idea of what it was like in 1492. Be sure to stroll around the Calle de la Judería, Callejón del Agua, Calle des Levis, and the Calle de Santa María, which may have been the main street.

■ The name of the Calle de la Susona attests an old legend concerning a *converso* uprising against the Inquisition led by a woman, La Susona,

The whitewashed facades, flowers, and patios make this a charming quarter and give us an idea of daily life in the Sepharad. Note, however, that the squares were opened up in the nineteenth century in order make the quarter more airy.

■ Inside the cathedral, the pedestal of the mausoleum built by Alfonso X for his father, Fernando III, has a Hebrew inscription giving the date of the king's death according to the Hebrew calendar. The cathedral treasury has the silver keys given to King Fernando III by the Jews. They bear two inscriptions in Hebrew announcing that "God will open, the King will enter" and "the King of Kings will open, the King of the whole earth shall enter."

[Cathedral and Treasury. avenida de la
Constitucion, 41001 Seville. ✆ 954563150.
Open Mon–Sat 11 A.M.–5 P.M.,
Sun 10 A.M.–2 P.M.]

■ Three seals belonging to Jewish figures in the twelfth century are on exhibit at the Archaeological Museum, and the Archive of the Indies has a copy of Abraham Zacuto's perpetual almanac, used by Christopher Columbus and Vasco da Gama.

[Archaeological Museum:
plaza de America, 41003 Seville.
✆ 954232401. Open Wed–Sat 9 A.M.–8 P.M.,
Sun 9–2 P.M., Tue 3–8 P.M.]
[Archive of the Indies:
avenida de la Constitucion,
41004 Seville. ✆ 954200234.
Open Mon–Fri 10 A.M.–1 P.M.]

Estremadura ■

It is likely the history of Spain's Jews began in Estremadura. Vestiges from the third century bear witness to them and, according to the twelfth-century chronicler Abraham ibn Daud, the Jews that Titus deported from Jerusalem settled in this old Roman province. However, as elsewhere, there are few traces left to indicate this long presence.

Cáceres

Cáceres had a fairly sizable Jewish presence after the Christian recon-quest. In 1479, 100 married Jews were listed in a community with some 650 members. They lived in two *juderías:* the "old" one was on the site of today's Casa de las Vele-tas, and the "new" one was around Plaza Mayor, where the Jews had most of their shops.

■ The San Antonio chapel is proba-bly an old synagogue that was trans-formed. Small, with a porch and single hall, it is built on the tradi-tional synagogue plan.

[San Antonio Chapel:
calle Barrio Judio, 10003 Cáceres.
Open during services.]

■ The chapel, now unused, serves as a conference room for the cultural center housed in the Palacio del Marques de la Isla. It too might once have been a synagogue.

[Palacio del Marques de la Isla (cultural center): calle de la Cruz 6, 10000 Cáceres. Open Tue–Sun 10 A.M.–2 P.M. and 4–8 P.M.]

Trujillo

The community of Trujillo is first mentioned in 1290. Just before the expulsion it had 150 members. All of them went to Portugal.

■ Not long ago, construction in the back of a pharmacy brought to light the site of an old synagogue. An in-scription from Psalms (118–20) reads: "This door is the door of the Lord: the Just will enter through here." The adjoining house has two vaulted rooms that are the disfigured remains of the old synagogue. Sadly, they cannot be visited.

[Solis Pharmacy: calle Tiendas 14,
10100 Trujillo. ✆ 927320216.
Open Mon–Fri 9 A.M.–2 P.M.
and 4:30–7:30 P.M. The back of the shop can be visited during the pharmacy's open hours.]

Plaza de Santa María, Cáceres.

Hervás

■ Although the *Judería* in Hervás was small, a local proverb that "in Hervás there are many Jews" made the quarter famous. It stood close to the Ambroz River near the town's exit. The Calle Rabilero and Calle de la Sinagoga are the most pictur-esque, with a fine fountain dedicated to Jewish-Christian friendship and two-story brick and chestnut-wood houses with many flowers. Local bakers continue to make an unleav-ened bread, *homazo*, possibly in memory of the **matzohs** eaten by the Jews at **Passover**.

אדם

שֵׁת אֱנוֹשׁ קֵינָן מַהֲלַלְאֵל יֶרֶד חֲנוֹךְ מְתוּשֶׁלַח
לֶמֶךְ נֹחַ שֵׁם וָפֶת בְּנֵי יֶפֶת גֹּמֶר וּמָגוֹג וּמָדַי וְיָוָן
וְתֻבָל וּמֶשֶׁךְ וְתִירָס וּבְנֵי גֹּמֶר אַשְׁכְּנַז וְדִיפַת
וְתוֹגַרְמָה וּבְנֵי יָוָן אֱלִישָׁה וְתַרְשִׁישָׁה כִּתִּים וְרוֹדָנִים
בְּנֵי חָם כּוּשׁ וּמִצְרַיִם פּוּט וּכְנָעַן וּבְנֵי כוּשׁ סְבָא
וַחֲוִילָה וְסַבְתָּא וְרַעְמָא וְסַבְתְּכָא וּבְנֵי רַעְמָה שְׁבָא
וּדְדָן וְכוּשׁ יָלַד אֶת נִמְרוֹד הוּא הֵחֵל לִהְיוֹת גִּבּוֹר
בָּאָרֶץ וּמִצְרַיִם יָלַד אֶת לוּדִיִּים וְאֶת עֲנָמִים וְאֶת
לְהָבִים וְאֶת נַפְתֻּחִים וְאֶת פַּתְרֻסִים וְאֶת כַּסְלֻחִים
אֲשֶׁר יָצְאוּ מִשָּׁם פְּלִשְׁתִּים וְאֶת כַּפְתֹּרִים
וּכְנַעַן יָלַד אֶת צִידֹן בְּכֹרוֹ וְאֶת
חֵת וְאֶת הַיְבוּסִי וְאֶת הָאֱמֹרִי וְאֶת הַגִּרְגָּשִׁי וְאֶת
הַחִוִּי וְאֶת הָעַרְקִי וְאֶת הַסִּינִי וְאֶת הָאַרְוָדִי וְאֶת
הַצְּמָרִי וְאֶת הַחֲמָתִי בְּנֵי שֵׁם עֵילָם וְאַשּׁוּר ט
וְאַרְפַּכְשַׁד וְלוּד וַאֲרָם וְעוּץ וְחוּל וְגֶתֶר וָמֶשֶׁךְ יו

Portugal

🕎 NORTHERN PORTUGAL 🕎 CENTRAL PORTUGAL |

🕎 SOUTHERN PORTUGAL |

Portugal BECAME AN AUTONOMOUS KING-
DOM under Henry of Burgundy, a prince of French
origin. His son, Alfonso I, was the first king of Portugal (1114–85). The history of its Jewish population differs from that of the Jews on the Iberian
Peninsula. Alfonso was aware of the importance of
the Jewish communities he had freed from the
Muslim yoke and granted them his protection, putting the chief rabbi, Yahia ben Yahia, in charge of
collecting taxes.

Until the end of the fourteenth century, the
Jews were reasonably well protected. The rivalry
between the two Iberian kingdoms resulted in the
accession of a new dynasty, the Avis. Their reign
began a period of great prosperity for the Portuguese Jews, whose ranks were soon swelled by
the Spanish Jews who began to arrive in 1391.
This golden age for the Jews paralleled Portuguese
exploration of Africa and the East Indies, which
anticipated the "great discoveries." In 1279 the
country had thirty-one *judarias*. Two centuries later
there were 135.

Hebrew Bible, The Book of the Chronicles, *Lisbon,*
late fifteenth century, Bibliothèque Nationale de France, Paris.

However, this period was not totally free of tension between Jews and Christians: Portugal's new merchant class was apprehensive of the influence of the Jews and their capital. Under the reign of João I (1385–1443), new laws obliged Jews to wear an identifying sign on their clothes and imposed curfews on the *judarias*. There were scattered outbreaks of violence, like the attack on the Lisbon *judaria* in 1445, in which many died. Many Jews subsequently converted. When the Catholic monarchs passed their edict of expulsion, King João II allowed the Jews to enter Portugal, offering a limited stay of eight months on payment of eight cruzados per head. Portugal's estimated Jewish population of 30,000 was thus swollen by some 30,000 to 60,000 Spanish Jews, the new total representing between 6 percent and 10 percent of the kingdom's entire population.

Until 1496 the Portuguese government steered an ambivalent course between the need to conciliate its powerful neighbor and a concern to keep a still-useful minority within its borders. After a series of extremely harsh measures, with children being separated from their parents to be brought up in the Christian faith, and considerable pressure on adults to convert, a decree of expulsion was issued in December 1496. However, lacking the number of ships needed to ensure their departure, King Manoel I decided to convert all the Jews to Catholicism in one comprehensive ceremony. Furthermore, in 1499 he closed the border to prevent them from crossing. He thus created a society of *cristãos novos* (new Christians) whose destiny was quite different from that of the Spanish *conversos*. For, in spite of the apparent unity of the two Iberian kingdoms, their ways of dealing with their Jewish populations were very different. These "new Christians"

formed a homogenous group who occupied important positions in Portuguese society while continuing to maintain their own cultural traditions. They
came to form a separate nation, and they were
called "men of the nation," or, after settling in Bayonne and Bordeaux, "Portuguese nation."

The Inquisition in 1547 authorized the prose-
cution of *cristãos novos* who still practiced Judaism
and, later, of the crypto-Jews. It was carried out
with varying degrees of conviction. The union of the
two kingdoms from 1580 to 1640 under Philip II
of Spain facilitated contact between *conversos* and
cristãos novos, who were linked by family and commercial networks far beyond the peninsula to Bayonne, Bordeaux, London, Amsterdam, and the
Ottoman Empire, where the Portuguese-Jewish
diaspora was present.

♕ JEWISH: A SYNONYM FOR PORTUGUESE

*The brilliant history of the Portuguese-Jewish
diaspora can be summed up in two symbolic
examples. The glory of Amsterdam's Jewish
community, which built a majestic synagogue
in 1666, is immortalized by the works of its
members: in 1650, Menasch ben Israel, who
had been raised in the Christian faith under the
name Manuel Dias, wrote* Esperança de Israel:
*Isaac Aboab de Fonseca set up a community in
Recife, Brazil, between 1645 and 1654; finally,
Baruch Spinoza elaborated a groundbreaking
philosophical system. The case of the "Senhora,"
Dona Gracia Nassi, the wife of a banker,
constitutes another illustrious example. She
lived in Antwerp, Italy, and later Constantinople,
where she developed her business interests and
fostered numerous charitable institutions. She
even founded a community of Spanish and*

Portrait of Dona Gracia Nassi, sixteenth century. Musée National du Moyen Âge des Thermes de Cluny, Paris.

Portuguese Jews in Tiberius, Palestine, thus reviving hopes of a return to Zion. At the time, there were Portuguese Jews throughout Europe, and "Jew" was often used as a synonym for "Portuguese."

Portuguese exploration opened new horizons for the kingdom, not least for the Jews, many of whom settled in the Americas. They also participated intellectually in this auspicious period: the rabbi Guedella Negro was made physicist and astrologer to King Don Duarte for the period 1433–1451; Jafuda Cresques, also known as Jaime of Majorca, the son of the cartographer and inventor of instruments of navigation Abraham Cresques, was asked by the infante Henry the Navigator to train navigators;

Abraham Zacuto, from Castile, published a perpetual almanac in 1496 used on many voyages, including Vasco da Gama's to the East Indies in 1497. Printing works flourished, including those of Eliezar Toledano in Lisbon and Samuel Orta in Leiria.

Yet it was not until the nineteenth century that Portugal's Jews were able to express their identity openly and live freely. Between 1820 and 1830, Jewish families from Morocco came to live in Algarve and in the Azores. In 1860 a synagogue was built in Faro. In 1904 the Shaare Tikvah (Gates of Hope) Synagogue, still in use today, opened in Lisbon. In 1920 Captain Barros Bastos founded the Jewish community of Porto and embarked on a campaign to persuade crypto-Jews to return to the Judaism of their ancestors. Working almost single-handedly, he organized circumcisions, published a journal, held talks, set up a school and built a superb synagogue. Opened in 1936, it continues to be used for worship. Unfortunately, Bastos was attacked by Portuguese fascists and a military tribunal condemned him on trumped-up charges; only in 1997 was his name rehabilitated.

During this same period the engineer Samuel Schwartz made the surprising discovery of a crypto-Jewish community in Belmonte (Guarda province), all but forgotten by both Judaism and history.

After his posting to Bordeaux in 1940, the consul Mendes Sousa perceived the Nazi threat and set about providing visas for refugees. His work during the weeks of the French collapse saved several thousand men and women from death. He was nonetheless discharged and discredited by the authorities, and died in poverty. In spite of Salazar's sympathy for the Nazis, Portugal remained neutral during the war and protected Portuguese Jews while providing support for those who managed to cross its borders. In 1948, with the agreement of the government, the American Jewish Joint Committee set up a camp to receive and organize the transit of Jews to the United States.

In 1977, the new Portuguese democracy established diplomatic relations with Israel. In 1993, the first stone was laid for the Belmonte Synagogue. It opened in 1996 as part of the ceremonies commemorating the expulsion of December 1496. Today there are several thousand Jews living in Portugal, mainly in the major communities of Lisbon, Porto, and Belmonte but also dotted around a few other towns.

→ **To call Portugal from the United States, dial 011 351** followed by the number of the person you are calling.

Northern Portugal ■

Porto

■ The name of the synagogue in Porto, Kadoorie, evokes the international reach of the Portuguese-Jewish community. Kadoorie is the name of a Portuguese-Jewish family that took English nationality and settled in Shanghai. Its members generously subsidized the construction of this fine monument with the help of the Portuguese communities in Lisbon, London, and Amsterdam in 1936. The synagogue has a capacity of 300 and offers all that is needed for religious service. It is to a large extent the work of Captain Barros Bastos, who tried to bring the region's crypto-Jews back to the faith of their ancestors.

[Kadoorie Synagogue:
340 rua Guerra Junqueiro, 4100 Porto.
✆ 226092789.]

☰ A PORTUGUESE DREYFUS

Raised in a Christian family in Porto, Barros Bastos rediscovered Judaism when he visited a synagogue in Lisbon. After his conversion in Tangier, he married a young Jewish woman. He traveled tirelessly around the villages of the Porto region, speaking to the crypto-Jewish inhabitants and inspiring them with his fervent call to courageously and openly affirm their Judaism after centuries of secrecy. He was particularly concerned with providing a Jewish education to children, seeing this as the only way of rejuvenating the old communities. To this end he set up a teaching college in Porto. He had many enemies in the Salazarist movement, however, and, when false charges were leveled against him, he was condemned and stripped of his rank in 1938.

He died in poverty in 1961. Portugal rehabilitated him in 1997, officially acknowledging his innocence and tireless devotion.

Belmonte

The little community of Belmonte of between 100 and 300 souls was "discovered" in 1920 by the engineer Samuel Schwartz. Its existence was revealed to the world by Frédéric Brenner's short film *The Last Marranos* in 1990.

The Jews of Belmonte are one of the last groups bearing witness to the precarious life of Jews hunted by an all-powerful Inquisition and Church. They lived without rabbis, synagogues, or books. The faith was passed on orally by the women, who chose the moment when their children seemed capable of learning about their com-munity identity. Socially, these Jews took full part in the village's Catholic life of baptisms, weddings, and fu-nerals. However, the non-Jewish population, especially the village priest, likely had some awareness of their secret practices. In any case, their rites were reduced to the bare essentials: Hebrew words and im-portant Jewish figures (Adonai, Es-ther) were included in prayers spoken in Portuguese; a discreet light was lit on Friday evenings; they fasted frequently and cooked **mazoth** at **Passover**. Prayers were spoken ei-ther at home with all the windows closed or in the woods or by the river. After a rather complicated re-turn to overt Judaism with the sup-port of the Israeli authorities, the community at Belmonte has been consolidated by the construction of a synagogue, paid for by a patron, Sa-lomão Azoulay, and seems to have returned to normal community life.

Central Portugal

Tomar

Although there was an organized community in Tomar at the turn of the fourteenth century, indicated by the inscription on the tombstone of Rabbi Joseph of Tomar, who died in Faro in 1315, it was not until 1430 that the Jews of Tomar had the means to undertake construction of the synagogue that still stands today. It was completed in 1460.

THE SYNAGOGUE

After the expulsion of 1496 the syn-agogue was converted to a prison, then used by successive owners as a

Synagogue, Castelo de Vide.

hay barn. In 1920 a group of Portuguese archaeologists identified the building as a synagogue. It was placed on the historical register in 1921. In 1923 the engineer Samuel Schwartz, who worked in the region's mines, heard about the building and bought it. In 1939, after carrying out initial restoration work, he donated it to the state with the proviso that it set up a Portuguese-Jewish museum there. Although this has yet to happen, his gift was not made in vain since it is possible to see this very bold example of synagogue architecture.

The synagogue is supported by four fine columns at the center, reminiscent of these in the Portuguese church at Ourem made by Hispano-Moorish craftsmen. Indeed, the same builders could well have been involved here. Recent excavation has revealed parts of the **mikvah**. Several coins from the age of King Alfonso V (1446–81) and everyday tableware have also been found.

The facade and entrance are modest and unremarkable. Upon entering, several steps lead down to the floor, which, being below street level, made it possible to reduce the height of the facade. Another noteworthy curiosity is the necks of vases built into the four corners. Apparently they were designed to amplify and improve the synagogue's acoustics. The synagogue is no longer used for worship.

[Synagogue: 75 rua Dr Joaquim Jacinto, 2300 Tomar.]

Castelo de Vide

The Jews who lived within the walls of the little hilltop town of Castelo de Vide were engaged in the traditional activities of commerce, crafts, and sometimes medicine. The population grew after 1492 with the arrival of Jews from Spain.

■ The former *judaria* is fairly easy to identify around the market square (Praço do Comércio). Between the fourteenth and sixteenth centuries the characteristic little streets led to the small synagogue. A niche, used as a church altar in the seventeenth century, might be a vestige of the *aron kodesh*. The municipality is currently conducting research into this movingly simple building.

[Synagogue: rua Judaria,
7320 Castelo de Vide.
Open Mon–Sat 9 A.M.–5 P.M.
Be sure to confirm these times with
the tourist office: ✆ 245901361.]

Lisbon

■ The Shaare Tikvah Synagogue, designed by the architect Ventura Terra, was built in 1904. Its discreet facade opens onto a courtyard. The interior, built on the traditional plan of **Ashkenazic** synagogues, is decorated in the neo-oriental style. There is also a

Attributed to Nuno Gonçalves,
Polyptych of Saint Vincent, *1465.*
Museu Nacional d'Arte Antiga, Lisbon.

small oratory frequented by Jews of Ashkenazic origin on Rua Elias Garcia.

[Hebrew Community of Lisbon and
Shaare Tikvah Synagogue:
55 rua Alexandre Herculano,
1250 Lisbon. ✆ 213881592.]
[Oratory (Israelite Synagogue):
110 rua Elias Garcia, 1200 Lisbon.
✆ 213885828.]

■ In the National Museum of Art (Museu Nacional d'Arte Antiga), note the figure carrying a book in Hebrew in the retable attributed to Nuno Gonçalves. This offers an image of a Portuguese Jew in the 1460s.

[Museu Nacional d'Arte Antiga:
rua Janelas Verdes, 1200 Lisbon.
✆ 213912800.
Open Wed–Sun 10 A.M.–6 P.M.,
Tue 2:30–6 P.M.]

■ Rua de la Judaria is the only remaining trace of the old Jewish quarter in the medieval Alfama district. It runs alongside the Visigoth city walls.

Southern Portugal ■

Faro

Faro was an important center of Jewish culture. It was here, notably, that the first printed book in Hebrew, a Pentateuch, was produced by Samuel Porteira. Today, the only sign of its brilliant past is in the old medieval cemetery.

Italy

THE EXCAVATIONS AT OSTIA, once the great imperial port of ancient Rome, have revealed the remains of an antique synagogue whose columns support capitals adorned with *menorot,* the traditional seven-arm candelabra of the Jews. Constructed toward the middle of the first century, perhaps even before the destruction of the Temple of Jerusalem, the synagogue attests to the more than 2,000 years of Jewish presence in Italy, especially in Rome. In the Eternal City, the synagogue preceded the Vatican. "Among the groups of Jews who emigrated from Palestine to settle in Europe, those who chose Italy are not only the most ancient, but also the only Jews who never had an interruption in their occupation of this new place of residence," writes Attilio Milano, the author of *Storia degli Ebrei in Italia* (The History of Jews in Italy).[2] According to Milano, long ago during fasting periods the Jews of the peninsula celebrated their adopted land as "the island of the divine dew," a rather liberal translation of the three Hebrew words *I-tal-yah.*

Although no specific supporting evidence exists, the first Jewish communities are thought to have settled in Rome and some urban centers of southern

Michelangelo, Moses, 1513–1516. San Pietro in Vincoli, Rome.

*Circumcision dish, Padua,
seventeenth century.
Musée d'Art et d'Histoire
du Judaïsme, Paris.*

Italy beginning in the second century B.C.E. The first official contacts were made in 161 B.C.E. when Judas Maccabeus, then struggling to liberate Palestine from the Syrian dynasty of the Seleucids, sent two ambassadors to the Roman Senate to ask for aid. The appeal had no immediate outcome because the rebellion was rapidly crushed. In the next century, however, Rome increasingly implicated itself in Judaea's affairs, until in 63 B.C.E. Judaea was finally conquered by Pompey and became a Roman protectorate. Thousands of Jews were brought to Rome as slaves, but on the whole, they obtained their freedom rather rapidly. The Jews' refusal to work on Saturdays and their dietary demands made them difficult to manage.

These *liberati* increased the numbers of their fellow believers in Rome, who were for the most part merchants and artisans attracted long ago by the wealth of the capital city. Their numbers are estimated to have been some tens of thousands in the last years of the republic. The Jewish community had become a significant population. In the civil war between Pompey and Julius Caesar, the Jewish community chose to massively support the latter, who showed his gratitude by granting them a number of specific rights. They were exempted from military service, and the communities obtained the right to regulate their internal affairs according to their own laws. They were also permitted to collect donations and send a part of them to Jerusalem for the support of the Temple there. According to Roman historian Flavius Josephus, when Julius Caesar was assassinated in 44 B.C.E., the Jews of Rome were among the most numerous to pressure the Forum to honor him who had given dignity to the former slaves.

Augustus confirmed and enlarged the privileges that Caesar had granted to the Jews. In the first years of the empire, the Jewish population in Rome is estimated to have been some 40,000 persons of a total population of 1 million inhabitants. However, the absolutist demands made by Augustus's successors that everyone worship in the cult of the deified emperor created growing problems. The emperors were determined to apply their demands to all, including the Jews. Caligula was the first to want to install a statue of himself in the synagogues before he was convinced to withdraw his project. Imperial power began to consider the Jews with their incomprehensible religion in an increasingly suspicious light, while their quarrels with Christians were judged stranger still. The Jews' situation became more delicate when revolts broke out in Judaea, bloodily repressed by Vespasian and his son Titus. In 70 C.E. Titus reconquered Jerusalem, destroyed the Temple of Jerusalem, and took more than 100,000 Jews into captivity. Among other things, he decided the money the Jews had been donating for the maintenance of their temple would henceforth be used to maintain that of Jupiter Capitoline.

The conversion of Constantine to Christianity in 312 and, shortly thereafter, the proclamation of Christianity as the state religion changed the fortune of Jews for the worse. The Church could not refuse the heritage of the Old Testament without thus denying itself; on the other hand it could not readily accept its affiliation with the community without risk of losing the prestige of its status as official religion. It decided that the Jews could continue to practice their religion in the capacity of living witnesses to the truth contained in the Old Testament, but that they should also perpetually expiate their sin of refusing Jesus Christ. In 325 the Council of Nicaea clearly separated the two religions by instituting Sunday instead of Saturday as the obligatory day of rest and creating the first discriminatory measures against the Jews that prohibited them from occupying positions of public governance or possessing real estate. After the barbarian invasions, the Jews numbered no more than a handful of citizens in a devastated Rome, reduced to some 10,000 inhabitants. Pope Gregory I the Great's coming to power in 590 reestablished the authority of the Church in the west. The papal bull *Sicut Judaeis* put in place some measures of protection for the Jews. Throughout the Middle Ages, Italian Jews experienced alternating periods of persecution and relative tranquillity.

The travels in Italy chronicled by Benjamin of Tudela, a Jew from Navarre, give us a good idea of Judaism on the peninsula in the middle of the twelfth century. At the time, there were few Jews in northern Italy, scarcely two families in Genoa, and not many more in Venice. An active community of some 200 families lived in Rome, respected by the rest of the population and not obliged to pay tribute. They worked as artisans and merchants, but also as literary figures and doctors welcomed in the papal court. The Popes did not impose on their city the severe measures applied to Jews in the rest of Christendom. However it was in southern Italy, in Naples, Salerno, and above all Sicily, that Jewish communities flourished even more. With more than 8,000 Jews of a population of 100,000, the Palermo of the Norman kings was then the great center of Jewish life in Italy. They excelled in the production and dying of silk. Born of this pluralistic culture, the emperor Frederic II of Souabe was the first modern prince of Europe at the dawn of the thirteenth century. The great enemy of the Popes, he instituted within his domains of Sicily and southern Italy the first laws protecting the Jews. He recognized especially their essential economic role. These measures did not survive his reign; rather the Fourth Lateran Council (1215) hardened the discriminations against the Jews.

The princes of Anjou and later the Spanish conquered Sicily and southern Italy in their turn, and over time the situation became more difficult for the Jews. Sicilian Judaism was wiped from the map at the same time as in Spain with the order to expel Jews in 1492. In an unusual case, the population and the local government of Sicily, and especially Palermo, protested against the Jews' arrest and defended them, although with little success. Those expelled left for Naples, whence they were again driven out a few years later.

In the sixteenth century, Italian Judaism was in a completely new situation. In Rome and in the Papal States, the persecutions had become more severe since the middle of the century. In 1555, the newly elected Paul IV released the *Cum Nimis*

Absurdum edict, which, in instituting a ghetto for the Jews of Rome, subjected them to difficulties without precedent in the Eternal City. For ready identification, men were forced to wear a yellow hat and women a yellow veil while in the city. Jews no longer had the right to have real estate or Christian servants. Authorized employment was limited to moneylending, and the bank owners no longer had the right to make loans at interest rates higher than 12 percent. In Rome, as in Ancona and all the territories administered by the papacy, Jewish communities began to sink into a long night that lasted three centuries. The principal gathering spots for Jewish life, reinforced by the arrival of Jews from Spain, Portugal, or Sicily, subsequently spread to the northern cities of the peninsula thanks to the relative tolerance of the princes or local powers such as the Gonzaga family of Mantua, the Este family of Ferrara, or even Venice, which was, however, the first city to institute a ghetto in 1516. In Tuscany, at first Cosimo I de' Medici welcomed numerous Jews in Florence and Siena before giving in to papal injunctions against them. His successor Ferdinand I decided to make Livorno a large trading port with the Levant and encouraged Jews to settle there, eventually making this city the ultimate haven of freedom for Italian Jews.

Reverberations of the French Revolution, which for the first time accorded Jews full equality with other citizens, shook up Italian Judaism. Considered as "the natural allies of the French and new ideas," the Jews were victim to uprisings fomented by the clergy in Livorno in 1790, and in Rome in 1793. When, in 1796, the soldiers of Napoleon Bonaparte crossed the Alps and slowly but surely toppled the walls of the ghettos as they advanced, they brought with them legal parity for the Jews of

the Piedmont, then Lombardy, Emilia, and finally
Venice, where the French troops entered in May
1797. Less than a year later, the troops marched
on Rome, where the Jews traded their yellow caps
for the tricolors of the French flag. The Roman
Republic proclaimed: "Jews who meet the pre-
scribed conditions for being Roman citizens will be
subject only to the law common to all citizens." The
soldiers swarmed the civil guard, one of whose bat-
talions was commanded by a certain Isacco Barraf-
fael. When French troops withdrew a year later,
retribution was swift and terrifying, subjecting the
Jewish communities to harsh punishment. Many
Jewish quarters were pillaged. However, in 1800
the soldiers of the tricolor retook control of the

Hanukkah lamp, Italy,
sixteenth century.
Musée d'Art et d'Histoire
du Judaïsme, Paris.

peninsula. For fourteen years Italian Jews enjoyed full civil rights. They bought land and opened shops outside the ghettos. A Jewish lyceum was created in Reggio Emilia. After the overthrow of Napoleon, the Congress of Vienna tried to turn back the clock a quarter of a century. Pope Pius VII returned to Rome, the Austrians to the north of the peninsula, and the Bourbons to the south. But the Restoration could not eradicate the new ideas. Italy discovered itself as a nation and the Italian Jews as free men. The Jews played an active part in the conspiracies and struggles that finally led, a half century later, to the unification of Italy under the guidance of the Piedmontese monarchy.

On 20 September 1870, Italian troops entered Rome through a breach in the Porta Pia, putting an end to the temporal reign of the Popes and thereby achieving the complete unification of the country. Rome's ghetto was eliminated. The Jews of the new capital became, like their fellow believers in the rest of the peninsula, separate but full citizens. Jews' attainment of full equality occurred later in Italy than elsewhere in the west, but they soon enjoyed conditions that "could not have been better," as Cecil Roth emphasizes in *The History of the Jews of Italy,* and assumed important roles in the new kingdom.[3] Isacco Artom, personal secretary of the Piedmontese prime minister Camillo Cavour between 1850 and 1860, was the first Jew to occupy a position of diplomatic importance. Luigi Luzzati, heir to a great Jewish family from Venice, became prime minister in 1910 after having worked in the Ministry of Finance for several years. General Giuseppe Ottolenghi, a Piedmontese Jew, was chosen by the king as a professor of military science for the crown prince before he became minister of war in 1903. Ernesto Nathan, a Jew and grand master of the Freemasons, was the mayor of Rome between 1907 and 1913. Numerous Italian Jews made names for themselves in the universities, in music, literature (Italo Svevo, Umberto Saba), and the plastic arts (Amedeo Modigliani). Communities concentrated in large cities built new temples, like the neo-Babylonian-style Grand Synagogue in Rome, thus demonstrating the harmonious integration of some 45,000 Jewish Italians into the bosom of the nation. Italy was almost entirely without anti-Semitism. Even the Fascists did not play this trump card, at least during the first decade in power.

Benito Mussolini never ceased repeating that, in Italy, "there isn't a Jewish problem." The Jews were members of the fascio since its creation. Margherita Sarfatti, a refined intellectual, biographer, and political adviser to Mussolini, was Jewish. If in

Parohket. *Jewish Museum of the Grand Temple, Rome.*

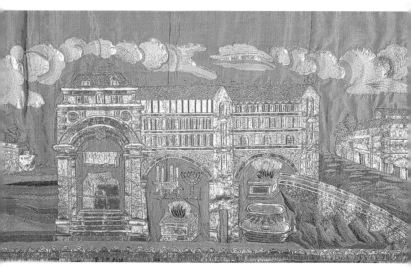

his speeches Mussolini lashed out at "the international Jewish plutocracy," he maintained relations with certain leaders of the Zionist movement in hopes of reducing English influence in the Near East. After 1933 and Hitler's rise to power, Fascist Italy welcomed several thousand Jewish refugees fleeing Nazi Germany, who then embarked for Palestine from Trieste. Nevertheless, beginning in the middle of the 1930s, the strengthening of the Rome-Berlin axis gave rise to an anti-Semitic Fascism that was increasingly virulent. It came to a head in July 1938 in the *Manifesto of the Race,* written in large part under the influence il Duce. Three months later the regime announced the first racial laws that robbed certain Jews of their nationality and banned all Jews from the army and administration. The laws also prohibited Jews' owning or managing businesses with more than a hundred employees. These infamous laws were rigorously applied. Italian Jews were humiliated, reduced to second-class citizens, but they were not killed.

The Final Solution was put into action after September 1943 in German-occupied central and northern Italy, as well as in the puppet Republic of Salo, proclaimed by Mussolini after he was overthrown by the grand Fascist council and the king. The massacres began in a few villages of the north where the Jews had found refuge. Soon after, the killing machine went into full swing. On 16 October 1943 the former Jewish ghetto in Rome was surrounded by the SS and 2,000 Jews were taken in three days of mass arrests. The victims, many of whom were children and the elderly, were soon deported. Only fifteen of them would return from

*Meeting between Pope John Paul II and Grand Rabbi Toaff,
13 April 1986. Grand Temple, Rome.*

the camps. Deportations also took place soon after in Florence, Trieste, Venice, Milan, Turin, Ferrara, and elsewhere. Aided by their fellow citizens, many Italian Jews succeeded in going into hiding, but ever at the mercy of betrayal, Jews had to change shelters ceaselessly. Some Jews managed to reach the Swiss border, while others joined the ranks of the partisans. In all some 85 percent of Italian Jews survived the war, the highest percentage after Denmark.

Close to 35,000 Jews live in Italy today (of a total population of 62 million). The strongest community is that of Rome, which is the most deeply rooted in its dialect, traditions, and cuisine. A number of Jews came from Hungary after the war, but especially Jews from Egypt, Tunisia, and Libya settled on the peninsula in the years 1950–1960. The community flourishes economically, with a high level of education and integration. Jewish writers and intellectuals—Carlo Levi, Primo Levi, Alberto Moravia, Natalia Ginzburg, citing only the most famous among them—have been or still are at the forefront of Italy's cultural life. Anti-Semitism remains almost nonexistent. Its most severe manifestation was the attack perpetrated on 9 October 1982 by Arab terrorists at the exit of the Grand Temple in Rome. A child was killed and forty injured. Since the Second Vatican Council launched by Pope John XXIII, and then by Pope Paul VI, the Church has never been more engaged in Jewish-Christian dialogue, turning the page on centuries of anti-Semitic doctrine. This new dynamic gained expression on 13 April 1986 with the historic visit of Pope John Paul II to the Grand Temple in Rome, where he gave homage in the name of Catholics "to their elder brothers."

→ **To call Italy from the United States, dial 011 39** followed by the number of the person you are calling.

Latium

Rome

The Jews in the capital of Italy are perhaps the oldest Romans of all. They have been settled in the same ancient neighborhoods in the heart of the Eternal City for 2,000 years, making their homes in the former ghetto, in Trastevere, and on both sides of the Tiber River where it is crossed by the Ponte Fabricio or Ponte Quattro Capi. Not only one of the oldest communities of the peninsula, Roman Jewry also represents one of the most important, lively, and deeply rooted communities today, with its own dialect containing Hebrew words and particular culinary tradition. This 2,000-year-old homeland, without equal with the exception of Israel, preserves numerous monuments dating from all periods, from the Jewish catacombs or the Ostia Antica Synagogue to the Grand Temple constructed at the beginning of the twentieth century on the location of the former ghetto. A visit to Jewish Rome merits at least five days. In this Christian capital, the rich remains of Jewish history proper are augmented by many things that attest to papal policy regarding the Jews. Some for the better and most for the worst, these physical records conditioned Jewish life in Rome—if not in the west as a whole.

THE FORMER GHETTO

The quarter where the Jews were forced to reside for three centuries until 1870 is at the center of the Italian capital, between the Largo Argentina, the Capitoline, and the Tiber. Almost nothing remains of the stifling, cramped streets of the old ghetto, which was destroyed, sanitized, and reconstructed in the first years of the twentieth century. The neighboring narrow streets, such as Via della Reginella or the beginning of Via Sant'Angelo in Pescheria,

JEWISH-ROMAN CUISINE

Certain Jewish dishes still make up part of Roman gastronomy and appear on the menus of numerous restaurants. A case in point is *carcioffi alla giudea* (artichokes Jewish style): the artichoke is fried in oil until the small leaves are marvelously crispy. The traditional cuisine of the Eternal City's lower classes is based on inexpensive ingredients, lower quality cuts of meat, and lots of vegetables. These characteristics are more markedly noticeable in dishes typical of the Jews in the capital, confined for three centuries in the ghetto. Many recipes, notably for fish, are *agro-dolci* (bitter sweet) with sugar, vinegar, pine nuts, and raisins, representing a tradition dating back to the Roman period. Fried dishes make up the lion's share of typical Roman cooking; aside from the artichokes already mentioned, these include *fiori di zucchine* (fried zucchini blossoms stuffed with mozzarella and anchovies) or the *fritto di baccalà* (salt cod croquette). The pasta and soup recipes are hearty, stick-to-the-ribs dishes like the traditional *ceci e pennerelli* (chickpeas and leftover meat morsels) simmered on a low fire for three hours.

give an idea of what the lives of the Jews in the city were like for three hundred years.

🍇 BECAUSE IT IS ABSURD AND INCONVENIENT . . .

The ghetto was established on 14 July 1555 by Paul IV with the Cum Nimis Absurdum *edict:*

"Because it is absurd and inconvenient to the utmost degree that Jews, condemned for their faults by God to eternal slavery, can with the excuse of being protected by Christian love, be tolerated living among us . . ." *The walls of the ghetto were constructed in less than three months. In 1816, the ghetto occupied some 325,000 square feet of which 250,000 square feet were inhabitable. More than 5,000 persons were living there when the walls fell little more than a century ago. This was one of the highest population densities in the capital, and in a disease-prone district inundated at each swelling of the Tiber. The buildings pushed heavenward, up to seven or eight stories high, and more and more overpopulated. Building collapses were frequent. "This entire ensemble of persecutions had fallen into disuse, but with the death of Pius VII [in 1823] everything began again: the Jews were shut up in their ghetto at 8 P.M.," noted Stendhal in 1827. Twenty-five years later, the writer Edmond About expressed his indignation at the terrible poverty and filth of the quarter:*

"In the Christian city, the rain washes the streets, the sun dries the waste, and the wind sweeps away the dust, but there is neither rain, nor wind, nor sun that can sanitize the ghetto."

■ The Portico of Octavius, constructed by Cecilius Metella in 146 B.C.E. remains one of the symbolic places of the former Roman ghetto. The remains of the fluted columns rise from among the enormous paving stones surrounding the large Temple of Juno on Via del Portico d'Ottavia. Restaurants set up their sidewalk tables from which the regulars take in the fresh air. This portal marks one of the five former entrances to this forced residential quarter. It was customarily barred at night with a great iron chain.

■ The Piazza delle Cinque Scole surrounds a fountain by Giacomo della Porta (erected in 1591, rebuilt in 1930) commemorating the five synagogues of the former ghetto (Catalana, Castigliana, Tempio, Siciliana, and Nova). These were all located in a single building that has since vanished but which was located on the present-day square at number 37. The current building is constructed on the site of the former Platea Judea, or "grand square," divided into two halves by the ghetto wall, which was the intersection of two ancient thoroughfares of the Jewish quarter, Via Pescaria and Via Rua. It was in the Platea Judea, at once inside and outside the ghetto, that the economic activities permitted to the Jews of Rome took place. These activities included trade in old clothing, used goods, and some artisanal work. In periods of tolerance these stalls were permitted to open on Sunday and the villagers who had come to the city and did not want to lose a day would come here to make their purchases.

THE PLATEA JUDEA

Fernando Gregorovius wrote, after his visit to the Jewish ghetto in Rome in 1833:

"It [the ghetto] is an indescribable chaos of scraps and debris. An entire world of shredded fabric flutters at the feet of the Jews. There is every kind and color: fragments of brocaded silk or velvet, golden fringes, old bits in red, azure, turquoise, black, or white. The Jews could outfit a harlequin with all that lies on the ground. In the middle of this sea of rags, they act as if they are searching for treasures."

The Piazza delle Cinque Scole, with its many shops, remains the heart of the quarter. Be sure not to miss a pasticceria called Boccione, which sells cakes typical of the Roman-Jewish tradition such as its extraordinary cheesecake made from ricotta. Menorah, a nearby bookstore, is well stocked with both old and new books on Judaism in Italian, French, and English.

[Menorah Bookstore: Via del Tempio 2, 00186 Rome. ✆ 066879297.

❶ libraria@menorah.it.

Open Mon–Thu 9 A.M.–7:30 P.M.,

Fri 9 A.M.–2 P.M., Sun 10 A.M.–2 P.M.]

■ Heading back up this narrow, shadowy street toward the Piazza Mattei, with its magnificent "tortoise" fountain constructed in 1581–84, it is possible to get an idea of what the ghetto was like. The blocks of buildings situated between Via Reginella and Via Sant'Ambrogio became part of the Jewish quarter when Pope Leon XII deigned to enlarge it a little in 1823.

■ Completely on the other side of the former Jewish quarter, and heading in the direction of the Tiber and the Grand Temple, stands the small church of San Gregorio alla Divina Pietà, constructed in the eighteenth century opposite one of the ghetto gates. Its facade features an inscription in Latin and Hebrew citing the prophet Isaiah speaking "to those rebellious people who act according to ideas in a way which isn't good, to those people who continually provoke my anger." This was one of the places where each Sunday, representatives of the Jewish community were obliged to listen to the Catholic Mass.

THE GRAND TEMPLE

The zinc dome of the Grand Temple rises 151 feet above the street and can be seen from anywhere in Rome among the other Baroque domes of the many churches in the Eternal City. It is easily recognized by its square shape. Constructed between 1901 and 1904, hardly more than thirty years after the closing of the ghetto, the Grand Temple celebrates the Italian Jews and their extraordinary integration. The style of the temple is oriental, though some have ironically described it as neo-Babylonian. "Between the Capitoline and the Janiculum, between the monument to Victor Emmanuel and that of Garibaldi, the two great masters of our Italy, stands this majestic temple surrounded by the pure, free sunshine that signals liberty and love," declared Angelo Sereni, president of the Jewish community, whose perhaps florid rhetoric on the occasion of the building's opening nevertheless expressed the state of mind of his fellow believers at the time. Surrounded by a lovely garden with palm trees, the building was constructed on a large, 32,000 square foot piece of land made available by the demolition of the former ghetto, which had been completely razed shortly before and replaced with the large liberty-style buildings. Since at the time there were no licensed Jewish architects, its two designers, Vincenzo Costa and Osvaldo Armani, were non-Jews. The facade is adorned with palms and has three large windows. Near its top, the building features a tympanum decorated with the Tablets of the Law, above which stands a seven-branched **menorah.**

Grand Temple, Rome.

The interior of the main hall is sumptuous, with marble columns in an oriental style. The *aron,* above the steps of a platform at the end of the nave, evokes the altar of a church, like many of the synagogues constructed just after the Jews' emancipation. Abundant light pours in through the large liberty-style windows. The interior of the large dome is decorated with oriental-style paintings (palms and a starry sky) by Annibale Brugnoli and Domenico Bruschi. In the halls of the Grand Temple many of the objects historically used in the five synagogues of the former ghetto have been assembled and are on display. Especially noteworthy are the magnificent marble-columned *aronot* from the Siciliana Synagogue of 1586 and that of the Castigliana Synagogue of 1642. The Spanish Temple, occupying since 1932 a large part of the Grand Temple, perpetuates the tradition of Jews who came from the Iberian Peninsula, while the majority of the services are now in Italian. The hall with its *aron* facing the *tevah* evokes the atmosphere of the former Roman Synagogue that has since disappeared. The Jewish Museum occupies one of the wings of the Grand Temple. Numerous silver religious objects, circumcision chairs, candelabras, fabrics, and manuscripts, including three volumes of poems in Judeo-Roman by Crescenzo del Monte (1868–1935), are on display in two vast rooms.

[Grand Temple: Lungotevere Cenci 9, 0186 Rome. ✆ 066875051.]
[Jewish Museum: Lungotevere Cenci 9, 0186 Rome. ✆ 066840061.
Open Sun–Thu 10 A.M.– 6 P.M.,
Fri 10 A.M.– 2 P.M. Closed Jewish holidays.]

Tiber Island, Rome.

TIBER ISLAND AND TRASTEVERE

■ The only island in the Tiber River as it snakes through Rome, Tiber Island was consecrated by the ancient Romans to Aesculapius, the god of medicine. Since the Middle Ages, it has been the site of hospices or hospitals. The island links the Jewish quarter on either side of the river; thus in the eleventh century both the Ponte Fabricio and the Ponte Quattro Capi were alternately called the Pons Judeorum. In 1870 the confraternities of the former ghetto settled here in order to create aid organizations for the newly emancipated Jews. On one side of the island's central street facing upstream stand the Israelite hospital and the Panzieri-Fatucci oratory, called the Tempio dei Giovani. The nineteenth-century wooden *aron* of the oratory originally came from the five synagogues. The brightly colored stained-glass windows representing Jewish holidays were completed in 1988.

[Panzieri-Fatucci Oratory: Piazza San Bartolomeo all'isola 24, 00186 Rome.]

■ On the other side of the river is the Trastevere (literally, "beyond the Tevere [Tiber]") district. In his travel journals during a trip to Italy in the twelfth century, Benjamin of Tudela, a Jew from Navarre, recounts that numerous Jews lived here under imperial Rome and during the medieval period. Traces of this past that survived the imprisonment of the Jews in the ghetto in 1555 are rare. At 14 Vicolo de l'Atleta stands a small brick building with two arches. A Hebrew inscription on a column of the loggia and a well in the courtyard indicate that it probably functioned as a synagogue in the Middle Ages.

The former cemetery was in the area of the Porta Portese, where the flea market is held every Sunday. After 1870, a large part of Roman-Jewish life once again moved to the Trastevere district, where today the majority of the community institutions are concentrated, including Il Pittigliani, the former Jewish orphanage, which has been transformed into a cultural center with a **kosher** snack bar and library possessing numerous documents on Jewish life in the capital.

[Il Pittigliani: Via dell'Arco de Tolomei 1, 00153 Rome. ✆ 065800539. Open Mon–Sat 9 A.M.–11 P.M.]

■ The headquarters of the Union of the Italian Hebrew Communities is located on the other side of Viale Trastevere, the large avenue dividing the district. It includes a documentation center on Jewish heritage and, a little further along, at numbers 14 and 12, the Hebrew day care and primary school respectively. The Roman Poets and Folklore Museum merits a brief visit to see the three paintings by Ettore Roesler Franz (1845–1907) depicting scenes of everyday life in the ghetto.

[Union of the Italian Hebrew Communities: Lungotevere Sanzio 9, 00153 Rome. ✆ 065803667.]
[Documentation Center:✆ 065803690. Open daily 9:30 A.M.–1:30 P.M.]
[Roman Poets and Folklore Museum: Piazza Sant'Egidio 1, 00153 Rome. ✆ 065813717. Open Tue–Sun 10 A.M.–8 P.M.]

THE FORUM

The center of power under the republic and later the empire was the Fori Imperiali, located between the Piazza Venezia and the Coliseum. In the Forum are also located two monuments directly tied to Jewish history.
■ The Arch of Titus celebrates the emperor's victory and that of his father, Vespasian, over the Jewish revolt in 70 C.E. Constructed after Titus's death in 81 C.E., the interior of the arch contains two large bas-reliefs illustrating the triumphal procession loaded with booty taken from the Temple of Solomon, including notably a seven-armed candelabra and silver horns. A symbol of defeat and the Diaspora, the Arch of Titus has naturally been a humiliation for Roman Jews. When the Nation of Israel was proclaimed in 1948, "they paraded under the arch in the

opposite direction of Titus's triumphal march," relate Bice Migliau and Michaela Procaccia in their book on travel in Jewish Rome and Latium.

At the other end of the Forum, heading toward the Capitoline, stands the ancient Mammertine prison with its lugubrious under ground cells where the enemies of Rome were imprisoned and executed after being led in shame through the city behind the chariot of the victor. A plaque recalls this was the fate one such prisoner, Simon bar Ghiora, a defender of Jerusalem in 70 C.E.

■ Leaving the Forum by the main entrance and going back up Via Cavour,

Detail of the Arch of Titus, Rome, first century.

you will find the Basilica San Pietro in Vincoli at the top of a large staircase. Originally constructed to hold the chains of St. Peter in the fifth century, it was altered at the beginning of the sixteenth century by Cardinal Della Rovere, the future Pope Julius II, to be a funerary monument. Here is located the celebrated statue of Moses by Michelangelo. Powerful and admonishing, the prophet, seated holding the Tablets of the Law, is represented at the moment when he has just descended from Mount Sinai and sees the idolatry of his people.

[Basilica San Pietro in Vincoli: Piazza San Pietro in Vincoli 4/A, 00184 Rome. ✆ 064882865.]

THE JEWISH CATACOMBS

The catacombs were constructed in the first years of the Christian era by Jews influenced by the Roman custom of entombing the dead in deep stone chambers. Six sites have been discovered around Rome. The first, Monteverdi, close to the Janiculum, was discovered in the seventeenth century. Only two Jewish catacombs are open today, that of the Villa Torlonia on Via Nomentana and that of Vigna Randanini, close to Via Appia Antica. The arrangement of the catacombs in galleries scarcely 3 ft. high x 7–9 ft. differs little from the Christian catacombs. "Considered as religiously impure places, the catacombs were not used by Jews for liturgical celebrations other than the burials," writes Attilio Milano in his *History of the Italian Jews.* The walls are decorated with inscriptions, most often in Greek, and with such symbols as the **menorah,** the Scrolls of the Law, the **shofroth,** and palm branches. Two rooms of the Vigna Randanini galleries are decorated with secular motifs (eagles, peacocks, griffins) and on the ceilings, a winged Victory and a personification of Fortune are represented. Some analysts interpret these figures as a result of the influence of the surrounding society; others emphasize that these catacombs were probably first pagan tombs and only later integrated into the Jewish burial complex.

[To visit for research or studies only, contact Dottoressa Maria Roserio Barbera at the Roman archaeological superintendency to obtain a permit: ✆ 064882364, fax 064814125.]

MEMORIAL TO THE ADREATINE MASS GRAVES

On Via Adreatina, just beyond its intersection with Via delle Sette Chiese and near Via Appia Antica, stands the Memorial to the Adreatine Mass Graves. On 24 March 1944 the SS troops of Herbert Kappler massacred on this spot 335 hostages, 70 of which were Jews. This mass execution was in retribution for the thirty-two German soldiers who were victims of the Resistance. The monument, *The Martyrs,* was sculpted in 1950 by Francesco Coccia. A cross and a Star of David rise above the wall of the burial plot.

Ostia

■ The excavations at Ostia (Ostia Antica), the great port of imperial Rome, bear impressive witness to Roman urbanism and deserve a visit to see the synagogue discovered there in 1962 when ground was broken for a new highway to Fiumicino Airport. The synagogue borders the northeastern edge of the archaeological zone, just beyond the Porta Marina. Its initial construction dates back to the first half of the first century C.E. and it was rebuilt several times until the fourth century. The synagogue complex includes a prayer hall, study room, and an oven for baking unleavened bread. There are three entrances: one for men, one for women, and the entrance to the mikvah, whose remains are still visible. One can still see the *aron* flanked by two columns whose capitals support the remains of a frieze decorated with *menorot,* palm branches, and shofroth. There is a small podium at the opposite end of the room that served as the bimah.

■ The Archaeological Museum features several lovely lamps decorated with seven-arm candelabras.

[Archaeological Museum: Viale dei Romagnoli 717, 00119 Rome. ✆ 0656358099. Open Tue–Sun 8:30 A.M.–6 P.M.]

Tuscany ■

With cities like Livorno and Florence, Tuscany represents an important part of the history of Jewish life in Italy, although evidence of the longstanding Jewish presence here is less abundant than in Venice and Piedmont. The large free port city of Livorno was the largest Jewish city of Italy between the seventeenth and nineteenth centuries. The powerful Spanish-Portuguese community had what was considered to be one of the most sumptuous synagogues in Europe along with that of Amsterdam. Florence's richly decorated Grand Temple, completed in 1882, stands as one of the most luxurious of those erected after the Jews' emancipation.

Small Jewish communities have lived in the region since the Middle Ages. Early records demonstrate a stable presence—thanks to the Modioio of Jewish moneylenders in Florence from the beginning of the fifteenth century. The Medicis remained well disposed toward Judaism for almost a century. Cosimo I readily welcomed the Jews fleeing the Papal States in 1555. Several years later, however, Cosimo I buckled to papal pressure and forced the Jews of the Grand Duchy to live in two ghettos, one in Florence and the other in Siena. In 1593, Cosimo's successor Ferdinand I took a more pragmatic and tolerant political stance and encouraged the Jews, especially those who had fled the Iberian Peninsula a century earlier, to settle in Livorno in order to develop the Grand Duchy's commerce with the Levant. The small city of Pitigliano, near the former border with the Papal States was another center of Judaism. Refugee Jews awaiting better times in Rome settled here in the sixteenth century.

Their descendants stayed in Pitigliano until the emancipation of the Jews in the middle of the nineteenth century.

Florence

The former ghetto of Florence was located in the heart of the old city center near the market in a zone totally destroyed at the end of the twentieth century, situated today between Via Brunelleschi, the Piazza della Repubblica, and Via Roma. Bernardo Buontalento, the grand duke's architect, was commissioned to design the ghetto. The streets accessing the residential blocks were walled, with the exception of two gates that were closed each evening. As in Siena, in

Florence Jews from all the villages and towns of Tuscany were confined inside a labyrinth of alleys and courtyards. The Jews were excluded from guilds, and hawking used clothing was the only occupation open to them. They remained in the ghetto for almost three centuries, until 1848. Its two synagogues, one with Italian services and the other with Spanish, were destroyed at the same time as the ghetto at the end of the twentieth century. Shortly before the opening of the Grand Temple, two small oratories were created in 1882. In use until 1962, one oratory held services in Italian; the other followed an **Ashkenazic** liturgy. Both of them are commemorated in a plaque on the building at 4 Via delle Oche, which was the offices of the Mattir Assurim confraternity.

Ghetto, Florence, 1880.

■ The imposing neo-Moorish Grand Temple (Tempio Maggiore) was unveiled in 1882 after eight years of construction. Designed by Marco Treves with the assistance of architects Mariano Falcini and Vincenzo Micheli, this synagogue with its majestic pink and white stone facade is dominated by a large green dome and two matching minarets on each side. The Tablets of the Law crown the pediment. The rich Moorish-style interior is sumptuously decorated

Grand Temple, Florence.

with arcades of slender columns, and in the center, there is a semi-circular apse where the *aron* and the **bimah** are enthroned, separated from the rest of the prayer hall by a finely wrought grille. The mosaics and frescoes of gold and azure are the work of Giovanni Panti. During the war, the Nazis used the temple as a military garage and attempted to dynamite it during their retreat, fortunately without substantial damage. Carefully restored, the synagogue was later victim to the great flooding of the Arno River in 1966, which filled it with seven feet of water. A large portion of the 15,000-volume library was severely damaged.

[Tempio Maggiore: Via Farini 4, 50121 Florence. To visit, contact the Jewish Community office: ✆ 055245252, fax 055241811.]

■ Opened in 1981, the Jewish Museum is on the second floor in a vast room divided into two parts: one houses a collection of photos, visual witnesses to Jewish life in Florence, and the other contains beautiful religious objects, especially silver pieces and textiles. You can also admire a beautiful old *rimmon* dating from the end of the sixteenth century. At the museum exit, a large plaque commemorates the 248 Jews from Florence who were deported and died in the death camps or were executed.

[Jewish Museum: same address as the Tempio Maggiore. ✆ 0552346654. Open Sun–Thu 10 A.M.–5 P.M., Fri 10 A.M.–2 P.M. Closed Jewish holidays.]

♜ THE FACADE OF THE BASILICA SANTA CROCE

The facade of the Basilica Santa Croce is decorated with a large Star of David that will probably arouse your curiosity. In their Guida all'Italia Ebraica *(Guide to Jewish Italy), Annie Sacerdoti and Luca Fiorentino tell of its strange origin: "In 1860, it was decided to renovate the church's thirteenth-century Gothic facade with polychrome marble. The work was entrusted to the architect Nicolò Matas, a Jew from Ancona who incorporated the large star as an element of the decoration. No one paid any attention to the architect's Jewish origins, even after he specified in his contract that he would not work on Saturdays. When he died, he put the Jewish community and the Franciscans in a difficult position by stating in his will his wish to be buried in the basilica. A compromise was finally reached: he was interred in a marble sarcophagus just outside the church under the flight of stairs facing the main entrance."[+]*

Pitigliano

Located at the extreme south of Tuscany among the hills and cypresses, the borough of Pitigliano rises from a rocky pinnacle. Once called "little Jerusalem" by Tuscan Jews, the nickname points to the historical importance of Pitigliano's Jewish community here, formed by those fleeing the Papal States after the edicts of 1555. The Jews remained here for almost four centuries, formally occupying a ghetto after 1622, but trading or even farming in almost perfect tranquillity. This calm was interrupted, however, in 1799 by anti-French

Ghetto, Pitigliano.

violence subsequently directed at the Jews, who with their new ideas, were accused of being in sympathy with the French. Of the 3,189 residents registered in the town census of 1841, 359, or roughly 10 percent, were Jewish. After the emancipation in 1859, the Jews in Pitigliano stayed until the beginning of the twentieth century, their positive sentiments evident in the custom of naming their children Garibaldi or Mazzini, names of the heroes of Italian reunification. Eventually many residents departed for Florence or the capital and the community languished.

■ The best white **kosher** wine in Italy and an old synagogue are among the remains of the Jewish community in Pitigliano. The synagogue, which dates from the sixteenth century and was last remodeled in the eighteenth century, was crumbling by the 1960s. Restored and reopened in 1995, it stands in the former Jewish quarter at the foot of Orsini Castle beside the former bread oven. Only one wall of the synagogue, that of the women's gallery, has remained intact. The rest of the synagogue has been carefully reconstructed with the gilt stucco, holy inscriptions in Hebrew, and plaques commemorating the visit of the grand dukes Ferdinand III and Leopold II to the temple at the beginning of the nineteenth century.

[Synagogue: Vicolo Manin,
58017 Pitigliano. ✆ 0564010390.]

Siena

Siena's ghetto was created at the same time as that of Florence in 1571. The large Jewish presence in the city is verified by documents from the beginning of the thirteenth century that mention a *universita iudarum*. The Jewish quarter is in the heart of the city, near the Piazza Campo and between the present-day Via San Martino and Via di Salicotto. The narrow little streets and tall houses were partly destroyed during the urban renewal projects of 1935, but certain of them have kept their original appearance, as with the buildings in Via delle Scotte near the synagogue and the names of streets like the Vicolo della Fortuna and the Vicolo della Manna.

■ The lovely neoclassical synagogue was built in 1756 according to the design of the Florentine architect Giuseppe Del Rosso. The construction lasted thirty years. At the center of the large, high-ceilinged hall is an elegant sculpted wood bimah decorated with nine-armed candelabras. The windows are surrounded by moldings in the shape of ionic columns, and among the Baroque stuccowork, the walls feature fourteen verses from the Bible. The beautiful eighteenth-century *aron* is surrounded by marble Corinthian columns.

[Synagogue: Via delle Scotte 14, 53100 Siena. Open the first Sun of the month. For information, contact the Jewish Community of Siena: ✆ 0552346654.]

■ Facing the synagogue, in Via degli Archi, stands the old fountain of the ghetto, which once boasted a statue of Moses. The statue was removed in the twentieth century due to pressure from indignant Orthodox Jews, who saw the statue as a transgression of the law forbidding representation of the human figure. It is now located in the local museum (Museo Communale), in a room that is, unfortunately, temporarily closed. Contact cultura@comune.siena.it for further information.

[Museo Communale: Piazza il Campo 1, 53100 Siena. ✆ 057749153. Open daily 10 A.M.–5:30 P.M.]

■ At the gates of the city on Via Certosa, one can see the old Jewish cemetery, whose oldest graves date to the sixteenth century.

[Old Jewish Cemetery: Open by appointment through the Jewish Community of Siena: ✆ 0552346654.]

Livorno

A visit to Livorno is required in the name of remembrance, even if the urban renewal projects of the early twentieth century around the port and the bombings of the Second World War in 1943–1944 have destroyed most of the old city center, including Jewish Livorno's Grand Synagogue. In no other Italian city did the Jews have such a significant role as in Livorno, where they were never forced to live in ghettos. They were the true founders of the city and architects of its splendor. The grand duke of Tuscany issued the edict *Livornina,* dated 10 June 1593, which guaranteed—for twenty-five years and with the option of the edict's renewal—the Jews free trade and the right to settle where they chose. They were not forced to wear an identifying sign as were other Jews in the duchy, and they were permitted to have Christian servants, ride in carriages, and, under Ferdinand I, were protected from the Inquisition: "During the said period we do not want any inquisition, inspection, denunciation, or accusation to be pronounced against you or your families, even if in the past they lived outside our dominions, whether as Christians or simply called such."

There were a large number of Jews of Portuguese and Spanish descent in Livorno. This small coastal city, ravaged by fevers, became, in just a few years, a flourishing port where the Jewish community had a prominent role. Spanish was the official language and Ladino the vernacular in use especially by those expelled from Spain to Thessaloníki, as with other ports of the Levant. Gradually the Livornese Jews created a new dialect, *bagitto,* a mix of Spanish, Hebrew, and the local dialect; it is spoken by elderly Jews of the city even today. The community reached its apogee in the seventeenth and eighteenth centuries. Its decline began with the arrival of Bonaparte's troops, however favorable this was to Jews throughout the rest of the peninsula: the blockade hurt the port. With Italian unification and the emancipation, the Jews of Livorno emigrated to Florence or Rome. By 1900, there were no more than 2,500 Jews in the city, a reduction by half in fifty years. The Second World War and the Nazi deportations struck a death blow to the Jewish community of Livorno, which today is reduced to some 800 members.

■ Completed in 1962, the new synagogue is a concrete, futuristic edifice designed by the Roman architect Angelo Di Castro that stands in the Piazza Benamozegh (the former Piazza del Tempio) in the location of the former synagogue destroyed by bombing in 1944. The magnificent delicately carved, gilt *aron* from the beginning of the eighteenth century came from the old synagogue of Pesaro in the Marches.

[New Synagogue: Piazza Benamozegh, 57123 Livorno. To visit, contact the Jewish Museum.]

■ The Marini Oratory (Draforia Marini) is located on the nearby Via Micali. During the period after the war and until the construction of the new synagogue, the oratory served as the location of worship. At the back of the almost square hall of the yeshiva, one can see an extraordinary gilt *aron* with finely carved floral decorations. It dates from the fifteenth century and probably came to Livorno with the Jews forced to flee Spain. Nevertheless, some experts date the creation of this masterpiece slightly later. The Jewish Museum is also located in this building; its collection of beautiful liturgical objects is housed in two display cases.

[Draforia Marini and Jewish Museum: Via Micali 21, 57100 Livorno. To visit, contact the Cooperativa "Amaranta": ✆ 0586839772.]

Pisa

The old Jewish community of Pisa grew with the arrival of Jews from Spain at the beginning of the sixteenth century, but, with the development of Livorno, steadily decreased in numbers during the seventeenth and eighteenth centuries.

■ The current synagogue, constructed in 1756, has been remodeled several times, most notably at the end of the nineteenth century.

[Synagogue: Via Palestro 24, 56127 Pisa. To visit, contact the Jewish Community of Pisa: ✆ 050542580. Bluereef organizes daily tours of Jewish Pisa (synagogue, cemetery, and Jewish community): ✆ 0509711383.]

Emilia-Romagna ■

The rich region of Emilia-Romagna is definitely worth a two- or three-day visit. Located to the south of the floodplain of the Po River, it includes cities like Bologna, home to a museum that is a model of modern installation techniques and location of the ruins of an ancient ghetto in the heart of the city, and above all Ferrara, once a very important center of Italian Judaism. A leisurely tour of the region will allow for a visit to its many monuments and evidence of a Jewish past that dates back to the Middle Ages. The history of the numerous small communities in the region varies considerably according to their location. In the Papal States, which include Bologna and Ravenna, severe persecutions began as early as the fourteenth century. The forced ghettoization of the Jews in the small towns of Romagna (Rimini, Forlì) erased the active communities of those towns. In Modena or Ferrara, possessions of the dukes of the d'Este family until 1598, the Jews fared much better, as the rich heritage they left behind attests today.

Bologna

The former Jewish quarter of Bologna lies near the famous Due Torri, in the area marked today by Via Zamboni and Via Oberdan. It consists of a warren of small streets whose eloquent names such as Via dei Giudei or Via dell'Inferno evoke the neighborhood's Jewish past. The ghetto was established in May 1556, just after that of Rome, with the edict of Pope Paul IV, and as in the Eternal City, the Jews were forced to wear a distinguishing mark so they could be easily identified and shut up in the ghetto at night. As authorized by the papal edict, only one synagogue was permitted to remain in operation; this synagogue was probably located at number 16 on Via dell'Inferno. Before this time, especially in the fourteenth and fifteenth centuries, the flourishing community boasted eleven synagogues, and Bologna possessed a renowned, rabbinical academy. The Jewish printing houses of the city were famous. Examples include those of the Montero family and Abraham ben Haim of the Tintori family, whose presses produced in 1482 the first printed version of the Pentateuch with commentaries by Rashi. The first expulsion of Jews from the city took place in 1569, several years after the establishment of the ghetto. They returned, in 1586, only to be banished again in 1593. There was no real Jewish presence in the city again until after the emancipation.

■ The Jewish Museum is housed in the Palazzo Pannolini, named after the family of wool producers and textile merchants that lived here in the fifteenth and sixteenth centuries. This modern museum, opened in 1999, permits the visitor to experience the history of the Jewish people since their origins by following an indicated route through numerous multimedia and video presentations. Several rooms are dedicated to the life of the Jewish community in Emilia-Romagna, traces of which have been uncovered in twenty-six urban centers of the region. The other rooms are centered on the history of Bolognese Jews. Worship centers are still active in five cities of Emilia-Romagna, including Bologna, Ferrara, Modena, Parma, and Soragna.

[Jewish Museum: Via Valdonica 1/5, 40126 Bologna. ✆ 0512911280. Open Sun–Thu 10 A.M.–6 P.M., Fri 10 A.M.–4 P.M.]

Ferrara

The Jewish quarter of Ferrara, along with that of Venice, is one of the largest and best preserved in Italy. The Jews of Ferrara were not forced to live in the quarter until the beginning of the seventeenth century. As the capital city of the d'Este dukes until 1598, the city was a center of Italian and European Judaism, with more than 2,000 Jews of a population of 30,000 during its golden age between the fifteenth and sixteenth centuries. **Ashkenazim** from Germany and **Sephardim** welcomed after their expulsion from Spain lived side by side under the protection of the local authorities; they were not required to wear any distinguishing sign and could freely choose where to live in the city. The large street that connects medieval Ferrara to the Renaissance city, the corso della Giovecca (or Giudecca), attests to this happy past. Prestigious rabbis and doctors lived in this city that was, like Bologna, a center of Jewish printing. It was here in 1555 that Abraham Usque published the famous Bible of Ferrara. The situation declined after 1597, when Duke Alfonso d'Este died without a male heir. The d'Este court abandoned the city and the papacy took control. The d'Estes left for Modena, followed by a number of Jews. The ghetto was created in 1627. Despite difficulties, and even after their emancipation in 1859, many Jews remained in the city until Mussolini imposed racial laws in 1938. This tragedy has been magnificently retold by the writer Giorgio Bassani, who has dedicated most of his books to Jewish Ferrara.

♔ THE GARDENS OF THE FINZI-CONTINI

"Only we, being Jews, of course, but Jews brought up in the very same religious rite, could really understand what it meant to have our own family pew in the Italian synagogue, up there on the second floor, and not in the German synagogue on the first floor, which, with its severe, almost Lutheran gatherings of prosperous Homburg hats, was so very different. . . . who, apart from us, could have been in a position to give precise details about, say, "the via Vittoria lot"?. . . all rather peculiar people, in any case, faintly ambiguous and inclined to keep themselves to themselves, people whose religion, which in the Italian synagogue had become popular and theatrical in an almost Catholic sense, a fact that was clearly reflect in the character of the people . . . had remained essentially a half-secret, exclusive cult best practiced at night, by a few people gathered together in the darkest, least know alley-ways of the ghetto."

GIORGIO BASSANI, TRANS. ISABEL QUIGLY, *THE GARDEN OF THE FINZI-CONTINIS* (NEW YORK: ATHENEUM, 1965).

■ The ghetto is located near the cathedral, around Via Mazzini (formerly Via dei Sabbioni), and has remained quite commercial. Most of the boutiques were owned by Jews until the Second World War. The three main synagogues in the city (German, Italian and Farnese) have always been located on this street in a large building purchased in the fifteenth century by a rich Jewish lender, Samuel Melli, who then donated it to the community. The building still houses the offices of the Jewish community, as well as the Jewish Museum.

■ The magnificent German Synagogue (Scola Tedesca) is used only for large ceremonies. Five windows opening onto a courtyard illuminate the hall of prayer. The opposite wall is decorated with medallions and stucco depicting allegorical scenes from Leviticus, probably the work of Gaetano Davia, who also decorated the town theater. Notice the lovely *aron* carved in dark wood in the seventeenth century. The **bimah,** originally in the center of the hall, was repositioned to the side of the holy arch in the nineteenth century.

■ The Farnese Synagogue (Scola Farnese) is located on the second floor beside the rabbi's apartments and the offices of the community. One enters the room via a richly carved wooden door that came from the former synagogue of the small town of Cento, as did the **bimah** and the lovely polychrome marble *aron* dating from the beginning of the eighteenth century. The synagogue also features gilt stucco citing the Ten Commandments.

■ The equally beautiful Italian Synagogue (Scola Italiana), which is no longer active, is at the top of another staircase and long gallery. On its far wall, three rare carved wooden lacquer *aronot* are on display. The gold and ivory one in the center is original to the Italian Synagogue while the two others, each with two magnificent swirling columns, come from the former Spanish Synagogue on Via Vittoria. The furniture in the vestibule is from the rabbinical academy.

[Synagogues and Jewish Museum: Via Mazzini 95, 44100 Ferrara. ✆ 0532210228. Visits to the synagogues by appointment.]

■ Continuing the visit to the former ghetto, you will notice behind the community building on Via Contrari—at one time outside the quarter—the walled-up windows that prevented the Jews from looking outside. The ghetto once had five entrances. A number of courtyards and passages permitted discreet travel from one building to another.

■ Those interested in Jewish manuscripts and antique books should not miss the chance to visit the Ariostea Library (Biblioteca Ariostea), which has numerous manuscripts, books, and engravings on Jewish Ferrara.

Synagogue, Modena.

[Biblioteca Communale Ariostea: Palazzo Paradiso, Via delle Scienze 17, 44100 Ferrara. ✆ 0532418200. Open Mon–Fri 9 A.M.–9 P.M., Sat 9 A.M.–2 P.M.]

■ The Jewish cemetery, in use since 1620, is located near the city walls. With its many tombs, both old and new, among the poplars, this is a very moving place.

[Jewish Cemetery: Via Fussato Mortara 80, 44100 Ferrara. ✆ 0532230111. Open daily 8 A.M.–5 P.M. Visits by appointment.]

Modena

Modena's former Jewish quarter became the ghetto in 1638. The narrow medieval streets have been completely opened up, widened during the vast urban renewal projects of the early twentieth century that give the city its appearance today.

■ A beautiful oriental-style synagogue stands in the Piazza Mazzini, which is located on part of the former ghetto. Constructed between 1869 and 1873 on plans by Ludovico Maglietta, the synagogue has a double facade: one opens onto the Piazza Mazzini, the other onto Via Coltellini. Inside, the circular prayer hall is surrounded by a colonnade of Corinthian columns that support the women's gallery.

[Synagogue: Piazza Giuseppe Mazzini 26, 41100 Modena. ✆ or fax 059223978. Visits by appointment.]

Piedmont ■

Unjustly slighted as a tourist destination, Piedmont is one of the richest regions of Jewish heritage in Italy, with magnificent small Baroque synagogues like those of Carmagnola, Casale Monferrato, Cherasco, Mondovi, and Saluzzo. In 1848, the Piedmontese Jews became the first in Italy to definitively obtain full equality. The main restrictions on their residence or authorized economic activities had been lifted since 1816 in the territories of the Savoy dynasty. The rulers had never dared to fully rescind the rights Napoleon had accorded to the Jews. With the emancipation, the Jews emigrated in greater numbers to large cities, beginning with Turin, and thus abandoned the small cities where the wealthy communities had lived until then. The Jews benefited from a relatively protected situation, and their place in the economic life was already well established. The ghetto in Turin was not created until 1679, and the ghettos in the other nineteen centers in the Piedmont region, where some 5,000 Jews lived, were not established until the beginning of the eighteenth century. In addition to moneylending and trade in used clothing, the Jews were allowed other economic activities such as goldsmithing, printing, and textiles, especially silk production.

Jews were fairly well represented in elite positions in the administration of the Savoy monarchy, which became the source of the first kings of a unified Italy. Piedmontese Jews also played a significant part in the economy and cultural life of the region. Large synagogues were built in the region toward the end of the nineteenth century: a neo-Byzantine synagogue in Vercelli, a neo-Gothic synagogue in Alessandria, and a large neo-Moorish structure in Turin. The local community in Turin had at first commissioned architect Alessandro Antonelli, who emulated the transalpine style of Gustave Eiffel in creating a "tower synagogue" in steel rising to a height of over 500 feet, whose purpose was to celebrate not only the Jewish community's newfound power but also its modernity. Lack of funds, however, forced the Jewish community to forfeit the half-finished work. The municipality revived the project and completed the Mole Antonelliana, which became the National Independence Museum.

Jews from the Piedmont paid a high price during the Second World War—there were 4,000 Jews in the region in 1939 and fewer than 2,000 in 1945. Despite this tragedy, the community remained active after the war and included such prominent members as the businessman Adriano Olivetti and the intellectuals and writers Primo Levi, Carlo Levi, and Natalia Ginzburg.

♇ MY ANCESTORS

"Rejected or given a less than warm welcome in Turin, they settled in various agricultural localities in southern Piedmont, introducing there the technology of making silk, though without ever getting beyond, even in their most flourishing periods, the status of an extremely tiny minority. They were never much loved or much hated; stories of unusual persecutions have not been handed down. Nevertheless, a wall of suspicion, of undefined hostility and mockery, must have kept them substantially separated from the rest of the population, even several decades after the emancipation of 1848 . . ."
PRIMO LEVI, *THE PERIODIC TABLE,* TRANS. RAYMOND ROSENTHAL (NEW YORK: SCHOCKEN BOOKS, 1984).

Turin

Turin, the capital of Piedmont, is a good point of departure for visiting other Jewish places of remembrance in the region.

■ The Grand Synagogue merits a short visit. Opened 16 February 1884 amid great pomp and ceremony, this majestic neo-Moorish building with its four onion-domed towers attests to the elation of Italy's Jews after their emancipation. The architect Enrico Petiti did not skimp on the decorations for the building, most of which, sadly, were destroyed when the Grand Temple caught fire in 1942 after an Allied bombing. A significant portion of the archives of the Jewish community of Piedmont was also destroyed. The synagogue was restored between 1945 and 1949.

[Grand Synagogue: Via Pio V 12, 10125 Turin. To visit, contact the Jewish Community of Turin: ✆ 0116692387.]

■ Some ten minutes away on foot from the synagogue and the community center, behind the animated Via Roma, one can still see traces of the former ghetto. In particular, notice the remains of the entrance gates at 25 Via Maria Vittoria.

Carmagnola

The most elegant of the region's Baroque synagogues is found in the little city of Carmagnola near Turin. The city's Jewish community was forced to live in a ghetto beginning in 1724.

■ The temple is on the second floor of an eighteenth-century house opposite the former entrance to the ghetto. Passing through a vestibule decorated with frescoes, you will enter a prayer hall almost square in shape (30 ft. x 33 ft.) with a coffered wooden ceiling and lovely ornamental windows. In the center stands a magnificent Baroque **bimah** sculpted of gold, black, red, and green polychrome wood with slender columns supporting a large crown. The richly decorated *aron* is surrounded by two columns and stucco. The walls are paneled mid-way in sumptuously carved dark wood. These decorations, apparently older than the synagogue itself, are oversized compared to the dimensions of the room. The woodwork dating from the sixteenth and seventeenth centuries is of exceedingly high quality and reminiscent of the furniture in the collections of the royal house of Savoy. "If these are not the same artisans, they belong to the same workshop," remarked art historian David Cassuto in his study on the Baroque synagogues of Piedmont.

[Synagogue: Via Bellini 9, 10022 Carmagnola. To visit, contact the Jewish Community of Turin: ✆ 0116692387. Closed temporarily, but can be seen from the street.]

Saluzzo

■ Saluzzo's small Jewish quarter maintains its former appearance in the area around Via Deportati Ebrei. In one of the courtyards on this street stands a building containing a synagogue on its third floor. Constructed in the eighteenth century and remodeled in 1832, the prayer hall was designed to accommodate more than 300 persons. Notice the beautiful carved door, as well as the gilt wood *aron* and the *tevah* dating from the eighteenth century.

[Synagogue: Via Deportati Ebrei, 12037 Saluzzo. ✆ 0116508332 or 0116508585. Visits by appointment.]

Cherasco

■ In the small town of Cherasco in the province of Cuneo, you can make an appointment to visit a very interesting synagogue on private property. Hardly bigger than a living room, the synagogue features magnificent woodwork and gilding. A plaque at the entrance commemorates the founding of the synagogue in 1797. The Baroque *tevah* in the room's center is made of polychrome wood. The *aron* has finely sculpted, gilded swinging doors.

[Synagogue: Via Marconi 4, 12062 Cherasco. To visit, contact the Jewish Community of Turin: ✆ 0116692387.]

Mondovi

■ The small synagogue of Mondovi is a jewel of Piedmontese Baroque architecture, more harmonious overall than that of the nearby administrative center Cuneo. A balustrade surrounds the octagonal carved wooden bimah in the center of the hall. Illuminated by five large crystal lamps, the right wall is decorated with fourteen trompe l'œil windows crowned with Hebrew verses that face the eighteenth-century *aron*.

[Synagogue: Via Vico 65, 12048 Mondovi. To visit, contact the Jewish Community of Turin: ✆ 0116692387.]

Asti

■ The synagogue of this administrative center is unique for two reasons. First, its liturgy is special: called *astigiano* in Italian and *Appam* in Hebrew, its language is named after the initials of the three small towns where it is still actively spoken (Asti, Fossano, Moncalvo). Annie Sacerdoti and Luca Fiorentino note in their *Guida all' Italia Jewish Ebraica* (Guide to Jewish Italy)[5] that it is a combination of **Ashkenazic** worship and the old provincial liturgy brought to the city by Jews of German and French origin. Second, the plan of this synagogue is unusual. The location of the *tevah* under a central dome supported by four columns is unique in Italy and is directly inspired by temples constructed in Bohemia and Hungary during the same period.

[Synagogue: Via Ottolenghi 8, 14100 Asti. ✆ 0141593094, 0141594271, or 0141593281. Visits by appointment.]

Casale Monferrato

■ The **Ashkenazic** synagogue of the lovely, rich city of Casale Monferrato on the floodplain of the Po River was constructed in 1596, in the center of the old Jewish quarter. It is one of

Synagogue, Casale Monferrato.

the oldest in Piedmont. The discreet exterior facade has nothing remarkable to recommend it, but the interior with its numerous gilt wood decorations and frescoes is one of the most remarkable in Italy. After extensive remodeling in the eighteenth and especially nineteenth centuries, the temple as we see it today is very different from what it was originally. The *tevah* was at the center of a rectangular hall illuminated by fourteen windows, like the synagogues of Central Europe that also have the pews for the faithful surrounding the *tevah.* In 1868, this arrangement was changed and the hall considerably enlarged. The *aron,* dating from 1787, remains in its original location.

It is decorated on both sides with large stuccowork depicting the city of Jerusalem. A fresco of the heavens and clouds occupies the center of the ceiling, with an inscription in Hebrew, "This is the door to heaven." Two gilt inscriptions on the walls recall difficult times in the history of the community. Another inscription recalls the statute of 1848 that granted the Piedmontese Jews legal equality. The synagogue was restored in 1969.

■ The Jewish Museum situated in the building connected to the synagogue brings together a collection of beautiful liturgical objects.

[Synagogue: Vicolo Salomone Olper 44, 15033 Casale Monferrato.]

[Jewish Museum: same address.

✆ 014271807. Open Sun 10 A.M.–noon and 3 P.M.–5 P.M. Mon–Sat visits by appointment.]

Lombardy ■

Milan

Until the middle of the nineteenth century and the unification of Italy, very few Jews lived in Milan (barely 200 in 1840), or for that matter in the duchy as a whole during the preceding centuries. Today, however, Milan represents the second largest Jewish population in Italy after Rome, with some 9,000 people of some thirty different origins. A large number of these Jews came from Egypt, Libya, and Iran. It is a dynamic community reflecting the energy of the Lombard capital itself.

■ All of Milan's synagogues are modern. The Grand Synagogue opened in 1892, burned down during World War II, and was later reconstructed with a lovely facade by Luca Beltrami. Of Milan's six other temples, two are Persian synagogues.

[Grand Synagogue: Via Guastalla 19, 20122 Milan. ✆ 025512029, fax 025512101.]

[Persian Synagogues: Noam Synagogue, Via Monteculoli 27 and Ohel Shalom Synagogue, Via Patti 3, 20122 Milan.]

Soncino

The only noteworthy place of remembrance in the area surrounding Milan is the small town of Soncino in the province of Cremona. In the fifteenth century a Hebrew printing house operated here, created by the rabbi and doctor Israel Nathan of Speyer, who was originally at this Rhenish city. The business was eventually forced to leave the duchy of Milan, but the Soncinos, the dynasty of printers who took the name of the city, continued to work in various cities in Italy (Pesaro, Brescia) and the Mediterranean (Thessaloníki, Istanbul).

■ A small museum now occupies the former print shop.

[Museum: Via Lenfranco 6, 26029 Soncino. ✆ 037484883. Visits by appointment.]

Mantua

Under the protection of the Gonzaga dukes, Jewish life flourished in the city of Mantua during the course of centuries. At the beginning of the seventeenth century, some 7,000 Jews lived in the city, representing 8 percent of the population. Nevertheless the walls of the ghetto, established in 1612, fell only with the arrival of Napoleon Bonaparte's soldiers. Unfortunately, not much remains of this rich and prestigious Jewish past.

■ Only one of the original six synagogues of the city remains, and has been restored to its original appearance. However, the Jewish quarter and much of the old city center were modernized at the beginning of the twentieth century. The synagogue is a faithful copy of the Norsa Torrazzo Temple and is classified as a national historic monument. The wall decorations, the sumptuous *aronot,* and the early eighteenth-century *tevot* are original and attest to the past splendor of this community.

[Synagogue: Via Gilberto Govi 11–13, 46100 Mantua.]

Veneto

Padua

In the fourteenth century, Padua was one of the great centers of medieval Judaism, with a celebrated rabbinical academy where students from all over Europe came to study. These students were also attracted to Padua by its very old medical school, the only one to accept Jews as students. The Venetian conquest in 1405 obliged the Jews to sell their homes and lands and limited the interest rates they could charge to 12 percent. In

1509, the conquest of the city by Maximilian of Austria's German mercenaries included the sacking of the Jewish quarter. When the Venetians retook the city a few months later, new pillaging ensued. Until 1560, the city celebrated this victory on the seventeenth of July with three races, one of which required the Jews to ride donkeys through the town as they were mocked and insulted. The ghetto was created in 1601, confining more than 600 people in a handful of narrow, dirty streets. The ghetto was eliminated only in 1797.

THE FORMER JEWISH QUARTER

■ Situated in the narrow streets near the Piazza delle Erbe, the former ghetto has kept much of its original appearance. At 9 Via San Martino e Solferino, where the offices of the Jewish community are located, stands one of the four gates to the ghetto crowned with the lion of Saint Mark. A little further away is Via delle Piazze, once the center of the quarter with two old synagogues, which have since disappeared.

■ In 1525, the Great "German" (Ashkenazic) Temple was opened in the corte Lenguazza, the primary synagogue of the city. Remodeled and embellished in 1683, the synagogue began using the Italian liturgy in the nineteenth century, when the large Baroque central platform was removed. Damaged by fires first in

1927 and later in 1943, when it was torched by local Fascists, only the temple's magnificent Baroque marble *aron* escaped the flames. In 1955, it was dismantled (weighing approximately forty tons) and reinstalled in Tel Aviv in the Yadan Eliahu Synagogue.

■ The Italian Synagogue, erected in 1548 on Via San Martino e Solferino, has remained the ultimate testimony to Jewish life in Padua. The *aron* and **bimah** face each other from the long sides of a rectangular hall measuring 60 ft. x 23 ft. Four columns of white-veined black marble surround the beautiful seventeenth-century *aron.*

[Italian Synagogue: Via Martino e Solferino 9, Padua 35122. ✆ 0498751106. Visits by appointment.]

■ In the Albergo Toscanelli on nearby Via Arco, one can still see a chimney decorated with a dove, the emblem of the Salom family. This was the headquarters of the rabbinical academy. The street with its tall, narrow houses evokes what the ghetto looked like in the past.

THE JEWISH CEMETERIES

One can also visit a section of Padua's seven Jewish cemeteries, which are located on the edge of the city. The oldest cemetery is close to San Leonardo and dates back to 1384. The tomb of the famous rabbi Meir Katzenellenbogen (1482–1565) is located here and continues to attract pilgrims. The cemetery of Via

Codalunga includes the grave of Isaac ben Juda Abravanel (1437–1508), minister of finance for Alfonse V of Portugal and, before that, for the kings of Spain.

[Visits by appointment. Contact the Jewish Community of Padua: ✆ 0498751106.]

Venice

On 20 March 1516, Zaccaria Dolfin, an influential Venetian patrician, announced a radical turn in the history of the Jews of the Serenissima: "It is necessary to send all the Jews *(zudei)* to stay in the *geto novo,* which is like a stronghold, and to make drawbridges and to surround it with walls so that there will be only one gate that will need to be monitored, and only the boats of the Council of Ten will stay through the night." After the council, the senate of the city voted 130 to 44 to enclose the Jews in a specific part of the city. On 29 March, a decree established the first ghetto in an unhealthy, outlying area that was the location of a former copper foundry *(geto* in Venetian, a plausible source of the word *ghetto*). Jewish quarters already existed in several cities in Central Europe, but the residential conditions were not as rigorously codified. The "geto" rapidly became famous, its name soon achieving the status of a common noun.

♛ THE ORIGIN OF THE WORD "GHETTO"

The noun "ghetto" appears to derive from the name of the islands where the first ghetto was established, having featured a foundry (geto or getto). *Although this etymology is generally accepted, it is perhaps too simplistic and leaves some skeptical, for it neglects to explain the shift in pronunciation from the initial sound "zh" of* geto *to the hard "g" of* ghetto. *This gutteralization could be due to the pronunciation of Venetian Jews of the period, who were in large part of German origin. Some scholars have suggested other origins for "ghetto": for example, from the Hebrew word* ghet *(repudiation or divorce).*

Until this time, the Jews of the Serenissimo had had few problems. Some Jews probably lived in Venice as early as the twelfth or thirteenth century, on Spinalonga Island (the reason it has been called Giudecca ever since). However, historians do not agree on this point. The republic needed money, and at the beginning of the fourteenth century it authorized Jewish moneylenders to settle in Venice. Arriving primarily from Germany, the Jews were forbidden to reside permanently in the city and were forced to wear a yellow, later red, beret for easy recognition. Most Jews chose to live in Mestre or in

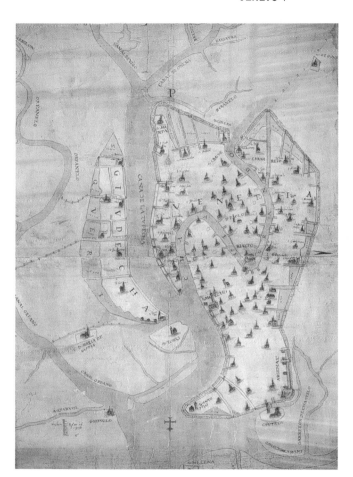

Cristoforo Sabbadino, Plan of Venice, *1557. National Archives.*

neighboring cities such as Padua. Beginning in 1509, the Jews began to arrive at the Lagoon in greater numbers, fleeing, as did thousands of other refugees, the victories of the papal and Austrian troops allied against Venice. It was in this dramatic context it was decided to create the *ghetto nuovo*, which held some 700 German and Italian Jews. Then, in 1541, the *ghetto vecchio* was created for Jews from the Levant and Spain, this last group being wealthier and engaged in maritime commerce. Among the Jews from

The Merchant of Venice, *nineteenth century. Private collection.*

Spain were many Marrtanos. In 1633, a new zone *(ghetto novissimo)* was added to the area where Jews were permitted to live in Venice. There rich Levantine or Spanish families settled. In 1589, some 1,600 Jews lived in the ghettos; by 1630 they numbered 4,870 people, or 3 percent of the inhabitants of Venice's city center, but with a population density four times higher than that of the rest of the city. The walls of the ghetto finally fell in 1797 with the arrival of Napoleon Bonaparte's troops. This ghetto was both the most infamous

and sumptuous in Europe; it has maintained almost totally its original structure. Its five synagogues from the sixteenth and seventeenth centuries are among the most beautiful in Europe. Scarcely 500 Jews live in the city today. A visit to Jewish Venice requires at least two days.

THE GHETTO

■ If you cross the small wooden bridge over the Rio del Ghetto Nuovo and then pass beneath a *sottoportego* (a little arched passageway under a building that is typically Venetian), you can still see the holes in the walls from the beams of the great doors that blocked the passage at night. Emerging from the *sottoportego,* you immediately find yourself on the large *campo* (square) of the *ghetto nuovo,* a trapezoidal space with a few trees and three wells made of Istrian stone that has remained almost unchanged since the time of the ghetto's occupation. Only the buildings of the Casa Israelitica di Riposo built on the north side in the nineteenth century have replaced the high facades that surround the rest of the *campo.* These buildings have eight or nine stories and are still among the tallest in Venice.

♨ A BABEL OF MEN AND LANGUAGES

"In the ghetto, one heard the most diverse sounds: not only Hebrew songs or dialects cut off

from their homelands in the Mediterranean but also the patois colored with Spanish, Turkish, Portuguese, Levantine, or Greek, not to mention the slang of a few Poles or German refugees and the various Italian dialects. A true Babel of men and languages where a few adventurers and shady Marranos stand out."

RICCARDO CALIMANI, *HISTORY OF VENICE'S GHETTO* (PARIS: STOCK, 1988).

The *campo* was the heart of daily life for Venetian Jews. Here money-lenders set up their tables in front of the houses or under doorways. Although Venice's Jews excelled in printing and medicine, the rows of *strazza* (used-cloth) vendors on the square engaged in the other occupation officially permitted to Jews. At number 2911 on the square, one can still see the signboard of the Banco Rosso (which also existed in yellow and green, and so was called depending on the color of the borrower's note given).

Crossing the Ponte delle Agnudi, one passes from the *ghetto nuovo* into the *ghetto vecchio,* which has a calmer atmosphere despite boutiques lining its narrow streets. In the past, every evening both ghettos emptied of all their non-Jewish pedestrians and clients before the doors shut on the enclosed Jews. They were forced to pay guards who, on foot and in boats, enforced their confinement.

The *campo nuovo* was the only large Venetian *campo* without a church or palace to define the space. The Scola Tedesca Grande, or Grand German Synagogue, is located at the southeast corner of the square on the second floor of a tall house with large windows. The Scola Canton and the Scola Italiana were located next door. The *ghetto nuovo* had its gaze turned toward its main synagogues and the land of Israel.

🕎 A CITY WITHIN A CITY

"There was one oven for baking bread and another for baking unleavened bread in each of the ghettos, numerous shops selling fruit and vegetables, meats, wines, cheeses, pâtés, and oil merchants, some frequented by the Germans and others by the Levantines. One found not only tobacco and candle wax shops but also barbers, hatmakers, wet nurses, tailors, booksellers, printers, a morgue for the dead, and an auberge for Jews passing through."

DONATA CALABI, *LA CITTÀ DEGLI EBREI* (THE CITY OF JEWS), WITH UGO CAMERINO AND ENNIO CONCINA (MILAN: MARSILIO EDITIONS, 1995).

THE SYNAGOGUES

None of the following five synagogues in the *campo* of the *ghetto nuovo* or the neighboring streets can be seen without a guided visit.

■ Constructed in 1528 by **Ashkenazic** Jews, the Grand German Synagogue (Scola Tedesca Grande) in the *ghetto nuovo* was the first of the ghetto's synagogues. The walls of the majestic great hall (46 x 23 feet) appear to be oval, but are actually trapezoidal. They are paneled midway with lovely walnut wood and gilding. Dating from 1666 and covered with gilt, the raised *aron* (with the Ark of the **Torah**) is accessed by four pink marble stairs. The golden **bimah** with its elegant Corinthian columns is from the same period. The *aron* and **bimah** face each other from the short walls of the room. The synagogue was drastically remodeled in the middle of the nineteenth century. In the original layout, the **bimah** was in the center of the room, as in the synagogues of Germany and Central Europe, which explains the absence of decorations on the floor in the center of the hall and the octagonal opening in the ceiling. Five large windows inundate the room with light during the day, symbolically representing the five books of the Pentateuch that illuminate the world. Like the other synagogues in the ghetto, this one is on the second floor in order to be closer to heaven and the stars. The Museum of Hebrew Art, opened in 1953, occupies two rooms in the same building as the synagogue. Beautiful silver religious objects, sacred decorations, and interesting manuscripts are on display.

[Museum of Hebrew Art: Cetneregio 29012/B, 30121 Venice. ✆ 041715359.]

■ The Canton Synagogue (Scola Canton) is located near the Grand German Synagogue. It is easily recognized from outside by its small gilt dome above a wooden square base erected in 1532 by Jews from the provinces. After crossing a long hallway that served as a "room for the poor" (for those who could not afford to pay for the service) at the top of a narrow staircase and passing through a swinging door, you will enter the lovely rectangular hall (43 ft. x 23 ft.) of the temple. The *aron* and **bimah** face each other from the shorter sides of the hall. The *aron* resembles that of the Grand German Synagogue and dates from the same period (1672), but it is even more splendid.

■ With its four-columned classical portal, the Italian Synagogue stands out on the *campo* of the *ghetto nuovo.* Its entrance is the same as that of the nearby residences. Constructed in 1575, the large, almost square (36 ft. x 33 ft.) prayer hall of the synagogue is located on the third floor. The worship hall is decorated less lavishly than that of the two mentioned temples. Lit by five windows and a small dome above the **bimah,** the hall is harmoniously proportioned. Dating from the eighteenth century, the imposing **bimah** rests on a raised platform reached by eight steps and surrounded by four gilded wood Corinthian columns.

Grand German Synagogue, Venice

■ With its simple but elegant seventeenth-century facade, the Spanish Synagogue (Scola Spagnola) stands on the Campiello delle Scole in what was formerly the heart of the *ghetto vecchio*. Established in 1541 for the **Sephardic** Jews banished from Spain who had subsequently settled in the Levant *(levantini)* or the falsely converted Marranos who stayed on Christian soil *(ponentini)*, the Spanish Synagogue was the first edifice in the ghetto erected according to real architectural plans and not simply a structure adapted to its location. Begun in 1555, the synagogue was remodeled circa 1635 under the influence of the great Venetian architect Baldassare Longhena, or clearly one of his students. His influence is equally evident in the structural design and in the interior decoration. The handsome *aron* with its black marble columns is separated from the rest of the hall by a wooden balustrade. It seems to be an almost exact copy of the great altar of the chapel of the cardinal patriarch Francesco Vendramin in the church San Pietro di Castello. At the other end of the large, well-lighted hall of worship (72 ft. x 43 ft.) stands the raised **bimah,** with two columns supporting a heavily decorated

Scola Levantina, Venice.

architrave. The rich decoration of the ceiling is particularly interesting with its carved wooden bas-reliefs and its stuccowork in a style close to that of the palace of Ca Pesaro.

■ On the other side of the small square stands the Levantine Synagogue (Scola Levantina), erected between 1528 and 1561 and renovated in around 1680. Although displaying the same architectural influences as the other synagogues, it is even more luxuriant. Decorated with dark wood, the large entrance vestibule contains two doors: one leading to the hall of worship on the second floor and the other down a short hallway to the Luzzato Synagogue (Scola Luzzato), a yeshiva with a gilded wood Renaissance *aron*—the oldest in the ghetto. The synagogue's prayer hall (26 ft. x 30 ft.) is imposing. The sculpted wood **bimah** made of black-stained walnut is the work of Andrea Brustolon, a cabinetmaker originally from Belluno whose work was fashionable at the time. The podium, accessed by a double staircase, is crowned with a baldachin supported by twisting columns of the type thought to have been in the Temple of Solomon. The polychrome marble *aron* at the other end of the room is undeniably simple.

THE FORMER JEWISH CEMETERY OF THE LIDO

Situated between the sea and the Lagoon in what was at the time the desolate outskirts of the city, the old Jewish cemetery is located on the property of the San Nicolo monastery. As attested by its oldest tombstone—belonging to a certain Samuel, son of Samson—the cemetery opened in 1389. It is difficult to imagine what the cemetery might have been like in the past. Time has bleached the gravestones and erased many of the inscriptions. Some of the stones have fallen over and are overgrown with ivy. The tombstones crowd and overlap each other; some of the sarcophagi are open, the slabs once covering them now pointing skyward. One can still make out, however, the symbols and emblems decorating many of the tombstones, especially those of the great families of Spain or Portugal. The rampant lions or crowned eagles of the Jesurum-Diaz family for example, are still visible. Other stelae bear more traditional motifs, such as seven-armed candelabra, ram's horns, palms, or hands in the gesture of blessing. The last burials occurred at the end of the eighteenth century, when the new Jewish cemetery opened on Via di Cipro.

[Equally as old as the Jewish cemetery in Prague, the Jewish cemetery of Lido is worth the effort to schedule a visit. To make an appointment, contact the Museum of Hebrew Art: ✆ 041715359.]

Conegliano Veneto

In this little town, as in so many other towns in Venetia, there was a small but flourishing Jewish community.

■ One can see the street of the former synagogue, whose interior ornaments and decoration were all sent to Israel after the war and installed in the Italian Temple Rehov Hillel in Jerusalem.

Friuli-Venezia Giulia

Trieste

A rich and influential Jewish community lived in Trieste, a large port city of the Austro-Hungarian Empire that became Italian only after the First World War. During the nineteenth century and the first half of the twentieth century, this community had a profound impact on the economic and cultural life of the city. Enclosed in the ghetto in 1661, the Jews enjoyed a de facto emancipation in 1782 through the *Toleranzpatent* of Emperor Joseph II. Consequently, the history of Trieste's Judaism mingles with that of Austria, especially Viennese Judaism, and shares all its

splendor. This is still in evidence today by the many palaces of large bourgeois families in the city, such as the Morpurgo de Nilma, the Hierschel de Minerbi, the Treves, the Vivantes, and others. This large commercial port was the empire's only access to the sea. It was also an intellectual capital, where the Jews, before and after 1918, had important roles as writers (Italo Svevo, Umberto Saba, the publisher Roberto Bazlen, or today Giorgio Voghera) and as painters (Isodoro Grünhut, Gino Parin, Vittorio Bolaffio, Arturo Nathan). The presence of Ernesto Weiss (1889–1970) in the city made it the cradle of Italian psychoanalysis. During

FRIULI-VENEZIA GIULIA

the Second World War, Trieste was also one of the ports of departure for Jews emigrating to Palestine. The *Shoah* was deeply felt by the Jews of this city.

THE GRAND SYNAGOGUE

Constructed in 1912 by a community that wanted to show its wealth and power, the synagogue of Trieste represents architecturally one of the most significant edifices of emancipated Judaism at the end of the nineteenth century. Somber, spacious, elegant, and free of any kitsch, the synagogue was designed by the architects Rugero and Arduino Berlam without any regard for expense. The decorations, in part inspired by those of certain Christian edifices of the Near East (i.e., Syrian), also show—in the mosaics, the starry dome and the splendid luminosity of the interior—the influence of the styles fashionable in Vienna at the beginning of the twentieth century.

[Grand Synagogue: Via San Francesco 19, 34133 Trieste. Visits by appointment only by mail or fax. Contact the Jewish Community of Trieste: ✆ 040371466, fax 040371226.]

JEWISH TRIESTE

■ The old Jewish cemetery remains the heart of Judaism in the city. It is accessible on Via del Monte, a street that crawls toward the hill of San Giusto. Located at 5 Via del Monte is the Carlo and Vera Wagner Museum.

This was formerly the location of an **Ashkenazic** oratory where German, Czech, and Polish refugees prayed before emigrating to Palestine between the wars. In fact, Jews called the port city of Trieste the "Door of Zion." The ornaments and gold objects on display here are in some cases quite old; many come from Bohemia and Germany as well as from Italy.

[Carlo and Vera Wagner Museum: Via del Monte 5, 34122 Trieste. ✆ 040633819. Call for opening times.]

■ Narrow streets such as Via Ponte, near the Piazza Borsa give an idea of what this former Jewish quarter might have been like a century ago, when it was inhabited by poor Jews and still had four synagogues, whose discreet facades hid richly decorated interiors. The buildings and synagogues were totally razed in the 1930s to the great joy of the Jewish community of Trieste, which had no desire to see the remains of their miserable past. Many of the synagogues' furnishings are now in Israel.

■ The Caffè San Marco near the Grand Synagogue, a favorite haunt of Triest's intelligentsia, remains one of the most memorable places in the city. Italo Svevo frequented Caffè San Marco, as did a number of artists and writers both Jewish and non-Jewish. The tradition continues today with authors such as Claudio Magris, who dedicated the magnificent pages of *Microcosmes* (Paris: Gallimard, 1998) to the café. The turn-of-the-century Viennese Succession–style interior is remarkable—as are the coffee and food.

[Caffè San Marco: Via Battisti 18, 34122 Trieste. ✆ 040363538.
Open Tue–Sun 8 A.M.–midnight.]

■ Renowned throughout the city for the quality of its products—not to mention its interior decor—the celebrated pastry shop La Bomboniera was also, until the 1930s, a **kosher** pasticceria whose **Purim** cakes made between February and March delighted Trieste's residents, Jewish and non-Jewish alike.

[La Bomboniera: Via 30 Ottobre 3, 34122 Trieste. ✆ 040632752.]

■ The poet and writer Umberto Saba's masterpiece *Canzoniere* was first published in his bookstore in 1921. The shop, which he managed until his death in 1956, has remained as it was during Saba's lifetime, when he was often found engaged in long discussions with the customers and friends he received there.

[Umberto Saba Bookstore:
Via San Nicolo 30, 34121 Trieste.
✆ 040631741. Open Tue–Sat 9 A.M.–
12:30 P.M. and 3:30–7:30 P.M.]

MORPURGO DE NILMA CIVIC MUSEUM

Installed in the palace he had built in 1875, the Morpurgo de Nilma Civic Museum is named after Carlo Marco Morpurgo, declared a valiant knight of the empire for his achievements. The palace suggests what daily life was like for a large Jewish family of Trieste. The private apartments are on the third floor and include a magnificent Louis XVI–style music room, a large azure reception hall decorated in the Venetian style, and a pink salon, among others. Other palaces once belonging to great Jewish families such as the Hierschel de Minerbi at 9 Corso Italia, or the Vivante at 4 Piazza Banco are located in the neighboring streets and have been transformed into apartment buildings or offices.

[Morpurgo de Nilma Civic Museum:
Via Imbriani 5, 34122 Trieste.
✆ 040636114. Open Tue–Thu 5–7 P.M.]

RISIERA OF SAN SABA

The Nazis established the only Italian concentration camp, Risiera of San Saba, in the buildings of a former rice-processing factory in an industrial zone. Between October 1943 and March 1944, convoys of Jews were deported from Risiera of San Saba to extermination camps, although 837 Jews lost their lives at the camp itself. The site was transformed into a memorial by the architect Romano Boico.

[Risiera di San Saba:
Ratto della Pilleria 43, 34148 Trieste.
✆ 040826202.
Open Tue–Sun 9 A.M.–6:30 P.M.]

The Marches ■

The presence of Jews in the Marches dates from as early as the twelfth century. The community developed especially after the expulsions of Jews from Spain, Sicily, and the Kingdom of Naples. There are still remains of Jewish streets and synagogues in a number of small towns in this region bordering the Adriatic coast. This area is off the beaten tourist path and very picturesque. The Jews were constrained by papal bulls in 1555 and 1569 to live in four cities: Ancona, Urbino, Pesaro, and Senigallia. An intense Jewish life was maintained in these cities until the nineteenth century and their synagogues are worth visiting.

Pesaro

Documents attest to a Jewish presence in Pesaro dating back to 1214. The expulsion of the Jews from the Papal States in 1569 led numerous Jewish families to Pesaro, which became the most important center of Jewish life in the Duchy of Urbino. The annexation of the Duchy by the Pope radically changed the Jews' situation. Three years later, in 1634, 500 Jews were forced to move into a ghetto. After the departure of Napoleon's troops in 1797, the ghetto and its two synagogues were pillaged

Pesaro occupies a special place in the history of Jewish printing. In 1507, Gershom Soncino opened his print shop and worked without interruption until 1520, printing among other things a complete Bible, twenty treatises on the **Talmud**, and the *Arukh* by Nathan ben Yehiel from Rome.

■ Only the **Sephardic** synagogue dating from the second half of the sixteenth century remains. It has been absorbed into a large edifice that opens onto the street of the Grand Ghetto, the present-day Via Sarah Levi Nathan. The building houses the schools of the **Sephardic** community, including a **yeshiva** and a school of sacred music. One can still see the **mikvah**, the oven used for baking unleavened bread, and a well. The prayer hall is surrounded by high windows. On the left side of the *tevah* is a painting of the Temple of Jerusalem; on the right is a painting of the encampment of the Jews at the foot of Mount Sinai. The carved, gilt wood *aron* was moved to the synagogue of Livorno, the *tevah* is now in Ancona's synagogue, and the grilles that separated the women's gallery are now in the synagogue of Talpiot in Jerusalem. The vaulted ceiling has been restored.

[Synagogue: Via delle Scole, 61100 Pesaro. ✆ 072167815. Please call for information on scheduling a visit.]

Paolo Uccello, The Legend of the Profanation of the Host, 1465–69. Galleria Nazionale delle Marche, Urbino.

Urbino

The first traces of a Jewish presence in Urbino date to the fourteenth century, when Daniel of Viterbo received authorization to work as banker and merchant. The Jewish community prospered under the liberal regime of Duke Federigo da Montrefeltro (1444–82), who was interested in Jewish culture and collected Hebrew manuscripts. This situation changed when the duchy came under the authority of the Della Rovere family in 1508 and was subsequently incorporated into the Papal States in 1631. Its ghetto had been established in 1570. In the eighteenth century, the community became considerably poorer. The arrival of Napoleon's armies brought Jews their freedom, but the troops' departure was followed in 1798 by anti-Jewish demonstrations.

The discrimination disappeared only in 1861 with the incorporation into the kingdom of Italy.

■ The synagogue is located in the former ghetto. It dates from 1633–34 and was restored in 1848. The prayer hall is located on the second floor of this edifice. The decorated *aron kodesh* and the *tevah* face each other and are well preserved. The furnishings and the prayer books are still in evidence.

[Synagogue: Via Stretta, 61029 Urbino. To visit, contact the Urbino tourist office, or the Moscati family: ✆ 07224767 or 071202638.]

■ The famous six-panel series *The Legend of the Profanation of the Host* painted in 1465–69 by Paolo Uccelo is located at the National Gallery of the Marches (Galleria Nazionale delle Marche). It depicts a Christian woman bringing a communion wafer to a Jewish moneylender as guarantee on her loan, only to have him throw it into the flames. The blood dripping from the host informs the population about the sacrilege. The woman is

condemned to be hanged, but pardoned at the last moment, while the Jewish moneylender and his entire family are burned at the stake.

Senigallia

The history of the Jews in Senigallia is similar to that of the Jews of Urbino or Pesaro. In the eighteenth century, the Jews numbered 600 of a total population of approximately 5,500 inhabitants. When French troops withdrew, the populace sacked the ghetto, killing thirteen Jews and forcing the others to flee to Ancona. In 1801, Pope Pius VII forced the Jews to return and rebuild their ghetto. As of 1969, only some thirty Jews remained in Senigallia.

■ The Italian-rite synagogue on Via Commercianti is no longer active. It was constructed at the time the ghetto was created in 1634, replacing the former synagogue found on Via Arsilli outside the Jewish perimeter. The prayer hall is located on the second floor. It still has its furnishings, which were remade after the ghetto's sacking, including the gilt *aron* and the *tevah* surrounded by a semicircular balustrade standing opposite it. The pews are still in place as well as the placards with the names of the community members when it was still functioning.

[Synagogue: Via Commercianti 20, 60019 Senigallia. ✆ 3357611247. Visits by appointment.]

Ancona

The Jews first arrived in Ancona around 1000 c.e. In the fourteenth century, the city hosted a significant Jewish community, whose activities were organized around the port and commerce with the Orient. In 1541, Pope Paul III encouraged Jews expelled from Naples and, in 1547, even the Marranos from Portugal to settle in Ancona, granting them protection from the Inquisition. A

hundred or so Marrano families took advantage of the Pope's offer. However, the 1555 papal edict *Cum Nimis Absurdum* was rigorously applied in Ancona. The Jews were confined within a ghetto and their commercial activity limited to trade in second-hand clothing. A papal emissary arrived to crack down on the Marranos. Some managed to flee to Pesaro or Ferrara. Twenty-five Jews were burned at the stake between April and May of 1555. This tragedy had a large and resounding effect on the Jewish world. At the request of Dona Gracia Nassi, the great Turkish sultan intervened several times. The Jews of the Levant threatened to boycott the port of Ancona and transfer their business to Pesaro. This movement failed mainly due to rabbinical authorities' fear of provoking the Pope to take even harsher measures. Finally, when the Popes expelled the Jews from papal lands in 1569 and 1593, the Jews were allowed to remain in Ancona. The community never recovered its previous prosperity, but through its relations with the rest of the Jewish world, it continued to attract rabbis and men of letters. Napoleon's troops abolished the ghetto and the discriminatory policies against the Jews, but after Napoleon fell from power in 1814, the ghetto was reestablished as the city returned to the Papal States. The ghetto was opened up in 1831, but full equality was not obtained until 1861.

■ Via Astagno forms the ghetto's principal artery. The Levantine-rite synagogue at 12 Via Astagno was constructed following the initiative of Moses Basola in 1549. Destroyed in the nineteenth century, it was rebuilt in 1876. The large prayer hall on the second floor is still in use. The Baroque *aron* is decorated with marble columns and faces the *tevah,* which originally came from Pesaro. Elements of the original interior of the Italian synagogue demolished in 1932 are arranged on the first floor.

[Synagogue: Via Astagno 10, 60121 Ancona. ✆ 071202638. Call to visit.]

Southern Italy ■

The communities of the southern peninsula were the wealthiest and best integrated in all of Italy during the Middle Ages. This was particularly true of Sicily, where more than 37,000 Jews lived, including a large number in Palermo. This is as many as are living in all of Italy today. The world of the Jews living under the Spanish crown was swept away within a few years after the forced expulsion in 1492. No trace remains, except perhaps a few place-names, like Via Giudecca in the San Pietro quarter of Trapani in Sicily, and a few rare monuments.

San Nicandro

It was in San Nicandro that the first mass conversion to Judaism since the end of antiquity took place. All the converts emigrated to Israel shortly after 1948, so unfortunately there is nothing left in San Nicandro recalling this incredible story.

Trani

Also in the region of Apulia, the small port of Trani on the Adriatic coast possesses two synagogues, which have since been transformed into churches.

■ Heading up Via Giudea and past the Old Synagogue (Vicolo Sinagoga), one arrives at the church of the Scola Nova, whose name comes from the Hebrew. The small neighboring church of Santa Anna was also wrought from the walls of an old synagogue.

Central Europe

Austria

Austria's present borders cover only a small part of the former empire, once a major continental power of Central Europe and heir to the Holy Roman Empire. The empire was formed through an alliance with the kingdom of Hungary, becoming the imperial and royal "double monarchy" *(kaiserlich und königlich, or "k. und k.")*. This chapter covers present-day Austria and Vienna in particular, a city that until 1918 was the capital of an immense, multiethnic state governing regions such as Bohemia, Moravia, Hungary, Transylvania, Galicia, Bukovina, and the Balkans, each of which contained sizable Jewish populations. These communities had an increasing influence on the ethnic balance of the Empire, especially in regard to the intellectual and cultural life of the capital. After the fall of the Austro-Hungarian Empire, Jewish intellectuals like Joseph Roth, born in Brody (Galicia), developed a deep nostalgia toward the former monarchy, as illustrated in their works.

The first written reference to a Jewish presence in Austria goes back to the twelfth century, when, after the first Crusades, Jews fled persecution or were expelled from the cities of the Rhine valley.

Seitenstettengasse Synagogue, Vienna.

During that time Emperor Frederick II issued his famous Charter of Privileges, which granted wide autonomy to Vienna's Jewish community. In the late thirteenth and throughout the fourteenth centuries, this community evolved into the most prominent one in all the Germanic states, as much for demographic reasons as for its heightened influence. The sway of the "Sages of Vienna" spread well beyond the city limits and endured for several generations. Outstanding personalities of the era included Isaac ben Moses (also called Or Zarua after the title of his primary work), his son Hayyim ben Isaac Or Zarua, Avigdor ben Elijh ha-Cohen, and Meyer ben Baruch ha-Levi. In 1348 and 1349, a time of successive persecutions at the height of the Black Death, the Viennese community was not only spared but even served as a refuge for Jews from other regions who had been accused of poisoning fountains.

Beginning in the late fourteenth century, persecution of Jews multiplied throughout Austria. In 1406, following a synagogue fire, citizens attacked Jewish houses. Several years later, in the wake of a pogrom, many Jews were massacred, while others were expelled from Vienna and their children were forced to convert. After such persecution, only a small number of Jews continued to live in Vienna, totally illegally.

By 1512, only twelve Jewish families remained in Vienna, a situation that persisted throughout the sixteenth century. Emperor Rudolph II (1576–1612), however, authorized the settling of Jewish "noble" families, and a new community formed, with an early synagogue (which no longer exists) and a cemetery that can still be seen on the Seegasse (in the Ninth *Bezirk,* or district), whose oldest grave dates back to 1582.

Ritual object of the Levites, Slovakia, eighteenth century. Max Berger Collection, Vienna.

During the Thirty Years' War (1618–48), the Jews suffered greatly during Vienna's occupation by soldiers of the imperial army. In 1624, Emperor Ferdinand II ordered the Jewish community to live in a ghetto located in the Unter Werd, in today's Second *Bezirk*. The ghetto, which existed until 1670, was actually one of the privileges granted the Jewish community and corresponded to a proud era of flourish and expansion. Among the prominent rabbis of the time were Yom Tov Lipman Heller, a disciple of Rabbi Loew of Prague, and Shabbetai Sheftel Horowitz, a survivor of the Khmelnitsky massacres that ravaged Poland in 1648. Jewish communities began to form also in provinces such as Burgenland, Styria, and Lower Austria.

In the mid-seventeenth century, a wave of anti-Semitic hatred engulfed Vienna once more. The poorest Jews were expelled from the city, while others, dispossessed of their belongings, were ultimately forced out as well during the month of Av, 1670. The Grand Synagogue was transformed into a Catholic church. A handful of Jews converted to Christianity to avoid forced exile.

In 1693, Vienna, now in financial disarray, decided to readmit the Jews within its walls. Only the wealthiest were permitted to return, however, and then only under the status of "tolerated subjects" burdened by heavy taxes. Practice of their religion was authorized only in private homes.

The founders and prominent personalities of the community were thus rich, "courtly" Jews, such as Samuel Oppenheimer, Samson Wertheimer, and Baron Diego Aguilar. Thanks to their efforts, Vienna became during the eighteenth century the largest Jewish diplomatic and philanthropic center under the Hapsburg Empire. Starting in 1737, moreover, a **Sephardic** community established itself here and prospered from the increased trade with the Balkans.

Under Archduchess Maria Theresa (1717–80), Jews suffered especially restrictive legislation. Her son Joseph II, however, issued the Toleranzpatent (1782), which effectively paved the way for their eventual emancipation. In 1793, a Hebrew printing press set up shop in Vienna, rapidly becoming the most prominent one in Europe. The first signs of social assimilation in the community also emerged during this era.

When Galicia was absorbed after the first partition of Poland in 1772, Austria inherited a sizable Jewish community (250,000 Jewish subjects were living in Galicia at the turn of the nineteenth century; 800,000 by 1900) that often filled an intermediary social stratum between the Polish aristocracy and peasantry. With the annexation of Bukovina (ceded to Austria in 1775 by the Sublime

Porte), Jews helped spearhead the Germanization of that distant province and others, most notably Czernowitz.

As the nineteenth century progressed, Austria's Jewish community enjoyed increasing freedom, which culminated in 1849 with the granting, in theory, of equal rights to different faiths. In the latter half of that century, Vienna's Jewish population grew rapidly with the massive arrival of Jews from the empire's other regions, including Hungary, Galicia, and Bukovina. While only 6,217 Jews lived in Vienna in 1857 (2.16 percent of the population), their numbers had already reached 72,000 by 1880 (10 percent), and over 100,000 by the turn of the twentieth century, the majority of them settling in Leopoldstadt in the Second *Bezirk*.

Simultaneously, anti-Semitism, then considered merely one political opinion among others (one famous adherent, Vienna's mayor, Karl Lueger) had begun to spread as well. In 1826, a magnificent synagogue—the first legal one here since 1671—had opened. By the turn of the twentieth century, Vienna had some fifty-nine synagogues of various denominations, as well as a wide network of Jewish schools. By 1923, Vienna's Jewish community had grown to become the third largest in Europe, with many Jews starting to gain access to the liberal professions. The Jewish community had reached the height of its cultural influence. Jews had begun to shine in every artistic and scientific field. Great figures of the era included the composers Gustav Mahler, Arnold Schönberg, and Anton Webern and the writers Franz Werfel, Stefan Zweig, Arthur Schnitzler, Joseph Roth, and Karl Kraus. Sigmund Freud discovered the unconscious and founded psychoanalysis in Vienna, while many other Jewish scientists had begun to excel in their respective fields.

*Arthur Schnitzler,
1927.*

Vienna was also the cradle of Zionism. Perets Smolenskin published the first Zionist newspaper, *Ha-Shahar,* in 1868, while Nathan Birnbaum founded Kadimah, the first Jewish student association here in 1884.

Theodor Herzl set up the headquarters of the Zionist Executive in Vienna, but, before 1932, Zionists never made up a majority of the Jewish community. Only after the First World War did the movement begin to gain influence among Vienna's Jews.

With the empire's dissolution in 1918, Vienna became the oversized but still lively capital of a minuscule state that continued to draw its strength from the former eastern provinces, a phenomenon that also helped augment the city's Jewish population.

After the Anschluss in March 1938, Vienna found itself in the clutches of the Nazis. The discriminatory laws began appearing within a year and were enforced through merciless terror and mass arrests. On Kristallnacht (9 November 1938), forty-two synagogues were destroyed, while thousands of apartments were sacked by the SA and Hitler Youth, often to the indifference of the city's other inhabitants. Some of Vienna's Jews managed to emigrate before the war, but those too poor to escape to the west merely returned to their former provinces (such as Galicia), where they were later recaptured by the Nazis.

From the very onset of the Second World War, deportations to Poland began. Jews were first sent to the Nisko concentration camp in the Lublin district (October 1939). The final mass transport took place in September 1942, first to Theresienstadt (Terezín) and then, for the majority of deportees, to Auschwitz. In November 1942, Vienna's Jewish community was officially dissolved.

Immediately after the war, DP (displaced-person) camps were set up in Austria for Jews who had survived the Nazi camps, the majority of whom emigrated to Palestine and other countries. For many years Vienna's Jewish community did not, strictly speaking, regenerate, faced with the latent anti-Semitism of Austrian society that was encouraged by mean-spirited allusions from certain politicians.

As the capital of a neutral state, Vienna became a stopping point in the 1970s for Soviet Jews emigrating from Russia, who were expected to continue their journey toward Israel or the United States. A number of them wound up staying, however. They can be seen in particular practicing various trades near the Mexicoplatz not far from the Prater (in the Second *Bezirk*), breathing life into the city's new Jewish community. In the year 2000, Vienna's Jews numbered 9,000.

→ **To call Austria from the United States, dial 011 43** followed by the number of the person you are calling.

Lower and Upper Austria ■

Vienna

The history of Vienna's Jewish community can be divided into several distinct periods, with the community itself settling in two specific neighborhoods: in a section of the city center in the First *Bezirk* and in Leopoldstadt in the Second *Bezirk*.

In the Middle Ages, the first Jewish community in Vienna established itself in what came to be known as the "Judenstadt" in the heart of the city not far from the cathedral, inside a perimeter roughly delimited by present-day Seitenstettengasse, Hoher Markt, Jordangasse, and Judenplatz. The Gothic-style synagogue, similar to the Altneuschul in Prague, was first mentioned in 1294 as the Schulhof, named after the spot on which it was built (now the Judenplatz) in immediate proximity to the

Court. In addition to the Judenplatz, there is nearby a different square called Schulhof, bordered by a Gothic church resembling the former synagogue and perhaps an exact replica of it, designed after its destruction in 1421. Between 1360 and 1400 the Jewish community ranged from 800 to 900 people, representing 5 percent of Vienna's total population. In 1421, however, they were all either expelled or forced to convert.

In 1624, the Jews were granted a new neighborhood, the Unter Werd, located along Taborstrasse in present-day Leopoldstadt, on the other side of the Danube. A new synagogue was built there; Leopoldskirche church stands on the site today. The Unter Werd ghetto, which included 132 houses, offered the Jews a certain amount of protection until it was destroyed and its residents exiled in 1670.

Beginning in 1782, with Joseph II's edict of tolerance, Jews settled in Vienna once more. In 1826, a new synagogue by architect Josef Kornhäusl was built on Seitenstettengasse, marking the community's effective return to its historical center of Jewish life of the Middle Ages. In 1858 another synagogue, the Leopoldstädter Temple, was built across the Danube not far from the former Unter Werd ghetto. This attracted Jewish settlers to the district, later called Mazzesinsel, or "Matzoh Island." Since the 1980s and 1990s, the Jewish community has once again concentrated its activity in these two neighborhoods.

In the city center, the Jewish Museum, Judenplatz Museum, and the synagogue are all well worth a visit (a single ticket allows access to all three in one day).

THE JEWISH MUSEUM

■ Vienna, site of the world's first Jewish museum in 1897, opened the current one in 1990. This museum, whose purpose is to act as a link between Jews and non-Jews, also serves as a window on the rich but lost world of Viennese Judaism. The first floor houses two permanent exhibitions. The first displays objects of Jewish liturgical life, while the second—the creation of New York artist Nancy Spero—illustrates Vienna's Jewish history. The second floor is for temporary exhibits, and the third provides a retrospective on Jewish life in Austria through twenty-one paintings. The fourth floor, in a room called the Schaudepot, "depot expo," is given over to hundreds of religious objects recovered after Kristallnacht. It resembles the back room of an antique shop.

[Jewish Museum of Vienna: Dorotheergasse 11, 1010 Vienna. ✆ 015350431 ext. 210. Open Sun–Wed and Fri 10 A.M.–6 P.M., Thu 10 A.M.–8 P.M.]

The library here tops those of all other Jewish museums in Europe. It preserves 25,000 volumes in German, Hebrew, **Yiddish,** and English.

[Library: Seitenstettengasse 4, 1010 Vienna. ✆ 015350431 ext. 410. Open Mon–Thu 10 A.M.–4 P.M.]

Located at the museum entrance is a bookstore well stocked in catalogues and texts (in German). On the same floor, Teitelbaum Café, among the city's best, serves Austrian **kosher** wines, Viennese pastries, and vegetarian dishes.

JUDENPLATZ

■ A monument by London artist Rachel Whiteread commemorating Austrian Jews exterminated during the *Shoah* was placed in the Judenplatz (former Schulhof) in October 2000. The piece consists of a square, closed room, the outer walls of which support shelves loaded with books.

■ The Judenplatz Museum in the Misrachi House is located behind the monument and has also been

In the Synagogue, *circa 1900. Max Berger Collection, Vienna.*

open since 2000. Its focus is the Jewish quarter of the Middle Ages, particularly the founding of the medieval Gothic synagogue (Or Zarua), rediscovered in 1995 during an archaeological dig. Two videos and computer-animated displays provide information about medieval Jewish life. At the museum entrance, a room equipped with computers allows visitors to look up the names of 65,000 victims of the *Shoah.*

[Judenplatz Museum: Judenplatz 8, 1010 Vienna. ✆ 015350431 ext. 310. Open Sun–Thu 10 A.M.–6 P.M., Fri 10 A.M.–2 P.M.]

■ The Stadttempel, Vienna's synagogue of 1826 by architect Josef Kornhäusl, was the only temple that avoided destruction during Kristallnacht. Kornhäusl, highly respected in his time, specialized in theaters; not surprisingly, then, the Stadttempel was designed like a small theater or Italian-style Baroque opera house, with a circular shape, a stage, three balconies, wings, and a foyer. It lacks only dressing rooms and ushers.

[Stadttempel: Seinstettengasse 4, 1010 Vienna. ✆ 01532040. Guided tours Mon–Thu at 11:30 A.M. and 3 P.M.]

■ The Judengasse, a little street linking the Seitenstettengasse to the Hoher Markt, was a main street

LOWER AND UPPER AUSTRIA

through the Jewish quarter of the Middle Ages, as its name indicates.

■ For a deeper understanding of old Jewish Vienna, you need only stroll through Leopoldstadt, an island in the Danube that was, in former days, so populated with Jews it was called Matzoh Island. Here and there along its streets, you will come across plaques marking former Jewish-community establishments.

■ The Leopoldstädter Tempel stood on the street still bearing the name Tempelgasse, at number 5. A plaque and four large columns by architect Martin Kohlbauer evoke the former synagogue. In its place today is the ESRA, a center dedicated to counseling the victims and witnesses of the *Shoah* and racism.

[ESRA: Tempelgasse 5, 1020 Vienna.

✆ 0121490140.]

■ At number 7 on the same street sits the Sephardic Center, which brings together associations of Jews from Bukhara, Georgia, and their respective synagogues.

[Sephardic Center: Tempelgasse 7, 1020 Vienna. ✆ 2162216 or 06643025840.]

■ Before the war the Turkish Temple, for the Jewish community from the Ottoman Empire, resided on Zirkusgasse (Circus Street). Built in 1885 in Moorish style, it was destroyed in 1938. Residential housing was built in its place in the 1950s. A strange

Tempelgasse Synagogue, 1858. Historiches Museum, Vienna.

plaque declares: *"Gesunde Wohnungen, glückliche Menschen"* (clean apartments, happy people), while another, smaller one, hidden beneath a balcony, notes: "The Turkish Synagogue was located here."

■ The Orthodox temple Polnische Schul, constructed with three naves, stood at 29 Leopoldgasse but was also destroyed on 9 November 1938.

FAMOUS ADDRESSES

It is not possible to fully grasp Jewish Vienna without stopping by the haunts of the major Jewish intellectuals who helped make Vienna one of Europe's most modern capitals at the turn of the twentieth century. These figures include Sigmund Freud, of course, as well as Arnold Schönberg, Joseph Roth, and Martin Buber.

■ The address 19 Berggasse is legendary. This was Freud's house, a spot of cult interest for all those fascinated by the history of psychoanalysis. While the furniture is original, his famous couch was moved to London when he emigrated there in 1938, a year before his death. Freud's house features a museum, the headquarters of the Sigmund-Freud-Gesellschaft, a library, and archives.

[Sigmund Freud Museum: Berggasse 19, 1090 Vienna. ✆ 013191596. Open daily 9 A.M.–5 P.M.]

■ Born in 1874, Arnold Schönberg founded the Vienna School along with Alban Berg and Anton Webern;

he was a composer of twelve-tone music. After converting to Protestantism in 1898 (just as Mahler had converted to Catholicism, the "entry ticket to European culture"), he returned to the Jewish faith in 1933 in Paris, with Marc Chagall as his witness. He then emigrated to the United States, where he died in 1951, aware that he would gain true recognition only after his death. The Arnold Schönberg Center opened in 1998, and it preserves manuscripts, scores, correspondence, and archives that are available for examination.

[Arnold Schönberg's birth house:
Obere Donaustrasse 5, Second *Bezirk*.
✆ 022364222323. Fri 9 A.M.–5 P.M.]
[Arnold Schönberg Center: Palais Fanto,
Schwarzenbergplatz 6 (entrance at
1-3 Zaunergasse), 1030 Vienna.
✆ 01712188830.
Open Mon–Fri 9 A.M.–6 P.M.]

■ Founder of the "philosophy of dialogue," Martin Buber was born in Vienna in 1878. Although he spent his childhood in Galicia, he later returned to Vienna. He died in Jerusalem in 1965.

[Martin Buber's House:
Franz-Josefs Kai 45, First *Bezirk*.
For further information on Martin Buber
contact ✆ 0049625293120.]

■ On Rembrandtstrasse sits the house where Joseph Roth lived. Born in Brody, Galicia, in 1894, Roth completed his studies in Lemberg (Lvov) and Vienna. The collapse of the Austro-Hungarian Empire was highly traumatic for him. His work blends social criticism with transfiguration of the Austrian monarchy. Novels that made him famous include *Job, the Story of a Simple Man* (1930), *The Radetzky March* (1932), and *The Emperor's Tomb* (1938). He died in exile in Paris in 1939.

[Joseph Roth's House:
Rembrandtstrasse 35, door 5,
Second *Bezirk*.]

Mauthausen

Twenty countries have participated in events commemorating the murder of 150,000 people here during the Second World War, one-third of whom were Jewish. Mauthausen was classified by the SS administration as a "Category 3" camp; this category of camp corresponded to the harshest possible treatment. The prisoners sent here were designated "return undesirable" and destined for "extermination through work." All activities in the camp gravitated around the stone quarry and the construction of tunnels in the infamous adjoining camps of Gusen, Melk, and Ebensee. The Mauthausen camp was liberated on 5 May 1945 by the American Eleventh Armored Division. A memorial ceremony takes place every year on that date.

Burgenland ■

Eisenstadt

The region's sovereigns, the Ester-házy dukes of Hungary, granted the Jews special protection within the seven districts of Burgenland. Since 1670, the region has been one of the most important Jewish cultural centers of central Europe. Schedule half a day to visit Eisenstadt, the capital of Burgenland.

A tour of the Austrian Jewish Museum recalling this region's highly unusual history is not to be missed.

Slovenia

A SLAVIC LAND UNDER GERMANIC RULE FOR MANY CENTURIES, Slovenia finally gained independence in 1991. The fate of the Jewish population here depended largely over the years on the good will of its princes. Nonetheless, the Jewish presence in the region goes back to antiquity. Archaeological digs have revealed a tomb engraved with a **menorah** at the Skocjan site, which likely dates back to the fifth century C.E. Traces in the region then disappear until the twelfth century, with documents that mention the arrival of immigrants from Central Europe and Italy. It is also known that a community prospered in Styria, where Jews owned vineyards and mills. At the time, Jews could be found living in ghettos in and around ten cities or localities, including Maribor, Piran, and the current capital of Ljubljana.

At the end of the fifteenth century, however, the Hapsburgs exiled the Jews, first from Styria and Carinthia and later from Ljubljana, confining them to a rural setting. In 1718, moreover, Emperor Charles VI ordered their complete expulsion. At the end of the eighteenth century, small communities began to reestablish themselves in the extreme

Tower and synagogue, Maribor.

northeast of the country, then under Hungarian domination: Jewish life began flourishing to an extent in or around Murska Sobota, Beltinci, and Lendava. The brief "Illyrian Provinces" interlude under Napoleonic domination, from 1808 to 1814, was not enough to convince a great number of Jews to return to the country. And in 1817, the Hapsburgs forbade them to settle in Carniola, the central region of present-day Slovenia. The total emancipation of the Jews in 1867 by the Austro-Hungarian Empire had little effect in Slovenia: the anti-Semitism was so virulent in the region that any large-scale return was discouraged.

In 1940, present-day Slovenia contained a Jewish community of 1,500 people. Germany annexed the region directly into the Reich, sending more than 90 percent of its Jews to their deaths. Only a small minority managed to flee to the Italian-occupied territory or into the underground Resistance. Today, Slovenia's Jewish community consists of fewer than 100 people.

→ **To call Slovenia from the United States, dial 011 336** followed by the number of the person you are calling minus the initial 0 (used only for domestic calls).

Central and Northeast Slovenia ■

Ljubljana

The only remaining traces of a prior Jewish presence in Ljubljana are the names of two narrow streets in the city center, Street of the Jews (Zidovska ulica) and Passage of the Jews (Zidovska steza), the place of the medieval ghetto until the 1515 expulsion.

■ The remains of a neighborhood of about thirty houses have apparently been found beneath the Baroque buildings here, constructed in the seventeenth century atop the medieval foundations.

■ Additionally, a monument to the victims of the *Shoah* has been put up in a corner of the municipal cemetery.

[Jewish Community of Slovenia: Trzaska 2, 1000 Ljubljana. ✆ 0612521836, fax 0612521836. ♁ jss@siol.net.]

Maribor

The Jewish settlement in the medieval fortress of Maribor, near the Austrian border, dates back to at least the thirteenth century. This Jewish community must have been rather prosperous, for in the fifteenth century several Catholic families of the city asked to convert to Judaism, a rare event certainly in Europe at the time.

After their expulsion by Austrian emperor Maximilian I, Maribor's Jews headed for Italy and Hungary. The Morpurgos, one of the most famous Jewish families in Trieste, Split, and even Gorizia, was among them: their name derives directly from Maribor, their city of origin.

■ The Regional Museum of Maribor features the tomb of the first rabbi known to have officiated in the city, a certain Abraham, who died in 1379.

[Regional Museum of Maribor:
Graeska 2, 200 Maribor. ✆ 022283551.
Open Tue–Fri 9 A.M.–5 P.M.,
Sat–Sun 10 A.M.–2 P.M.]

■ The former Jewish district, located in the southwest section of the old city near the outer walls, has its own Street of the Jews. A project is under way to restore a synagogue here. The building, whose dimensions measure 65 ft. by 39 ft., was converted into a church in the sixteenth century, following the expulsion. The only remnants today of its use as a synagogue are a wide recess for the Ark of the Covenant as well as a number of fragments bearing Hebrew inscriptions.

You will also find the "Jewish Tower" here, now a photo shop. Not far from the synagogue, it most likely owes its name to its role in defending the Jewish quarter during attacks against the city.

[The archaeological remains of both the Synagogue and tower are located on Zidovska Street in the old city.]

Murska Sobota

■ The Jewish cemetery of Murska Sobota no longer exists; it was demolished in the 1990s. The site features, however, a small monument erected in memory of the city's Jews murdered during the war.

Lendava

The Lendava city council is working to renovate the old synagogue, built in 1866, and turn it into a cultural center featuring a permanent exhibition on local Jewish history. Seriously damaged by the Germans during the war, the synagogue was later sold to the city by the Federation of Yugoslav Jewish Communities, which then used it as a warehouse. The former Jewish school, active until the 1920s, was located next to the synagogue.

[Synagogue: Spodjna ulica 5, Lendava.]

■ The Jewish cemetery, which dates back to the late nineteenth century, was renovated in 1989 after vandals damaged around 40 gravesites. In all, it contains 176 graves and features a memorial to the victims of the *Shoah* put up shortly after the war by survivors.

[The cemetery is located near the village of Dolga Vas, on the road leading toward the Hungarian border.]

Italian Border and Istria ■

Nova Gorica

Nova Gorica was divided between Italy and Slovenia after the Second World War.

■ It is on the Italian (Gorizia) side that one should look for major evidence of a past Jewish presence.

■ In the Slovenian section, however, there is a Jewish cemetery dating back to the fourteenth century. With one and a quarter acres of surface area, it contains nearly 900 gravestones, the oldest of which date to the seventeenth century, and they are still legible. The most recent tombstones date from the Second World War. The grave of the philosopher and painter Alberto Michelstädter, who died in 1929, is found here as well.

The cemetery has no caretaker, though it is apparently kept up regularly thanks to the gracious efforts of the Italian-Jewish community.

[The cemetery is located in the Rozna Dolina (Valley of Roses), several hundred yards from the main border passage point. Entry is free, and the gate is unlocked.]

Piran

Piran is a former possession of the City of Doges, which explains its Venetian atmosphere. It contains some beautiful architecture, including a replica of the Campanile in the Piazza San Marco.

■ This charming little coastal town has preserved its medieval ghetto square, Zidovski Trg, which can be entered through an arcade. The square is surrounded by several multistory houses that undeniably resemble those of the Venetian ghetto.

Croatia

JEWISH SETTLERS HAD TO WAIT until the death of Austria's Catholic and very anti-Semitic Arch-duchess Maria Theresa and the ascension of her more tolerant son, Joseph II, to gain the right to establish communities in northern Croatia, which at the time had been Hapsburg territory for nearly three centuries.

Except for the probable existence of a synagogue in Osijek (Roman Mursa) and a few rare references in documents between the twelfth and fifteenth centuries, a prior Jewish presence in the region was unremarkable. Before Joseph II's 1781 edict of tolerance, however, a few cities, like Križevci, Koprivnica, Bjelovar, and Osijek, did permit Jewish merchants to spend a maximum of three days here during fairs, but only in exchange for a hefty tax. Then, in 1688, the Austrian army deported 500 Jews from Belgrade to work as slaves in Osijek, which had just been taken back from the Turks. A few decades later, Jews were allowed to settle in certain cities temporarily in order to guarantee a good supply of garrisons.

It was not until 1867, the year the Jews achieved total emancipation under the Austro-Hungarian Empire, that their communities began to develop in

Jewish tombstones embedded in the outer wall of the city, Dubrovnik.

Hungary, of which northern Croatia formed an integral part at the time. Croatian Jews numbered 13,500 in 1880, and reached 20,000 by 1900, the vast majority of them **Ashkenazic**. Jewish fathers devoted to intellectual and commercial pursuits were succeeded by sons who were lawyers, doctors, and journalists. For these younger generations, moreover, Croatian had quickly become a maternal language.

After the First World War, the country was absorbed into the Serbian kingdom. This change, coupled with an upsurge in anti-Semitism fueled by local nationalism and right-wing extremism, made assimilation more difficult. Zionists took control of the community's major institutions, while a segment of the Jewish youth was drawn to the underground Communist movement.

When Germany invaded Yugoslavia in April 1941, it installed an independent puppet government in Zagreb led by Fascist nationalist president Ante Pavelic. Soon after, the Ustashis, German army auxiliaries living throughout the Yugoslavian territory, attacked the Jewish community, seizing property, executing or sending residents to concentration camps (most notably in Jasenovac)—all with the aim of effecting a Final Solution. In the spring of 1943, Croatia's concentration camps were emptied of their Jewish prisoners, who were soon exterminated in Auschwitz. The Roman Catholic Church managed to spare a few hundred Jews married to Christians; others fled to the Italian-occupied zone, while a few hundred more joined the ranks of the Resistance. At the time of the liberation, over 80 percent of the 25,000 Jews living in Croatia in 1941 had been killed. Meanwhile, half the survivors quickly emigrated to Israel. The country's Jewish community, though still active, consists today of fewer than 2,000 members, half whom live in Zagreb.

→ **To call Croatia from the United States, dial 011 385** followed by the number of the person you are calling minus the initial 0 (used only for domestic calls).

Zagreb and Surrounding Areas ■

Zagreb

Built at the turn of the twentieth century by architect Franjo Klein, the Grand Šynagogue of Zagreb was entirely destroyed in 1941 along with Croatia's approximately thirty other active synagogues.

■ Today, a far more modest establishment, located on the same site as the Jewish Community Center headquarters serves as a place of worship. Besides a collection of religious artifacts, the community's offices also house one of the largest Jewish libraries in the Balkans, which has collected over 20,000 volumes, some of which date back to the fifteenth century.

[Jewish Community Center: Palmoticava 16, 10000 Zagreb. ✆ 01434619, fax 014922692 or 014922693.]

■ Built 120 years ago on the city's north side, the Mirogoj cemetery

rivals the most beautiful in Europe. Its sizable Jewish section has the unique quality of featuring Christian and non-Christian tombs side by side. Over time many Jewish graves were sold to Christians after their leases expired due to the disappearance of entire families during the war, and this accounts for the unusual arrangement. Also remarkable are the burial stelae of local upper-middle-class families, including those belonging to the Deutsch-Maceljskis, the Alexanders, the Priesters, and the Ehrlichs. The Jewish area begins immediately to the right of the main entrance, and at the back of the cemetery, there is a monument depicting Moses holding the Ark of the Law in commemoration of the *Shoah*.

[The Mirogoj cemetery is located on Grobna Avenue, on the north side of the city. Open daily from sunrise to sunset. To get there, take the bus from in front of the cathedral.]

Karlovac

Synagogue, Zagreb, 1867

Karlovac counted around 500 Jews before the war.

■ Karlovac's Jewish cemetery has been the recent target of Fascist vandals, who have painted swastikas and slogans glorifying the Ustashi regime. It contains around 200 graves.

[The cemetery is located at Velika Svarca, near the Military Cemetery.]

Slavonia ■

Varaždin

■ The synagogue, which dates back to 1862, has since been turned into a movie theater.

■ The city also includes a neglected Jewish cemetery dating back to 1810.

[The cemetery is located on the main road to Koprivnica.]

Osijek

In 1847, fifty or so families helped found the community in Osijek, Slavonia's main city. A school and synagogue were quickly built, presided over by Rabbi Samuel Spitzer, author of religious, cultural, and historical books. His son, Hugo Spitzer, became a pioneer of Zionism in Yugoslavia at the turn of the twentieth century.

The community consisted of 2,600 members in 1940, 90 percent of whom were killed in the Jasenovac, Djakovo, and Loborgrad camps in Croatia, as well as in Auschwitz.

■ At the headquarters of the city's small Jewish community, a museum houses the remains of objects rescued from the main synagogue, destroyed during the war.

[Community Headquarters and Museum: brace Radica 13, 31000 Osijek. ✆ 031211407.]

■ In Osijek's main square, there is a monument dedicated to the victims of the *Shoah*.

Djakovo

■ Created in 1879, the Jewish cemetery in Djakovo possesses the unique feature of containing individual burial sites for victims of the *Shoah*. A total of 566 Jewish victims of Djakovo's Ustashi concentration camp, murdered in 1942, are interred here. A collective monument has been erected as well.

[The cemetery is located on the ulica Vatroslava Doneganija near the central municipal cemetery.]

■ The illuminated registry of the burial society *(Hevra Kadisha)* of Djakovo, which dates back to 1860, is preserved in the Jewish Historical Museum of Belgrade (see page 488).

Istria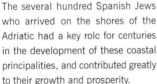

Rijeka

The **Ashkenazic** synagogue, built in the nineteenth century after a design by Hungarian architect Lipot Baumhorn, was destroyed in 1944. ■ The **Sephardic** synagogue, built in 1928, is still used by the city's Jewish residents. The community today consists of around a hundred members, as compared to the nearly 2,000 it numbered before the war.

[Community and Synagogue: ulica Ivana Filipova 9, 51000 Rijeka. Contact Mr. and Mrs. Vlado Biba, heads of the community: ✆ 051336032.

Dalmatian Coast ■

The several hundred Spanish Jews who arrived on the shores of the Adriatic had a key role for centuries in the development of these coastal principalities, and contributed greatly to their growth and prosperity.

Exploiting their relationships with fellow Jewish settlers in Venice and Constantinople, the Jews of Dalmatia provided an invaluable service to the small cities of the region; pressed up against the mountains, these towns managed to survive thanks only to the delicate interplay between the Ottoman Empire and the City of Doges. Keeping to their own districts but rarely subject to containment within ghettos, the Jews nevertheless warmly greeted the early effects of the French Revolution, or rather its Napoleonic extension. A decree issued by France's Marshal Marmont, duke of Raguse (Dubrovnik) on 22 June 1808 guaranteed them the same rights as other citizens.

When Austria took possession of the territories in 1814, it immediately revoked such progressive legislation. Not long afterward, however, Jews won complete emancipation.

The region saw a clear decline over the course of the nineteenth century, due to the enclosed nature of its location and the spiraling breakdown of the neighboring Ottoman Empire. The local Jewish community, already losing its numbers, maintained its meager presence by virtue only of the influx of fellow Jews from Turkish Bosnia, who were escaping an even less enviable economic situation.

REVERSAL OF FORTUNE

Moshe Maralio made the best of his bad luck when the archbishop of Dubrovnik refused him the post of head doctor in the local government. For this Italian Jew, who had emigrated from Barletta in 1494, what mattered was keeping his private practice afloat, for he already enjoyed the respect of both the whole city and beyond: Turkish dignitaries from surrounding Bosnia regularly requested his services. Unfortunately, Maralio fell victim to the rare allegation of having committed a "ritualistic crime," an accusation sometimes leveled against the Jews of the Dalmatian coast. His trial and that of nine fellow Jews, as pieced together from Dubrovnik's archives, took place 5–11 August 1502. Indicted for having torn out an old woman's heart, half the defendants were tortured to death and the rest burned alive, despite the seeming utter lack of proof.

During the Second World War, Dalmatia served as a temporary refuge for Jews persecuted elsewhere in Yugoslavia. Mussolini had convinced Hitler to yield him the coast, given that two of its cities, Rijeka (Fiume) and Zadar, had already been under Italy's control since the end of the First World War. When the Italian government surrendered in September 1943, the German army rushed to the coast and hunted down all remaining Jews. One segment of the community, however, managed to find shelter in the zones liberated by Yugoslavian partisans. A Jewish battalion even succeeded in forming on the island of Rab, where the Italians had interned some of the community's members. Generally speaking, the Yugoslavian Jews who were able to escape the Ustashis and the Nazis took an active part in the Resistance, providing Tito's troops the bulk of their health service.

Split

Archaeologists have recently unearthed traces of a Jewish presence in Salona (Solin), capital of Roman Dalmatia and sister city to Split, that dates as far back as the first centuries C.E. Salona was destroyed in the seventh century, and its survivors, some of whom were Jewish, took refuge behind the solid walls of Emperor Diocletian's palace, the origin of present-day Split. Substantial evidence suggests that a synagogue was soon built in the southern section of the new city. In fact, until the sixteenth century, this section of the city was called "The Synagogue" by its inhabitants. Trace of it disappears during the Middle Ages, as Dalmatia's Jewish communities are rarely mentioned in surviving texts, but when they are they are referred to as *zueca*, a term used to designate areas occupied by tanners and dyers.

With the arrival of Jews from Spain and Portugal in the sixteenth century, Judaism in the region began expanding rapidly. One Spanish Jew, Daniel Rodriga (a name derived from the Spanish "Rodriguez"), played an essential part in the city's evolution. He set in motion a number of development projects, including a *lazareth* (infirmary), and managed to convince his contemporaries to favor the land route across the mountains, which was far safer than navigating south of Split toward Turkey and the rest of Asia. His talents were recognized by the Republic of Venice, which in turn sought to raise the status of the city's Jewish community. Jews were even allowed to engage in the food industry, which was forbidden everywhere else in Europe at the time.

Although Split's Jews throughout the ages made up only 2 to 3 percent of the local population, they did not hesitate to prove their loyalty to the city in the wars against the Turks. During the Turkish siege of 1657, Jews distinguished themselves by successfully defending Fort Arniro, the northwest wing of Diocletian's palace, from then on called the "Jewish Fort."

On the eve of the Second World War, the Jewish community of Split consisted of around 300 members. Half of them were killed, either through deportation or in combat against occupying forces.

■ The synagogue, which was completely ravaged by the Ustashis in 1942, is located in a building that also serves as headquarters to the small Jewish community. It sits in the city center on a tiny little street, or passage, near the People's Square (Narodny Trg).

[Community of Split: Zidovki prilaz 1 ("Jewish Alley"), 21000 Split. ✆ and fax 021345672. Starting from Narodny Trg, take Bosanska Street several dozen yards and turn right down the alleyway.]

■ In the People's Square you will notice the Morpurgo bookstore. First opened in 1860, the shop features a plaque in memory of its founder, Vid Morpurgo (1834–1911), whose life marked Split in the nineteenth century.

Vid (Vita) Morpurgo is best known for his participation in Croatia's growing national movement. He also established Split's first lending library, founded a bank, and was soon invited to preside over the local chamber of commerce.

[Morpurgo Bookstore: Narodny Trg 16, 21000 Split. ✆ 021346843. Open Sun–Fri 8 A.M.–8 P.M., Sat 8 A.M.–1 P.M.]

■ Built in 1578, Split's Jewish cemetery sits on the slopes of Mount Marjan in an ideal setting. In magnificent surroundings, it contains over 200 tombs, many gravestones of which remain legible; the most recent ones are written in Italian. The names of some of the region's famous *ponentini* (Venetian "western" Jews) can be observed here, such as

Synagogue, Split.

the Tolentino and Camerici families, and even the grave of a certain medical doctor, Raffael Valenzin, who died in 1878 at the age of thirty. It is also on Mount Marjan that Vid Morpugo is buried. The most recent graves date from the start of the Second World War. The cemetery entrance is located beside a house that once functioned as a **mikvah,** transformed today into a café.

Dubrovnik

The earliest refugees from the Iberian Peninsula arrived in Ragusa (present-day Dubrovnik) at the end of the fifteenth century, at a time when the republic, still under nominal supervision by Hungary for a few more decades, had reached its apex.

The early years were tumultuous: forced exile in 1515 was followed by a return several years later. With reinforcements of fellow Jews coming in through Greece and Albania, the city's small Jewish community would be recognized in 1538 as *Univeritas Haebroru* or *Università degli Ebrei* (Hebrew University), since Ragusa's education leaders used Latin as much as Italian as an official language. Doctor Amatus Lusitanus, of Portuguese origin (as his name suggests), wrote seven books during this time describing the 700 illnesses he had treated.

The ghetto was created several years later, in 1546, on Zudioska Street, enclosed by gates at both ends. A 1745 census reveals, however, that 78 people were living in the ghetto's nineteen houses while 103 others were permitted to live outside. During this period, moreover, Jews earned a status near that of the rest of their fellow citizens, as proven by their passports: the passports were printed in Italian for voyages across the Mediterranean and in Serbian for trips toward the Ottoman lands.

The size of the Jewish community remained steady until the Second World War, when more than 1,000 Jews from Yugoslavia and other countries under the Reich's domination flooded into the Italian zone. Soon transferred to internment camps on the islands off the coast, several hundred Jewish prisoners managed to escape before the Italian debacle in September 1943 and the region's subsequent seizure by German troops.

Only a few dozen people of Jewish origin still live in Dubrovnik, where the presence of tourists is often necessary to form a **minyan** at the synagogue.

THE SYNAGOGUE

The three-story building, whose origins date to the fourteenth century, has served as a house of worship since 1408. In fact, it is one of the oldest **Sephardic** sites in the world. It can be distinguished from the other houses on Zudioska Street only by its slightly larger second-story windows with their traditional Arabic trim. In the seventeenth century, the synagogue benefited from passageways through the other houses on the block, which allowed ghetto dwellers to come and go without breaking curfew.

Among the religious artifacts that managed to remain hidden during the war are three scrolls of the **Torah** dating back to the first **Sephardic** immigration. A little under 24 inches wide, their outer layers are made from linen and rolled lengthwise, knotted in a particular way called "Ragusa point." The scrolls also bear the names of their likely donors: the Terni, Maestro, and Russi families. A silk, cotton-padded bedspread of undeniably Iberian origin is also on display at the synagogue.

Seriously damaged by a Serbian bombardment during the 1992-95 war, the synagogue has since been restored.

[Synagogue and Community Center: Zudioska ulica 3, 20000 Dubrovnik.]

THE CEMETERY

The current cemetery dates to only the nineteenth century. In 1911, however, every grave from the old Jewish cemetery, including those from the early sixteenth century, was transferred here. Unfortunately, during the First World War, most of the gravestones were used to reinforce the citadel walls, and only thirty of them remain today.

Some are flat and rectangular in classic **Sephardic** style, with Hebrew inscriptions and pseudo-heraldic decorations (coats of arms, crowns, and fleurs de lys), of obvious Italian influence. Others are more eastern-inspired and feature images of the sun, moon, or stars. The remaining ones are obelisk-shaped and reminiscent of the Austro-Hungarian period, their Hebrew inscriptions proving to be their only distinctively Jewish aspect.

[The cemetery is located in the Boninovo area, just beyond the ramparts.]

Hungary

AT THE JEWISH MUSEUM OF BUDAPEST, a replica of a tombstone dating from the third century bears the image of a **menorah**. This relic attests to nearly 1,700 years of Jewish presence in the Carpathian basin, predating that of the Magyar tribes who broke free from the confines of the Ural Mountains during the ninth century. The modern history of Judaism in Hungary goes all the way back to settlement by Bohemian, Moravian, and German Jews here during the eleventh century. Under Ottoman occupation (1526–1686), tens of thousands of **Sephardic** Jews from Spain took refuge within the empire's borders. The country was then taken back in 1686 by the Hapsburgs, unleashing a wave of pogroms. Considered as collaborators with the forces of Ottoman occupation, Jews were either massacred or expelled. They did not return until the late eighteenth century, encouraged by Joseph II's policy of tolerance. From that point until the twentieth century, two distinct Jewish communities coexisted in Hungary. One, of Moravian and German origin, settled in both the country's western regions and in Budapest; the other, made up mostly by **Hasidism,** settled in the Northeast.

Hungarian Jews, late nineteenth century.

In 1840, Jews in Hungary became the first to enjoy freedom of trade within the Hapsburg Empire. The nation counted around 340,000 Jews at the time, many of whom enlisted in the army during the war of independence from Austria in 1848 and 1849.

The 1860s saw the rapid development of the city of Pest, where Jews had a significant presence. Meanwhile, the community's poorest members were leaving their villages for the city to earn a living.

A sort of tacit "social contract" was developing: the Magyar nobility restricted itself to administrative and political careers, gladly leaving the industrial and financial spheres to the Jews, who possessed both capital and know-how. With the passage of the 1867 law of emancipation, Jews were granted full civil rights. They were called upon in exchange to assimilate and "Magyarize"—the Hungarian language defining nationality at the time. But as François Fejtö has pointed out in his work *Hongrois et juifs: histoire millénaire d'un couple singulier* (Hungarians and Jews: 1,000-Year-old History of a Singular Couple [Paris: Balland, 1997]): "The historical Magyar class had another reason to grant Jews civil rights. This was their desire to reinforce the weight of Magyar speakers in a country where Hungarians . . . held only a weak majority of 51.4 percent at the turn of the century, and this thanks to the support of assimilated Jews and Germans. Thus the Jews' choice of language took on special meaning, causing the demographic balance to tilt toward the Magyar side," a fact of primary importance, for the Magyar kingdom faced an upsurge in nationalism by other minority groups living under its control.

Despite the 1870 schism between the progressive Neolog Jews and the Orthodox community, the turn of the twentieth century marked a golden age of assimilation. In 1900, 72 percent of Jews were listed as Magyars. In 1910, Jews numbered 203,000 in Budapest—not including converts—or 23 percent of the city's population, while in Vienna and Prague they made up respectively only 8 percent and 5 percent of the population.

Between the wars, they represented only 6 percent of the population, though half of all merchants, manufacturers, and bankers were Jewish. In 1940, Jews owned 40 percent of the property in Budapest.

In 1919, the dismemberment of the Hapsburg Empire altered the political landscape. Mutilated by the 1920 Treaty of Trianon, Hungary lost two-thirds of its territory. The conservative regent Horthy took the reins of the country, while Jews were becoming the target of increasing anti-Semitism. Hungary became the first European country to reintroduce anti-Jewish legislation, notably the *numerus clausus* of 1920, though this law was unevenly applied. Horthy's irredentist politics, meanwhile, led him into an alliance with Hitler. When the war began, this approach paid off, as Hungary quickly regained all its lost provinces. Although Horthy managed to resist Hitler's pressure for a time, he was forced to appoint a pro-Nazi government when German troops occupied the country in March 1944, resulting in the deportation of hundreds of thousands of Jews.

Allegory to the Glory of Joseph II, *circa 1782. Musée d'Art et d'Histoire du Judaïsme, Paris.*

Veesenmayer, Hitler's plenipotentiary in Hungary, declared not long after: "Thanks only to the zealous and full participation of the Hungarian police apparatus have we succeeded in completing our task in less than three months."

Dispossessed of their belongings, 600,000 Hungarian Jews—of a total 900,000—were deported. Practically every Jew from the provinces was liquidated, though half of those from Budapest (around 120,000) managed to survive the *Shoah*.

Today, the Hungarian-Jewish community is estimated at around 100,000, centered mostly in Budapest. There has been an undeniable reawakening of Jewish identity here. The newfound presence of newspapers, schools, organizations, and **klezmer** bands attests to a cultural rather than religious renaissance. Hungarian society has not yet settled its accounts with history; as François Fejtö has remarked: "No one has yet expressed, in the name of the nation, condemnation or shame regarding Hungary's complicity, and history books remain surprisingly quiet on the subject."

Mishnah Torah, thirteenth century. Bookstore of the Hungarian Academy of Sciences.

→ **To call Hungary from the United States, dial 011 36** followed by the number of the person you are calling minus the initial 0 (used only for domestic calls).

Budapest and Northwest Hungary ■

Budapest

Visiting Jewish Budapest requires at least three days. The capital was born from the unification of three cities: Buda and Óbuda on the western shores of the Danube, and Pest on the eastern shores. Although wars and urbanization have left few traces of the Jewish presence in Buda, Pest contains an old Jewish quarter that still houses a portion of the community.

BUDA

"There are a few Jews here and they speak French well; many were expelled from the kingdom of France," Bertandon de La Brocquière noted in his 1433 *Chronique de voyage à Boude* (Chronicle of My Trip to Buda).[6] The earliest arrival of Jews

from Vienna certainly began as far back as the eleventh century. King Béla's 1251 charter granted Jews the right to settle there, which offered them protection until the Ottoman era. Of the medieval period, only vestiges of a synagogue remain in the Baroque castle district.

■ In the late fourteenth century, Jews built a large synagogue at 23 Táncsics Street, which was formerly called "Jewish Street." The ruins here have yet to be restored.

■ Somewhat smaller, the synagogue at number 26 was a house of prayer, a temple serving the capital's **Sephardic** community. Propped up by two Gothic pillars, the prayer room shelters two beautiful frescoes. One depicts a bow turned toward the sky, the other a Star of David. The caption reads: "Powerful men equipped with bows were corrupt, while the

Clothing Market, Budapest, 1933.

weak were invested with power." The other Hebrew inscriptions, featuring Turkish stylizations, relay the fears of **Sephardic** Jews under Christian attack. Such fears were not unfounded: on one of the synagogue walls, the reproduction of a painting illustrates how the Jews of Buda were massacred in 1686 after the Turks' defeat by the Austrians; they had been accused of collaborating with the Ottomans. Under Turkish occupation, **Sephardic** and **Ashkenazic** Jews had lived in harmony in Buda.

[Synagogue: Táncsics Mihály utca 26, 1014 Budapest. Open May 1–Oct 31, Tue–Sun 10 A.M.–5 P.M. From Moskva tér (square), take the minibus leading toward the castle (it has no number, but bears an icon of a castle) to the second stop (Bécsi Kapu); you can also take ❶ 16, terminus above the castle. If starting from below near the Danube, take the funicular at Clark Adám tér, which leads to the castle (one stop only).]

🕎 THE JEWS OF BUDA

"In the Jewish quarter of Buda one could buy almost everything: Persian carpets, kilim, velvet, muslin, fine linen, atlas, felt, aba cloth, frieze cloth, Moroccan leather. Fruits, even the most exotic ones that grew in the remotest corner of the Sultan's empire, were sold there, as well as cattle, hide, flour, salt, timber. Credit was also available, against promissory notes. Jewish merchants played an important role in the ransoming of Christians who had been taken captive. Servants, too, were sold on the market.

Trade in wine, however, was prohibited even to the Jews. In

order not to tempt the virtues of the Moslem population, the Turkish authorities forbade the use of wine, even in Jewish ceremonies."

GÉZA KOMOROCZY, ED., *JEWISH BUDAPEST: MONUMENTS, RITES, HISTORY* (BUDAPEST: CENTRAL EUROPEAN UNIVERSITY PRESS, 1999).

PEST

Jews settled north of Pest's current center, Deák Square, around a market where they sold grain, cattle, wool, and hides. In 1800, they numbered more than 1,000 and soon built a synagogue in the Orczy House (destroyed) on the site of Madach square. Besides the synagogue, a rabbinical school was founded here, along with other schools, baths, housing, and shops. Letter-writers rubbed elbows with matchmakers. The famous Café Orczy opened in 1825, where **cantors** were regularly recruited. Enriched by trade and industry, the nascent Jewish middle class soon wanted a temple worthy of its rank. The synagogue on Dohány Street was opened in 1859, only a few years before the Jewish community gained full emancipation.

Here begins a tour of Pest's Jewish quarter, delimited roughly by three synagogues that form a sort of triangle and represent the three branches of modern-day Judaism.

👑 THE ASSIMILATION OF HUNGARIAN JEWS

Starting in the latter half of the nineteenth century, many Jews "Magyarized" their names. "The teacher turns two pages. Maybe he has reached the letter K. Altmann who at the beginning of this term had his family name changed to the

Hungarian Katona, now *bitterly regrets this rash act."*
FRIGYES KARINTHY, *PLEASE SIR!*, TRANS. ISTVÁN FARKAS (BUDAPEST: CORVINA PRESS, 1968).

■ The synagogue on Dohány Street was designed by Austrian architect Ludwig Förster. Inspired by Vienna's Tempelgasse synagogue and the Solomon Temple, Förster created an imposing structure, adding two towers to echo the columns of the Temple of Jerusalem. The outer, light-red brick walls are decorated with eastern- and Byzantine-inspired motifs and are of a Moorish style very popular at the time. Förster's work features a striking mix of Greco-Roman, Roman, and Byzantine elements, integrating modern techniques: thin pillars of tempered steel support the upper galleries and roof, while the lighting comes from above. Certain features are reminiscent of Christian church architecture. Unlike in Orthodox synagogues, the **bimah** here is not found in the center but in the extension of the richly decorated *aron,* and it is modeled like an altar. A huge arch (40 feet in diameter) separates the sanctuary from the nave. One detail that scandalized Orthodox believers of the era was the presence of an organ, despite the traditional ban of musical instruments during **Shabbat.** The "Jewish Cathedral," as some of its detractors have called it, symbolized the triumph of Neolog Jews, partisans of assimilation and modernization of Judaism. It is today the largest synagogue in Europe (245 ft. x 88 ft.) and served as the model for the one on East Fiftieth Street in New York City. Restored in the early 1990s by the Hungarian state, the synagogue can accommodate as many as 3,000 people. It is packed during major celebrations **(Yom Kippur, Rosh Hashanah),** where women can freely mingle with men.

[Synagogue: Dohány utca 2, 1077 Budapest. ✆ 013428949. Open Mon–Thu 10 A.M. to 5 P.M., Fri and Sun 10 A.M.–2 P.M. Closed Sat and Jewish holidays.]

■ The small adjacent museum has on display beautiful ritual objects, sacred decorations, and photos taken during the *Shoah.* Between the synagogue and museum, the remains of a redbrick wall signal the border of the ghetto built in late November 1944 and liberated by the Soviets on 18 January 1945. Through the arcades of the courtyard, the mass graves of Jews who died in the ghetto can be seen. Here also stands the Temple of Heroes: built in 1929 as a memorial to soldiers fallen during the First World War, it serves today as an everyday house of worship.

[Museum: same address as the Temple of Heroes (a single ticket is good for entry to the museum and Temple of Heroes). Open Mon–Thu 10 A.M.–4 P.M., Sun 10 A.M.–1 P.M. The archives can be consulted by appointment.] [Temple of Heroes: Wesselényi utca 5, 1077 Budapest. Open daily 10 A.M.–3 P.M.

Synagogue on Dohány Street, Budapest.

It serves as a house of worship in winter only, services on Fri at 6:30 P.M. and Sat at 9 A.M. Tours are given to groups only. Contact ✆ 013422353.]

■ Behind the synagogue, a *Shoah* memorial stands in the middle of an open courtyard. The work of sculptor Imre Varga (1990), this steel and granite weeping willow is in fact an inverse **menorah**. The black marble arch symbolizes the Ark of the Law, hollowed out by the annihilation of

Shoah Memorial, Budapest.

the *Shoah*. The park is dedicated to Swedish diplomat Raoul Wallenberg, who saved thousands of Jews during the war. *Saving Angel,* an ormolu sculpture on Dob Street, has been erected in honor of another righteous soul, Swiss consul Carl Lutz.

■ The synagogue on Rumbach Street, a major work by Austrian architect Otto Wagner, was built in 1872 for the traditionalists who refused to take sides in the dispute between Neologs and Orthodox Jews. In Romantic-Moorish style, the building's exterior is decorated with numerous Arab-inspired motifs and two turrets shaped like minarets. Currently closed, the splendid interior can only be glimpsed through the windows: an octagonal room with thin columns rising to the vault, richly decorated in blue, mauve, and gold motifs.

[Synagogue: Rumbach Sebestyén utca 11-13, 1075 Budapest. 🚇 Deák tér (lines 1, 2, or 3).]

■ The Orthodox synagogue is pure Art Nouveau, built in 1913 according to plans by the Löffler brothers. Severely damaged during the war, it has been almost entirely restored to its original state. The superb ceiling is decorated with eastern-inspired floral motifs, palms, and lotus flowers typical of late Jugendstil. The stained-glass windows, in a ring, diffuse an optimal light, while very stylized *menorot* decorate the galleries, banisters, and windows. The gilded marble *aron* is the work of Italian masters. In the courtyard, you will notice the *huppah,* a dais of forged iron under which Orthodox **Ashkenazic** Jews celebrate outdoor marriages. The courtyard also houses a small prayer room (only holidays are celebrated in the synagogue), a **kosher** dining hall, a **yeshiva,** and a butcher shop.

[Orthodox Synagogue: Kazinczy utca 27, 1075 Budapest. 🚇 Deák tér (lines 1, 2, or 3). For visiting hours, contact the Community Center: ✆ 13510525. The offices are in the courtyard. The synagogue is temporarily closed for restoration.]

■ The only functioning **mikvah** in Hungary is located at 16 Kazinczy Street. At number 41 (in the courtyard), the **kosher** delicatessen Dezsö Kövari seems taken right out of a film from the 1930s. The proprietress stands stone-faced behind her counter, on which an immense red slicer holds the place of honor.

■ A stroll through the somber streets with their peeling façades hints at the splendors of times past. The door of 16 Sip Street is shaped like a **menorah,** while that of number 17 hides a stylized tree of life. The Neolog community's headquarters are located at 12 Sip Street. The cultural center itself is found near the opera.

[Mazsihisz: Sip utca 16, 1075 Budapest. ✆ 013421335. 🚇 Deák tér (lines 1, 2, or 3).]

[Bálint ház Cultural Center: Révay utca 16, 1065 Budapest. ✆ 013119214. 🚇 Opera (line 1).]

■ A required stopping place for a bite to eat is the Fröhlich Bakery, where you can sample exquisite *Kindli* and *Flodni,* **Purim** cakes made with poppy seeds and nuts. Taking Dob Street up to Klauzál Square, you will find Kadar restaurant, a cult hangout. A **Yiddish** proverb maintains that "it takes two to eat a chicken, me . . . and the chicken."

This is precisely the ambience that prevails in this cramped bistro where you will have to share your table with the regulars. On the wall hang photographs of famous actors, most notably of Marcello Mastroianni, who stopped here for a hearty meal. Students and artists come to savor, at ridiculously low prices, Jewish cuisine . . . Hungarian style. While they do serve a copious **cholent** here, a **Shabbat** dish made from red beans, there is nothing **kosher** about it. They serve the dish on Fridays and Saturdays, embellishing it with bacon or smoked breast; it is also offered with roasted goose or chicken. On the menu, other Jewish specialties—boiled beef with cherries—line up alongside undeniably Magyar paprika stews. Kadar is a temple of gastronomic assimilation.

[Fröhlich Bakery: Dob utca 22, 1074 Budapest. ✆ 012672851. Open Mon–Thu 9 A.M.–6 P.M., Fri 7 A.M.–2 P.M., and Sun 11 A.M.–4 P.M.]

[Kadar: Klauzál tér 9, 1072 Budapest. ✆ 013213622. Lunch only Tue–Sat 11:30 A.M.–3:30 P.M. ❶ 4 or 6, Wesselényi utca stop.]

🕎 THE HISTORY OF **CHOLENT**, TRADITIONAL SHABBAT DISH

"[a dish of] Central European Jewry; the best, the most satisfying; made especially for the poor, who could keep it in their kitchens for three or four days, or even longer, without fear of its going bad.

It was a concoction of dried beans, eggs, rice and goose-flesh (sometimes beef or lamb instead), and was cooked in the oven in a big saucepan, its lid fastened with fine string to which was fastened a label bearing the name of the family who owned it. This was because the sciolet needed a whole night's cooking and was therefore placed in the big communal oven. No private house could burn and keep watch over a fire for that length of time."

GIORGIO AND NICOLA PRESSBURGER, *HOMAGE TO THE EIGHTH DISTRICT⁸: TALES FROM BUDAPEST,* TRANS. GERALD MOORE (LONDON: READERS INTERNATIONAL, 1990).

■ Not far from the Jewish quarter, Andrássy Street is worth a stroll for its splendid mansions, two-thirds of which were inhabited by Jewish families at the turn of the twentieth century. At number 23 lived the banker Mor Wahrmann: a rabbi's grandson, he became president of the Chamber of Commerce and Industry, and the first Jewish deputy elected to Parliament in 1869. He advocated emancipation, but for the leisure class alone.

[🚇 Bajcsy-Zsilinszky or Hösök tere (linc 1). Andrássy utca is located between the two stations.]

Franz Liszt Music Academy, Budapest

IN THE FOOTSTEPS OF JEWISH ARTISTS

Throughout the city, Jewish artists have left their mark.

■ We should not overlook Miksa Róth, who designed the stained-glass windows for innumerable buildings, including the Gresham Palace, the magnificent Franz Liszt Music Academy, and the Museum of Agriculture.

■ The architect Béla Lajta cleverly blended Art Nouveau, Jewish motifs, and Hungarian folk style in his buildings: gates were often adorned with *menorot,* six-pointed stars, and biblical motifs like the tree and the serpent, or Noah's Ark. The staircases he designed for the Institute for Neurological Research (founded in 1911) resemble towers. At the top, a complex structure of wooden beams is reminiscent of Transylvanian architecture. The Institute for Handicapped Children and the hospital on Amérikai Street are two other remarkable examples.

[Institute for Neurological Research and Hospital: Amérikai utca 57, 1145 Budapest.]

[Institute for the Blind: Mexikói utca 60, 1145 Budapest. 🚇 Mexikói utca (end of the line); then walk or take 🚌 69 for Amérikai utca, 🚌 67 for Mexikói utca.]

■ Lajta also designed several mausoleums for the Rákoskersztúr cemetery. The mausoleum of the Schmidl family, for example, is impressive; its decor—majolica and mosaics made of glass and marble—was inspired by the sepulcher of Galla Placidia in Ravenna.

[Rákoskeresztúr Cemetery: Kozma utca 6, 1108 Budapest. ✆ 012652458. Open daily 9 A.M.–6 P.M.]

Györ

■ The immense gray dome of Györ's synagogue stands out against the industrial landscape. Completed in 1870, the structure reflects the prosperity of the city's Jewish middle class—lawyers, bankers, and manufacturers of German or Moravian origin. The massive bronze pillars supporting the octagonal building contrast with the subtlety of the eastern-inspired decor of the galleries, beams, and frescoes. The adjacent building, a former Jewish school, houses the Széchényi art high school.

In a sorry state, the building is slowly being restored by the dynamic Jewish association that also organizes concerts and festivals here: in the last week of April through May 2, Györ welcomes a cultural festival called "Mediawave," presenting films and shows from around the world. Concerts (folk and ethnic music or jazz) are held in the synagogue.

[Synagogue: Kossuth Lajos utca 5, 9021 Györ. ✆ 096329032.]
[For information about Mediawave, e-mail mail@mediawavefestival.com]

■ The peaceful, fir-lined Neolog cemetery is located on the bank of the Rapca River beside the Catholic cemetery. It is remarkably well kept—unusual for Hungary—by the caretaker couple who live at the site, Mr. and Mrs. Sandor Seles.

[Cemetery: Temetö utca 33, 9025 Györ. ✆ 0696324791.]

■ Along the road leading from Györ to Sopron, not far from the city limits, a statue on the right stands in honor of the great Jewish poet Miklós Radnóti. He died from exhaustion—or perhaps was gunned down—after a forced march from the Balkans to Austria in November 1944.

☙ RAZGLEDNICE

"I fell beside him; his body turned over,
  already taut as a string about to snap.
  Shot in the back of the neck.
  That's how you too will end,
  I whispered to myself:
just lie quietly.
  Patience now flowers into death.
  Der springt noch auf,⁹ a voice said above me.
  On my ear, blood dried, mixed with filth."

MIKLÓS RADNÓTI'S LAST POEM, 31 OCTOBER 1944, IN MIKLÓS RADNÓTI, *THE COMPLETE POETRY,* ED. AND TRANS. EMERY GEORGE (ANN ARBOR: ARDIS, 1980).

Sopron

Within this Baroque city, where splendid thirteenth-century houses have been transformed into museums, restoration projects have brought two medieval synagogues back to life.

■ Built in the early thirteenth century, the synagogue on Új Street is the oldest one in Hungary. So closely does it resemble the one in Miltenberg (Bavaria) that historian Ferenc David suspects Sopron's Jews originated there. Emigrating from Germany and southern Bavaria, they possibly took up residence in Sopron, a royal and independent city at the time where monarch Laszlo IV had granted privileges to bankers and merchants—the only professions Jews were allowed to practice.

Like many medieval synagogues, the building, which in times past served a scaled-down but flourishing community, is set back from the street. The raised entrance opens onto a Gothic-style room. The magnificent stone-sculpted *aron* is surrounded by a frieze adorned with grapes and fig leaves in homage to wine, a symbol of life and celebration of the **kiddush** during the **Shabbat**. To its right, a boarded up window was enlarged to allow barrels to pass through. After the Ottoman occupation, the Jews were expelled in 1526 and their businesses transformed into residential housing. The adjoining room, added later (in the fifteenth century), was reserved for women, who could only observe ceremonies through narrow openings, a kind of horizontal loophole. In the courtyard, a **mikvah** dates from 1420.

[Synagogue: Új utca 22, 9400 Sopron. Open May–Aug, Wed–Mon 10 A.M.–6 P.M.; and Sep, Wed–Mon 10 A.M.–2 P.M.]

■ Located at number 11 on the same street—formerly "Jewish Street," where Jewish and Christian merchants lived side by side—a small synagogue was built in 1350 modeled after the one that preceded it. More precisely, it was a private prayer room belonging to the rich banker Israel and his family.

[Synagogue: Új utca 11, 9400 Sopron. Open Mon 1–5 P.M., Wed and Thu 9 A.M.–3:30 P.M., Fri 9 A.M.–noon. In winter, ask for the key at the Storno Museum, a short distance away off the main square.]

Carpathian Foothills ■

This region of rolling hills punctuated by vineyards merits a two-day visit for memory's sake. There remains, in fact, little evidence of Jewish life here, as most of it was eradicated by the *Shoah*.

Tokaj

In the seventeenth century, the Jews of Galicia and Silesia (modern-day Poland and Ukraine) were drawn to this region by trade in *tokaj,* a syrupy, amber-tinted wine very popular at the courts of Louis XIV and Peter of Russia. Jews gradually settled here, producing wine for Jews and non-Jews alike, and a crowd of other small trades followed subsequently. In this very Orthodox region, **Hasidism** took root and Jews here resisted assimilation until the Second World War.

♦ THE MEMOIRS OF BER, JEWISH MERCHANT OF BOLECHÓW (TODAY IN UKRAINE)
"Once Poniatowski (the local count) said to Saul: 'I should like to send someone to Hungary to buy me a considerable quantity of good wine. If you know of a fellow-Jew, a trustworthy person who understands the business, I will send him.' [. . .] He accordingly decided to send my father for the wine and handed him 2000

ducats, that is 36,000 gulden. He also sent with my father the tutor of his sons, in the capacity of a clerk, in order to register the purchase of the wines and the daily expenses, so that a proper account might be kept. The clerk was named Kostiushko. My father did as he was requested by Poniatowski. He bought 200 casks of Tokay wine of the variety called máslás. When they both returned from Hungary and brought the wines to Stryi, Poniatowski was very pleased with the purchase; he gave my father 100 ducats for his trouble, and for keeping the accounts properly the clerk Kostiushko was promoted to be steward of our native town Bolechów . . ."
RUTH ELLEN GRUBER, *UPON THE DOORPOSTS OF THY HOUSE* (NEW YORK: JOHN WILEY & SONS, 1994).

■ The Grand Synagogue on Achim Street, built in 1890, accommodated 1,800 of the faithful. Damaged by a fire in 1999, it cannot be visited, but it is possible to explore the old Jewish quarter surrounding it: the L-shaped **yeshiva, mikvah, beth hamidrash** (a study room, in the small white building), and bakery (with orange walls, on the street side). The poor lived by the river's edge, those of the middle class toward the city center.

🕎 POLISI!

*In the nineteenth century, Jews acquired vineyards and got rich from industry. At the same time, the poor continued immigrating to Hungary. In 1927, Albert Londres sketched the appalling misery of these **Hasidism** who came from the north, scornfully labeled* polisi *(Poles) by the wealthy Jews of Budapest:*

"The babies were dressed in shirts, their bare feet pressed against the ice. . . . The mothers held their shawls open, revealing milkless breasts and fleshless ribs. Twice the husband of one such tried to make it down to the cities to find some bread, and twice he collapsed in the street, exhausted. In two years, misery here has increased tenfold. Before the most recent peace treaties, these Jews worked three months every summer on the infamous Hungarian plain. The border separated the plain from the mountain. Hungary has refused passports to its former subjects, who have now become Czechoslovakian subjects. Three months of work was all these Jews needed to live for the rest of the year. All year long now, they will have only the meager fruit of the trees of the Carpathian Mountains!"

ALBERT LONDRES, *LE JUIF ERRANT EST ARRIVÉ* (THE WANDERING JEW HAS ARRIVED) (PARIS: LE SERPENT À PLUMES, 2000). SEE ALSO, *THE JEW HAS COME HOME*, TRANS. WILLIAM STAPLES (NEW YORK: R. R. SMITH, 1931).

■ Located on a wooded island in the middle of the Bodrog River, the very moving old cemetery is worth a visit. The scores of mossy graves here are disturbed only by ducks. The community acquired the land when Jews were forbidden to live in the city by Archduchess Maria Theresa in the eighteenth century.

[The island is accessible by ferry in summer. For access to the ferry, the only choice is to contact local historian Lajos Löwy, who aids visitors and can arrange the crossing. ✆ 047352550 (8 A.M.–5 P.M.). In winter, a nearby riverside resident can help you cross by motorboat. Make sure to leave a tip for gas.]

Mád

■ Built in 1795, the synagogue looms over the old Jewish quarter with its elegant white facade. With the Protestant church on the other side of the small valley, it symbolizes the religious balance of a large wine-making village, a quarter of whose inhabitants were Jews at the end of the nineteenth century. It represents a very beautiful and rare example of a Baroque synagogue in Hungary.

The interior, though in terrible shape, is splendid, and the harmony of its proportions is striking. The graceful, wrought iron **bimah** is located in the very center beneath a supporting architrave on four columns, in accordance with Orthodox tradition. The refined *aron* is sculpted from stone and decorated with a beautiful medallion (lions and griffons surround the Ark of the Law and cherubs hold *rimmonim*). Engraved on the fragments of stone surrounding the steps can be seen the prayers of Yom Kippur and the new moon, as well as a text written in Aramaic. The multicolored frescoes were added later.

[To visit the synagogue, request the key at the city hall, located on the main street, Rókóczi utca 50-52, 909 Mád. ℘ 647348016.]

■ Make sure to visit the old cemetery. It is even older than the synagogue, with some graves dating from 1650.

[To find the cemetery, ask for directions at the city hall.
Open Mon–Fri 8:30 A.M.–4:30 P.M.]

Sátoraljaújhely

The region is famous for its rebbes, heads of **Hasidic** communities whose followers revered their thaumaturgical and magical powers.

■ The city of Sátoraljaújhely, where 4,000 Jews lived in 1939, houses the mausoleum of Moses Teitelbaum. Born in Poland in 1759, he founded a dynasty of rebbes in Hungary, Galicia, and Romania. Every day, legend has it, Teitelbaum dressed in rags and climbed Mount Šator to see if the Messiah had come.

■ The archives in the city hall contain documents in Hebrew available for examination.

[Contact Mr. Istvan Högye: Kossuth Lajos utca 5, 3980 Sátoraljaújhely. ℘ 0647321353.]

Southern Hungary ■

Kecskemét

■ Kecskemét is worth a stop for its two synagogues. The largest is in (nineteenth-century) Romantic style. Today it houses the Technology Center, where expositions and conferences are regularly held on technical subjects. The second contains a small Museum of Photography.

[Technology Center: Szabadsag tér 7, 6000 Kecskemét. ℘ 075481459.
Open Mon–Fri 10 A.M.–4 P.M. Closed weekends and for private gatherings.]

[Museum of Photography: Katona Jozsef tér 12, 6000 Kecskemét. ℘ 076483221.
Open Wed–Sun 10 A.M.–6 P.M.]

Szeged

■ Half a day will suffice to see the synagogue in Szeged, one of the most interesting ones in Hungary (1903). With its Baroque dome, Roman columns, and Byzantine-inspired bellows, the monumental building is a hymn to eclecticism. At the entrance, two plaques honor rabbis Lipot, a

Synagogue, Szeged.

Reform pioneer who was the first to deliver his sermons in Hungarian, and Immanuel Loew, son of the former whose passion for botany inspired the floral motifs of the decor. On both sides of the nave, beautiful stained-glass windows count out the Jewish holidays. Everything exudes opulence: the *aron* and **bimah** are made out of marble from Jerusalem, while the *menorot* are made from ormolu set in semi-precious stones. Jews prospered here thanks to commerce and the wood and paprika industries. The dome's superb stained-glass windows are by the famous Jugendstil artist Miksa Róth. Concerts are sometimes held here, with the money going to maintaining the synagogue.

[The synagogue's postal address (Gutenberg utca 20, 6722 Szeged) does not correspond to its actual site, which is located about fifty yards away, at the corner of Gutenberg utca and Jósika utca. ✆ 062423849. Open Sun–Fri 10 A.M.–noon and 1–5 P.M. The foundation overseeing the synagogue is open 9 A.M.–noon.]

Slovakia

T HE HISTORY OF JEWS IN SLOVAKIA—dating
from the sixteenth century under the protection of
the Hapsburgs—intersects that of their fellow
believers in Hungary and the Czech Republic. Jews
in these three countries experienced the same vicis-
situdes of discrimination, expulsions, and, in the
seventeenth century, the acquisition of some civil
rights. Numerous Jews from neighboring Moravia
flocked to Bratislava and nearby cities. At the time
a part of northern Hungary, this region was called
"Magyar Israel." Just after the installation of the
double Austro-Hungarian monarchy in 1867, the
Hungarian Parliament passed a law emancipating
the Jews and granting them full civil rights equal to
those of other citizens. Their "Magyarization" accelerated, notably in the western cities. The great
majority of Slovakian Jews, in contrast, lived in the
east in the heart of small, introverted communities
following the model of the shtetl of Galicia or Ukraine.

Anti-Semitism in Slovakia is more virulent
than in the Czech Republic, where the nationalists
reproach the Jews for being of German cultural
background. In Slovakia, they denounce Jewish
assimilation into Hungarian culture. Slovakian

Jewish quarter in a southern city.

Judaism is itself marked by the struggle between Reform and Orthodox Jews.

With the birth of Czechoslovakia after World War I and the Treaty of Versailles, the Jews also obtained the right to be recognized as a specific nationality. Jewish cultural life bloomed in the new democratic state, where the Jews enjoyed a major economic role, especially in Bohemia-Moravia. They held more than one-third of industrial investments. In contrast, 65 percent of Slovakian Jews still lived in the countryside in 1930.

The Munich Accords of 1938 and the capitulation of London and Paris in the face of Hitler's demands led to the dismantling of Czechoslovakia. The Czech territory was separated from the Sudetenland. Slovakia in its turn lost eastern and southern territories to Hungary, regions where some 40,000 Jews lived, and became an autonomous region. Less than a year later, in March 1939, Slovakia proclaimed its independence under the protection of Nazi Germany. Slovakia elected Father Josef Tiso as president, and as prime minister Andrej Hlinka, the leader of the Slovakian Peoples' Party. This religious and extremely right-wing party quickly became the only political party in the country. From the first, discriminatory measures were taken against the country's 135,000 Jews and were hardened in September 1941 with the promulgation of anti-Jewish legislation in 270 articles. This legislation forced Jews to begin wearing the Star of David and institutionalized forced labor. The deportation of the Jews to death camps (primarily Auschwitz) followed soon after. By the end of 1942, more than three-quarters of Slovakian Jews had been exterminated. The deportations and massacres resumed in April 1944, during the repression of the Slovakian Resistance movement, in which a number of Jews participated. At the end of the war there were no more than 5,000 Jews in the country, who had been able to hide themselves with false papers. At most only some 20,000 Slovakian Jews survived Nazism.

Bratislava was a large center for Jewish culture, and flourishing communities existed in small cities such as Košice or Prešov; in the main, however, most Jews traditionally resided in the small western villages of what is today contemporary Slovakia. Some vestiges still exist of the close to 200 synagogues

Synagogue, Bratislava.

and 630 cemeteries within the boundaries of this new nation, which came into existence 1 January 1993 as part of an amiable separation from the Czech Republic. Most of the remains of a Jewish presence in Slovakia are buried under modern reconstructions or have been left in ruins. Ultimately, these ruins are the last clues to a world that has all but disappeared. Before the war, 135,000 Jews (4.5 percent of the total population) lived within the boundaries of contemporary Slovakia. Today there remain no more than some 4,000 Jews, mainly elderly. Of this greatly reduced community, 1,000 live in Bratislava.

→ **To call Slovakia from the
United States, dial 011 421**
followed by the number of the person
you are calling minus the initial 0
(used only for domestic calls).

Bratislava
and Surrounding Areas ■

Bratislava

Bratislava, capital of Slovakia and a large city of more than 500,000 inhabitants, is located on the banks of the Danube River not far from the Hungarian and Austrian borders. Although Jews are thought to have lived here since the Roman period, the first mention of a community dates back to the second half of the thirteenth century. The Jews of Bratislava have been expelled from the city several times in its history, notably in 1360 and in 1526. At the beginning of the eighteenth century, a census counted 120 Jewish families in the city. During this period the community began to grow, notably with the influx of Jews coming from Moravia. With the arrival of Rabbi Moses Schreiber, known as the "Hatam Sofer" (1762–1839), the city even became a center of Euro-

pean Judaism. At the very end of the nineteenth century, many Jews arrived in the capital city from the villages of western Slovakia. More than 15,000 Jews lived in the city at the dawn of The Second World War. Many buildings in "Jewish Bratislava" were destroyed during the war and the great urban renewal of the Socialist period.

■ The Grand Orthodox Synagogue, constructed in an oriental style in 1863 on Zamoska Street, was largely destroyed in 1945. Its remains were razed in 1980.

The large Moorish-style Reform synagogue, so much a part of the landscape near present-day Paulinyho Street, was knocked down in 1970 to make way for a parking lot and highway ramp. Zidovska Street ("Street of the Jews") wound its way between the walls of the city and the castle. Several fires (in 1913, for example) destroyed a number of seventeenth- and eighteenth-century houses, the last of which were cleared away after 1945. The Jewish Museum is housed in one of the few buildings that survived this period.

■ Deprived for many years of a spiritual leader, Bratislava's small Jewish community (at most 1,000 members) has, since the fall of Communism, been under the direction of Rabbi Baruch Myers, educated in Brooklyn within the ultra-Orthodox, **Hasidic** Lubavitch (chabad) movement. Information about Slovakian Judaism is available at the Institute of Jewish Studies.

[Jewish Community of Slovakia:
Kozia ulica 18, 81441 Bratislava.
✆ 0254416949.]
[Institute of Jewish Studies:
Commenius University, Panenska ulica 4,
81103 Bratislava. ✆ 0254416873,
fax 0254416867. ❶ ij@ij.uniba.sk.]

■ The Jewish Museum constitutes a section of the National Museum of Slovakia. Since 1991, it has been housed in an urban villa dating from the late Renaissance that has been remodeled several times after fires ravaged the street in the seventeenth and nineteenth centuries. The collections of the Jewish Museum in Prešov are now contained here. Objects of worship and antique books, some from the Hatam Sofer library, are on display. The galleries of the museum illustrate the life of Slovakian Jews during the last five centuries and celebrate important figures

of the community. The permanent exhibition ends with a commemoration of the victims of the *Shoah*.

[Jewish Museum: Vajanského nábr 2,
81006 Bratislava, P.O. Box 31.
✆ 0254418567. Open Mon–Fri 9 A.M.–1 P.M.
Permanent exhibition:
Zidovska ulica 17, 81101 Bratislava.
Open Sun–Fri 11 A.M.–5 P.M.]

■ Only one synagogue remains in Bratislava. An austere but elegant building in an oriental style, it was constructed for the city's Orthodox Jews in 1923 following the plans of architect Arthur Szalatnai-Slatinski. It is open for **Shabbat** services as well as Monday and Thursday mornings.

[Synagogue: Heydukova ulica 11-13, 81447 Bratislava. Closed in winter.]

■ Perhaps the most moving and symbolic monument in Bratislava is the mausoleum of the Hatam Sofer in the so-called Vajanskeho Nabrezy. The tomb stands in a large underground crypt beneath a highway. It remains one of the important pilgrimage sites for Orthodox Jews in Central Europe. Rabbi Moshe Schreiber, called Hatam Sofer for his great wisdom and penetrating interpretations of the Law, was one of the primary leaders of early modern Orthodox Judaism. The twenty-three tombs and forty-one gravestones are the last vestiges of a Jewish cemetery that was in use until the middle of the nineteenth century. It was razed during the war.

[Mausoleum of Hatam Sofer: Visits by appointment. Call the Jewish Federation of Bratislava: Kozia ulica 1, ✆ 0254412167.]

■ Not far from the mausoleum, some 600 feet up the hill (the entrance is on Zizkova Street), is an Orthodox cemetery established in 1846 and still in use today. Many of the 7,000 tombstones here are from older cemeteries elsewhere.

Synagogue, Trenčín.

320

Trenčín

■ Trenčín is a city of roughly 60,000 inhabitants, and you will find on Vajanskeho Street a beautiful synagogue dating from the beginning of the twentieth century. Although now an exhibition space, its decorations remain, and a plaque recalls that the building was once the location of worship for the 1,300 Jews in the city, most of whom were exterminated during World War II.

[For information contact the tourist office: ✆ 0327433505.]

Eastern Slovakia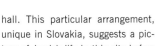

There are a few significant vestiges of Slovakian Judaism in some of the small cities beyond Bratislava. An initial appointment at the offices of the Jewish Community of Slovakia for information and an orientation to the region is required.

[Jewish Community of Slovakia:
Kozia ulica 18, 81447 Bratislava.
✆ 0254416949.]

Košice

The capital of eastern Slovakia, Košice is a large industrial city of 250,000 inhabitants. Its sizable Jewish community was almost totally annihilated during the Second World War. The city is now home to 800 Jews.

■ The spacious nineteenth-century synagogue is in a building adjacent to the community headquarters. The building also includes a **mikvah**, a **kosher** butcher shop, and a prayer hall. This particular arrangement, unique in Slovakia, suggests a picture of Jewish life in this city before the *Shoah*.

[Jewish Community of Košice:
Zvornaska ulica 5, Košice.
✆ 0556255503, fax 0556224834.]

Prešov

Not far from Košice, Prešov was also an important center of Jewish life. More than 6,000 Jews from the city and surrounding villages were killed during the war. Today fewer than 100 Jews live here in Prešov.

■ The area from near the old city center with its Renaissance homes and palace to beyond the city walls once marked the extent of the Jewish quarter. Close to the Jewish community center near the city walls stands a beautiful synagogue from the last century. A monument commemorating the victims of the *Shoah* stands in the center of the quarter. Remnants of two cemeteries, one Orthodox and the other Reform, can be found near the Catholic cemetery.

[Community and Jewish Museum:
Svermova ulica 32, Prešov.
✆ 0517731638.]

Bardejov

Bardejov possessed a large Jewish quarter where some 5,000 Jews lived before World War II. This small medieval city of 35,000 inhabitants lies thirty-seven miles north of Prešov near the Polish border. Most of Bardejov's Jewish community was wiped out during the war.

■ Despite the devastations of the war and postwar reconstruction, a few houses and an interesting eighteenth-century Polish-style synagogue remain. The synagogue is now a warehouse.

[There are only two remaining members of the Jewish community, found at the Komenskeho ulica 20, Bardejov. In order to visit the former synagogue, contact Meyer Spira ✆ 544724729 or Karol Oimonoviè ✆ 544723014.]

Stropkov

Approximately thirty miles northeast of Prešov, the small city of Stropkov had one of the largest Jewish communities in the region and was an important center of Judaism. Many of its Jews arrived from Poland in the seventeenth century, victims of pogroms who were in search of the relative security in lands belonging to the Hapsburg Empire. Although allowed to work in the city, they did not have the right to live there or bury members of the community within the city limits. For decades, the Jews were thus compelled to bury their dead in the cemetery of the neighboring village of Tisinec. Stropkov's Jewish community experienced significant growth in the eighteenth century. Stimulated by the teachings of famous rabbis such as Chaim Yosef Gottlieb and Yekutiel Yehuda Teitelbaum, Stropkov became one of the most prestigious centers for the study of the **Torah** in all of greater Hungary and Galicia. Today there is not a single Jew left in the city. Most of the houses and shops of the Jewish quarter were razed after the war. And the memory of this community lingers in but a few scattered tombstones.

Czech Republic

B ELOW THE BELL TOWER OF PRAGUE'S JEW-
ISH CITY HALL, there are two clock faces. One displays Roman numerals, and the other Hebrew
letters. The hands of the first clock revolve in the
normal clockwise direction while those of the second turn counterclockwise, following the customary
manner of reading Hebrew right to left. Such clocks
are rare, and this is the only one of its kind adorn
ing a public building. Apollinaire and Blaise Cen-
drars, like many poets and writers, were fascinated
by the clocks, which evoked "a time that seems
to forever turn backward." Just opposite the tower
one sees the large triangular, jagged facade of the
Stare-Nova (Old-New) Synagogue constructed in
the thirteenth century. A few steps away is the
entrance to the former cemetery and its 12,000
graves. Although no more than 1,200 Jews remain
in the Czech capital, before the war there were over
32,000. The 700 Jewish communities in the cities
and villages of Bohemia and Moravia were almost
completely annihilated by the *Shoah*. Synagogues
and cemeteries outside Prague, where Nazi destruction was concentrated, largely escaped damage.
With the extermination of the Jews, much of their

Jewish cemetery and Klaus Synagogue, Prague,

heritage was pillaged, making these monuments, in the end, a "museum of a vanished people." The Czech Republic, with its remains of the Zidovske Mesto, the former Jewish quarter of the capital, and many small ghettos of the provinces, holds the richest and most compelling ensemble of Europe's Jewish heritage.

The first records of a Jewish presence in the Czech lands date from the ninth and tenth centuries. The Jewish-Arab merchant and traveler Ibrahim ibn Jacob described Prague in 965 as a large commercial city: "The Russians and Slavs came there from their royal cities with their goods. Muslims, Jews, and Turks also arrived from the land of the Turks with goods and money." As is evident from this famous text, a number of Prague's early Jews came from the east adding to those from German and Italian lands. Early Jewish settlement concentrated on the left bank of the Vltava, at the foot of the hill where Prague's castle would later be erected. Massacres and forced baptisms are mentioned as early as 1096, at the time of the first Crusade, but such tragedies remained isolated. A charter signed by Prince Sobeslav II in 1174 assured Jews the same rights and privileges as other foreign merchants. Jews also had the right to move freely about the city and settle along the large commercial routes. They were active in trade and the import of luxury goods from the Orient. Representatives of the flourishing community were given frequent audience at court. Around this time the Jewish community extended to the right bank of the river, establishing itself in an enclave north of the old city that would later become the Jewish quarter. Prague thus became one of the most important centers of Jewish culture in Europe. Such well-known **Talmud** scholars as Isaac ben Jacob and his disciple Abraham ben Azriel were members of this community.

As in the rest of Europe, the fortunes of Czech Jews changed after the Fourth Lateran Council (1215), which forbade them to possess land and drastically limited their economic activities. Jews were forced to live in separate areas and permitted only moneylending as a livelihood. Their lives improved, however, when King Přemysl Otakar II, following the example of Pope Innocent IV in Rome, enacted in 1254 more favorable legislation that placed the Jews under the direct protection of the crown. It was during this period the New Synagogue was constructed, later called Stare-Nova (Old-New), the oldest building for worship in the Czech capital.

In the course of the following decades, despite Charles IV's reaffirmation of these guarantees, the persecutions and massacres amplified. The most terrible was the Easter pogrom of 1389, which coincided with the two last days of Passover. Thousands of Jews were accused of having profaned the Host and were massacred by a fanatical crowd, encouraged by their priests. "Many were killed; to number them is an impossible task—young women, youths, old men, and babies. O you, God of all souls, not one of them needs you to recall him, you will judge all and you will know all . . ." So wrote Rabbi Avigdor, who, as a child, witnessed the carnage that claimed also his father. This elegy is read every Yom Kippur in the Stare-Nova Synagogue.

The Hussite wars that ravaged the Czech lands between 1417 and 1439 also adversely affected the lives of the Jews. The doctrine of Jan Hus made reference to early Christianity to demonstrate the abuses of the Church. "Catholics considered the Hussites to be a sect of Judaism, and the Hussites themselves, notably the most radical of them from Mount Tabor, saw themselves as an extension of biblical Israel," notes historian Arno Parik, conservator of the Jewish Museum in Prague. He emphasizes that this anti-feudal revolt movement showed a certain indulgence to local Jews despite some exceptions.

The development of a monetary economy gradually marginalized the Jews. They were forced out of a number of towns in Bohemia and Moravia by a growing bourgeoisie desirous of eliminating Jewish competition in banking and lending. Although protected in the first decades of the sixteenth century by Kings Vladislav Jagiello, Ludwig Jagiello, and the Hapsburg emperor Ferdinand I at the beginning of his reign, Jews in the capital also suffered worsened conditions. In 1541, with the sovereign's approval, the Diet voted to expel the city's Jews. Only some fifteen families escaped banishment by bribing officials. Gradually, and for a large sum, Jews began returning to the city. In 1551, Ferdinand I forced the Jews of Bohemia to "wear a characteristic mark that would permit them to be distinguished from Christians" and to live within the walls of the ghettos. In 1558, the Jews of the capital were again threatened with expulsion and had to pay in order to remain. This precarious situation lasted nine years, until Emperor Maximilian II issued a new decree authorizing the Jews already present in Prague and other Bohemian towns to stay where they were. The sovereign reinstated their freedom to engage in commerce and circulate freely. These measures were extended by the successor of Maximilian II, the flamboyant Rudolf II (1552–1612). This "wise fool and mad poet," great protector of scholars, astrologists, and artists, settled in Prague with his entire court after six years on the throne.

During this period Prague's Jewish community reached its height in the Baroque efflorescence of

Hans von Aachen, Portrait of Rudolf II, *c. 1600. Kunsthistorisches Museen, Vienna.*

this heart of European intellectual life, as the great Slavic Italian writer Angelo Mario Ripelino masterfully described it in his work *Praga magica* (Paris: Plon, 1993). Leading Jewish personalities included, for example, the mathematician and astronomer David Glans and the scholar and chronicler Rabbi Yehuda ben Betsalel, who, according to later legend, created the golem, a manlike clay creature who escaped his creator. The legendary rabbi, whose tomb is still revered, even received an audience, on 16 February 1592, with Rudolf II, who was curious about **kabbalistic** rituals. Another great figure, the financier and philanthropist Mordecal Marcus

328

The Golem, *German film directed by Paul Wegener and Carl Boese, 1920.*

ben Samuel Meisel, as mayor of the Jewish quarter
enlarged the cemetery and had the Jewish city hall
and new synagogues built. Jacob Bashevi, an
adventurer and successful financier from Italy, was
given the name von Treuenburg, and thus noble
status, by his protector, the infamous condottiere
Albrecht de Wallenstein. The Jewish banker
believed himself justly rewarded for his loyalty to
the emperor, a faithfulness shared by the majority
of his community.

The splendor of Jewish Prague continued until
the beginning of the seventeenth century under
Ferdinand II, when the revolt of the Czech lands
converted by the Reformation was crushed in 1620
in the Battle of White Mountain. The Counter-

Reformation triumphed throughout the Hapsburg Empire. Prague's Jews survived the attempts to expel them that affected the communities in the provinces, but a plague epidemic in 1680 and great fire in 1689 devastated the ghetto. Some Jews considered moving to another district, but finally the new ghetto was reconstructed on the ruins of the old. The situation nonetheless remained precarious, with explosions of anti-Semitism in 1694 resulting from the Simon Abeles affair (a twelve-year-old boy who wanted to convert to Catholicism was killed by his father and one of his father's friends).

At the beginning of the eighteenth century, approximately 12,000 Jews resided in Prague, making it the site of the largest Jewish settlement in Christendom. Life for the Jews became very difficult, however, under Emperor Charles VI (1711–40), who decided to drastically limit their numbers in the city. In 1726 he organized a census and enacted legislation putting a ceiling on the number of Jewish families living in Czech lands (8,541 in Bohemia and 5,160 in Moravia). Only one son per family— usually the eldest—had the right to marry and set up a household; other male children wanting to marry had to emigrate or wait for the departure or death of other family members. The ascension of Maria Theresa (1740–80) to the throne aggravated the status of Czech Jews, especially those in Prague. To punish their alleged disloyalty during the Silesian War against the Prussians, the bigoted archduchess issued a decree in 1744 banning all Jews from the capital. The measure elicited far-reaching public outcry in Europe, but Maria Theresa remained inflexible, and 13,000 Jews left the city for the surrounding areas in March the following year. The archduchess then

demanded they leave the Czech territories altogether. She finally relented, however, and after
exacting exorbitant payments as restitution—equivalent to ten times the normal yearly taxes—the
Jews were allowed to return to Prague in 1748–49.
They lived under the threat of new expulsions in a
dirty, overpopulated ghetto that contained on average 738 inhabitants per acre—a population density
three times that of the rest of the city. Fires were
unavoidable, and one in 1754 destroyed a large
part of the quarter, including six synagogues. Only
at the end of the century, with the ascension of
Emperor Joseph II (1780–90), did the Jews see
their fortunes improve.

The old Jewish quarter in Prague is still called
Josefov, in honor of the enlightened sovereign who,
with the *Toleranzpatent* (Tolerance edict) of 1782
abolished some of the discriminatory measures
against Jews. This decree accorded Jews and
Protestants a measure of religious freedom as well
as most of the rights enjoyed by other citizens of
the empire. Only sixty years later, however, did
full equality become a reality. The modernizing
reforms of Joseph II, which instituted, among other
things, military service and German as the language of instruction, profoundly impacted not only
the empire but also the daily lives of its Jews.
Thereafter Jews had access to secondary and even
higher education, but the communities of Bohemia
and Moravia nevertheless had to create primary
schools whose language of instruction was German.
Traditionalists such as the extreme critic of the
Haskalah Rabbi Ezekiel Landau denounced the
assimilatory trends of by the Jewish Enlightenment
then spreading among German communities. The
Jews were forced to give in, however, and the first
German-language Jewish school opened in Prague

on 2 May 1782. An elite, modern Jew was thus born and nurtured, and drawn to leave the ghetto, whose walls did not officially come down until the middle of the nineteenth century.

Virulent anti-Semitism remained in the general population, as demonstrated by riots in 1844, when angry textile workers destroyed Jewish-owned factories. In 1848, as the great wave of revolution swept across Europe and the Czech lands, the army had to intervene in Prague to protect Jewish property. With the establishment of the first Austrian constitution in the same year, the discriminatory laws were abolished and the empire's Jews finally won full and equal citizenship. It was another ten years, however, before they gained the right to own property outside the old ghettos.

The Jewish population grew considerably from the middle of the nineteenth century. By 1890, 94,599 Jews were living in Bohemia and 45,324 in Moravia. An ever greater number of Jews streamed into Prague and other industrial centers from the outlying towns and villages. A Jewish bourgeoisie formed, but integration proved difficult. This was due as much to the Jews feeling obliged to choose between their own culture and the Germanic world surrounding them as it was to the Czech nationalism that was increasingly suspicious of German culture and openly anti-imperialistic. "For the young Czech nationalists, the Jews were Germans. For the Germans, the Jews were Jews," emphasizes Ernst Pawel in his biography of Kafka, who experienced this conflict directly *The Nightmare of Reason: A Life of Franz Kafka* (New York: Farrar, Straus, Giroux, 1984). Hatred of Jews represented the only point of agreement between the most radical of the German and Czech nationalists. It is therefore not surprising that a number of the first militant Zionists came from the Czech lands. On the occasion of the first language census of 1880, which could be considered as a veritable declaration of faith for one or the other of these two identities, only a third of the Czech Jews declared Czech as their principal language. Ten years later, 55 percent chose Czech, although in fact almost all Jews spoke German. Although under some pressure to do so, choosing the Czech language showed Jews to have an attachment to the burgeoning Czech nation.

The Czech nationalist youth movement slid easily into anti-Semitism: during the riots of 1897, after overrunning the most well-known German cultural and commercial establishments, for three days the crowd attacked Jewish shops and synagogues and anyone who appeared to be a Jew. This rage took an even more malicious form in 1899 with the Hilsner Affair, eastern Europe's equivalent of the Dreyfus Affair in France. As Pawel notes, "Such was the hate-filled atmosphere of Kafka's world. But he had never known anything else, and it took some time before he understood why it was so difficult for him to breathe."

THE HILSNER AFFAIR

A young woman was found murdered on 1 April 1899, the night before Easter, near the hamlet of Polná, where she lived. For the villagers, it was clearly a Jewish ritual murder. A small anti-Semitic newspaper in Prague took the news item and amplified it into a public campaign accusing Leopold Hilsner, a Jewish cobbler in the village, of the crime. He was arrested, tried, and condemned to death without proof, thus unleashing a wave of anti-Semitism throughout the empire.

Tomáš Masaryk, the future first president of Czechoslovakia, was the only politician to have the courage to go against the tide of public opinion: in a small pamphlet, he demonstrated in minute detail all the inconsistencies of the investigation. Student demonstrations succeeded in forcing him from the university. The booklet was banned, and he was labeled a traitor. Nevertheless, the Left was roused, as well as some of the intelligentsia. A new trial took place, with, however, the same verdict, but the death penalty was commuted. The cobbler was finally pardoned in 1918.

Around this time the destruction of the old Jewish ghetto began as part of a vast project to clean up the oldest neighborhoods of the city. The new Jewish elite, like that in many other European cities, had little interest in preserving the houses and sordid little streets that only reminded them of the horrors of the recent past. The urban renewal operation, which lasted until 1905, wiped away not only the run-down hovels and old buildings, but also small synagogues.

Prague's German-speaking Jewish intelligentsia occupied a highly visible place in Czechoslovakia around the time of the First World War, especially in the world of literature as exemplified by Franz Kafka, Max Brod, Franz Werfel, Leo Perutz, and other members of the "Prague Circle." In this city the poet Paul Kornfeld called "an asylum for the metaphysically alienated," three cultures, German, Jewish, and Czech, intermingled, making Prague one of the great cultural capitals of Europe. Jews had key roles not only in the arts and industry but also in the political life of the new country. A representative example is Adolf Stransky, publisher since 1893 of the prestigious Czech daily *Lidové Noviny*. President Tomáš Masaryk even traveled to Palestine in 1927 in order to visit Jerusalem and the Jewish colonies. Unfortunately, the democratic and humanist Czech Republic that he succeeded in creating would last only twenty years.

In September 1938 Hitler imposed the Munich Accords on a Czechoslovakia abandoned by London and Paris. The accords amputated from Czechoslovakia the western Sudetenland, forcing thousands of Jews and Czechs to flee. Soon after, part of southern Slovakia was ceded to pro-Nazi Hungary, and German troops installed themselves in the rest of Slovakia, which in turn proclaimed itself an independent state allied with the Reich. In March 1939, what was left of Bohemia-Moravia was occupied by the Nazi army and placed under the direct control of the Reich. At the time, some 118,000 Jews lived in this territory. With the immediate imposition of the Nazi race laws, Jews were banned from all public positions and Jewish doctors were forced to limit their practice to Jewish patients. Jewish businesses were confiscated, Jews had to register all their belongings, and their capital and assets were seized. In 1940 they were forced to begin wearing the yellow star.

The Final Solution began in the Czech lands in October 1941 with the first convoy of 1,000 people to a Polish ghetto. A few months later, a ghetto was created in the small town of Terezín (in northern Bohemia), which had been emptied of all its inhabitants. Czech Jews were held there for weeks or months before transport to extermination camps in Poland. In all, approximately 89,000 Jews from Bohemia and Moravia were deported, of which 80,000 perished. After the war Jewish refugees from the east, especially Ruthenia, streamed into Prague. Approximately 19,000 Jews emigrated to Israel. Another wave of 15,000 departures followed in 1968 with the crushing of the Prague Spring by Soviet tanks. Today no more than some 6,000 Jews remain in the Czech Republic.

German troops, Prague Castle, 15 March 1939.

♛ LEAVE?

*"I've been spending every afternoon outside
on the streets, wallowing in anti-Semitic
hate. The other day I heard someone call the
Jews a 'mangy race.' Isn't it natural to leave
a place where one is so hated? (Zionism or
national feeling isn't needed for this at all.)
The heroism of staying on is nonetheless merely
the heroism of cockroaches, which cannot be
exterminated, even from the bathroom.*

*I just looked out the window: mounted
police, gendarmes with fixed bayonets, a
screaming mob dispersing, and up here in the
window the unsavory shame of living under
constant protection."*

FRANZ KAFKA, *LETTERS TO MILENA,* TRANS. PHILIP BOEHM
(NEW YORK: SCHOCKEN BOOKS, 1990).

Although Prague's rich Jewish heritage eclipses that of the country as a whole, Jewish institutions and tourists unduly overlook the outlying areas. In the small towns of Bohemia-Moravia, it is still possible to see extraordinary Jewish cemeteries, like that of Kolín, and well-preserved ghettos, as in Třebíč. The Nazis almost completely eliminated the small Jewish communities of the Czech territories, and a half century of neglect under Communism destroyed much of what remained of this heritage. Many synagogues have been transformed into shops, warehouses, or municipal buildings, and new structures have been placed atop former cemeteries. Still, numerous traces remain of the some 118,000 Jews who, until 1939, lived in Bohemia-Moravia, evidence discovered and catalogued through the patient work of historians and conservators.

→ **To call the Czech Republic from the United States, dial 011 420**
followed by the number of the person you are calling minus the initial 0 (used only for domestic calls).

Bohemia

Prague

Stuccoed in pink, green, or yellow, grand neo-Renaissance and neo-Gothic buildings line the Parizká, the Avenue of Paris. Since the fall of the Wall, elegant boutiques have been flourishing on this major traffic artery, which lacks none of the cachet that it had at the beginning of the century. Here the legendary ghetto of Prague was located until the renovation of the city center between 1897 and 1905. All that remains are the shadowy alleys abandoned by the growing number of Jews at the time of their emancipation in 1850. Only the poorest and most pious stayed in the former Jewish quarter, "with its shelves of old clothes, scrap metal, and other nameless things on display," as Apollinaire wrote in *Le Passant de Prague* (The Wandering Jew). It is the smallest district of old Prague, covering an area scarcely 86,000 square feet, and there is not a single tree except for those in the old cemetery. Deserted by its former inhabitants, these small, dirty islands of residential space were gradually invaded by the poor, the marginalized, and the city's prostitutes. In the first years of the twentieth century, the bordellos with their red lanterns and the disreputable taverns multiplied among the places of worship and buildings still inhabited by Orthodox Jews. On **Shabbat** evenings, the prayers and sacred songs of the Jews mingled with the blaring music of the gambling houses. This universe has disappeared. It survives only in the main synagogues, now museums, which still stand only steps away from the grand, straight avenues born of modern urban planning. In the past, these synagogues, with their mysterious, otherworldly facades, stood out among the sordid hovels that seemed ready to overwhelm them. Not long after the demolition of the ghetto, the poet Jaroslav Vrchlický wrote, "You are like widows, gray synagogues/Clothing torn and head covered with ashes/But when night with her black **tallit** descends on earth/I see your windows shine with candlelight and scarlet." The ghetto was razed, but its memory lives on, as Franz Kafka recalled in his conversations with Gustav Janouch.

☸ IMPRESSIONS OF THE GHETTO

"The picturesque aspect of the Ghetto (as we see it in yellowed photos and in the paintings of Jan Minařík, Antonín Slavíček and other artists from the beginning of the twentieth century) was a result of its daredevil architecture, the dense interweaving and overlapping of misshapen, damp, run-down, tainted hovels, nests for the King of Mice and his subjects. It was a bizarre labyrinth of filthy, unpaved alleyways as narrow as mine shafts, where sunbeams rarely swept away the refuse of the shadows; ugly, fetid alleyways running through the belly of a dilapidated tenement only to end like bats on a blind wall; alleyways like crevices crisscrossed by patches of mould and foul smells; zigzag alleyways with streetlamps on the corners, cesspool-like puddles and arched wooden doors; alleyways, whose bends and curves lent them a certain drunken, wobbly, dreamlike quality."

ANGELO MARIA RIPELLINO, *MAGIC PRAGUE*, TRANS. DAVID NEWTON MARINELLI, ED. MICHAEL HENRY HEIM (BERKELEY: UNIVERSITY OF CALIFORNIA PRESS, 1994).

Ghetto, Prague.

BOHEMIA

"In us all it still lives—the dark corners, the secret alleys, shuttered windows, squalid courtyards, rowdy pubs, and sinister inns. We walk through the broad streets of the newly built town. But our steps and our glances are uncertain. Inside we tremble just as before in the ancient streets of our misery. Our heart knows nothing of the slum clearance which has been achieved. The unhealthy old Jewish town within us is far more real than the new hygienic town around us. With our eyes open we walk through a dream: ourselves only a ghosts of a vanished age."

GUSTAV JANOUCH, *CONVERSATIONS WITH KAFKA*
(LONDON: QUARTET BOOKS, 1985).

*Torah cover, 1593.
Jüdisches Zentralmuseum, Prague.*

THE JEWISH MUSEUM

The Jewish Museum of Prague, created in 1906 as a symbol of Czech Jews' assimilation, manages the synagogues and the old Jewish cemetery. It possesses some of the world's richest collections of religious and domestic objects, manuscripts, paintings, and engravings gathered before the war, as well as numerous pieces that were pillaged by the Nazis in Bohemia and Moravia to be displayed in their "museum of the vanished race" that served their anti-Jewish propaganda machine in Prague. This stratagem ended up saving valuable objects and the several dozen intellectuals employed to classify them.

The idea for the museum had been nurtured by certain Jewish communities in the Czech lands that managed, with considerable difficulty, to convince the occupation authorities of the worthiness of their plan. The majority of the employees of the Jüdisches Zentralmuseum were finally deported in 1944, but the collections were saved. Under Communism it became the State Jewish Museum. The collections and so the heritage of the Jewish community of the Czech Republic were handed back in 1994. A selection of objects, the oldest ones, are displayed in the Meisel Synagogue and depict the history of the Jews in Bohemia-Moravia from their origins to the time of their emancipation. The rest of the exhibition, devoted to Jewish life from the eighteenth century until the end of the Second World War, occupies the rooms of the Spanish Synagogue, restored in 1998. The Pinkas Synagogue has a memorial bearing the names of the some 80,000 Jews of Bohemia-Moravia who were victims of the *Shoah*.

[Jewish Museum of Prague: Ustoveskooy 1, 11000 Prague 1. ✆ 0224819456. Open Sun–Fri 9 A.M.–6 P.M.]

THE OLD JEWISH QUARTER

A visit to the old Jewish quarter and its monuments requires at least a full day, although the sites are all concentrated in a few streets between Parizkà and Kaprovà avenues. Tickets valid for the entire tour can be bought at the entrance to the cemetery or the Jewish Museum. The synagogues and the cemetery are open every day except Saturday and Jewish holidays.

[🚇 Staromestskà (line A). 🚋 s17 or 18.]
■ The jagged brickwork of the Stare-Nova Synagogue's pediment looks as though it were pulled from an Expressionist film set. Now crowded on all sides by the surrounding buildings, this medieval synagogue set among the little streets of the ghetto has intrigued travelers and passersby for centuries with its narrow windows and strange facade. Today this synagogue is the oldest north of the Alps. Built in approximately 1280,

it is even older than the Saint Guy cathedral of Prague. It was first called the "New," and later the "Old-New" Synagogue when other grand synagogues were erected in the quarter in the sixteenth and seventeenth centuries. None of the other synagogues, however, have so many legends attached to them. One legend claims the celebrated synagogue was built with stones of the Temple of Jerusalem brought by Jews from Palestine at the time of their exodus. Another version of this tale recounts that the stone blocks were transported to Prague by angels. Other legends assert that when work began on the foundation, the synagogue suddenly rose from the ground after only a spadeful of earth had been dug. Abundant local romantic literature assserts that the golem's remains were located for many years in the synagogue's rafters under its great, steep roof.

Although it remains the most important and moving place of Jewish worship in Prague, the synagogue today is overrun with tourists. Located on the Cervenà ulicka (Red Street), the street name recalls the numerous butcher shops that existed on the small square nearby before the destruction of the ghetto. The re-plastering and other restorations of the synagogue have erased the patina created by centuries of lamp-oil smoke. The mildew stains on the walls that some had seen as traces of blood from the thousands of victims of the pogrom of 1389 have likewise vanished. The synagogue's interior plan is oblong, a borrowing from medieval monastic architecture. Two octagonal pillars support Gothic arches and separate the space into two naves. The interior layout is similar to that of the synagogue of Worms (1175) in southern Germany, which was torched by the Nazis. For many years the nave was reserved for men; women followed the services from the hallway and through small windows. Standing between two columns, the fifteenth-century **bimah** is surrounded by a large Gothic grille and the wooden seats of the faithful. The first seat to the right of the pulpit, bearing the number 1 and crowned by a Star of David, once belonged to Rabbi

Stare-Nova Synagogue and city hall, Prague.

Loew. The *aron* of the eastern wall features two Renaissance columns. Finely carved stone floral-motifs decorate the tabernacle. The prayer hall is illuminated by large wrought iron lamps. Carved grapes and vines adorn the magnificent tympanum of the great door to the prayer hall. These motifs are similar to those found in the famous Cistercian abbeys of southern Bohemia. Some historians believe that the same artisans worked on the structures of both faiths. The building's heavy masonry has protected it from the many fires that have ravaged the ghetto over the centuries.

[Stare-Nova Synagogue: Cervenà ulicka 1, 11000 Prague 1. ℭ 0222310302. Open Sun–Fri 9 A.M.–6 P.M.]

■ The Jewish city hall stands on Maislova Street, one of the ghetto's principal arteries and at one time named the Zlata ulicka (Street of Gold). The building was constructed circa 1560 with funds given by Mordecai Meisel, the financier and philanthropist who was the quarter's first mayor. In gratitude for their loyalty and courage during the siege of Prague by the Swedes, in 1648 the Jews were granted the right to add a belfry. Devastated by a fire in 1754, the edifice was rebuilt according to the rococo-style plans of architect Josef Schlessinger. The city hall is crowned by a small tower with two clocks, one with Roman numerals and the other, beneath it, with Hebrew numbers and hands that revolve counterclockwise. This building is now the administrative center for the rabbinate and the institutions of the Jewish community. Decorated with stuccowork and Stars of David, the large "Hall of Advisers," has been the home of a **kosher** restaurant, Shalom, since 1954. The restaurant is managed by the community and serves up generous portions.

[Jewish City Hall /Administrative Offices of the Rabbinate: Maislova ulicka 18, 11001 Prague 1. For information call Jewish City Hall ℭ 0224800803 or rabbinate ℭ 0224900812. No visits.]
[Shalom: Open noon–2 P.M.]

■ Across Cervená Street, one of the few remaining little streets of the ghetto, and opposite the Stare-Nova Synagogue is the Vysoka (High) Synagogue. It belongs to the same ensemble of buildings as the Jewish city hall and was built during the same period, in 1568, by the same architect, Pankratius Roder, from South Tirol. Damaged by several fires, notably that of 1689, it was remodeled at the end of the seventeenth century. The large prayer hall on the second floor retains its original appearance, with graceful arches of a mixture of late-Gothic and Renaissance styles and three beautiful windows on the northern wall and two on the eastern wall. The magnificent Baroque *aron* is located between the two windows of the eastern wall and dates from 1691. The synagogue was active until World War II, and again between 1946 and 1950. It has since

BOHEMIA

become an exhibition space for a collection of sacerdotal vestments belonging to the Jewish Museum.

[Vysoka Synagogue: Cervená ulicka 4–10, 11001 Prague 1. For information, contact Jewish City Hall ✆ 0224800803 or rabbinate ✆ 0224900812.]

■ The Meisel Synagogue was erected at the edge of the ghetto by Mordecai Meisel, who bought a piece of land there in 1590 for the construction of a private synagogue. An inscription, almost completely effaced, celebrates the many charitable deeds of the philanthropist. Constructed in 1591–92 after a design by Yehuda Goldschmied de Herz and Josef Wahl, Meisl's synagogue was the most elegant and richly decorated synagogue in the ghetto. It was destroyed by a fire in 1689, and rebuilt on a more modest scale. Again in 1754 the synagogue was devastated by fire. It was reconstructed in 1864, and made over yet again, this time from 1893 to 1905 in a neo-Gothic style by architect Alfred Grotte, when the entire zone was cleaned up. The synagogue was restored in 1994, and it has served as one of the main exhibition spaces of the Jewish Museum since the early 1960s. On display are extraordinary pieces of old silverwork—decorated Torah scrolls, goblets, chandeliers—collected from all 153 Jewish communities of the Czech lands, most of which have disappeared.

[Meisel Synagogue: Maislova ulicka 10, 11001 Prague 1. Open Apr–Oct, Sun–Fri 9 A.M.– 6 P.M.; Nov–Mar, Sun–Fri 9 A.M.–4:30 P.M.]

■ The Klaus Synagogue was built in 1694 right next to the entrance of the Jewish cemetery and on the former site of the Klausers. The Klausers were three small buildings, one of which was a synagogue erected in 1564, and another of which was Rabbi Loew's school. All three were destroyed in a major fire of 1689. The current synagogue takes its name from the Klausers, whose place it occupies. It was the second most important house of worship in the Jewish community. The building has been renovated several times, notably in 1883 by the architect Bedrich Münzberger, who enlarged the original structure and added a women's gallery. The majestic prayer hall, which features an impressive *aron* dating from 1696, currently serves as a repository of manuscripts and early printed works for the Jewish Museum. On the western wall, there is a magnificent *aron* of carved wood originally from the synagogue of Podboransky Rohozec.

[Klaus Synagogue: Stareho Hrbitova ulicka 3a, 11001 Prague 1. ✆ 0222310302. Open Apr–Oct, Sun–Fri 9 A.M.–6 P.M.; Nov–Mar, Sun–Fri 9 A.M.–4:30 P.M.]

■ The Pinkas Synagogue was built on the edge of the old cemetery in the fifteenth century for the Horowitz family and later enlarged in the middle of the sixteenth century. Completed in 1535, it was rebuilt in a late-Renaissance style between 1607 and 1625. The current building preserves the original plan, but the large Gothic nave with its rich polychromatic decorations have totally disappeared in the numerous renovations, especially those from the beginning of the seventeenth century designed by the architect Yehuda Goldschmied de Herz. The synagogue was altered again more than a century later, in 1862. The *aron* is Renaissance-Baroque in style. The stone **bimah** is enclosed by a lovely metalwork grille dating from the eighteenth century. Off to the side you can see the main remnants of a **mikvah**. In 1960 the walls of the synagogue were inscribed with the names and birth and death dates of the 77,297 Jews from Prague and the surrounding Czech lands killed by the Nazis. The synagogue was closed

for about thirty years and was restored only in the late 1990s.

[Pinkas Synagogue: Sirokà ulicka 3, 11001 Prague 1. ✆ 0222326660. Open Apr–Oct, Sun–Fri 9 A.M.–6 P.M.; Nov–Mar, Sun–Fri 9 A.M.–4:30 P.M.]

■ The Moorish-style Spanish Synagogue was built in 1867 and occupies the place where the oldest synagogue of Prague once stood. The Old School, as it was called, served the Byzantine community of Jews in the twelfth and thirteenth centuries. They had their own small ghetto separated from the Jewish quarter and near the Church of the Holy Spirit and a convent. The synagogue was destroyed by pogroms, including that of 1389, and several fires and rebuilt, each time to its original plan of a long hall covered by a steep roof.

Pinkas Synagogue, Prague, 1905.

BOHEMIA

THE SYNAGOGUES IN AND AROUND PRAGUE

Other small synagogues were constructed during the same period in a variety of districts in Prague and its suburbs. Most of them, including Kralovske Vinorady, were destroyed during the air raids of World War II. The others were deconsecrated and transformed into warehouses or stores. Nevertheless, one can still admire the very interesting oriental style functionist building built in 1930 for the neighborhood Jewish community on Strupeznického Street in Smíchov (about two miles southwest of Prague). In Karlín (one and a half miles east of Prague) a tiny neo-Renaissance synagogue was constructed in 1860 and then transformed into a Hussite church. It can still be found on a small street in the countryside called Vitkova Street.

It became the first Reform synagogue in the city at the beginning of the nineteenth century, and an organ was installed. In 1868, it was decided to raze the older and set in its place a larger place of worship symbolic of the new role the most modern fringe of the Jewish community began to have in Czech society. Architect Vojtech Ignac Ullmann, who had designed important public buildings such as the current headquarters of the Academy of Science, chose the Moorish style so fashionable among Jewish communities (especially those of Germany) at the time. Erected according to architect Bedrich Münzberger's plans on a square plan with a large dome, the interior of this synagogue is richly decorated with stuccowork inspired by the Alhambra of Granada. The synagogue has been restored and serves today as an exhibition hall for the Jewish Museum.

[Spanish Synagogue. Vezecka ulika 1, 11001 Prague 1. ✆ 0224194464.

Open Apr–Oct, Sun–Fri 9 A.M.–6 P.M.; Nov–Mar, Sun–Fri 9 A.M.–4:30 P.M.]

■ Around the time of the great urban renewal projects of the former ghetto at the beginning of the twentieth century, three small synagogues were destroyed: the New Synagogue (end of the sixteenth century); the Tzigane Synagogue (seventeenth century, modified in the eighteenth), where the young Franz Kafka had his Bar Mitzvah at the age of thirteen; and the Synagogue of the Great Court (1626). The Synagogue of the Jubilee replaced these three and was constructed outside the old Jewish quarter in the Nove Mesto (New City). Erected in 1905–06, it celebrated the integration of Jews into Prague society at the beginning of the century. Constructed according to plans by the architect Alois Richter, it melds the Moorish style with Art Nouveau elements, especially in its interior design.

[Jubilee Synagogue: Jerusalemska ulicka, 11000 Prague 1. To visit contact the Jewish Community of Prague ✆ 0224800803.]

■ Although the cemetery's well-marked walkways have been cordoned off to prevent the tens of thousands of tourists who file through it each year from walking on the graves, the old Jewish cemetery in Prague remains the most famous and interesting in Europe. It is best to visit it either very early or very late in the day, or outside the tourist season altogether, in order to capture the poignant nostalgia of the place. Some 12,000 gravestones are piled one upon another—sometimes three or four deep or more. The grounds are a hodgepodge of crooked stones, like swaying drunkards, buried almost to their tops, covered in ivy, and swallowed up by the damp, black earth. A few trees, mostly alders and elms, manage to grow in this mass of stones, their inclining trunks recalling the gravestones worn by the weather and caresses of the faithful. You can still make out the inscriptions in remembrance of the dead, and often the bas-reliefs symbolizing a family name, occupation, or the virtues of the deceased. Hands in a gesture of blessing indicate the tomb of a **Kohen** (or Cohen, Kohn, Kahn, or Kagan), descendants of Aaron and the great priests of the Temple, the **Kohanim.** The pitcher or basin adorning many gravestones marks the final resting places of the Leviyim, or the **Levites** (descendants of Levi), the second group in line after the **Kohanim** to read from the **Torah** during celebrations at the synagogue. Other motifs, such as palm leaves, recall the verses from the Psalms, "The good man will flourish like a palm tree" (Psalm 92:13). A bunch of grapes symbolizes abundance and the kingdom of Israel. Despite the prohibition against representing the human figure, there are a few rare feminine silhouettes carved onto tombs dating from the seventeenth and eighteenth

RABBI LOEW

Physician, astronomer, and mathematician, Rabbi Loew was born in 1512 (or 1520) near Poznań (in present-day Poland). The most respected Jewish thinker of his time, Loew was a renowned interpreter of the **Talmud** and the Law. Though above all a scientist, in the popular imagination of the nineteenth century he became a great **Kabbalist,** even a Jewish Faust, who had created a golem, an artificial man of clay who escaped from his creator. He was invited to meet Rudolf II on 16 February 1592, and according to legend, made shadows of the great figures of Genesis and the Patriarchs appear on the walls of the room. It was also reported that he succeeded in avoiding death for several years by tearing from Death's hands the list containing the names of those slated to die. Death did manage to catch up to him, hidden in a rose his granddaughter gave him to smell.

centuries, symbolizing, according to the tradition, the desire of God to enter the hearts of men. Other, more prosaic images represent an occupation, such as a boat for merchants, tweezers for doctors, or scissors for tailors. There are also many sculptures of animals, first and foremost the lion, representing the royal kingdom of Judah and the twelve tribes of Israel or recalling the name of the deceased (Löwe, German for "lion," or Leyb in **Yiddish**). The bear also figures in this stone bestiary, suggesting the search for honey that symbolizes the Jew immersed in the sweetness of the **Torah.** Also depicted are the doe and the gazelle ("because God runs to the synagogue to hear the prayers of Israel"), as well as birds.

The oldest tomb is that of Rabbi Avigdor Kara, which dates to 1439. An older cemetery, desecrated at the time of the pogrom of 1389, was found near the present-day Vladislavova Street in the Nove Mesto. The last tombs were erected in 1787, the year the cemetery was closed at the command of Emperor Joseph II. Small stones are placed on the most celebrated tombs, such as the one decorated with lions of the wise and holy Rabbi Yehuda Loew ben Betsalel (1512–1609), called Maharal and reputed to have performed miracles even after his death. Pilgrims slide slips of paper with their requests and prayers in the crevices of the red stone. Another venerated tomb is that of Mordecai Meisel

(1528–1601), the philanthropic financier who was mayor and benefactor of Prague's Jews. The epitaph on his tomb recalls that "his generosity was without limits and his charity was given with all his heart and soul."

[Jewish Cemetery: Starého Hrbitova ulica 17, 11001 Prague 1. ✆ 0222310302. Open Apr–Oct, Sun–Fri 9 A.M.–6 P.M.; Nov–Mar, Sun–Fri 9 A.M.–4:30 P.M.]

THE ZIZKOV CEMETERIES

■ The earliest graves of the Old Zizkov cemetery date to 1680, but

Jewish Cemetery, Prague.

the cemetery really began to grow after 1787 with the closing of the one in the old ghetto. In the restored section one can see lovely Baroque and classical sepulchers. The last burials date from 1890. Part of the cemetery has been transformed into a park. There is also a television transmission tower on the grounds.

[Old Cemetery of Zizkov: Fibichova ulicka. Open Tue and Thu 10 A.M.–noon]

■ The new cemetery, established in 1890, is Prague's only Jewish cemetery still in use. The large hall, which also houses the administrative offices, was constructed in a neo-Renaissance style at the end of the nineteenth century. The cemetery includes magnificent tombs in the Art Nouveau, neo-Gothic, and neo-Renaissance styles. Franz Kafka is interred here beside his parents. The tomb is crowned by a sober gray stone stele where visitors often leave small stones in homage. Opposite is the grave of the writer Max Brod, Kafka's friend and confidant, who, after Kafka's death, refused to burn Kafka's writings despite the demand in his will.

[New Cemetery: avenue Jan Zelivsky. ✆ 0272738387. Open Apr–Oct, Mon–Fri 9:30 A.M.–5:30 P.M. Nov–Mar, Mon–Fri 9:30 A.M.–4:30 P.M.]

THE FRANZ KAFKA HOUSES

A visit to the nostalgic sites of Jewish Prague would not be complete without a trip to the places where the most famous Jewish author lived. All his life, despite his parents' many changes of residence and his own, Franz Kafka stayed within a narrow perimeter of the old city center around the large square, some three hundred feet from the former Jewish quarter.

■ Kafka's birthplace (at 5 Radnice Street) is situated on the northeast side of the large square. He was born here 3 July 1883. Of the original building destroyed in a fire in 1896, only the main entrance remains. A bust commemorating the writer was placed there in 1965.

■ Two years after their son came into the world, Kafka's parents moved. After some wandering around the quarter, they settled in the U Minuti House on the old city square, near the great clock. The facade of this seventeenth-century building is decorated with biblical scenes and classical legends from antiquity. Kafka lived here from age six to thirteen; his three sisters Elli, Valli, and Ottla, who died while being deported, were born here.

■ In 1896, the Kafka family moved into a lovely old home, "In the Name of the Three Magi," at 3 Celetnà Street. Kafka, whose bedroom faced the street, remained here until the time of his law studies. His father's first store, Hermann, was a little further away at number 8 of the square on the north side, but it has not been preserved. A few years later, Kafka's father moved his business to Celetnà Street, and then, in 1912, to the ground level of the imposing Kinsky Palace on the square. The German lyceum that Kafka attended was located in a wing of this building.

■ In 1907, about the time Kafka had begun working at Assicurazioni Generali, the family settled at 36 Niklasstrasse (now Parizkà Street) in an elegant building constructed on the ruins of the former ghetto. The house, zum Schiff (like a boat), was very close to the Vltava. Here he wrote three of his masterpieces, *The Judgement, Amerika,* and *The Metamorphosis.* The building was destroyed in 1945.

■ In 1913 the Kafka family returned to the old city square to live in the Oppelt House (Starometseke Náměsti): Kafka's bedroom faced Parizkà Street.

■ In 1914, Kafka left for nearby 10 Bilkova, lent him by his sister Valli and where he began to write *The Trial.*

■ Beginning in May 1915, Kafka lived alone for the first time in the "House of the Golden Pike" (now 16 Dlouhà Street). "Without a broad view, without the possibility of seeing a big swath of the sky, or at least a tower in the distance to compensate me for the lack of open, empty countryside—without all that, I am an unhappy man, a man oppressed," he wrote to Felice Bauer at the time.

■ He next lived for a few months on the other side of the river in a little house at 22 Zlata Street (Little Street of the Alchemists), near Prague Castle. In May 1917, he also rented an

Franz Kafka, 1914.

Kafka's house, Alchemists' Street, Prague.

apartment in the magnificent Schön-born Palace (15 Trziste), today the location of the American embassy.

JEWISH SITES IN CHRISTIAN PRAGUE

Some of Prague's extraordinary architectural heritage is directly tied to the Jewish past.

■ On the Charles Bridge, the third statue on the right coming from the old city represents a Christ bearing a large golden inscription in Hebrew ("The Holy One, the Lord") paid for as a fine in 1696 by a Jew accused of having blasphemed the name of Jesus.

■ In the Church of Saint-Mary-of-the-Tyn in the old-city square, there is a plaque commemorating a "hero" of the Counter-Reformation. "Solemnly buried here is the fellow believer of the Catechism, Simon Abeles, killed in the name of hatred of the Christian faith by his own father, a Jew," states the text, recalling the young Jewish boy, aged twelve, who, tempted to convert, was killed by his father and his father's friend 21 February 1694. Arrested in the old city, Lazar Abeles, the father of the victim, hanged himself by his prayer shawl in his cell in the city hall. The corpse was dragged outside the city walls, drawn and quartered, mutilated, and his heart was placed on the mouth of his slain son. His accomplice, one Löbl Kurthandl, was tortured on the wheel until he renounced his faith, after which he was put to death. The remains of the child were found intact in the Jewish cemetery—a sign of a miracle—and were laid out for a month in the church of Tyn. During this time, the village and the clergy filed past the body to pay their respects. In the years between the two world wars, several historians, including Egon Erwin Kisch, examined records of the trial and forever put to rest the legend forged by the Jesuits in the seventeenth century. The circumstances surrounding the death of the child remain unclear, but the charges were entirely fabricated in order to force the guilty to convert.

Drevikov

In the village of Drevikov, roughly sixty miles southeast of Prague, it is possible to see how Jews lived in the villages of Bohemia at the end of the nineteenth century, before their immigration to cities and industrial centers. About thirty Jewish families lived in the two-story houses on the "Jewish street" of this village.

■ The school and small synagogue of the community, now a store, can still be seen. The old cemetery is nearby at the edge of a wood. The Jewish houses, partly of wood, the small synagogue, and the **mikvah** are to the village's south.

■ Velká Bukovina, further away, is another rural ghetto that is well preserved.

Kolín

The city of Kolín, one of the most important places of Jewish remembrance in the Czech lands, is worth a trip to see the small streets of the Jewish quarter and the magnificent cemetery. Overrun with vegetation, the cemetery's atmosphere recalls that of Prague's old Jewish cemetery before it became a usual stop for large tour groups. The Jews settled in this town close to the Kutná Hora and its gold mines as early as the fourteenth century. Expelled and then allowed to return in the sixteenth century, the Jews' homes stood in what was probably already the ghetto dating from the time they first settled

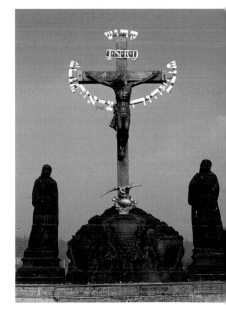

Christ on the cross,
Charles Bridge, Prague.

in the city. The Jewish section was in the western corner of the city's old walls near the large central square.

■ Zidovska ulicka (Street of the Jews), lined with small Baroque and classical houses, has been transformed into two streets, Na Hradbach and Zlata streets. You can still see the building housing the school and synagogue, constructed in 1642 and enlarged in the eighteenth century, with the addition of decorative stuccowork on the arches. The Baroque *aron* is also eighteenth century. Active until World War II, it is now no longer in use. A small portion of its ornaments and religious objects are preserved in a synagogue in Colorado in the United States.

[Synagogue: 152/7 Na Hradbach. Contact the local tourist office: ✆ 0321748111.
❶ sekretariat@mukolin.cz.]

■ The old cemetery is accessible from Slunecni Street; the former main entrance on Kmochova Street is now closed. The cemetery was enlarged several times during its history until its closure in 1887, and it contains more than 2,600 gravestones. The oldest graves date from the beginning of the fifteenth century. The new Jewish cemetery, which is at the edge of the city in the neighborhood of Zálabí, is not particularly interesting.

[The keys to the old cemetery are available by request from the regional museum. For more information, contact the local tourist office: ✆ 0321748111.
❶ sekretariat@mukolin.cz.]

Čáslav

Those with a healthy curiosity should make a quick detour to the small town of Čáslav, located forty-four miles southeast of the capital. Forbidden to Jews until the middle of the nineteenth century, the communities in the neighboring villages began to settle here after the Jews' emancipation. To the northeast of the large square on Fucikova Street one can see an unusual synagogue in a neo-Moorish style with an odd rounded pediment and a beautiful painted-wood interior.

Golcuv Jenikov

The small town of Golcuv Jenikov near Čáslav had a significant Jewish quarter of some fifty homes to the south of the town's central square. Most have kept their original appearance. Of interest is that Christians also lived in Golcuv Jenikov's Jewish quarter.

■ The oriental neo-Romanesque synagogue was constructed in the middle of the nineteenth century.

■ The Jewish cemetery has some interesting Baroque tombs.

■ The nearby little town of Heřmanuv Městec had a significant ghetto close to the current Havlickova Street. Its synagogue now serves as a warehouse, but the *aron* has been preserved.

Březnice

In Březnice in western Bohemia one can still see the former Jewish quarter created in 1570 by the local lord, Ferdinand of Loksany, and enlarged a century and a half later. The two streets and small square of the quarter are lined with low houses. Březnice's Jewish quarter is located to the north of the town's central square.

■ Its most beautiful building is the Popper Palace, a manor house with courtyard that belonged to the celebrated Jewish merchant and financier of the eighteenth century, Joachim von Popper, one of the first Jews in the Czech lands to receive a noble title.

■ The synagogue, constructed in 1725 and remodeled a century later, still exists and is located on the square of the former ghetto, although it is now used for storage. Despite the new building and road construction projects, the town's small Jewish quarter preserves its original plan and architecture.

■ At the edge of the city on the way to the village of Přední Poříčí is a Jewish cemetery active until World War II that has some interesting Baroque-style tombs.

Kasejovice

There is a small Jewish quarter of about ten houses to the southwest of Kasejovice's central square, linked to the rest of the city by a narrow, straight street.

■ The synagogue, in the heart of the Zidovske Mesto, was built in 1762 in the rococo style and redone a century later. With its striking *aron* and painted decorative features, it is one of the most interesting and best preserved in the region.

Plzeň

Plzeň is the principal center and beer capital of western Bohemia. The Jews were expelled from the city in 1504 and not permitted to return for more than two centuries. Following the industrial and urban development in the nineteenth century, a Jewish community resettled here and flourished. In 1921 more than 3,000 Jews lived in Plzeň.

■ Three synagogues were built in Plzeň in the nineteenth century. The most interesting of the three stands to the west of the historic city center on Nejedleho Sady. Crowned by two towers, this magnificent neo-Romanesque building dates from 1890. No longer active, it is slated to become an exhibition space about Jewish life in western Bohemia. A small prayer hall was established at 80 Smetanovu Sady, in 1988.

■ The neighboring villages still have traces of the life of the small local Jewish communities, especially Radnice (approximately twelve miles northeast), which has a small Jewish

BOHEMIA

Synagogue, Plzeň.

quarter, an eighteenth-century synagogue (now a storage facility), and a small cemetery. Rokycany (about nine miles east of Plzeň) also merits a visit.

Roudnice nad Labem

The large village of Roudnice nad Labem twenty-five miles from Prague was one of the first small centers of Judaism in Bohemia and merits a brief visit. The oldest Jewish quarter, destroyed in the seventeenth century, stood beside the village's lovely Baroque castle.

■ The "new ghetto" is to the west of the castle in what is today Havlickova Street. It contains ten or so homes, eventually sold to Christians. The quarter spread while remaining separated from the rest of the town by a barrier. The homes on the south side of Havlickova Street have maintained much of their appeal.

■ At one time Roudnice nad Labem had three synagogues. Not a trace remains of the oldest synagogue. The second, erected in 1613 and remodeled in 1675, was destroyed at the end of the nineteenth century to make way for the train station. The third, to the north of Havlickova Street, was constructed in 1852 in a neo-Romanesque style and was in use until World War II. It now functions as a warehouse.

■ Three cemeteries also existed in Roudnice nad Labem. The most moving of them extends roughly 1,200 feet from the existing synagogue and contains interesting tombstones from the seventeenth and eighteenth centuries.

Terezín (Theresienstadt)

The lovely little garrison town of Terezín in the same region was created at the end of the eighteenth century during the reign of Joseph II. In 1942, the Nazis totally emptied the city of its 7,000 inhabitants — with the exception of Jewish families— and transformed it into a ghetto and transit center for Czech Jews of the capital and surrounding lands. Some 57,000 Jews were held in Terezín's newly formed ghetto. As many as 152,000 deported Jews of fifty-three different nationalities passed through the town, including 74,000 Czechs. More than 30,000 of the imprisoned died in the ghetto. Approximately 87,000 departed from Terezín to the death camps, of which only 3,000 returned. A quarter of the ghetto's inhabitants died of illnesses related to lack of hygiene and malnutrition. Despite the terrible conditions and mass arrests, the prisoners succeeded in maintaining a minimum of organization and social life, with centers for study and prayer. Of the some 150,000 Jews transited through Terezín, the 3,000 who stayed there several years received a basic education, in secret since schools were prohibited. The brightest stars of the Jewish-Czech intelligentsia were sent to this ghetto, including sculptors, painters, musicians, writers, and other intellectuals, whose presence was used as part of the Nazi propaganda machine. A delegation of the International Committee of the Red Cross was authorized to visit the ghetto in June 1944. When the camp was liberated on 8 May 1945 by the Red Army, 6,800 Jews were still in detention.

■ A memorial was erected in 1955 in the eastern part of the cemetery with text in Hebrew and Czech. Close to 13,000 persons—in 11,250 individual graves and 215 communal burial pits—were buried between 1941 and 1942 in the ghetto's cemetery, beside the municipal cemetery. The crematorium constructed by the Nazis at the time has been transformed into an exhibition space. At the end of 1944, the ashes of the 22,000 victims were thrown into the nearby Ohře River. A small burial mound in memory of those who died has been erected on the riverbank.

[Cemetery and Crematorium:
℘ 0416782442.
Open Sun–Fri 10 A.M.–5 P.M.]

■ On a hill above the city stands the Kleine Festung (small fortress). This former Austrian prison served as a Gestapo interrogation center where some 35,000, including a number of Resistance fighters, were questioned and imprisoned. The remains of 26,000 of these prisoners are buried in the national cemetery in front of the center. Since 1962 the town of Terezín and its fortress have been national museums.

[Guided tours only. ℘ 0416782225.
❶ manager@pamatnik-terezin.cz.]
[Kleine Festung: Open Oct–Mar, daily 9 A.M.–4:30 P.M.; Apr–Sep, daily 8 A.M.–6 P.M.]
[Ghetto: Open Oct–Mar, daily 9 A.M.–5:30 P.M.; Apr–Sep daily 9 A.M.–6 P.M.]

Moravia ■

Třebíč

■ The city of Třebíč is located thirty-one miles north of Brno on the other side of the Jihlava River. Its Jewish quarter, near the city center, was one of the largest in the country: in the middle of the nineteenth century, it counted more than a hundred houses. The quarter grew beginning in the sixteenth century, and even today many of its residences retain some traces of their Baroque or Renaissance origins.

■ The Old Synagogue, on Tiché Square west of the former ghetto, was erected in the eighteenth century on the remains of a very old wooden synagogue. Destroyed several times by fire, it was rebuilt in a

Synagogue, Třebíč.

neo-Gothic style and enlarged for the last time in the nineteenth century. After the war it became a place of worship for the Hussite Church.

■ The New Synagogue on Blahoslavova Street was probably also built on the remains of a wooden building dating from the eighteenth century. It was remodeled in 1845 and 1881. Now an exhibition and concert hall, it retains part of its interior decoration, most notably its stuccoed ceiling.

■ Although no trace remains of the former cemetery near the castle, it is possible to visit the large cemetery—with over 3,000 gravestones—on Hradek Street not far from the Old Synagogue. The oldest stones date back to the beginning of the seventeenth century.

Boskovice

Boskovice is located nineteen miles north of Brno. This large center of Jewish culture and study of the **Torah** was for many years the headquarters of the Chief Rabbinate of Moravia.

■ The fifteenth-century Jewish quarter extends from the present-day Bilkova and Plackova Streets, near the large square. The original plan, with the ghetto gate always visible and the tiny streets lined with two-story houses, has remained almost completely intact despite the renovations and restorations undertaken in the nineteenth century.

■ The Grand Synagogue is on Traplova Street, in the heart of the former ghetto. The original seventeenth-century building was remodeled in the nineteenth century in a neo-Gothic style.

■ The cemetery is one of the largest in Moravia. There is a new (small) museum that can be visited.

[Cemetery: Plackova 6, Boskovice. Contact the director for information and opening hours: ✆ 602249400. ❶ muzaum@boskovice.cz.]

Mikulov

After Prague, until the nineteenth century the largest Jewish community in all the Czech lands lived in the city of Mikulov, south of Brno. Its *yeshivoth* were renowned throughout the region, even to Galicia. The ghetto extended to the west of the old city around the present-day Husova and Zameskà streets, but only a few houses dating from the ghetto's heyday still stand. In the nineteenth century—and before the demolitions of 1950–60 the Jewish quarter had some ten prayer halls and three synagogues.

■ Only one of Mikulov's synagogues remains: the Old Synagogue, built in 1550 and destroyed by fire nearly two centuries later. It was reconstructed in 1723. The only Polish-style synagogue of its kind in the Czech Republic, it has four columns at the center of the large prayer hall surrounding the **bimah.**

MORAVIA

JIRI FIEDLER: ARCHAEOLOGIST OF MEMORY

Born in Olomouc in Moravia, the historian Jiri Fiedler worked almost completely alone for many years despite the indifference or even hostility on the part of Communist authorities, compiling a list of the last vestiges of some 700 Jewish communities—proof of their presence in Czech lands over many centuries. "Today there are 200 synagogues in this country. There were 300 more than that after the war," states Fiedler. His book *Jewish Sights of Bohemia and Moravia* (Prague: Sefer Ed., 1991) is an indispensable guide and exhaustive catalogue of a constantly threatened heritage. Over the years dozens of small village synagogues have been transformed into shops or storage spaces. Those in use as warehouses have been destroyed either by the state or by their owners. The small Jewish cemeteries dotting the Czech countryside are attacked by vandals convinced there is gold to be found in Jewish tombs.

[Old Synagogue: Zamek ulicka 1, Mikulov. Contact the Jewish Community of Brno for information:✆ 0545244710.]

■ Some of the tombs of this large city cemetery date to 1608. As in Prague, the grave markers in the oldest part of the cemetery are piled up in several layers. There are roughly 2,500 tombstones here, some richly decorated. The entrance to the cemetery is on the Hrbitovni Square.

Poland

$\mathbf{P}$OLAND REPRESENTS THE MOST ILLUSTRI-
OUS AND TRAGIC CHAPTER in European Jewish
history. For centuries, this country was the most
welcoming to Jews fleeing Germany, Spain, and
southern Europe; the continent's largest Jewish
community was born here, enjoying privileges and
autonomy granted by the different kings and developing an incredibly rich culture of its own. Ultimately, however, Poland wound up the largest
Jewish cemetery in Europe, the place where the
Nazi dream of "exterminating the Jewish race"
was almost perfectly realized. Two numbers are
enough to grasp the magnitude of the disaster:
there were 3,500,000 Jews in Poland in 1939, or
10 percent of the population; a maximum of 2,000
to 3,000 live here today. Touring Jewish Poland
resembles an archaeological dig conducted after a
Pompeii-style cataclysm, a search for traces of a
lost civilization alive today only in literature and the
memories of those who emigrated in time or miraculously survived.

The earliest remnant of a Jewish presence in
Poland dates to the tenth century: a traveler from

*Sculpted wooden doors of the hekhal of a Polish synagogue,
seventeenth century, Wolfson Museum, Jerusalem.*

Toledo, Ibrahim ibn Jacob, wrote the first major report dealing with Poland in 965. In 1098, during the Crusades, Jews expelled from Prague settled in Poland. Jewish communities were mentioned in Płock in 1237, Kalisz in 1287, and Kraków in 1304. In 1264, the king of Poland, Boleslas the Pious, issued the "Kalisz statute," which guaranteed Jews religious freedom and security of person and property. In the fourteenth century, under Casimir the Great, these privileges were reaffirmed in 1364 and 1367, and then once more in 1453 by Casimir Jagiello; they remained effective for Jews until Poland was divided in the late eighteenth century. Jewish communities here were virtually autonomous, enjoying the right to dispense justice and build synagogues and schools, making Poland the most tolerant country to Jews in Europe.

Starting in the mid-sixteenth century, Jewish exiles from Germany found refuge in Poland. Jewish quarters began forming in Lvov (1356), Sandomierz (1367), and Kazimierz near Kraków (1386); in all, communities were reported in eighty-five cities. Refugees continued flowing in throughout the sixteenth and early seventeenth centuries not simply from the Germanic countries but also from Spain, Italy, and Turkey. Centers of Jewish life began shifting eastward through the country.

In 1581, the first "Diet of the Four Countries" convened in Lublin (Sejm Czeterech Ziem, or in Hebrew *Vaad arba aratsot*) and continued to meet every year until 1764. The Sejm, or Vaad, governed the Jewish communities of Poland and Lithuania: it issued rulings, collected taxes, and worked to protect the community. It was the Vaad that voted to erect fortified synagogues in Brody, Buchach, Lesko, Lublin, Shargorod, Stryy, Szczebrzeszyn, Zamość, Żółkiew, and other towns. In 1648, the Jewish pop-

Polish Jews, *circa 1865. Bibliothèque des Arts Décoratifs, Paris.*

ulation in Poland was estimated at 500,000 inhabitants, or already 5 percent of the total population.

A fifth of Poland's Jews were massacred by the Cossacks under Bohdan Khmelnitsky. The **Hasidic** religious revitalization movement was born and flourished in Poland and Ukraine as an indirect consequence of these massacres and of the impoverishment of those who survived them. Jews would have to wait until the eighteenth century for their communities to form again and grow. In 1790, after the first division of Poland, their number reached about 900,000, or 10 percent of the population.

From 1795 to 1918, Poland was erased from the map, split between the three neighboring powers (Russia, Austria, Prussia), except during the years

1807–15, at which time Napoleon created the Grand Duchy of Warsaw. The vast majority of Jewish communities in Poland found themselves under the Russian Empire and so lost all the privileges they had enjoyed during the Polish era. Community self-governance was suppressed, as the czar relegated the Jewish population to the Pale of Settlement and imposed other serious restrictions on them. A large proportion of Jews also lived in the section of Poland annexed by Austria (Galicia); though they did at first see some of their privileges abolished, they benefited from favorable local governments in certain cities. From 1867 to 1868, all subjects under the Austrian monarchy, including Jews, were granted equal rights. In Galicia the assimilation of Jews was greatest: a number of Jewish intellectuals turned toward German culture, such as Karl-Emil Franzos (born in Czortkov) and Joseph Róth (born in Brody), while others embraced Polish culture, such as Bruno Schultz (born in Drohobych).

After the First World War, an independent Poland was re-created with enlarged eastern borders containing "borderlands" *(kresy)* in Galicia, Volhynia, Belarus, and Lithuania.

The "Jewish question" was increasingly posed: this was not merely a national and religious question but a social one, considering the teaming, poverty-stricken masses that lived in Poland's ghettos. The Polish government between the wars, dominated by anti-Semitic National Democracy, burdened them with taxes and prevented their social ascent. Tensions were mounting, and when the "rising threat" and German occupation arrived, the Jews were slowly but surely abandoned by the Poles, themselves subject to severe repression and concerned with their own survival.

Jewish quarter of Kazimeirz in Krakow, *nineteenth century. Max Berger Collection, Vienna.*

What followed is too well-known to be related here in detail. On 1 September 1939, the Germans invaded Poland and created ghettos in which they gathered together the Jewish population, strictly separating the Jews from the "Aryan" districts and imposing sweeping restrictions aimed at exhausting them through work and lack of food.

Starting in 1941 and throughout 1942, the ghettos were liquidated one by one, their populations transferred to newer camps in Chełmno, Bełżec, Sobibór, and Treblinka explicitly designed for extermination, or to already existing ones like Auschwitz or Majdanek, set up both for labor and extermination. The entire Jewish population of Poland, with few exceptions, perished in these death camps. The best known of all the camps is

Auschwitz, today the symbol of the *Shoah*. It was there that the industry of death was taken to its extreme. However, we will only touch on Auschwitz in this guide, precisely because its history is so well-known and because it is so much visited and so depressing. We have chosen to stop at Poland's more beautiful sites, to discover and tour with pleasure and emotion places like Kraków, Lesko, Zamość, and Lublin, and to present lesser known but equally moving camps like Sobibór, Treblinka, and Chełmno, where a visitor can reflect more easily than among the throngs of tourists at Auschwitz.

The postwar history of Polish Judaism demonstrated once again misunderstandings between Jews and Poles. Besides the rare survivors of the ghettos, the only other Jews still living were soldiers in the Soviet zone who had joined the Red Army and participated in their country's liberation. When they returned, they found the ghettos deserted, their homes destroyed, their relatives all exterminated. The first wave of emigrants to Israel began, growing in 1947 after the Kielce pogrom. Every jolt of Polish nationalism or national-Communism from then on provoked new waves of Jewish emigration, notably in 1956 with Gomulka's arrival to power, and in 1967 and 1968 after the Six Day War. This tide of emigration almost completely emptied the country of its Jewish population: of the 300,000 or 400,000 still living in Poland in 1945, there remain merely a few hundred today, concentrated in Warsaw, Kraków, Wrocław and Łódź, their communities so depleted they often cannot even gather a **minyan**.

→ To call Poland from the
United States, dial 011 48
followed by the number of the person
you are calling minus the initial 0
(used only for domestic calls).

Mazovia

Warsaw

Warsaw: the name alone evokes the martyrdom of the ghetto following the April 1943 insurrection. Events here shall remain firmly fixed in the conscience of humanity.

Jews settled in Warsaw beginning in 1414, the year their presence was first mentioned. In 1792, on the eve of Russian domination, they numbered 6,750 here, or 9.7 percent of the population. Their population increased considerably during the nineteenth and early twentieth centuries, when new synagogues, Jewish schools, and a rabbinical school were opened. In 1864, they already numbered 72,800, or 32.7 percent of the population, and in 1917, 363,400, or 41 percent. Daily newspapers appeared in **Yiddish,** such as the *Yidishes Tageblat.* In 1878, the Grand Synagogue on Tłomacka Street was built. In 1939, Warsaw contained nearly 400,000 Jews, a figure that

reached 500,000 when the ghetto was created in the fall of 1941, a veritable concentration camp in the middle of the city.

The Germans appointed, as in every ghetto, a *Judenrat,* at the head of which presided Adam Czerniakow. The Ghetto was separated from the rest of Warsaw, the "Aryan city," by high walls, and it was forbidden for anyone to enter or leave without a pass. Those Jews "fit for labor" *(Arbeitsjuden)* worked for German businesses (the shops). Food rations were scarce, as the Germans had requisitioned the furs, clothing, gold, and anything else they could get their hands on to sustain the Wehrmacht's war effort. In a single year, from the summer of 1941 to that of 1942, 100,000 Jews died of hunger, cold, and typhus. Death was a daily spectacle in the streets of the ghetto. Carts passed regularly to collect the corpses. Beginning 22 July 1942, German demands became inconceivable: they ordered Czerniakow to deliver 6,000 to 7,000 Jews each day for a so-called "population transfer to the east" *(Umsiedlung)*.

☙ 22 JULY 1942

"They told us that, with the exception of a few cases, all Jews, regardless of age or sex, would be evacuated to the east. Today we have to hand over a contingent of 6,000 people before 4 P.M. And it will be the same, if not more, every day." [22 July 1942]
ADAM CZERNIAKOW, *YOMAN GETTO VARSHA*
(WARSAW GHETTO DIARY):
6.9.1939—23.7.1942, ED. N. BLUMENTAL, ET. AL.
(JERUSALEM: YAD VASHEM, 1968).

Czerniakow understood what the Germans intended and committed suicide. Throughout the summer of 1942, in unprecedented raids the Germans "cleaned out" the ghetto, street by street, driving the Jews to a sorting center called the Umschlag-platz; from there, each morning trains left for Treblinka, only to return, empty, to Warsaw in the evening. In this way, nearly 300,000 Jews were deported and immediately gassed. The deportations slowed, and then picked up again in the spring of 1943, after the Wehrmacht's defeat at Stalingrad. On 19 April 1943, on **Passover** day, the ghetto uprising broke out; led by Mordecai Anielewicz, the rebels stood up to their German oppressors for four weeks. It was eventually crushed in the blood and

fire of General Stroop's incendiary tactics. When the ordeal had ended, the latter, victorious, wrote to Berlin: "There is no more Jewish quarter in Warsaw."

THE FORMER
JEWISH QUARTER

To understand where the quarter used to be, several days and two maps are needed: the first from the ghetto era, the second a current one. Warsaw's former Jewish quarter, which corresponded mainly to the Muranów district but extended as far as Swiętokrzyska Street (Holy Cross), is unrecognizable today, as it was 99 percent razed; not one of its houses has survived, as postwar reconstruc-tion transformed the area down to its very street layout and zoning map.

■ The Grand Synagogue on Tłomacka Street no longer exists. All that re-mains is the adjacent building, the former Institute of Jewish Sciences, founded in 1920 and today the Jew-ish Historical Institute. Here you will find a small museum, a library, and archival documents.

[Jewish Historical Institute:
ul Tłomacka 3–5, 00-900 Warsaw.
✆ 0228278372. Open Mon–Fri 9 A.M.–3 P.M.]

■ The only active synagogue here is the Nożyków on Twarda Street. It was built in 1903 on land offered to the community by Zelman Nożyk. It was restored in the 1980s and returned to the congregation. Services are held regularly, bringing together several

Jewish quarter, Warsaw, late 1930s.

generations as well as foreigners and those working in Warsaw. Beside the synagogue, a school for Jewish children has been established, as well as an "information point for Jewish visitors" (Ronald S. Lauder Foundation). The editorial offices of the review *Midrasz* have also been set up here.

[Nożyków Synagogue:
ulica Twarda 6, 00-104 Warsaw.
✆ 0226200676.
Normally open Sun–Fri 9 A.M.–5 P.M.
Ask permission to pray.]
[Ronald S. Lauder Foundation:
same address. ✆ 0226522150.]

Not far away, in Grzybowski Square, is located the Jewish State Theatre (Panstwowy Teatr Żydowski), bearing the name of Rachel Kaminska, its 1950 founder. Yiddish-language productions are regularly offered here, covering the entire classical and modern repertory, from Sholem Aleichem, Shalom Asch, and S. An-Ski to Isaac Bashevis Singer, and passing through adaptations of Itzhak Katzenelson's "Song of the Murdered Jewish People" or evenings of Yiddish songs interpreted by Golda Tencer. The Cultural Association of Polish Jews has its headquarters in the same building, alongside the bimonthly *Dos Yidishe Vort* (or *Słowo Żydowske*), a small newspaper half in Yiddish, half in Polish. Note as well several houses that appear to date back to the time of the ghetto.

[Panstwowy Teatr Żydowski:
plac Grzybowski 12–16, 00-104 Warsaw.
✆ 0226207025.]
[Cultural Association of Polish Jews:
same address. ✆ 0226200554.]

THE GHETTO

The ghetto itself was a bit further away.
■ Take Jana Pawla II (John Paul II) Street and stroll around the Hala Mirowska (Covered Market), where the former ambiance of this populous quarter can still be glimpsed. In the courtyards of houses dating to the 1950s and 1960s, mounds reveal how the field of ruins that was once the ghetto in 1943 and 1944 was never completely cleared away. Take Nowolipie, Karmelicka, Nowolipki, Dzielna, and Pawia and try to imagine how the ghetto once appeared, even if nothing shows through today. Drop by Krochmalna Street as well, where Isaac Bashevis Singer's novel takes place, *In My Father's Court.*[10]
■ At the intersection of Jana Pawla II and Dzielna streets once stood the Pawiak, a sinister prison where many Resistance fighters were tortured.
■ Further up, the street crosses Mordecai Anielewicz Street (formerly Gęsia Street). A right turn leads to a large, undeveloped square, at the far end of which sits the Monument

ISAAC BASHEVIS SINGER

Isaac Bashevis Singer was born in Radzymin in 1904 and died in New York in 1991. The Nobel Prize winner for literature in 1978, he was one of the most important Yiddish writers of the twentieth century, in the tradition of Sholem Aleichem and Itzhak Leybush Peretz. A rabbi's son, he lived in Warsaw until 1933, then emigrated to the United States, where he continued to write Yiddish stories with the life of Poland's shtetlach and emigration as their backdrop. Nearly all his works have been translated into English.

to the Heroes of the Ghetto. Erected in 1948, the memorial features a sculptural group by Natan Rappaport with the inscription, "From the Jewish nation to its combatants and its martyrs." On the back of the monument, the simple bas-relief is both more moving than the grandiloquent sculpture and less marked by its Stalinist style. In 1972, Chancellor Willy Brandt knelt before this monument, a gesture transcending normal protocol.

With Jewish tourism on the increase in Warsaw over the past ten or so years, a foundation has started raising funds for a museum devoted to Polish-Jewish history, planned near the monument on Lewartowskiego Street.[11]

■ Behind the monument, take Zamenhofa Street (named after the Jewish linguist Ludwik Lazar Zamenhof, born in Białystok and founder of Esperanto), where in 1988 stones were placed approximately every 300 feet representing a "memorial route of the Jewish martyrdom and struggle." Leading to the Umschlagplatz, the markers evoke the most illustrious names of the ghetto uprising: Jozef Lewartowski, Michal Klepfisz, Arie Wilner ("Jurek"), Mordecai Anielewicz, Meir Majerowicz ("Marek"), Frumka Plotnicka, and Itzhak Nyssenbaum.

■ At the corner of Zamenhofa and Mila streets, formerly at 18 Mila Street, was located the bunker where Anielewicz and his comrades led the insurrection, sealed themselves off, and met their death on 8 May 1943.

Monument to the Heroes of the Warsaw Ghetto.

A tombstone has been erected here atop a mound. Along Stawki Street, the path continues toward Dzika Street, with blocks of granite memorializing Janusz Korczak—the writer, educator, and doctor for the Warsaw Jewish orphanage who boarded the train of death with his children when the latter were deported—and Itzhak Katzenelson, the Yiddish poet who miraculously managed to escape the Ghetto and flee to France. After writing his famous "The Song of the

Murdered Jewish People," Katzenelson was handed over to the Germans and deported to Auschwitz.

☙ MIŁA STREET

There is a street in Warsaw,
it is Miła Street.
O, tear out your hearts
from your chests
and put stones there
in place of your hearts.
Tear out from your faces
your moist eyes
and put there shards of glass,
as if you had never seen,
as if you knew nothing.
Plug up your ears
and hear no more—be deaf!
I speak to you of Miła Street.

ITZHAK KATZENELSON, *THE SONG OF THE MURDERED JEWISH PEOPLE.* IN C. DOBZYNSKI, *LE MIROIR D'UN PEUPLE, ANTHOLOGIE DE LA POÉSIE YIDDISH*, (PARIS: GALLIMARD, 1987). SEE ALSO ITZHAK KATZENELSON, *THE SONG OF THE MURDERED JEWISH PEOPLE.* TRANS. NOAH H. ROSENBLOOM (TEL AVIV: HAKIBBUTZ HAMEUCHAD PUBLISHING, 1980.)

■ At 5-7 Stawki Street, a plaque indicates the building where the SS commander oversaw the Umschlagplatz selection, while at numbers 6–8 stood the Jewish hospital where Jews were assembled just before "boarding."

■ Just across the street, a 1988 monument, a marble door, commemorates the Umschlagplatz. Engraved on its ten-foot-high wall are 400 Jewish first names representing the 300,000 for whom this was their final train platform. The ramps were located right behind the monument, platforms where the cattle cars waited each morning to take their offering to Treblinka. Not far from here sits the Warsaw-Jerusalem restaurant, opened by an Israeli chef.

[Warsaw-Jerusalem Restaurant:
ulica Smocza 27, 00-115 Warsaw.
✆ 0228383217 or 0226363371.]

THE JEWISH CEMETERY

The Jewish cemetery on Okopowa Street is both beautiful and impressive, and miraculously avoided destruction by the Germans. Built in 1799 and covering eighty-one and a half acres, it contains around 200,000 graves. A stroll through its alleys among the gravestones and vegetation provides an inkling of the Jewish community's size before the war. Certain graves stand out, such as those of Ludwik Lazar Zamenhof, actress Rachel Kaminska, and *Judenrat* president Adam Czerniakow. The cemetery also features a sculpture depicting Janusz Korczak, who died at Treblinka, and a plot dedicated to the ghetto insurgents.

[Jewish Cemetery:
ulica Okopowa 49–51, 00-110 Warsaw.
Open Sun–Thu 10 A.M.–3 P.M.]

Góra Kalwaria

Jews began settling in Góra Kalwaria (Calvary Mountain) in 1795, and by a century later they had attained more than 50 percent of the city's population. The **Tsadik** Isaac Meir Rothenberg Alter, brother-in-law to Menahem Mendl of Kotzek, settled here in 1859. The Jews called Góra Kalwaria "Gur," or the "New Jerusalem," so well-known were the **tsadik** Alter and his dynasty. During the occupation, all the Jews of Góra Kalwaria were transferred to the Warsaw Ghetto, and from there to Treblinka.

♖ ALBERT LONDRES'S ACCOUNT

Albert Londres visited Góra Kalwaria in 1929: "Two thousand inhabitants, but one of the navels of eastern Jewry. Here, the famous zadick [sic] Alter, successor to Baal Shem Tov, the one who took the Zohar across the Carpathian Mountains in a car, sought contact with God, just like our fans of wireless radio seek the airwaves."

ALBERT LONDRES, LE JUIF ERRANT EST ARRIVÉ (THE ERRANT JEW HAS ARRIVED). (PARIS: LE SERPENT À PLUMES, 2000).

■ Today, the edifices of two synagogues remain, at Pijarska Street 5 and 10–12, converted today into stores. The Jewish cemetery dates to 1826 and often receives visitors from the United States.

[The cemetery is located at the end of Kalwaryjska Street.]

Łódź

Łódź is a large Polish industrial city where a significant Jewish working class, along with merchants and rich industrialists, were concentrated in the nineteenth century. A fine representation of the reality of life in nineteenth-century Łódź can be seen in Andrzej Wajda's 1974 film *Ziemia Obiecana* (Promised Land).

Under the occupation, the Łódź ghetto (with more than 150,000 people) was, just like the one in Warsaw, a concentration camp in the middle of a city, where the Germans deported Jews from other towns in Poland and Germany. (The Germans had renamed the city Litzmannstadt.) The *Judenrat* was headed by Chaïm Rumkowski, an authoritarian man and controversial figure to the Jewish community. Rumkowski's policies allowed him to survive a year longer than did Jews in the other cities. Although the first deportations to the Chełmno camp began in 1942, it was not until August 1944, only just before the liberation, that the remaining Jews of Łódź (76,700 people) were deported and exterminated in Auschwitz. Only 800 Jews here managed to survive until the end of the war, and almost none remain today.

■ Łódź's main street, Piotrkowska, forms the link between the city center and the Jewish quarter, located in the northern section near Rewolucji Street 1905r. The synagogue still stands on this street in the courtyard of number 28 and is supposedly operational when a **minyan** is gathered. From the street, you can still see its beautiful facade and sign in Russian and Polish. In the courtyard, a smaller building features a stained-glass window and a Star of David.

[Synagogue: ulica Rewolucji 1905.
(formerly Poludniowa 28),
90113 Łódź.]

■ On Piotrkowska Street near Zamenhofa Street, there was a Jewish community building dating back to 1899, serving first as a place of ritual slaughter and later as a synagogue. After the war, it was converted into a shop and then a printing house.

■ The enormous Jewish cemetery is truly impressive. Built in 1892 on ninety-nine acres, it features a beautiful, railed gate and around 180,000 graves, including those of relatives of the poet Julian Tuwin and pianist Arthur Rubinstein.

[Cemetery: ulica Bracka and
ulica Zmienna, 90-250 Łódź.]

Treblinka

Arriving in Treblinka by train recalls the horror of the Warsaw Ghetto inhabitants' final trip from the Umschlagplatz to the gas chambers. To reach Treblinka from Małkinia, the railway line follows hairpin switches: the train must therefore stop and travel in reverse, with the locomotive pushing the cars toward the camp, as explained by railroad worker Henryk Gałkowski in *Shoah,* a train conductor who made the trip three times a week over an eighteen-month period.

■ The railroad line crosses the Bug, then a rather thick pine and conifer forest. At the Treblinka station, an unused and rusted freight train still sits, as if parked there since its final trip. The site of the camp is located almost immediately past the station, at the end of a short path leading into the forest toward a concrete ramp designed to resemble railroad ties. Nothing remains of the camp but information panels in several languages, as the Germans destroyed it all to cover up their crime.

■ At the very end sits a large, circular space covered with tombstones, each symbolizing a **shtetl,** small Polish town scoured of its Jews. The stones bear the place names of hundreds of towns from the Warsaw, Białystok, Vilnius, Minsk, and Mazowiecki regions, among others. There is a stone dedicated to "Janusz Korczak and his children." In the center, a stone edifice has carved on it a seven-branch candelabra. The site is extremely still and encourages reflection.

Mémorial, Treblinka.

Lower Vistula ■

Chełmno

Located on the bank of the Ner, a tributary of the Warta in the region the Germans called Wartheland, Chełmno is where "gas trucks" were tested beginning in 1941, an early form of what later became the gas chambers. Jews were assembled in the Catholic church and from there sealed in trucks, with the exhaust pipe turned inward. The number of miles between the village and forest and the truck's speed were calculated in such a way that upon arrival, the Jews would have died from asphyxiation; they needed only to be buried in previously dug graves. A large part of the Łódź ghetto was exterminated in this way in Chełmno.

It is in Chełmno that Claude Lanzmann begins his film *Shoah.* A man is seen, a rare *Shoah* survivor named Simon Srebnik, as he returns to places where, as an adolescent, he sang for the Germans while they conducted their sorrowful work. He sang so well, in fact, that his life was spared, and the Polish peasants of the region could all remember him.

■ Chełmno's church still stands, towering over prairies where animals graze along the Ner. One almost expects seeing that rare survivor sailing in his small boat, as depicted in Lanzmann's film. At the church's entrance, a plaque recalls the fate of the region's Jews.

■ A mile or two from here, in the forest, is the camp, the extermination site where large, rectangular mass graves were dug to bury the cargo from the gas trucks. A monument has been erected here: a path leads through the various grave sites, lined with stelae evoking what happened and recalling the names of the **shtetlach** that vanished here.

Podlasie

Białystok

From Treblinka, rather than return to Warsaw in the evening, you can travel on to Białystok, near Belarus, a city with a Jewish tradition so strong that in 1913, Jews numbered 61,500, or 70 percent of the population.

■ Of the one hundred synagogues and houses of prayer—the three main ones being the Groyse Shul on Szkolna Street, the Chorszul (Choral Synagogue) on Żydowska Street, and the Pulkowa Synagogue—there remains almost nothing left to see, except for the nineteenth-century synagogue at 3 Piękna Street, today the House of Youth and Culture.

Tykocin

From Białystok, a detour toward Tykocin is imperative: it has effectively preserved the structure and architecture of an old **shtetl.** This town, tiny today, was in times past more important than Białystok, with a larger and older Jewish community. The community dates back to 1522 and was, in the seventeenth and eighteenth centuries, one of the most

Synagogue, Tykocin.

prominent in Poland. Like Białystok, in September 1939 Tykocin fell under the Soviet-occupied zone connected to Belarus. In August 1941, the Germans executed 1,400 Jews here and sent the rest to the Białystok ghetto, where 50,000 of their fellows were confined. In November 1942, Mordechai Tenenbaum of Warsaw began to organize a resistance, but the ghetto was liquidated beginning in February 1943 and the armed uprising crushed. All of the ghetto's inhabitants were exterminated in Treblinka and Majdanek.

■ The magnificent synagogue here, built in 1542, is still remarkable with its very tall, late-Renaissance frame and Baroque roof. It has been restored and transformed into a Museum of Judaism. The interior is splendid, with a large **bimah**, frescoes depicting exotic animals, inscriptions with beautiful Hebrew lettering, and stuccowork.

In front of the museum, at 4 Kozia Street, the Tejsza restaurant offers Jewish cuisine. Behind the museum, old Jewish houses still stand on Kozia, Kaczowska, and Pilsudskiego streets.

[Museum of Judaism: ulica Kozia 2, 16-080 Tykocin. ✆ 08857181613. May–Sept, open daily 10 A.M.–5 P.M. Oct–Apr, Tues–Sun 10 A.M.–5 P.M.]

Galicia

Kraków

In 1335, King Casimir the Great founded an independent city near Kraków, Kazimierz, in which he permitted Jews to settle around Sukiernikow (Clothier) Street (now called Jozefa Street), next to the Christian quarter.

They built the Stara Synagogue, a **mikvah,** hotel, and wedding chapel on the main street called Szeroka (Wide) Street. In the sixteenth century, a large number of Jews arrived here from Bohemia. In 1553, Jews bought the land located between Wąska (Narrow) Street and the city wall to construct houses, as well as a plot on Jakuba Street for the "Rema" cemetery and synagogue. At the time, three gates provided access to the Jewish quarter: one near the city wall and the Stara Synagogue, a second near the cemetery, and a third on Jozefa Street, between the Christian and Jewish areas. The Wysoka (High) Synagogue was later built near the third gate.

In 1564, the Jews obtained from King Sigismund August the privilege of *non tolerandis christianis:* the Christians were forbidden from buying plots of land on these streets and, conversely, Christian owners could not sell plots to anyone other than Jews. In 1635, all the land located on these few streets in Kazimierz was owned by Jews.

In the seventeenth century, the growth of the Jewish community required the building of new synagogues: the Popper Synagogue on Szeroka Street, founded in 1620 by a rich merchant, Wolf Bocian; the Ajzyk Synagogue, named after founder Isaac Jakubowicz in 1644; and the Kupa Synagogue. At the time, Kazimierz was one of the largest Jewish cities in Europe, with 4,500 residents, as compared to the 5,000 in the city's Christian section. As in Kraków, the wealthier Jews of Kazimierz had architects design new stone houses, and reconstruct the Stara Synagogue, destroyed by a fire in 1557.

After Poland was divided, Kraków and Galicia were annexed by Austria. In 1800, the Austrian government reunited Kazimierz and Kraków.

In 1867, the Austro-Hungarian constitution put an end to discrimination against Jews and even allowed them to freely choose their place of residence. The poorest and most religious Jews remained in Kazimierz at the edges of the former ghetto. The more assimilated built a Reform synagogue, the Temple, on Miodowa Street, beyond these limits.

During the occupation, the Kraków ghetto suffered the same fate as the

GALICIA

Mordecai Gebirtig, born in Kazimierz in 1877, was the most talented of the Yiddish singer-author-composers of the twentieth century. He was a carpenter in the Kraków ghetto, where he was murdered in 1942. His nostalgic songs, like *"Kinderyorn"* (Childhood Years), still sound in our ears. In 1938, he composed a premonitory song, *"Unzer Stetl Brent"* (Our Shtetl Is Burning), which was to become a hymn for ghetto combatants: "It is burning, little brother, it is burning! / Oh, our poor shtetl is burning."

other Polish ghettos. It was liquidated in 1943, its inhabitants exterminated in Bełżec or in the Płaszów camp. The Jewish quarter of Kraków, Kazimierz, is the best preserved of all in Poland, with considerable cultural value for tourists. Long neglected and repressed in Polish consciousness after the disappearance of its residents, it has reemerged as a valuable piece of Jewish heritage thanks to Steven's Spielberg's filming of *Schindler's List* here. Since 1991, moreover, the city has been putting on an annual Jewish cultural festival here, normally from June to July.

[Festival Office: ulica Józefa 36, 31-056 Kraków. ✆ 012431535 or 0124311517, fax 0124312427. ❶ www.jewishfestival.pl.]

KAZIMIERZ

■ The tour begins on Miodowa (Honey) Street, accessed from Szeroka Street, the ghetto's main street. At the intersection of these two streets stands the beautiful building that housed the old mikvah,

dating to 1567, converted today into a restaurant.

[Klezmer-Hois: ulica Szeroka 6, 31-053 Kraków. ✆ 0124111245.]

■ Szeroka Street is, in fact, a large, rectangular square, around which extend the majority of Jewish community buildings, houses, and Jewish restaurants, with the cemetery and the Rema Synagogue on the right, the Stara Synagogue straight ahead, and the Popper Synagogue on the left. At the center of the square a little park is surrounded by an enclosure featuring seven-branch candelabras. The rest of the square is now a parking lot.

■ The Stara Synagogue is the oldest preserved temple in Poland. Built in Gothic style during the fifteenth century and inspired by synagogues in Worms, Prague, and Ratisbon, it was reconstructed in Renaissance style following a design by the Florentine Matteo Gucci after a fire in 1557. Today it houses the Kraków Jewish History and Culture Museum.

The magnificent interior perfectly re-creates the atmosphere of an old

Stara Synagogue, Kraków.

synagogue, especially with the circular wrought iron **bimah** in the center, a sort of temple within a temple. To the sides and in the rooms adjacent to the prayer area, works of art and religious objects are on display, as well as photographs depicting old Kazimierz.

[Stara Synagogue and Kraków Museum of Jewish History and Culture: ulica Szeroka 24, 31-052 Kraków. ✆ 0124220962. Open Wed–Thu 9 A.M.– 3:30 P.M., Fri 11 A.M.–6 P.M., Sat and Sun 11 A.M.–3:30 P.M.]

■ Founded in 1620, the old Popper Synagogue is located behind the courtyard. It was destroyed during the war, then reconstructed, and finally converted into an art center for children and adolescents. At the entrance to the synagogue courtyard are located the Ariel café-gallery and a Jewish restaurant-café.

[Popper Synagogue/Art Center: ul Szeroka 16, 31-052 Kraków. ✆ 0124212987. Open Mon–Fri 9 A.M.–noon]
[Alef Restaurant: ulica Szeroka 17, 31-052 Kraków. ✆ 0124213870. Open Mon–Fri 9 A.M.–11 P.M.]
[Ariel: ulica Szeroka 18, 31-052 Kraków. ✆ 0124217920.]

■ The Landau House dates back to the fourteenth century, one of the oldest and largest stone houses of the former ghetto. Its architecture is distinctive and immediately attracts attention. Inside, there is a café and the Jarden Jewish bookstore, which offers guidebooks to Kazimierz and organizes guided tours of locations filmed for *Schindler's List*.

[Landau House and Jarden Bookstore: ulica Szeroka 2, 31-052 Kraków.

✆ 0124217166. Open daily 10 A.M.–6 P.M.]

■ The Rema Synagogue was founded in 1553 by Israel ben Josef Isserles, who hailed from Ratisbon. It bore the name of his son, philosopher and famous rabbi Moses Isserles (1525–72), also known as Reb Moses or Rema. Its monumental front door is also that of the cemetery! With the latter, this synagogue in fact forms an important fifteenth-century Jewish architectural ensemble, comparable to the Altneuschul and cemetery in Prague. Inside, it is relatively small. It, too, possesses an interesting wrought iron **bimah**. Besides the one in Lublin, this is the oldest Jewish cemetery in Poland, and worth a careful visit. Here one finds numerous graves of personalities famous in their time, notably those of Moses Isserles and his family, but also Eliezer Achkenazi, a rabbi in Cairo and later Poznań; rabbi and **Kabalist** Nathan Spira; and Yomtov Lipman Heller, a rabbi in Vienna, Prague, Nemirov, and finally **yeshiva** director in Kraków. The grave of Moses Isserles, just behind the synagogue, is one of the most remarkable: it is covered with small stones that visitors leave as a sign of tribute. A bit further on, the cemetery rises up, forming a hill, which is,

in reality, an accumulation of tombs. The cemetery wall, near the entrance, is made up of concrete gravestones.

[Rema Synagogue: ulica Szeroka 40, 31-052 Kraków. ✆ 0124221274. Open for Shabbat services and holidays, but can be toured outside services Mon–Thu 9 A.M.–4 P.M., Fri 9 A.M. until the service begins.]

■ Taking Szeroka Street to its end, you will reach Jozefa Street, where, at number 38, across from a small square at the intersection with Wąska Street, stands Wysoka (High) Synagogue, its name owing to the second-floor location of its prayer room. Built between 1556 and 1563, it was destroyed by the Germans, rebuilt after the war, and donated as a historical monument. Despite its beautiful exterior, nothing much remains inside.

■ From Jakuba Street can be seen the back side of the impressive Ajzyk Synagogue, at the intersection with Izaaka Street facing the cemetery wall. Founded by rich merchant Isaac Jakubowicz (also known as Reb Ajzyk ben Jekeles), it dates to 1638. Its facade and monumental staircase face Kupa Street. Destroyed by the Germans but now rebuilt, it is a place of memory featuring an exhibit about Polish Jews. Films about Kazimierz are also shown here.

[Ajzyk Synagogue: ulica Kupa 18, 31-057 Kraków. ✆ 0124305577. Open Sun–Fri 9 A.M.–7 P.M. Closed on Jewish holidays.]

■ The Kupa Synagogue is located on Warszauer Street at the end of Kupa Street. Built in the early seventeenth century at the site of the ghetto's outside wall, it is currently closed to the public. It supposedly contains beautiful paintings depicting the cities of Palestine. Further on is the very picturesque New Square (Nowy Targ), also called Jewish Square, where a circular covered market, or okrąglak, has been set up and where ritual slaughter was at one time performed.

■ The Talmud Torah school used to be at 6 Estery Street.

Continuing on to Meiselsa Street, the magnificent interior courtyard of a Jewish house can be seen at number 15, featuring galleries running through the second floor and a porch overlooking Jozefa Street. In the background looms the bell tower of the Church of Corpus Christi. A courtyard entered at Jozefa 12 Street was the location of a scene from *Schindler's List*.

■ From Bozego Ciała Street, Miodowa Street leads to the Reform Templ Synagogue (at the intersection with Podbzezi Street), which is remarkable for its beautiful stained-glass windows.

[Templ Synagogue: ulica Miodowa 24, 31-057 Kraków. Open Sun–Fri 11 A.M.–4 P.M.]

■ Behind the railroad tracks on the other side of Miodowa Street is the new Jewish cemetery. It was built in 1800 after the Rema cemetery was closed. Its extensiveness recalls the large Jewish community that was here before the war. At the entrance, a monument assembled from numerous gravestones and commemorative plaques has been put up in memory of the victims of the *Shoah*.

[New Cemetery: ulica Miodowa 55, 31-052 Kraków. Open Mon–Thu 10 A.M.–3 P.M. (10 A.M.–5 P.M. in summer), Fri 10 A.M.–2 P.M.]

■ By taking Starowisla Street, on the other side of the Vistula, you will reach what used to be the ghetto during the German occupation, around Bohaterow Getta (Heroes of the Ghetto) Square and Lwowska, Josefinska, and Limanowskiego streets. A museum is located in the Pod Orlem pharmacy, whose owner, Tadeusz Pankiewicz, greatly helped the Jews of the ghetto. On Lwowska Street a fragment of the ghetto wall can be observed, resembling an alleyway of gravestones.

[Museum: plac Bohaterów Getta 18, 30-457 Kraków. ✆ 0126565625. Open Mon–Fri 9 A.M.–4 P.M., Sat 9 A.M.–2 P.M.]

■ Further on, in Płaszów (on Kamienskiego Street), a monument stands in honor of the victims deported from the Kraków ghetto to the concentration camp built on this very spot.

Tarnów

In Tarnów, half of the population was Jewish: between 20,000 and 25,000 people worked principally in

Kupa Synagogue, Kraków.

AUSCHWITZ (OŚWIĘCIM)

Auschwitz remains the most horrible symbol of the *Shoah,* a symbol periodically threatened either by denial or by revisionism. In the Communist era, each country was permitted to construct refugee camps, but nowhere was it written that almost all the deportees had to be Jewish or Gypsy. All were presumed to be potential Communist Resistance fighters. Today, a large cross sows greater confusion, attempting posthumously to Christianize the victims.

A tour is required for anyone who might still doubt the reality of the Final Solution or imagine that it was merely a "detail" of the Second World War. More than 800,000, perhaps even over 1 million, victims died in Auschwitz. The tour comprises two camps: the main camp of Auschwitz (Oświęcim) and the one in Birkenau (Brzezinka), where the gas chambers were located. Although the tour is trying and exhausting, it is essential to see both camps. It is advised to visit Auschwitz during the day, using Kraków as a base, rather than having to spend the night in a place of such absolute horror. Expect the tour to take four to five hours.

[Information is provided in Jarden Bookstore in Kraków (see p. 381)]
[Panstwowe Museum w Oświęcimiu (Camp Museum):
ulica Więzniów Oświęcima (of the
Prisoners of Auschwitz) 20,
32-603 Oświęcim. ✆ 0338432022,
fax 0338432227.
Open daily 8 A.M.–5 P.M. or 7 P.M.,
depending on the time of nightfall.
Closed Dec 25, Jan 1, and Easter.]

Photograph of prisoners,
Auschwitz camp.

the clothing and hat industries (sixty or so businesses), arts and crafts, and trade. Some were rich merchants, lawyers, and doctors who owned beautiful houses still dominating Wałowa Street. The others, poorer, were concentrated mostly in the populated districts around Żydowska, Warynskiego, Lwowska, and Szpitalna streets. Renowned intellectuals were born or lived in Tarnów, including Warsaw Ghetto eulogist Adolf Rudnicki (1912–90).

■ The most important remnant, but also the most "trivial" of earlier Jewish life, is the **bimah** from the old synagogue on Żydowska Street: the synagogue itself was razed, leaving only a patch of green, in the center of

which sits the former stone **bimah**, reminiscent of a fountain.

■ Behind the **bimah**, take Rybna Street to see the former Jewish houses with courtyards crisscrossed by upstairs galleries. Beyond Wałowa Street, on Goldhammer Street, stood the Jewish community's prayer house, where services have not taken place since 1980 for lack of a **minyan**. A bit further on, in what used to be the ghetto, lie Więzniów Oswięcima (Prisoners of Auschwitz) and Bohaterów Getta (Heroes of the Ghetto) squares, where a monument stands to the victims of the *Shoah*, not far from the old **mikvah**, today a spa.

■ Nowodabrowska Street leads to the Jewish cemetery on Słoneczna Street. The cemetery dates to 1583 and is one of the oldest in the region. It remains active, though devastated: the most luxurious gravestones have been destroyed or stolen. At the entrance stands a column that came from the Nowa (New) Synagogue commemorating the massacre of 25,000 Jews of Tarnów, on the spot where the first mass executions took place on 11 June 1942.

Rzeszów

Jews began settling in Rzeszów in the fifteenth century and, in the seventeenth century, built two synagogues, both of which remain, almost side by side. They are fairly easy to find, located right in the city center.

■ The Stara (old) Synagogue, dating from the first years of the seventeenth century, today houses the city archives. It is rather small, but well restored on the outside. A Star of David can still be seen on one of the walls.

[Stara Synagogue/Archives:

ulica Boznicza 2, 35-959 Rzeszów.

✆ 0178529350. Tours are not given.]

■ The Duza (large) Synagogue is from 1686. It is more imposing, with large bearing walls reinforced by pillars that give it the look of a fortress. Rebuilt in the 1960s, today it houses an art gallery office in the main room and an upstairs café in the galleries for women. A visit to the site offers a glimpse of what the interior looked like before the war, when 14,000 Jews lived in Rzeszów. They were all deported to Bełżec or Auschwitz.

[Biuro Wystaw Artystycznych (Gallery Office and Café, Duza Synagogue): ulica Jana III Sobieskiego 18, 35002 Rzeszów.

✆ 0178533811. Exhibition room open Tue–Sun 10 A.M.–5 P.M. The café is open until 11 P.M.]

■ On Rejtan Street, a large Jewish cemetery remains, its many graves damaged, however, with overturned tombstones, and sometimes overgrown with vegetation.

Lesko

■ The small city of Lesko possesses one of the most beautiful fortified synagogues in the region, built in the sixteenth and seventeenth centuries,

with a turret that gives it the look of a little castle. Destroyed during the war, it was rebuilt in 1980; the interior mannerist decor has been redone, as well as the eighteenth-century iron gate and *aron kodesh*.

[Galeria Sztuki Synagogue:

ulica Berka Jozelewicza 18, 38600 Lesko.

✆ 0134696695. Open daily 10 A.M.–5 P.M.

Cross street: Moniuszko.]

■ The Lesko cemetery is almost across the street from the synagogue. It dates from the seventeenth century, is very large, and contains many old graves with beautiful decorative motifs.

Rymanów

Jews settled in Rymanów so long ago that there exists no document mentioning their arrival. A synagogue already existed here in the sixteenth century. In 1765, a thousand Jews lived in Rymanów, or 43 percent of the population. In the nineteenth century, Rymanów became a center for **Hasidism** in western Galicia, under the influence of the **tsadik** Menahem Mendel (also known as Mendel of Rymanów), who was a student of Elimelech of Lyzhensk and Shmelke Horowitz of Nikolsburg (Mikulov). In 1942, the entire Jewish population of Rymanów was exterminated in the Bełżec camp.

■ The synagogue, built between 1700 and 1726, is now a beautiful ruin, which unfortunately risks vanishing

Synagogue, Lesko.

one day if it is not restored. Located right near the *rynek,* on Piękna Street at the intersection with Kilinskiego Street, it attests, by its architectural importance, to the status the Jewish community once held in the city.

♔ THE LEGACY OF RABBI ELIMELECH

"Before he died Rabbi Elimelech laid his hands on the heads of his four favorite disciples and divided what he owned among them. To the Seer of Lublin he gave his eyes' power to see; to Abraham Yehoshua, his lips'

power to pronounce judgment; to Israel of Koznitz, his heart's power to pray; but to Mendel he gave his spirit's power to guide."

MARTIN BUBER, *TALES OF THE HASIDIM: THE LATER MASTERS,* TRANS. OLGA MARX (NEW YORK: SCHOCKEN BOOKS, 1948).

Łańcut

Łańcut is a small, pleasant city known for its Renaissance castle once belonging to the Lubomirskis.

■ The town also possesses a Baroque synagogue, one of the most beautiful in Poland. Built in 1761, destroyed during the war, and rebuilt during the

1960s, it has long served as a regional museum. In the 1980s and 1990s, it was completely restored once more, including the magnificent interior decor, the **bimah,** and the *aron kodesh,* where the Ark of the Law is kept. It houses today the Jewish Museum.

[Jewish Museum: ulica Zamkowa 2, 37-100 Łańcut. ✆ 0172252008-126. Open daily 9 A.M.–4 P.M. Will open for groups outside of these hours if a visit is arranged.]

■ On Traugutta Street, at the site of the former cemetery, a plaque commemorates the execution of hundreds of Jews during the German occupation.

Przemyśl

The last Polish city before the Ukrainian border and former Austrian fortress that fell to the Russians in the First World War, Przemyśl is also a city with a strong Jewish community going as far back as the twelfth century, perhaps even the eleventh century. Before the Second World War, 20,000 Jews lived here, or 40 percent of the population. In September 1939, after several days of German occupation, Przemyśl was handed over to the Soviet-occupied zone. The Russians deported or evacuated 7,000 Jews to the interior of the Soviet Union. In June 1941, the Germans occupied the city, created a ghetto, and then deported its inhabitants—first to Bełżec, then to Auschwitz.

■ The Jewish quarter stretched across the slopes of "Castle Mountain," between the San River, the marketplace, and Jagiellonska Street. The oldest synagogue in Przemyśl, built in 1579 and designed by an Italian architect, was located at the intersection of Żydowska and Jagiellonska streets. Another stood on the banks of the San; a third, the new Scheinbach Synagogue on Słowackiego Street, today serves as a library.

■ The synagogue in Unii Brzeskiej (Union of Brest) Square was built in the eighteenth century and reconstructed in 1963. Near the fortress, a monument commemorates the spot where the Jews of Przemyśl's "little ghetto" were executed.

[Former Synagogue: plac Unii Brzeskiej 6, 37-700 Przemyśl.]

■ In the cemetery on Słowackiego Street, a plaque has been mounted in remembrance of the mass executions that occurred from 1941 to 1945.

Lublin Plateau ∎

Lublin

An important city in eastern Poland, Lublin has preserved a very pictur-esque old quarter that offers a glimpse of what life was like here in the seventeenth century, with a city hall in the middle of the *rynek,* a Dominican church, fortifications, and various city gates. Lublin also fea-tures a castle surrounded by a park plucked straight out of a tale from *The Thousand and One Nights.* The castle and its park are accessible from Zamkowa Street.

Large numbers of Jews began set-tling in Lublin in the fourteenth cen-tury, first in the Kazimierz Żydowski district, later near the castle. The Grodzka Gate was called Brama Ży-dowska (Jewish Gate). The sixteenth and seventeenth centuries were the high point of Lublin's Jewish com-munity: a Hebrew press was founded in 1547, followed by a second one in 1578; the town also featured a renowned Talmudic school directed by major figures of the era—Solomon Luria, Mordecaï Jaffe, and Meir ben Gedaliah. (It is also where Moses Is-serles completed his studies.) In the nineteenth century, Lublin became a major center for **Hasidism,** centered around the **tsadik** Yaakov Yitshak, known as the Seer of Lublin and a disciple of the Great Maggid and Elimelech of Lyzhensk.

When war was declared in 1939, 45,000 Jews lived in Lublin. They had seven synagogues, two *mikva'ot,* a hospital, a library, and schools. The ghetto was created in March 1941,

Jewish quarter, Lublin.

Ul Podwal *Lublin*

and in March 1942, 30,000 Jews were deported and exterminated in the Bełżec camp, while the rest were executed on the spot or taken to the camp in Maidanek.

THE JEWISH CITY

■ First, absorb the atmosphere and take the pulse of this neighborhood with its *rynek,* its city gates, Grodzka Street, Po Farzu Square, and the old Jewish gate. To the right, heading down Grodzka Street, was located the Jewish community's retirement home *(dom starców),* marked by a commemorative plaque.

■ The little streets running off Grodzka Street are the former Jewish alleys, often still neglected, which lead to Lubartowska Street and Ofiar Getta (Victims of the Ghetto) Square, with a monument in memory of the murdered Jews of Lublin. The synagogue was located at 10 Lubartowska Street, transformed today into "An *isba* (room) to the memory of Lublin's Jews": a small museum with photographs and historical documents on display. At number 83 of the same street once stood the rabbinical school, Yeshivat Khachmei Lublin, today part of the Academy of Medicine, and, next door, the Jewish hospital.

[Izba to the Memory of Lublin's Jews: ulica Lubartowska 10, 20-900 Lublin. Open Sun 1–3 P.M.]

■ The two Jewish cemeteries are worth visiting, especially that on Kalinowszczyna Street, built in the sixteenth century. A number of personalities are buried here: Rabbi Shalom Shakhna, founder of the Talmudic school, who died in 1558; **Talmud** scholar Yehuda Leybush ben Meir Aszkenasi, who died in 1597; Rabbi Itzhak Aizyk Segal, who died in 1735; and above all, the **tsadik** Yaakov Yitshak, who died in 1815 and whose grave is covered with small stones of homage. The other cemetery, the one on Wałecznych Street, dates from the nineteenth century. It is large and contains beautiful graves as well.

[Ulica Kalinowszczyna Cemetery: contact the synagogue for the key.]
[Ulika Wałecznych Cemetery: free access.]

THE MAIDANEK CAMP

You cannot leave Lublin without stopping at the Maidanek camp, which is located today in a suburb of the city. It is easily visible from the road facing Chełm. The activities of the camp could be easily seen or guessed at from the city. A careful tour of Maidanek, where the barbed wire, barracks, gas chambers, and crematorium have all been preserved, is particularly moving and impressive, comparable to that of Auschwitz (with fewer tourists, however).

[Panstwowe Muzeum na Majdanku (State Museum): ulica Droga Meczenników Majdanka 67, 20-325 Lublin. ✆ 0817442647. Open in winter Mon–Fri 8 A.M.–3 P.M.; in summer every day 8 A.M.–6 P.M. Expect the tour to take around three hours. ❶ 22 or 🚌 30.]

Kazimierz Dolny

■ If one stop along the road from Lublin to Warsaw is a must, it is in the city of Kazimierz Dolny on the Vistula, first because it is a tourist city, with old houses, a magnificent *rynek* lined with Renaissance or Baroque facades, a large church, and castle, but also because it has been marked by an important Jewish presence, of which there remain a few remarkable traces, most notably the eighteenth-century synagogue, just behind the large square at 4 Lubelska Street. Rebuilt after the war, it serves as a cinema today. On one of the walls, a plaque recalls the memory of the 3,000 Jews of Kazimierz Dolny murdered by the Germans.

■ When you leave the city, if you take the road toward Opole Lubelskie, you can see what remains of the former Jewish cemetery on Czerniawy Street. On the hillside, overtaken by the forest, several beautiful gravestones still stand, as well as a moving roadside monument made from hundreds of pieces of destroyed tombstones.

Zamość

Zamość is a magnificent example from the Polish Renaissance era. Built in the sixteenth and seventeenth centuries

by Italian architects in the service of Kings Sigismund and Casimir, the city offers a distinctive architectural unity, with its wide-stepped city hall, central square lined with beautiful Renaissance and Baroque mansions, and its crisscrossing of old, narrow streets arranged around the city wall and gates.

The Jewish community began settling here in 1588, after the waywode Jan Zamojski allowed **Sephardic** Jews from Italy, Spain, and Turkey to come to his city, and even granted them privileges. In the seventeenth century, they arrived in even greater numbers. During the eighteenth and nineteenth centuries, the **Haskalah** developed in Zamość, the Jewish enlightenment and emancipation movement imported from Berlin and Vilna (Vilnius). When Poland was divided, Zamość fell within the Russian Empire. **Yiddish** writer Itzhak Leybush Peretz was born here in 1851, and he remained for thirty-six years before moving to Warsaw. The revolutionary Rosa Luxemburg, murdered in Berlin in 1919, was also born here, in 1870. In 1856, 2,490 Jews lived here; in 1921, they numbered 9,383 (or 60 percent of the population) and, just before the war, 12,000. They were all deported to Bełżec in April and May 1942.

■ The former Jewish quarter was located around Zamenhofa and Pereca streets. The synagogue at 9 Zamenhofa Street was built between 1610 and 1620 in late Polish Renaissance

Synagogue, Zamość.

style, like other important buildings in Zamość. Destroyed during the war, restored in the 1950s and 1960s and again in 1980, it still boasts its Renaissance-style gate. On its exterior walls, a frieze bears images of envelopes, but this is not a post office: it is a public library.

The Jewish community house *(dom Kalhany)* and a **mikvah** dating to 1877 are located beside the synagogue.

Szczebrzeszyn

A Jewish community sprang up in Szczebrzeszyn in the sixteenth century, while the synagogue was built here in the seventeenth century. In the nineteenth century, the community experienced important growth, jumping from 1,083 members (31 percent of the population) in 1827 to 2,450 (44 percent) in 1897; it also became a center of **Hasidic** influence centered around the **tsadik** Elimelech Hurwitz. Before the war, 3,200 Jews lived in Szczebrzeszyn; they were all deported to Bełżec in May 1942.

Szczebrzeszyn is today a small, tranquil city, with a Catholic church and city hall downtown.

■ Right near the central square (on Sadowa Street), you will see a tall, distinctive building, squarely set with a sloping roof: this is the synagogue, today a "house of culture." A plaque indicates that it is one of the oldest synagogues in Poland. It is also

Itzhak Leybush Peretz (Icchok Leib Perec in Polish) is considered, with Sholem Aleichem and Mendele Moykher Sforim, one of the classic authors of **Yiddish** literature. Born in 1851 in Zamość, he began writing in Polish, then Hebrew but, in 1888, settled on **Yiddish,** at the time considered merely a jargon, *mameloshn.* He spent more than ten years here working as a lawyer, then set out for Warsaw, where he strove to define **Yiddish** culture and founded a daily newspaper, *Der Veg.* His funeral procession in 1915 included 100,000 people. French novelist Georges Perec, whose parents hailed from Lubartów near Lublin, maintained he was a great-grandnephew of Peretz (see *W, or the Memory of a Childhood* [London: Harvill Press, 2000]).

protected as a national monument. It was burned down in 1940 and rebuilt in 1957.

■ A path behind the synagogue leads to the Jewish cemetery, which has been swallowed up by the forest. You will have to clear your way through the ferns and shrubs to visit its many very old graves. In the center, a monument commemorates the execution of the Jews of Szczebrzeszyn in this very spot.

Józefów

■ The city of Józefów possesses a beautiful late-seventeenth-century synagogue. It can be seen almost immediately upon arriving in the village, on the right and set back a bit in relation to the city center at the intersection of Górnicza and Krótka streets. It was rebuilt in the 1990s and converted into a public library with one distinctive feature: upstairs, a doctors office and hotel are located in the former women's gallery.

Ukrainian Border ■

Włodawa

Jews began settling in Włodawa in the seventeenth century. By the turn of the twentieth century, they numbered 3,670 (66 percent of the population), then 4,200 (67 percent) in 1921, and 5,650 (75 percent) in 1939. The Germans created a ghetto to which they deported 800 Jews from Kraków and 1,000 from Vienna, before exterminating them all in the camp near Sobibór, a mile or two from here in the forest, beside the Bug River.

Włodawa contains one of Poland's most important Baroque synagogues. Built in 1762, it features a square shape with a high upper floor and sloped roof. Destroyed during the occupation, it was restored after the war. A scene from the film *Shoah* by Claude Lanzmann takes place here: the synagogue appears in close-up while the director interviews a witness from the era, Pan Filipowicz.

[Museum (synagogue):
ulica Czerwonego Krzyza 7,
22-200 Włodawa.
✆ and fax 0825722178.
Open Mon–Fri 8 A.M.–3 P.M.,
Sat and Sun 10 A.M. –2 P.M.]

Synagogue, Włodawa.

✡ *SHOAH* (EXCERPT)

"There was a synagogue in Włodawa?"

"Yes, there was a synagogue and it was very, very beautiful. When Poland was still controlled by the czars, the synagogue was already here. It is even older than the Catholic church. It is no longer active. There are no more believers around here."

CLAUDE LANZMANN, *SHOAH,*
(PARIS: GALLIMARD-FOLIO, 1997)..

Sobibór

For the purposes of this tourist and cultural guidebook, we will not linger on the extermination camps, which are "documents to barbarity," as Walter Benjamin put it, and not to culture. Yet we must mention some of

them at least, as we seek to comprehend the incomprehensible, to grasp through their images that which ultimately cannot be grasped.

In Sobibór, there are in a sense two different villages. Sobibór proper is a sleepy, peaceful little town with a small Catholic church along the Bug. To see what remains of the camp, you need to go to Sobibór-Stacja Kolejowa (Sobibór Railway Station), a mile or two from here, accessible only through the forest. The forest is huge and, one must admit, magnificent. If, as Claude Lanzmann put it, every landscape in Poland breathes the *Shoah*, this is especially true around here.

■ On the other side of the forest, the road is blocked by a barrier. A sign reads SOBIBÓR; in the station, another sign reads WAITING ROOM. Besides the station agent and a woodworking company, the place is completely desolate. It was here that for a year and a half, from March 1942 to October 1943, convoys arrived from Poland and beyond, packed with 250,000 Jews who were immediately gassed. All that remains today are the ramp, a monument, and a small museum. A short walk to the site of the camp itself yields only a sort of circular tumulus.

The site was well documented in the film *Sobibór, October 14, 1943, 4 P.M.* by Claude Lanzmann.

[Sobibór Museum: Muzeum byłego hitlerowskiego obozu zaglady w Sobibórze stacj kolejowa, 22-200 Włodawa. ✆ 0825719867. Open daily 9 A.M.–2 P.M.]

Southeast Europe

Romania

T HERE IS LITTLE EVIDENCE OF A JEWISH PRESENCE on the coasts of the Black Sea before the arrival of Roman legions in the early second century C.E. Vestiges, coins, and inscriptions preserved in a museum in Bucharest, however, attest to the existence of Jews in the region throughout the first millennium. Near the end of the thirteenth century, the great voyager Benjamin of Tudela had already noted their presence in southern Wallachia.

Romania is made up of three distinct historical regions that extend beyond the country's current borders. Wallachia is located between the southern stretch of the Carpathians and the Danube, Moldavia is enclosed between the eastern Carpathians and the Pruth River, while Transylvania neighbors simultaneously Ukraine, Hungary, and, along its southernmost province (Banat), Serbia.

Each of these regions saw different destinies under three bygone empires: the Ottoman, Russian, and Austro-Hungarian. It was not until 1859 that Wallachia and Moldavia came together as part of the small Danubian kingdom. After the First World War, they were joined by the Austro-Hungarian and

Synagogue, Braşov

Russian provinces, where Romanians happened to form a majority. These regions included Bukovina and Bessarabia, centers of Romanian Judaism at the time but defunct today.

THE THIRTEENTH TRIBE?

Before and after the withdrawal of the Roman administration under Aurelian in 217 C.E., the Romanized Dacians north of the river were steamrolled by migratory inflow. According to an audacious and as-yet unverified hypothesis advanced by Arthur Koestler in his book *The Thirteenth Tribe,* the Khazars, whose empire in the eighth to tenth centuries stretched from the Volga to the Carpathians, might be the ancestors of millions of Jews living in eastern and Central Europe before the *Shoah.* [12]

Out of the 800,000 Jews who settled in Romania between the wars—the third most important Jewish community after Poland and the former Soviet Union—only about 12,000 remain today. Remember that in 1940, after the German-Soviet Nonaggression Pact, the Soviet Union annexed Bessarabia and Bukovina, while Hungary helped itself to a good half of Transylvania. Around 400,000 Jews lived in these provinces before their massive liquidation, either by the Romanian army allied with the Nazis in the war against the Soviet Union (in Bessarabia, Bukovina, and Trans-Dniestria) or in Auschwitz, handed over by the Hungarian authorities installed in occupied Transylvania. Those living in the territories that remained Romanian, however, though stripped of their belongings and marginalized, largely survived the *Shoah* despite pogroms in Bucharest, Dorohoi, and Iași. Over the following decades, they emigrated to Israel, the United States, or western Europe.

→ **To call Romania from the United States, dial 011 40** followed by the number of the person you are calling minus the initial 0 (used only for domestic calls).

Wallachia

Although its underground petroleum resources are today largely exhausted, Wallachia remains the country's economic center. This region was first dominated by Hungary, but in 1330 it fell under Ottoman influence. A number of Jews expelled from Hungary in the mid-fifteenth century settled on the Wallachian slopes of the Carpathians, and were followed, after 1492, by those expelled from Spain by that country's Catholic monarchs. Warmly received in regions controlled by the sultan (the Mediterranean shores and the Balkans) and the Wallachian princes, who encouraged trade, Jews in the late fifteenth century nonetheless fell victim to the cruelty of Vlad the Impaler, better known by the name of Dracula. If their economic importance grew during the seventeenth and eighteenth centuries, the law, which remained medieval, advocated their clear separation from the Christians. While their security was guaranteed under the reign of the Phanariot princes (Christians recruited by the Sultan in Istanbul's Greek quarter to govern the Danubian countries), already widespread anti-Semitism of Orthodox Christian inspiration led to accusations of ritual murder, abusive tracts, and finally pogroms.

With Moscow's stranglehold on the Romanian principalities following the 1829 Treaty of Adrianople, the Jews' legal standing, which mirrored exactly contemporary laws within the czar's empire, began to deteriorate with the arrival of large numbers of Jewish immigrants in eastern Moldavia, also annexed by Russia. The revolutionary upheaval of 1848, which elsewhere in Europe had called for equal rights for all, failed to live up to its promise. Over the course of the eighteenth century, Wallachia had been acquired by Austria, then passed on to Russia. In 1859, the region was united with Moldavia, forming a new realm that gained independence in 1878.

Despite pressure from French deputy Adolphe Crémieux and other western democracies, and despite Jewish participation in both the war for Romania's independence and the First World War alongside the Allies (1916–18), civil equality and respect for the minority rights of Jews were not granted until later, by the 1923 constitution. In that era, large Magyar-speaking Jewish populations from Transylvania, German-speaking ones from Bukovina, and **Yiddish-** or Russian-speaking ones from Bessarabia were all united within Greater Romania by the Treaty of Versailles. Fifteen years later, these gains were jeopardized by the anti-Semitic legislation of the Goza-Cuza government. The country's dismemberment, which began in the summer of 1940, combined with its entrance into war on Hitler's side against the Soviet Union and then, after defeat, the installation of a hard-line Communist government here, ultimately sounded the death knell for Romanian Judaism.

Bucharest

Jewish Bucharest has almost completely disappeared. Of a population estimated at 158,000 souls in 1948, there remain only 2,000 people today. Spread out across the four corners of the capital, they are doubtlessly too old or in too precarious an economic situation to contemplate emigration.

THE OLD JEWISH QUARTER

The old Jewish quarter was located near the Unirei (Union) Square on the other side of Sfânta Vineri Street. To the southeast, Dudesti and Vàcàresti streets resounded with the joys and color of Jewish life. These streets no longer exist. In their place stretches a vague, rubble-strewn terrain the locals call "Hiroshima." Ceauşescu reduced it all to nothingness in order to build a mad, improbable "City

Jewish quarter, Bucharest.

of the Future." A lone house attests to the Jewish presence in these parts: the Jewish State Theater. This is where actors—non-Jewish ones, for that matter—continue to learn **Yiddish** and interpret works by the great Jewish playwrights in the original language.

[Jewish State Theater:
Strada Dr. Julius Baras 15, sector 3,
74212 Bucharest. ✆ 013234530.]

SYNAGOGUES

Few active synagogues remain in Bucharest. At the turn of the twentieth century, however, the city contained at least sixty-six of them, **Sephardic** as well as **Ashkenazic**.

■ The Choral Temple remains the city's most important religious site today. Built in 1866 according to a design by the architects Endele and Freiwald in the Viennese style (just like the synagogue on Dohány Street in Budapest), it was rebuilt in 1933 and then in 1945, after it was vandalized by the Iron Guards during a January 1941 pogrom.

[Choral Temple: Strada Sfânta Vineri 9–11,
sector 3, 70478 Bucharest. ✆ 013155090.]

■ The Grand Synagogue, which catered to the **Ashkenazic** community, was built in 1846 by a congregation of Polish Jews. It stands on Vasile Adamache Street, one of the oldest streets in the capital, alongside miraculously preserved low houses. In 1992, this synagogue was transformed into a museum.

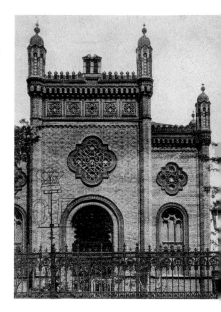

Choral Temple, Bucharest.

Here you will find religious objects, documents, and precious incunabula that retrace the history of Romania's former Jewish communities. In the center sits a statue in honor of the tens of thousands of Trans-Dniestrian Jews, victims of pogroms and deportations. During the war, 200,000 Transylvanian Jews were sent to Auschwitz by the Hungarian authorities, never to return.

[Grand Synagogue: Strada Vasile
Adamache 9–11, sector 3, 70494 Bucharest.
✆ 013150846.]

[Synagogue Mamulari: Strada Mamulari 3,
sector 3, 70468 Bucharest. ✆ 013150837.
Open Mon–Fri 8 A.M.–3 P.M.]

THE CEMETERY

The austere **Sephardic** cemetery Calea Serban Vodà also bears the scars of the pogroms and mass exterminations suffered by Romanian Jews in Moldavia, Bukovina, Bessarabia, and Trans-Dniestria.

[Cemetery: Sos. Giurgiului 2, 76305 Bucharest. ✆ 016853280. Open Sun–Thu 8 A.M.–2 P.M., Fri 8 A.M.–1 P.M. Closed Jewish holidays. 🚇 Eroii Revolutiei (line 2).]

JEWISH LIFE TODAY

■ The dynamic Federation of Jewish Communities of Romania publishes—in Romanian, English, and Hebrew—the excellent bimonthly *Réalitatea evreascà* (Jewish Reality). The catalogue of Hasefer, perhaps the only remaining Jewish publishing house in eastern and Central Europe, contains works by Sholem Aleichem, Martin Buber, Bernard Malamud, and Simon Dubnov, as well as those by Romanian-born authors Elie Wiesel, Carol Lancu, and Mihail Sebastian.

[Federation of Jewish Communities of Romania: Strada Sfânta Vineri 9–11, sector 3, 70478 Bucharest. ✆ 01356090. Open Mon–Fri 8 A.M.–3 P.M. 🚇 Pitaza Unirei (line 2).]

[Hasefer: bd. I. C. Bràtianu 35, 3rd floor, sector 3, 70478 Bucharest. ✆ 013122284. Open Mon–Fri 8 A.M.–2 P.M. 🚇 Piatza Unirei (line 2).]

■ There is only one **kosher** restaurant left in Bucharest.

[Kosher Restaurant–Cantina: Strada Popa Soare 216–18, sector 3, 70303 Bucharest. ✆ 013220998. Open noon–4 P.M. 🚇 Piatza Unirei (line 2).]

Moldavia

Founded in 1329 by Bodgan I, the principality of Moldavia pitted all those who coveted it against one another—Turks, Austrians, Poles, Cossacks and Russians—for over five centuries. Deprived of its northern section, Bukovina, annexed by the Hapsburgs in 1775, and Bessarabia, its eastern province later yielded to Russia, Moldavia gained them back when greater Romania was formed after the First World War. At the end of the Second, however, it lost them all once more.

Whereas, in Wallachia, the early waves of Jewish immigration were overwhelmingly **Sephardic,** those that settled in Moldavia were Polish- and Ukrainian-born **Ashkenazic** Jews. Warmly accepted by Prince Stephen the Great in the latter half of the fifteenth century, they were

MOLDAVIA

THE ART OF APPEASEMENT

If the Jews of Wallachia were sharp and efficient, the Moldavian Jews liked to weigh their words and take their time before making major decisions. Of a dreamy, ironic temperament, they proved on every occasion their rare spirit of conciliation, as demonstrated by a joke told on the train from Bucharest to Iaşi, the capital of Romanian Moldavia.

"Once upon a time, in Piatra-Neamt (one of the hubs of Moldavian Judaism), there was a young rabbi who loved to play chess with the owner of a local **kosher** butcher's shop. One day, the rabbi disappeared, only to return half a century later. Flabbergasted, his chess partner, now aged and skinny, called out to him:

'But where have you been for all these years, rabbi? Why did you abandon us?'

'I was up there, on top of the mountain,' said the rabbi, smiling.

'And what does a rabbi do over fifty years, all by himself, up there, on top of a mountain?' the frustrated butcher grumbled, trying to keep his calm.

'Oh, well, to be exact, way up there on top of the mountain, a rabbi reflects on his life,' replied the rabbi.

'And what conclusion did you reach?' the butcher exclaimed, now at the point of losing all composure.

Stroking his beard, the rabbi answered: 'My friend, life is like a fountain.'

This time, the butcher could not contain himself: 'In the name of . . . ! Fifty years all alone on top of the mountain to reflect, only to come up with such a stupid answer? Have you gone mad?'

The rabbi stopped stroking his beard, and said in a low voice: 'Fine, if you insist, life isn't like a fountain!' "

---

nonetheless segregated from the Christian population. In the seventeenth century, they were massacred by Bohdan Chmielnicki's Cossacks during their revolts against Polish rule. Over the next two centuries until the time of unification, Jewish community institutions truly began to take root, both in the capital, Iaşi, as well as the many Jewish townships that had multiplied under the Phanariot princes. In 1941, Romania joined the war on Germany's side, which led to pogroms in Iaşi and Dorohoi. The Jewish populations of Bessarabia and Bukovina were deported to the other side of the Dniester, where they were victims of hunger, illness, and mass executions perpetrated by the Romanian army.

Galaţi

The city of Galaţi has been a major Romanian trade hub since the seventeenth century. In 1868, it was the theater for acts of vandalism against Jews following accusations of their having committed ritual murders.

■ The imposing "Synagogue of Artisans" was the only temple to remain standing out of the twenty-nine that were active here during the 1930s.

[Synagogue of Artisans: Strada Dornei 9, 6200 Galaţi. ✆ 036413662. Open daily 8 A.M.–2 P.M.]

■ Galaţi still has a **kosher** restaurant.

[Kosher Restaurant: Same address as the synagogue. Open noon–4 P.M.]

Iaşi

The city of Iaşi, Moldavia's capital since the sixteenth century, is surrounded by little towns of pastel-colored houses and whitewashed, thatched cottages. Long ago, places like Bivolari, Harlau, Podul Iloaei, and Târgu-Frumos were abandoned by their Jewish inhabitants. In the 1920s, it was Iaşi that contained this eastern region's most important Jewish community. Populated by artisans, **kabbalists,** merchants, and **Talmudists,** the city counted 43,000 Jews at the time, or half its total population, and no fewer than 112 synagogues.

It was here that, in 1876, Abraham Goldfaden staged his first production, the foundation of European Jewish theater. French-language poet Benjamin Fondane was born here as well, in 1902. It was also in Iaşi that some of Romania's most virulent anti-Semitic movements developed. Iaşi was thus chosen, on 8 November 1940, as the seat for the Iron Guards, a Fascist and fiercely anti-Semitic organization outlawed after its January 1941 uprising against General Ion Antonescu. This very dictator, after putting a stop to the Bucharest pogrom, turned around and supported in June of the same year the massacre of some 12,500 Jews in Iaşi and Dorohoi (a tragedy described by Curzio Malaparte in his remarkable book *Kaputt*).[13]

What remains today of Iaşi's Jewish community, which once rivaled the communities of Poland, Ukraine, and Russia? In the late 1960s, fewer than 2,000 families still lived in Iaşi, and only eleven synagogues remained here. Today, only a few dozen people belong to this community, which runs the **kosher** restaurant and the Museum of History and Art.

[Jewish Community of Iaşi: Strada Elena Doamnei 15, 6600 Iaşi. ✆ 32114414.]

[Kosher Restaurant: Same address. Open noon–2 P.M.]

[Museum of History and Art: Strada Synagogilor 7, 6600 Iaşi. Open upon visitors' request.]

■ The Grand Synagogue is the oldest one in the region. Built in 1671 on the order of Rabbi Nathan Hanover, it

MOLDAVIA

THREE IDENTITIES, ONE DESTINY

Benjamin Wechsler, Fundoianu or Fondane?

Three distinct identities—Jewish, Romanian, and French—struggle for primacy in the work of this prophetic poet. It was the first of the three that brought about his death in Birkenau at the end of May 1944.

Born in 1898, poet, essayist, philosopher and filmmaker Benjamin Fondane left his native city, Iaşi, for Paris in 1923. "Locked in a memory like an obscure line of poetry/In an emptiness run through with flags and dreams / I await your arrival, trumpet of Catastrophic Fear," he wrote in 1922. Imprisoned at Drancy in 1944, he refused a pardon offered him after his wife and friends (Emil Cioran, Stéphone Lepanscu, and Jean Paulhan) intervened on his behalf. He instead chose to accompany his sister on her final journey.

---

was first restored a century later, then modernized in 1864. Proudly blending **Ashkenazic,** Byzantine, and **Sephardic** architectural elements, it attests its kinship not only to ones in Bohemia, Poland, Ukraine, and Russia, but also to those in Greece and Bulgaria.

[Synagogue: Strada Elena Doamnei 15, 6600 Iaşi. Open daily 8 A.M.–2 P.M. Services held for Shabbat and Jewish holidays.]

■ Note that gravestones from the old Jewish cemetery on Clurchi Street have been transferred to the cemetery on Pàcurari Street, where a monument commemorates the victims of the June 1941 pogrom.

[Cemetery: Strada Pàcurari, 6600 Iaşi. ✆ 022163098. Open Sun–Fri 9 A.M.–4 P.M.]

Elsewhere in Moldavia

Moldavia, with its **shtetlach** deserted and hundreds of synagogues long closed or destroyed, can be considered a remarkable museum to eastern European Judaism.

■ First, in Bukovina, several splendid eighteenth- and late nineteenth-century synagogues can still be found in towns such as Rădăuţi, Vatra Dornei, Câmpulung Moldovenesc, and Botosani. Further southward in Piatra-Neamţ, a rare wooden synagogue dates back to the sixteenth century.

[Rădăuţi Synagogue: Strada 1 Mai 14, 5845 Rădăuţi. ✆ 030561333.]

[Vatra Dornei Synagogue: Strada Eminescu 54, 5975 Vatra Dornei. ✆ 030371967.]

[Campulung Moldovenesc Synagogue: Strada Cantemir 8, 5950 Câmpulung Moldovenesc. ✆ 030312510.]

[Botosani Synagogue: Strada Marchian 1, 6800 Botosani. ✆ 031514659.]

[Piatra-Neamț Synagogue:
Strada Dimitri Enrnici 5,
5500 Piatra-Neamț. ✆ 033233815.]
[The synagogues are ordinarily open
Mon–Fri 8 A.M.–2 P.M.]

■ One of the region's three **kosher** restaurants is located near the synagogue in Bacău. The city also contains a Museum of Jewish History.

[Synagogue: Strada Stefan cel Mare 29,
5500 Bacau. ✆ 034134714. Open Sat only.]
[Kosher Restaurant: Strada Gheorge
Apostu 11, 5500 Bacau. Open noon–10:30 P.M.]
[Museum of Jewish History:
Strada Erou GH. Rusu 2, 5500 Bacau.
Open Sun–Fri 8:30 A.M.–2 P.M.]

■ The most moving testimony to the Jewish presence in Moldavia undoubtedly remains the sixty some cemeteries located between the wooded hills of the northwest and the plains in the southeast. Among them, the cemetery in the town of Siret (formerly a prince's residence during the nineteenth century, located between the Ukranian cities of Chernivtsi and Suceava in Romania) easily rivals the most beautiful ones found in Slovakia, Moravia, Bohemia, and even Prague.

Transylvania

North of Wallachia and west of Moldavia, at the center of the Carpathian arc, stretches Transylvania—the land "beyond the mountains," also called Erdely in Hungarian and Siebenburgen (The Seven Cities) in German.

Dacian warriors resided here until the year 107, when they were subdued by Trajan's Roman legions, including the Thirteenth Gemina recruited in Judaea. In 217, however, the Roman administration abandoned Dacia after a surge of migrations that culminated with the arrival of the Magyars in the tenth and eleventh centuries. The twelfth and thirteenth centuries saw an influx of Anglo-Saxon colonists and Swabians from the Holy Roman Empire. They settled at the request of the Hungarian kings to protect against the Turkish and Tatar threat, sheltered by the northern slopes of the Carpathians.

Subject to the Magyar kingdom, then an independent principality, later occupied by the Turks, Transylvania was incorporated into the Austrian Empire in 1691. Starting in 1867, when the region became Hungarian under the dual Hapsburg monarchy, the largely majority Romanian population living here sought reattachment to Romania; the Treaty of Trianon granted their wish after the First World War. In 1940, due to pressure by Nazi Germany and Fascist Italy, Bucharest was forced to cede Transylvania's northwest section to Hungary. The region became Romanian once again at the conclusion of the Second World War.

Although a small number of Jews most certainly appeared with the Roman legions, the first major arrival of those of **Sephardic** origin took place after the fifteenth century. They came via trade routes, either from the Danubian principalities or the Ottoman-controlled Balkans. It was not until much later, after annexation by Vienna, that the **Ashkenazic** immigration from Poland began.

Transylvania's Jewish population was split between the strictly traditional **Yiddish**-speaking communities living in the north (between Sighet Marmaţiei and Baia Mare, cradles of the often rival **Hasidic** and **Ashkenazic** Orthodoxy) and the somewhat Reformist Hungarian- and German-speaking ones to the west and south in cities like Oradea and Arad, Timişoara and Cluj, Sibiu and Braşov.

Under the reign of the late Hapsburgs, Transylvanian Jews enjoyed the same rights as the empire's other citizens, suffering neither discrimination nor marginalization. It was only when the region united with Romania that they had to struggle, with eventual success, for recognition of their civil and minority rights. In the late 1930s, this victory was called into question. From September 1940 to March 1944, the Jews living in northwest Transylvania found themselves under the authority of Hungarian chief of state Horthy,

by which they were subject to anti-Semitic laws as inhumane as those suffered by the Jewish community that remained in General Antonescu's Romania, whose lives were miraculously spared. In the spring of 1944, practically the entire Jewish population of occupied Transylvania was deported to Auschwitz and gassed. Only a tiny number survived.

Cluj

Cluj today is Transylvania's most important city. The Jewish presence became significant here only starting in the late eighteenth century. The community, divided between those of Orthodox faith and Reformists, was uniformly annihilated in Auschwitz

Temple of the Deportees, Cluj.

following imprisonment within the city's ghetto.

■ Only a few dozen Jews live in Cluj today, the rare survivors of the *Shoah* here having mostly emigrated to Israel in the years following the war. The town still features a **kosher** restaurant, however.

[Jewish Community Center:
Strada Tipografiei 25, 3400 Cluj.
Open Mon–Fri 8 A.M.–2 P.M.]
[Kosher Restaurant: Strada Paris 5–7,
3400 Cluj. Open noon–4 P.M.]

■ Make sure to visit Cluj's very beautiful synagogue, referred to as the Temple of the Deportees. Built in 1866, transformed into a warehouse under the Horthy regime, and later damaged by the Nazis during their retreat, it has been subject to a number of restoration projects.

[Temple of the Deportees:
Strada Horea 25–23, 3400 Cluj.
Visits granted upon request.]

[Small Synagogue:
Strada David Francisco 16, 3400 Cluj.
Open Mon–Thu 9–9:30 A.M., Fri 5–5:30 P.M.,
and Sat 9 A.M.–11:30 P.M.]

Oradea

Dating back to the fifteenth century, Oradea's Jewish community was exterminated, too, during the war.

■ Today, a **kosher** restaurant and Reform synagogue are still active for the city's small Jewish population.

[Community Center:
Strada Mihai Viteazul 4, 3400 Oradea.
✆ 059134843. Open Mon–Fri 8 A.M.–2 P.M.]
[Kosher Restaurant:
Strada Mihai Viteazul 4, 3400 Oradea.
Open 8 A.M.–3 P.M.]
[The synagogue nearby is open every day.]

Synagogue, Oradea.

Sighet Marmaţiei

At the northern border of Transylvania lies Sighet Marmaţiei, unquestionably the region's most original and charming little city, where Romanian, Hungarian, Gypsy, and Ruthenian populations all coexist. Nobel Peace Prize winner Elie Wiesel was born in this **Hasidic** township, half of whose population was Jewish until 1944.

■ Sighet Marmaţiei's single synagogue, the Klaus Wijnitzer Temple, features a stunning blend of Romantic, Baroque, and Moorish styles.

[Klaus Wijnitzer Temple:
Strada Basarabia 8, 4925 Sighet Marmaţiei.]

Southern Transylvania ▨

The spirit of Austro-Hungarian Cacania still breathes within the medieval cities that lie on the Transylvanian side of the Carpathians, populated until recently by Swabians and Saxons. Lynxes and bears still haunt the high valleys surrounding Timişoara, the capital of Banat, and the neighboring towns of Sibiu, Sihisoara, Braşov, and Rasnov, characterized by their stocky, Baroque houses of soft lilac, pink, yellow, or pale green colors.

In this region, the majority of Jews spoke German and practiced Reform Judaism, in contrast to Jews to the north. The region stayed Romanian during the Second World War and the Jewish population, though stripped of their belongings and subject to merciless anti-Semitic legislation, survived before emigrating en masse to Israel and other countries.

So strange a fate for that heterogeneous Jewish community of 100,000, having escaped within Romania's shrunken borders after the terrible summer of 1940! How to explain such a large percentage of survivors, the largest, perhaps, besides those in Denmark and Bulgaria? Why their mass exodus to Israel and elsewhere, and how was this possible under repressive Communist regimes?

With their customary humor, Romanian Jews admit owing their special situation to a pair of miracle-making rabbis. The unshakable faith of Alexander Safran, chief rabbi of Romania from 1939 to 1947, succeeded in thwarting the annihilation of many fellow Jews. He managed to convince the Vatican, ambassadors from neutral countries, and certain members of the political elite (including the queen mother and young King Michael) to beseech dictator Antonescu to postpone indefinitely deportation of "his" Jews.

His Communist-appointed successor, Moses Rosen, a shrewd diplomat with a manipulative mind, opened the doors of Israel to Romania's Jews. Rosen managed to convince yet another tyrant, Nicolae Ceauşescu, to allow Romania's Jews to emigrate there after years of harassment for being "bourgeois" and dabbling in "cosmopolitanism." In exchange for considerable financial compensation, many Jews left Romania for Israel in the early 1960s.

Timişoara

■ In Timişoara, the Temple of the Citadel was modeled after the famous synagogue on Dohány Street in Budapest. It was consecrated in 1867 with Emperor Franz Josef in attendance. Like the two other synagogues still active in Timişoara (2 Colonie Street and 55 Resita Street), it rivals the Orthodox Christian cathedrals in beauty, bringing together Baroque, Byzantine, Gothic, and Moorish architectural elements.

[Community Center: Strada Gh. Lazar 5, 1900 Timişoara. ✆ 056201698.]

[Temple of the Citadel: Strada Màràsesti 6, 1900 Timişoara.]

[Kosher Restaurant: Strada Màràsesti 10, 1900 Timişoara. Open noon–4 P.M.]

Sibiu

■ The Grand Synagogue of Sibiu has been declared a historical monument by the Romanian Academy. With its elegant interior and Renaissance facade enhanced by Gothic elements, it remains a popular tourist attraction.

[Synagogue in Sibiu: Strada Blanarilor 15, Sibiu.]

Braşov

At the foot of huge Postavarul Mountain and the Poiana Braşov ski station, Braşov unquestionably remains Transylvania's most fascinating city, with its citadel, ramparts, and medieval center, the latter today closed to cars.

■ The late-nineteenth-century synagogue here was sacked during the Second World War by pro-Nazi locals. It was rebuilt in 1944 but seriously damaged again in a 1977 earthquake. It was then restored once more, and now serves as a center for what remains of Jewish life in this city. A kosher restaurant, retirement home, mikvah, and community housing are all located nearby. Several hundred Jews, the majority of whom belong to the Reform tradition, still live in Braşov.

[Community Center and Synagogue: Strada Poarta Schei 27, 2200 Braşov.]

[Kosher restaurant: same address. Open noon–4 P.M.]

Synagogue, Sibiu.

Remember that in times past, Orthodox Jews practiced agriculture in the remote region of Maramureş, following the example of their Romanian and Hungarian neighbors. They have all but disappeared. Memory of them is gradually fading, along with that of their protectors and friends, the late Hapsburgs.

Bulgaria

IN A MEDIEVAL MINIATURE, Bulgarian Czarina Sara figures beside her husband, Czar Alexander, and two children, Shishman and Tamara. A Jewish queen, Sara of Tŭrnovo was obliged to convert to Christianity, adopting the name Theodora. In the fourteenth century such a union shocked no one in Constantinople, though it would have been inconceivable to the leaders of Rome.

Jews first landed on the banks of the Danube over 1,000 years ago, long before the arrival of the Slavs and Huns. Engraved with a **menorah** and Latin inscriptions, a Roman-era stele has been discovered in Nikopol, in the northern part of the country. The Jewish Diaspora, moreover, took refuge in this stopping ground and melting pot called Bulgaria. Expelled from the heart of the Byzantine Empire, Jewish colonists took root here over centuries of relative tolerance.

In the early days, Judaism and Christianity competed in the conversion of the Bulgarians, most of whom were still atheist at the time. The Christians won out, even if the faith of early Bulgarian Christians was in large part syncretic, borrowing from both Judaism and lingering pagan rituals.

Synagogue, Plovdiv.

Around 860 C.E., Bulgarian emissaries were still asking Pope Nicholas I whether they ought to choose Saturday or Sunday as their day of rest. The first names of the earliest Bulgarian princes—David, Moses, Aaron, and Samuel—also reflect Jewish influence on Bulgarian life.

Already enjoying trade relations with their fellows in Italy and Dubrovnik (Ragusa), local Jews—a majority of whom were still of the Romaniote (Byzantine) tradition—benefited from royal privileges that included the right to hold the post of torturer! Rabbi Yaakov ben Eliyahu once recounted to his apostate cousin, the Spaniard Pau Christiani, how the good Bulgarian king Ivan Asen II had commanded two Jews to avenge their people by tearing out the eyes of Salonae's governor, Theodore I Angeleus; known as the "Greek Devil," the latter had made a name for himself through his hatred of the Jewish faith. But taken with pity, the pair refused their monarch's enucleation order. In response, Ivan Asen II had the two thrown off a mountaintop.

Fleeing persecution in western Europe, Jews flooded into Bulgaria in successive waves throughout the fifteenth century, first from Hungary and Bavaria, and later from Spain after their 1492 expulsion by Catholic monarchs Ferdinand and Isabella. Falling under Turkish domination, Bulgaria, like neighboring Greece, proved to be one of the most accommodating countries for **Sephardic** Jews from Spain. More numerous, cultivated, and prosperous than Bulgaria's other communities, the **Sephardim** quickly gained a foothold here, progressively transmitting to the rest of the population their unique language, *Judezmo*. According to historian of Bulgarian Judaism Vicki Tamir, after the fifteenth century, **Yiddish** was no longer heard on the streets of Sofia.[14] Four hundred years later, Iberian culture still thrived among the Jews of Bulgaria, who now spoke old Castilian and prepared the same Spanish dishes that had decorated Cervantes's table. This all occurred, moreover, inside the mosaic of the other Greek, Turkish, Albanian, Armenian, and Gypsy minorities.

☙ CANETTI REMEMBERS

"The first children's songs I heard were Spanish. I heard old Spanish romances; but the thing that was the most powerful, and irresistible for a child, was a Spanish attitude. With naïve arrogance, the Sephardim looked down on other Jews."

ELIAS CANETTI, *THE TONGUE SET FREE: REMEMBRANCE OF A EUROPEAN CHILDHOOD,* TRANS. JOACHIM NEUGROSCHEL (NEW YORK: THE SEABURY PRESS, 1979).

Exiled from his native Toledo, the eminent rabbi Ephraim Caro chose to settle in Nikopol. His son Joseph, author of the *Shulhan Arukh,* one of the greatest treatises codifying Jewish law, moved on to the Palestine city of Safed. Within the vast Ottoman Empire, where they saw little persecution but suffered heavy taxation, Jews enjoyed prosperous trade relations with the other communities spread across the Dalmatian coast, the Balkans, and the Levant.

The nineteenth century saw an upsurge in Balkan nationalism, while the Jewish elite itself became gripped by the Enlightenment and its egalitarian claims. When the 1877–78 Russo-Turkish War broke out, a precursor to Bulgarian independence, many Jews joined the national liberation movement that was largely controlled by the Russians.

Paradoxically, the emergence of Bulgarian nationalism was concomitant with the spread of anti-Semitism, with many locals viewing Jews as henchmen of the formerly occupying Turks. Massacres and pillages ensued, perpetrated by both the Bulgarian-Russian military and the Turkish *bashibazouks*. The communities in Nikopol, Kazanlŭk, Svishtov, and Stara Zagora were forced to flee en masse; the brand new synagogue in Vidin was destroyed by Russian artillery. Thousands of Bulgarian Jews found shelter in regions that were spared from war, or beyond in Andrianopolis and Constantinople.

Following Turkey's defeat, the 1878 Treaty of Berlin required that the newly created Balkan kingdoms, Bulgaria included, grant full civil rights to their Jewish minorities. And yet, whereas Jews were subject to the military draft like the rest of their fellow citizens, they were barred from attending the Military Academy and excluded from the higher spheres of government.

Bulgaria's economic difficulties after its defeat in the First World War (it had sided with the Central Powers in that conflict) not only affected the Jewish minority here but stoked local anti-Semitism as well. It was in this era that the famous French reporter Albert Londres kept his readers on the edge of their seats with his coverage of the brutal Comitadjis, Bulgaria's fiercely anti-Semitic underworld composed of partisans bent on annexing recently independent Macedonia. Jews in Bulgaria were therefore less inclined to assimilate than those in other European countries at the time (such as Austria, Germany, and Hungary), where anti-Semitism was otherwise more deeply rooted.

This did not prevent younger generations from abandoning the *Judezmo* tongue for Bulgarian, however. The country's first Jewish newspaper, *Chelovecheski prava* (Human Rights) was published in Bulgarian; another community periodical,

La Alborada (Dawn), initially published in *Judezmo*, eventually switched to the national language, too. That said, the Zionist movement also proved to be wildly successful in Bulgaria, dominating the entire community here between the wars, including the consistory. More than 7,000 Bulgarian Jews emigrated to Palestine before 1948.

Allied with Nazi Germany, in 1940 the kingdom of Boris III enacted harsh anti-Semitic laws, quickly depriving Jews of all means of subsistence through a series of bans, confiscations, and forced-labor decrees. However, when Adolf Eichmann's services demanded the final liquidation of the Jews in 1943, the fate of the armed conflict had begun turning against the Axis powers. The Battle of Stalingrad marked a turning point in the war, the Allies had landed in North Africa, and the question of a front opening up in the Balkans had arisen.

Gravestone, Jewish cemetery, Vidin.

Bulgaria nevertheless handed over 12,000 Jews from its annexed territories (Macedonia, Thrace, Pirot in Yugoslavia) without batting an eyelid, but retained its own nationals due to the intervention of a segment of the intelligentsia and hesitation by the state apparatus, sensitive to warnings issued by the Allied powers. The country's 50,000 Jews escaped extermination.

Several years later, Bulgaria's new regime had still not returned to Jewish citizens property confiscated from them during the war. Bulgarian Jews eventually formed one of the largest contingents of emigrants to Israel, with 90 percent of the community moving there. Since 1990, Shalom, the new organization of Bulgarian Jews (consisting of no more than around 3,500 members) has sought the return of "nationalized" Jewish goods, and breathed new life into a community today presided over by only a single rabbi.

→ **To call Bulgaria from the United States, dial 011 359** followed by the number of the person you are calling.

Sofia
and Surrounding Areas ■

Sofia

Jews reached Sofia during the first centuries C.E., the era of Roman domination. **Ashkenazic** Jews emigrating from Hungary and Bavaria were joined in the fifteenth century by **Sephardic** Jews fleeing the Spanish Inquisition. Until 1890, they lived in a sort of ghetto, later torn down by the new capital of independent Bulgaria. Although one section of the city is still called the "Jewish quarter," nothing along its main street remains of the many shops with signs blending Spanish, Hebrew, and French.

Synagogue, Sofia.

■ Opened in 1909, the Grand Sephardic Synagogue still looms above the heart of Sofia. The third most important temple in Europe besides the synagogues in Budapest and Amsterdam, this synagogue is best described in stylistic terms as both Byzantine and Hispano-Moorish; it strongly resembles the famous Viennese synagogue on Leopoldsgasse destroyed by the Nazis. Its construction was entrusted to Austrian architect Friedrich Grünanger. Seriously damaged during an Allied air bombardment in 1944, it never received any significant restoration under the Communist regime. Important work has been accomplished in recent years, however, thanks to donations from Israel. Open for worship, it is visited by only fifty or so of the faithful, though it was designed to accommodate thirty times that number. Adjacent to the synagogue, a small museum is dedicated to the last-minute rescue of the Bulgarian Jewish community during the Second World War.

[Synagogue: 16 Ekzarkh Josif Street at the corner of George-Washington Street. ✆ 29831273. Open daily 9 A.M.–5 P.M.]
[Shalom Organization: Boulevard Samboliiski 50, Sofia 1303. ✆ 29265301.]
■ The Jewish cemetery, dating to the end of the nineteenth century, is still in use.
[Take tram number 2 to the end of the line.]

Samokov

Some of the richest **Sephardic** families in Europe made their fortune in the small city of Samokov, located about thirty-seven miles south of Sofia. A branch of the Apollo family, which originated in Vienna, founded a veritable empire here, with ventures in metallurgy, tanning, weaving, banking, and real estate.
■ The beautiful synagogue, today a national historic monument, along with a number of other public works (bridges, public fountains, etc.) were built by the Arieh family.
[Synagogue: General Velyaminov Street, Samokov.]

ACKNOWLEDGMENT OR LOVE

The Arieh family, after settling for a while in Vienna, had to leave the Hapsburg capital one day because the wife of tolerant Joseph II (1765–90) had set her sights on one of the clan's most handsome, eligible bachelors. The Ariehs first moved to Vidin, then to Sofia, and finally Samokov.

Midhat Pasha, a reformist pasha of the 1860s, one day told an assembly of the city's Jews that he knew of no people "in either Sofia, Kyustendil or Dupnitsa, whether they be Turks, Bulgarians, or Jews, who are as intelligent as the Ariehs."

Synagogue, Samokov.

Bulgarian Plains ■

Plovdiv

■ The Zion Synagogue dates from the nineteenth century. It is still active, but only a small minority of 300 to 400 Jewish inhabitants are still practicing. Under restoration, the synagogue is adorned with a delightful Venetian-glass chandelier and a richly decorated dome. In the sur-rounding area, traces of what was once a sizable Jewish quarter can still be found, including Stars of David engraved on certain gates.

[Zion Synagogue: 13 Tsar Kaloyan Street, Plovdiv. For information about opening hours, contact the Shalom Organization's local branch: 20 General Zaimov Street, Plovdiv. ✆ 32622509.]

Jewish store, Burgas.

Burgas

■ The synagogue here has been transformed into an art gallery. Built at the turn of the century following plans of the Italian architect Ricardo Toscani, during the 1960s it was completely remade into an exhibition space for some 2,500 works by contemporary Bulgarian painters, as well as for a collection of old icons.

Ruse

Twenty-five hundred members strong before the war, the Jewish community of Ruse, on the banks of the Danube, was reduced to barely 200 people after mass departures to Israel in the late 1940s. Since the fall of Communism, however, the Shalom organization has attempted to revitalize and return the **Ashkenazic** Synagogue here to service, the last one built in Bulgaria, in 1927.

The Sephardic Synagogue, which dates from the late nineteenth century, is also no longer active. Both buildings are closed to the public.

■ It was in Ruse in 1905 that Nobel Prize–winning writer Elias Canetti was born. He lived at number 13 on Gurko Street, where the former Sephardic Synagogue is located.

[Shalom Organization in Ruse: Ermustakov, 7000 Ruse. ✆ 082270457.]

Marchant   Juif.

Turkey

IN THE BEAUTIFUL SYNAGOGUE OF AHRIDA, one of the oldest in Istanbul, the *tevah* assumes the shape of a caravel symbolizing not only Noah's Ark but also the vessels that in 1492 transported the Jews banished from Spain to the shores of the Ottoman Empire. A royal edict issued in Granada, only recently recaptured from the Arabs, gave the Jews no choice but conversion to Catholicism or exile. Five years later, the Portuguese nobility followed the example of their counterparts in Madrid. A millennium of Jewish presence on the Iberian Peninsula was thus swept away. Sephardic Judaism, one of the most splendid manifestations of Judaism at the end of the Middle Ages, was dispersed throughout the Mediterranean basin and as far north as the United Provinces.

Many Jews chose to accept the hospitality of Sultan Bajazet II, who "had heard about the wrongs that the Spanish sovereign had inflicted upon the Jews and learned the Jews were looking for a safe haven." The sultan was also said to have declared, "Can you call such a sovereign wise and intelligent? He impoverishes his country and enriches mine." Such sympathetic tales from Jewish historiography,

Engraving after Nicolas de Nicolay, Jewish Merchant of Turkey, *1568. Musée d'Art et d'Histoire du Judaïsme, Paris.*

such as the chronicle of Rabbi Elijah Capsali (six-teenth century), are not corroborated by Ottoman sources, but in any case, they attest to the Jews' enormous gratitude toward the sultans of their adopted homeland. The Jews prospered for many years under the sultans' protection and remained loyal subjects until the end of the Ottoman Empire.

"In contrast to their counterparts in the west or northern Africa, the **Sephardim** of the Balkans overwhelmed the native community. They intro-duced Judeo-Hispanic culture to such a degree that cities such as Istanbul, Andrianopolis, Smyrna, Thessaloníki, and Sarajevo absorbed these influ-ences and in them a sort of **Sepharad** was trans-planted and re-created," notes an important study on Ottoman Judaism, *The Jews of the Balkans: the Judeo-Spanish Community, 15th to 20th Centuries.*[15] Today, however, traces of a Jewish presence in Turkey before the arrival of the Spanish exiles are literally concealed by the cities them-selves. The remains of a classical synagogue, dat-ing from the third century C.E., for example, was discovered in the ruins of Sardis, near İzmir. A bronze column found at Ankara lists the rights the emperor Augustus conferred upon the Jewish com-munities of Asia Minor. These Hellenistic Jewish communities, called Romaniotes, settled particu-larly in the large coastal cities of the Aegean.

The Jewish communities persisted during the Byzantine period despite numerous persecutions. Byzantine emperors simultaneously wielded both political and religious power. As a result, the sever-ity of discrimination against the Jews quickly esca-lated in Byzantium as compared with the West. Humiliated, restricted to certain economic activi-ties, and confined to living in specially designated neighborhoods, the Jews no longer even had the right under Justinian (527–65) to say in their prayers, "our God is the only God," a phrase considered an insult to the Holy Trinity.

In 422, the Jews were thrown out of Byzantium by Theodosius II. They returned to the capital only in the ninth century, settling along the southern banks of the Golden Horn, close to the Marmara Sea and the defensive walls of the city. The anti-Semitism of the Byzantine authorities never weakened. At the beginning of the fourteenth century, the patriarch Athanasius I complained about the presence of a synagogue in the capital to the emperor Andronicus II Paleologue: "Not only are the masses allowed to continue to live in ignorance, but they are being contaminated by the presence of the Jews."

At the same time, the inexorable advance in the fourteenth century of the Ottomans across Anatolia, and later through the Balkans, was enthusiastically welcomed by the Romaniote Jewish communities. "It meant an immediate liberation not only from oppression, persecution, and humiliation, but even from slavery," writes Stanford J. Shaw, who emphasizes that, in 1324, many Jews from the city of Bursa helped Sultan Ohran capture this large city in northwestern Anatolia, which would become the first Ottoman capital.[16] From the beginning, however, the tolerance of the Ottomans toward the Jews was one dictated by reasons of a vested interest. The Ottomans were a society of warriors and peasants whose burgeoning state bureaucracy left them little time for other activities. Commerce, most notably, was left to Christians and Jews. As in other Islamic lands, the Ottomans had a policy of *dhimmi,* or protected peoples, found both in the Koran and in the *sunna* (the "tradition") that provided for governing peoples of the Book who could not be converted by force. This policy guaranteed the security of individuals and their property, but non-Muslims were required to pay a tax to the state. And although non-Muslim communities were permitted self-governance under the authority of their religious leaders, the policy made non-Muslims second-class citizens subject to a number of discriminatory measures. These were mostly of a symbolic nature relating to clothing or domestic architecture, the forbidding of nonbelievers to bear arms or keep certain esteemed animals—all practices meant to show the superiority of the true believers. The policy could be applied in a more or less humiliating fashion. In the main, however, the Ottoman sultans were open and pragmatic. From the fourteenth century onward, European Jews streamed in from the lands that had expelled them, from Hungary in 1376 and France in 1394. Others arrived from Sicily at the beginning of the fifteenth century. Most of them settled in Adrianopolis (present-day Edirne), then capital of the empire. "I assure you, Turkey is a country of abundance where, if you wish, you will find rest," wrote the rabbi Isaac Zarfati in a famous letter to his fellow believers still living in Christian lands.

The Ottoman authorities forced small Jewish romaniotes communities to resettle in conquered areas in order to supply their cities with artisans and merchants. This policy was implemented for example in 1453 for colonizing Istanbul. The *surgün,* as the deported peoples were known, were differentiated from the *kendi gelen,* or people coming of their own free will, such as the Jewish exiles coming from the west. Jewish exiles remained an active group for many years. The steady stream of Jews arriving from Spain lasted for several decades. Some of them arrived directly, while others only after long journeys, notably by way of Italy. Either way, the trend was set.

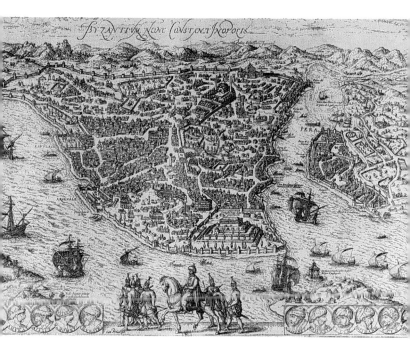

Map of Constantinople, sixteenth century.

Censuses undertaken by the Ottoman authorities in 1520–30 counted 1,647 Jewish households in Istanbul, some 10 percent of the city's population, and 2,645 households in Thessaloníki, of a population of 4,863 family units. Thirty years earlier there had not been any Jews in this large Balkan port city that was to remain the capital of the Judeo-Spanish world until the end of the Ottoman Empire. In Istanbul, Jews from the Iberian Peninsula did not become a majority in the local community until the seventeenth century, but they had a major role there due to their energy and prestige. They could also count on the goodwill of the Ottoman authorities' vested

Jewess of the Court, *Turkey, eighteenth century. Bibliothèque des Arts Décoratif, Paris.*

interest in their prosperity. As the historian Bernard Lewis explains, "From the Turkish point of view, the Jews, especially those that came from Europe, presented a number of advantages. . . . Abreast of European affairs but relatively uninterested in them, the Jews were able advisers in the relations the Ottoman Empire maintained with western powers. . . . Finally, and above all, the Ottomans had no *a priori* reason to suspect treason or suspicious sympathies with their primary enemy, the Christian Occident." Pillars of the empire, the Jews opened the first printing presses in Istanbul and Thessaloníki in the fifteenth century. However, Turkish authorities forbade them to use the Arabic alphabet in order to keep it from being profaned, and so that Turkish scribes and calligraphers would not be deprived of work. Jews introduced theater to the Ottoman Empire, which until then had been totally ignored. They brought with them new techniques of navigation and weapons production, as well as capital. Nonetheless, it was in the economic sphere where Jewish contributions were most significant. Jews had key roles in tax administration, in the Empire's finances, in the textile industry, and in banking. For example, the sultan benefited from the management skills and immense wealth of the rich Portuguese Jew Joseph Nassi, who, by the end of Suleiman the Magnificent's reign, had distinguished himself in his diplomatic activities with Poland, Italy, and Spain.

After Nassi's death in 1579, Jews were no longer to occupy such elevated government positions. However, two professions allowed Jewish influence to persist in the life of the empire: as doctors for political figures and, above all, as attendants in Turkish harems. As keepers of the jewels, clothing, or perfume of the sultan's favorites or their powerful mothers, such women as Esther Handali or Esperanza Malchi secured close friendships with the influential women of the harem.

♛ PILLARS OF THE EMPIRE

Jews occupied a crucial place in the flourishing Ottoman Empire of the sixteenth century. This fact was noted by numerous Western chroniclers, such as Michel Febure (quoted by Robert Mantran), who lamented, "They are so adroit and industrious they make themselves indispensable to everyone. There is not a single wealthy family among the Turks and foreign merchants where one does not find a Jew in their employ, whether to appraise merchandise, or to serve as an interpreter and to give advice about everything that happens. Regarding any location in the city they are able to recount in detail everything that is available for sale, its quality and quantity. . . . Other Oriental nationalities, such as the Greeks or Armenians, lack this talent and would not know how to attain such shrewdness: this is what obliges merchants to make use of the Jews, despite the slight aversion that one feels."

ROBERT MANTRAN, *ISTANBUL AU TEMPS DE SOLIMAN LE MAGNIFIQUE* (ISTANBUL UNDER SULEIMAN THE MAGNIFICENT) (PARIS: HACHETTE, 1994).

The decadence of Ottoman Judaism in the seventeenth century accompanied and anticipated that of the Empire. One of the causes of this phenomenon was the end of Jewish immigration from Europe that had afforded the Ottoman administration contact with the western world. Christian minorities, beginning with the Greeks and Armenians, began at this time to fulfill the roles of intermediaries between these two worlds. The marginalization and withdrawal of the Jewish community from secular functions were accelerated by the crisis of the false messiah Sabbataï Zevi that so shook Judaism within the Ottoman Empire.

Jacket, Ottoman Empire. Musée d'Art et d'Histoire du Judaïsme, Paris.

SABBATAÏ ZEVI (1626–78) AND THE *DEUNMÉS*

The hot-headed **Kabbalist** Sabbataï Zevi was born in Smyrna (present-day İzmir) in 1626 into a family of drapers hailing from Peloponnese. Convinced that he was the Messiah, he created upheaval in the Jewish community that led to its persecution by the Ottoman Empire. According to Gershom Sholem, the most penetrating modern commentator on Zevi, this religious and insurrectional movement developed out of a background of **Kabbalist** mysticism, the dominant form of Jewish piety of the period. From the time of their exile from Spain, Jewish thinkers sought answers to the tragedy of the expulsion, a catastrophe they likened to the destruction of the Temple of Jerusalem. A rabbi in Rhodes proposed in 1495, "I think these trials are the birth pains of the coming of the Messiah." One can thus understand the enthusiasm and hopes the sudden messianic movement in Smyrna aroused, despite Zevi's excommunication by the rabbis of Jerusalem. In 1665, Sabbataï Zevi departed for Istanbul. He was arrested by the Ottoman authorities and forced to choose either martyrdom or conversion to Islam. The false Messiah chose to submit. Some considered this apostasy as an indispensable step in the realization of his mission and also converted to Islam, all the while maintaining their Jewish faith and practicing its rites in secret. The community of *deunmés* (those who turned) resigned themselves to going to Turkey at the empire's end. Even today, certain great *deunmé* families occupy an important place in publishing or industry. Hiding for many years and continuing their low profile during the first seventy years of Kemal's secular republic, Turkey's *deunmés* have begun to openly reclaim their identity and history.

Portrait of Sabbataï Zevi, nineteenth-century after a seventeenth-century painting.

In the traumatized and despairing communities, the rabbis took on enormous power and effectively precluded any possibility of more liberal tendencies to develop. The Ottoman authorities began to regard the Jewish minority, which until then had attracted no particular concern, with growing suspicion. By the next century, when the Ottoman Empire was forced by western powers to begin modernization, the Jews of the Levant had become a scorned and impoverished minority. Far from the great intellectual debates around **Haskalah,** religious reform, Zionism, or the renaissance of the Hebrew language, Jews had fallen into obscurity. Western travelers who passed through the Jewish quarters of Istanbul or the Golden Horn recounted a miserable reality, totally opposite to what voyagers had described two centuries before. Turkish Jews kept to themselves in their communities, earning their living as shop owners, artisans, or low-level employees. Worse, an anti-Semitism encouraged by Christian minorities such as the Greeks began to develop: the first accusation of ritual murder suddenly occurred in Damascus in 1840.

♆ THE PARIAHS

"I never saw the curse denounced against the children of Israel more fully brought to bear than in the East [. . .] Where they are considered rather as a link between animals and human beings, than as men possessed of the same attributes, warmed by the same sun, chilled by the same breeze, subject to the same feelings, and impulses, and joys, and sorrows, as their fellow-mortals.

There is a subdued and spiritless expression about the Eastern Jew, of which the comparatively tolerant European can picture to himself no possible idea until he has looked upon it. . . . It is impossible to express the contemptuous hatred in

Wandering tinsmith, Constantinople.

which the Osmanlis hold the Jewish people; and the reriest Turkish urchin who may encounter one of the fallen nation on his path, has his meed of insult to add to the degradation of the outcast and wandering race of Israel."

Julia Pardoe, in a description of The City of the Sultan *(1836).*

BERNARD LEWIS, *THE JEWS OF ISLAM* (PRINCETON: PRINCETON UNIVERSITY PRESS, 1984).

Salvation came from outside. Western governments increased their pressure on the sultan's regime to accelerate its liberal reforms intended to guarantee the Ottoman Empire's integrity but also western economic interests. The 150,000 Jews living in Ottoman territories in the middle of the nineteenth century benefited from these initiatives, as did other minorities. In 1856 and later in 1869, decrees specifying and amplifying the first reforms of 1839 guaranteed the equality of all citizens before the law. The concern of Occidental Jewish communities over the welfare of their fellow believers in the Levant gradually awakened Turkish Judaism from its stupor. A small group of elite Jews played an essential part as intermediaries. They supported the *francos,* Jews of foreign origin who benefited from the privileges accorded to western expatriates by the sultans. The conflict between the Conservative rabbis and the small modernist elite first crystallized over the opening of a new school in 1858 under the patronage of banker Abraham de Camondo, "the Rothschild of the Orient." Two years later Reform sympathizer Jacop Avigor was elected the grand rabbi of the empire. Conservatives countered with the support of much of the working class. Violent upheavals in 1862 prevented authorities from intervening. Soon after, the traditionalists came back into power and excommunicated Abraham de Camondo. Three years later the Ottoman administration reversed its previous position and imposed on Jewish communities a more liberal policy that limited the power of the rabbis. But resistance continued and the *francos* established their own so-called "Italian" community. This community worked actively to introduce the schools of the Universal Israelite Alliance, based in Paris, into the lands of the Levant. The first such schools opened in Istanbul in 1870. French replaced **Ladino,** first among the elites and, gradually, among the majority of the empire's Jewish population. By 1912, every **Ladino** community of more than 1,000 persons had been granted an Alliance school. This organization increasingly replaced the weakened existing community institutions. In 1908, an Alliance supporter, Haim Nahum, became the head of Judaism in an empire where the triumph of the Young Turk Revolution had installed a constitutional monarchy. One of the centers of the movement was the great Jewish city of Thessaloníki. Nonetheless, its Jews played only a marginal part in the new democratic regime. The first Ottoman assembly elected in 1908 included only four Jews. The Balkan Wars of 1912–13, Greece's conquest of Thessaloníki, the First World War, and the crumbling of the empire marked the end of Ottoman Judaism. Thereafter, Judaism in Turkey was divided among several hostile, if not rival, nation-states. The First World War and the war for independence devastated other minorities. The Armenians were massacred in 1915 and the Greeks hunted down in the context of the great migration of populations that followed the Treaty of Lausanne in 1923.

According to a census taken in 1927, 81,872 Jews lived within the boundaries of the Turkish republic claimed by Mustapha Kemal, most concentrated in the cities of Istanbul and İzmir. Traumatized by the defeat of 1918 and the crumbling of the empire, the Turks attempted to forge a specific national identity, regarding minorities with suspicion. The new republican political system, directly inspired by the Jacobin model, had a major effect on the living conditions of the Jewish community. The new republic was above all determined to encourage the formation of a national middle class.

The Universal Israelite Alliance schools were forced to break their foreign ties, and Turkish was made the language of instruction. The militant secularism of Kemalist institutions suffocated the last Jewish community schools. The Jews were reminded that they were "guests" and that it behooved them to show their gratitude by integrating as quickly as possible.

Although in principle Jews were guaranteed full equality under the law, reality was otherwise. Public posts of a certain level remained off limits to Jews until the years 1945–50. As Esther Benbassa and Aron Rodrigue have observed, "This authoritarian, non-liberal nation-state left the Jewish community deprived of its own institutions while not permitting it to integrate into social and public spheres."[17] This discriminatory policy toward minority populations intensified during the Second World War. It is true that Kemalist Turkey which remained neutral during the war welcomed a number of Jews affiliated with German universities after they were forced out by the Nazis in 1933, and it permitted refugees furnished with an entry visa for Palestine to travel across its territories. Nonetheless, in 1942 it instituted an "exceptional tax" that in fact was conceived to bring about the economic ruin of its minority populations. They were divided into four groups (foreign residents, non-Muslims, Muslims, deunmés) and taxed accordingly. The official estimate of individual means was most often completely arbitrary. On average, the tax was 5 percent for Muslims and 150–200 percent for Greeks, Armenians, and Jews. Most had no way to pay such exorbitant taxes and were forced to sell their belongings. Those unable to pay were then condemned to work camps in the far reaches of Anatolia. The tax

Spanish-Jewish couple, Smyrna.

was finally abolished in March 1944. But its effect on Turkish Jews was traumatic and prepared the way for a massive emigration to Israel beginning in 1948 and continuing during the years 1950–60. Emigration increased with each nationalist initiative despite the reinstallation of a multiparty system and the democratization of republican institutions.

Today 26,000 Jews live in Turkey, mainly in Istanbul. Good relations between Ankara and Israel, the only two democracies of the region and both faithful allies of Washington, permit this community to live without major problems. It is the only significant Jewish community resident in an Islamic nation. Friendly to the west and secular, Turkey is Islamic but not Arab. Surrounded by hostile neighbors, it has obvious strategic interests in common with Israel, which led in 1998 to the signing of a military agreement. The authorities in Ankara have willingly reclaimed traditional Ottoman hospitality toward the Jews. Turkey celebrated the 500-year anniversary of the welcoming of Spanish Jews with great pomp. Still, Turkey's Jews remain concerned by the rise of Islamic fundamentalism in their country and fear being the target of terrorist attacks, such as that on 6 September 1986 at the Neve Shalom Synagogue in Istanbul, which left twenty-three dead.

→ **To call Turkey from the United States, dial 011 90** followed by the number of the person you are calling minus the initial 0 (used only for domestic calls).

Istanbul and Surrounding Areas ■

Istanbul

Sumptuous and decadent, immense and frenetic, Istanbul is "the world in one city," as it is often described by Western travelers overwhelmed by the city's splendor. The skyline of Istanbul is punctuated by hundreds of minarets, majestic onion domes, and bell towers. "An aged hand covered with rings held out toward Europe," according to Jean Cocteau, the great city of the Bosporus mixes the heritage of Byzantium and the Ottoman Empire, of the Orient and Europe. In this extraordinary mixture of the vestiges of centuries, the Jewish presence can appear quite discreet. There are hardly more than 20,000 Jews in Turkey today, a drop in the bucket compared to the 12 million inhabitants of Istanbul. The Jews, like all the inhabitants with old roots here, are drowned out by the mass of Anatolian immigrants that have streamed into the city in the last thirty years. More often than not, Istanbul's Jews speak Turkish among themselves, even if most know French. Only the very elderly remember **Ladino,** their old language to which the Hebrew weekly *Shalom* (circulation of 3,500) still dedicates

El Nacional, *established by David Fresco in Constantinople, later became* El Telegrafo *in 1871.*

one or two pages in each issue. The number of **kosher** restaurants can be counted on one hand and are often located in hotels for Jewish tourists passing through. Of the sixteen synagogues still in existence, only a handful are active.

Although Turkish Judaism and its monuments and cemeteries were spared the *Shoah* and the devastation of Nazism, real estate speculation and grand-scale urban renewal projects have destroyed a number of memorials. A highway passes through the middle of the old cemetery of Hasköy atop the Golden Horn. The sumptuous tomb of the Camondo family is thus surrounded by the roar of traffic. Jewish Istanbul still exists, however. One sees it in the summer when Jewish families, most now dispersed in different parts of the city, run into each other at Büyükada (Prinkipo), a traditional vacation spot on the largest of the Princes Islands in the Sea of Marmara. Prosperous merchants, businessmen, famous industrialists, and reputable doctors, Istanbul's Jews have almost all forsaken the former *judería* (Jewish quarter) of Balat, Hasköy, Kuzgunçuk (on the Asian side), and even the European old town next to Galata and Beyoğlu in order to settle in the new residential neighborhoods. Still, fascinating vestiges of Istanbul's secular pluralism remain. Less visited by tourists than other European cities,

Chiviti (decorative plaque) depicting a map of Jerusalem, eastern wall of a synagogue in Istanbul, 1853. Jewish Museum, New York.

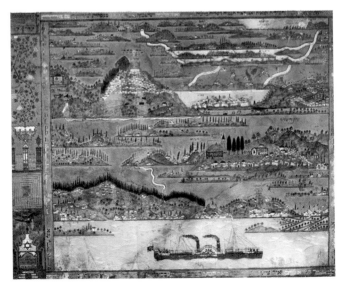

Istanbul's monuments are no less moving. As Esther Benbassa has written, "These streets have their own language, and in them history is preserved."

Visiting Jewish Istanbul merits at least two days. It is necessary to contact the Foundation for the Rabbinate's Synagogues at least twenty-four hours in advance for reasons of security and because many places of worship are closed. We have divided the tour of Istanbul's Jewish heritage into four large zones.

[Foundation for the Rabbinate's Synagogues: ✆ 02122938794, fax 02122441980. Visits by appointment for all Istanbul synagogues arranged with the faxed receipt of the first page of your passport a week before you wish to visit.]

BEYOĞLU AND GALATA

Lying atop a hill dominating the Bosporus to the north of the Golden Horn, the "European city" of Pera grew up in the middle of the nineteenth century. A place where earlier one could find the shop counters of Genoese merchants, the architecture of Beyoğlu, as the Turks call it, is western. Its grand structures such as the covered passages recall those of Paris, London, or Berlin. Western nationals, taking advantage of the privileges granted by the sultan to those doing business with the empire, settled here and were followed by a number of "minority" populations, including Greeks, Armenians, and Jews. The

only remaining part of Istanbul that has no significant mosque, Pera is located across from Stambul, the old city on the other side of the Golden Horn. In contrast, one finds numerous Orthodox, Catholic, and Protestant churches close to its large street, today called Istikal Street.

■ According to the travel guides from the era when this quarter became the sixth arrondissement of Istanbul in 1857, Beyoğlu was an "extension of Europe" characterized by embassies, wine merchants and milliners, cabarets and theaters, luxury hotels such as the Pera-Palas, and Western-style educational institutions such as the Francophone Galatasaray. An intellectual, political, and diplomatic center of the cosmopolitan Ottoman capital in the last decades of the Empire, Pera was also the residential neighborhood of choice for elite Jews open to the ideas and models of the west. Connected by a subterranean funicular to Galata-Karaköy near to the passengers' port on the Bosporus, Pera is also the home of the Neve Shalom Synagogue, the largest synagogue still active. The Italian Synagogue, Ashkenazic Synagogue, and the administrative offices of the rabbinate are also located here.

[Rabbinate: Yemeneci sokak 23, Beyoğlu/tünel, Istanbul. ✆ 02122448794.]

■ The Neve Shalom Synagogue is situated on a small street near the famous Galata Tower (Galata Kulesi). It was built by Genoese in the fourteenth century in a lively quarter that is still at the center of Jewish life in Istanbul. Near the synagogue one encounters typical Jewish homes of the period decorated with a Star of David on the pediment. The house at 50 Büyük Hendek Street is a good example. The houses at 5 and 7 Timarci Street have their date of construction engraved on a foundation stone calculated according to both the Hebrew and European calendars. A few of the last surviving grand homes typical of the **Ladino** way of life remain in this quarter. As Ilan Karmi notes in his guide to Istanbul, "Constructed around a central courtyard, these homes, commonly called *yahudi hani* (Jewish houses), could be comfortably inhabited by a large extended family or a congregation."[18] One of the best-preserved houses of this type is located at 56 Serdari Ekrem Street.

The Neve Shalom Synagogue, designed by the architects Elio Ventura and Bernard Motola, was built in 1951 on the site of a small prayer hall that it replaced. The elegant building has a large hall able to hold as many as 500 people and is decorated with a splendid rose window on the facade imported from Great Britain. Be sure to notice the magnificent woodwork on part of the walls.

Neve Shalom Synagogue, Istanbul.

The *tevah* and *aron* are elevated and face the worshippers' benches, as in most of European synagogues dating from the late nineteenth and twentieth centuries. In the entrance is a plaque recalling the terrible attack on 6 September 1986 that left twenty-three dead. Two Arab terrorists managed to enter the prayer hall during **Shabbat** services, and after killing the old *shamash* (the "bedaud"), who tried to stop them, opened fire on the congregation. The strong reaction of the Jewish community to the trauma remains acute, despite the solidarity immediately shown by the authorities and the near-total support of public opinion. The synagogue was restored and reopened in May 1987. Each year a special commemorative service is held for the victims.

[Neve Shalom Synagogue:

Büyük Hendek sokak 67, Şişhane.

✆ 02122936223. Visits by appointment.]

■ Near the Neve Shalom Synagogue at 87 Büyük Hendek Street is the site of the former Kneset Israel Synagogue in what is now a sports club. A little further down the street is a Jewish elementary and high school complex constructed in 1915 during the war, when the Universal Israelite Alliance schools were not permitted to operate: as Francophone institutions, they were naturally the enemy of the Ottoman Turks allied with Germany.

■ The Italian Synagogue is discreetly located in a harmonious building behind the wall of a small courtyard.

Largely remodeled in the early 1930s, the design preserves the original structure dating from 1887. The centuries-old presence of Italian Jews in the Ottoman capital is attested by the memory of the ancient synagogues of Puglia (Apulia) and Messina, which have since disappeared. In 1866, the Italian Jews separated from the rest of the Jewish community, which they judged to be too traditionalist. Supported by the Italian embassy, they obtained the right from Sultan Abdulaziz to form an autonomous congregation, similar to what already existed for the **Ashkenazic** community and the Karaites. The facade of the synagogue is restrained but harmonious with its rectangular pediment and brick double staircase leading to the entrance. The prayer hall is painted completely white and is surrounded by the women's gallery on the second floor. Today the Italian community numbers only a few hundred faithful.

[Italian Synagogue:

Sair Ziya Pas a Yokusu sokak 27, Karaköy.

✆ 02122937784. Visits by appointment.]

■ Imposing and rather austere from the outside, the **Ashkenazic** Synagogue stands in the middle of the large street connecting Pera to the lower section of the Galata neighborhoods near the Bosporus. This area is the former banking and financial section of the city, revealed by the names of the streets (Bankarlar Street, for example). In the nearby Voyvoda Street, above the sumptuous staircases that he had constructed, you will find the former neighborhood of the great financier Abraham de Camondo. The current synagogue, called the German Hebrew Synagogue according to the plaque on its facade, is the last of the city's three **Ashkenazic** temples. It is located in an area where Jews from Hungary, Germany, and France settled beginning in the fourteenth century. Approximately 2,000 **Ashkenazic** Jews live in Istanbul today. The building was constructed in 1900 following a design by architect Gabriele Tedeschi. The beautiful facade is composed of three richly decorated grand arcades crowned by two domes. It recalls the facades of numerous synagogues built in the nineteenth century in cities of the Austro-Hungarian Empire by emancipated bourgeois Jews. And this is not accidental, since many of Istanbul's **Ashkenazim** arrived here from Austria, Bohemia, and Hungary and remained Hapsburg subjects. The plaque at the entrance to the synagogue commemorates, among other things, the fiftieth birthday of Emperor Franz-Joseph, whose wife gave to the synagogue the magnificent *aron* made of carved alder and inlay and crowned by a wooden dome decorated with gold. The ensemble is of an obvious oriental style with carved wood decorations blending Hebrew letters with plant motifs. The large rectangular hall can hold 1,000 people and is crowned with an azure dome flecked with golden stars. The women's gallery extends on two floors. In all, the building has seven halls. Four are in the basement, which contains a dining area, the **mikvah, Midrash,** and a small room for morning prayers.

[Ashkenazi Synagogue:
Yüksek Kaldirim sokak 37, Karaköy.
✆ 02122938794. Visits by appointment.]

■ The beautiful Zulfaris Synagogue, which now houses the Jewish Museum of Istanbul, stands at the end of a small street near the entrance to the funicular (tunnel) and the famous Galata Bridge at the mouth of the Golden Horn. It is an elegant four-story building with a brick neoclassical facade and two marble columns at the entrance above a small flight of steps. Closed for more than ten years and reopened in 2000, the current building was remodeled in 1890 with a donation by the Camondo family and replaces most of the original edifice dating from the seventeenth century. Like other synagogues of the "European city, " the Zulfaris Synagogue takes its inspiration from Western models of emancipated Judaism. The imposing marble *aron* has two arrows on the side and is neo-Gothic in style. It was conceived by one of the architects who constructed Saint Anthony, the Pera quarter's large, beautiful Catholic church. The lovely rectangular hall measures 50 ft. x 23 ft. Its second-floor gallery houses a permanent exhibition on the life and history of Turkey's Jews. Naim Guleryuz, the museum curator and the community's historian, explained: "We wanted to illustrate six centuries of harmonious existence and to show our fellow believers and others that the Jews of Turkey have actively participated in the life of this country." Several Sifrei **Torah** crowned with the crescent and star are on display, as well as religious objects decorated with Ottoman symbols. You will discover in the display cases and on the walls examples of the flourishing Jewish and **Ladino** press from the end of the nineteenth and beginning of the twentieth centuries, as well as portraits of famous Jews of the time in diplomacy, the arts, and even the military. The museum gives information on Jewish scholars who fled Hitler's Germany and found refuge in Turkey, as well as Turkish diplomats such as the consul of Rhodes, Salahattin Ülkümen, who saved many Jews during the war by giving them Turkish papers.

[Jewish Museum of Istanbul: Perçemli sokak, Karaköy. To visit, contact the Foundation of the Rabbinate's Synagogues: ✆ 02122938794.]

THE GOLDEN HORN: BALAT

The Golden Horn is a small estuary created by two rivers that flow into the Bosporus. From one side of the Golden Horn to the other extend traditional Jewish neighborhoods that arose beginning at the time of Jewish settlement in Istanbul in the Byzantine period. Even at the beginning of the twentieth century more than half the population of the Balat was Jewish, although many were already leaving the cramped houses of this humid district for the "European city." The neighborhoods of the Balat, on the right bank, and of Hasköy, on the other side of the river, have remained vibrant and rather exotic in memories of Istanbul—places where **Ladino** was spoken and one lived according to the rhythms of Jewish festivals and the **Shabbat**. The names of synagogues, many of which have since disappeared, recall the Sepharad that everyone keeps close to their hearts (Gerouche-Castile—the exiles of Castile—Catalan, Aragon, Portugal, Senioria . . .). Many European travelers of the nineteenth century gave terrible descriptions of this quarter. Edmondo De Amicis, for example, described it as, "the vast ghetto of Balat stretching out like a foul serpent along the Golden Horn with its mold-encrusted huts." Marie-Christine Varol offered a more even-handed portrait in her monograph on the Balat: "All manner of social classes are found mixing in the Balat, from well-off merchants to the most humble street peddlers and rag-pickers."[19] As in the rest of Istanbul, the many wood houses were vulnerable to devastating fires. The volunteer fire brigade thus held a key place in the life of the community. The houses near the docks (the Karabaş area) have been knocked down to make room for a park and an embankment. Recent Anatolian immigrants occupy most of the small buildings abandoned by the Jews. Only a few Jews still live in the area, notably close to the Ahrida Synagogue. These are mainly poor families living on aid from the community. Some Jewish doctors keep an office in the area, near the large Jewish hospital Or ha-Haïm, which is still active. The inscriptions on the stone facades of the houses and several synagogues still standing in the area evoke memories of its former life. A visit to Balat and Hasköy necessitates a full day.

THE FIRE OF 1911

"In 1911 a part of the Or ha-Haïm hospital located in Balat burst into flames and was engulfed in fire. The entire Dibek quarter, including the Gerouche Synagogue and the two Israelite Alliance schools, a part of the Sigri quarter with its synagogue Pol Yacham, the entire Hevra quarter and its synagogue and Talmud Torah, and a large part of Balat fell prey to the flames. Caption: 520 buildings destroyed, 1,000 families without shelter . . . Outside the municipal and communal aid, the gifts of strangers are rapidly amounting to more than 60,000 francs."

AVRAM GALANTÉ, *HISTOIRE DES JUIFS DE TURQUIE*, (HISTORY OF THE JEWS OF TURKEY) 9 VOLS. (ISTANBUL: ISIS, 1985).

■ The lively main street of Kürkçü Cesmesi, like the nearby Leblebciler and Lapincilar, is the center of commercial Balat and animated every day except the **Shabbat**. On Saturdays the area is dead, a place where even the Turkish and Greek merchants respect the sacred day of rest. Most of the shops at the front of the houses are owned by Jews. The area was known for the manufacture of the fez until this traditional headpiece was outlawed by the republican authorities in 1928. There are also cobblers and makers of Turkish slippers, often Jews from Georgia *(los gurdjis)*. At 6 and 8 Eski Kasap, the street perpendicular to Kürkçü Cesmesi, you can still see two lovely Jewish homes, with a Star of David on the corbelled facade and the inscription, "Prosperity on the family."

■ The Ahrida Synagogue is the oldest continuously active synagogue in Istanbul. Founded in the fifteenth century by Jews from the Macedonian city of Ohrid, it is also incontestably the most beautiful. The synagogue has kept the name of the small Romaniote community that established it, even though this community was absorbed by Jews arriving from the Iberian Peninsula, who gave the temple its splendor. According to legend, the false Messiah Sabbataï Zevi once preached here.

The main building was rebuilt at the end of the seventeenth century and restored several times thereafter, each time keeping the general outlines

ISTANBUL AND SURROUNDING AREAS

Ahrida Synagogue, Istanbul.

of the original design. The large rectangular prayer hall is crowned by a wooden dome, and its ceiling is painted with elegant, typically Ottoman floral motifs. Resplendent with eight columns and ten large windows, the synagogue is luminous. The most recent large-scale restorations, completed in 1992, have returned the hall to its former design, most notably by getting rid of the women's balcony. As in earlier times, women follow the service from an adjacent hall separated from the main worship space by perforated panels. A unique *tevah* stands in the center of the hall. Made of varnished

wood in the form of a ship, it represents Noah's Ark and also explicitly evokes the caravels that carried Jews fleeing Spain. The prow points toward the *aron,* which features magnificent ivory and mother-of-pearl inlaid wood doors. Two other buildings are located in the garden, the **Midrash** and a heavy stone and brick structure, the old *odjara* The latter today serves as a hospice.

[Ahrida Synagogue: Kürkçü Cesmesi sokak 15, Balat. ✆ 02122938794. Visits by appointment.]

■ Several hundred feet from the Ahrida Synagogue stands the Yanbol Synagogue, the other main synagogue preserved in Balat. Bearing the name of the small city in Bulgaria where the members of the founding community originated, the synagogue was rebuilt in the eighteenth century and restored several times subsequently. Illuminated by its numerous windows, the large hall is crowned by an elegant wooden ceiling decorated with floral and other landscape motifs. The capitals of the columns are finely carved and painted. The *tevah* in the middle of the hall faces the *aron,* whose wooden doors are inlaid with mother-of-pearl and ivory like those of the Ahrida Synagogue.

[Yanbol Synagogue: Ayan sokak 1, Balat. ✆ 02122938794. Visits by appointment.]

■ Nearby, at the corner of Feruh Kahya and Mahkme Alti streets, you can visit the old Cavus Hammami, frequented by Jews of the quarter, who called it "el banyo de Balat." In both the men's and women's areas of the facility, there is a basin reserved as a **mikvah** for purification.

■ Going back up the hill toward Balat and the Saint-Savior-in-Chora (Kariye Camii), famous for its mosaics, you will come to the impressive Ichtipol Synagogue. Made completely of wood, the synagogue has a beautiful round stained-glass window bearing two interlaced Stars of David. It was established in the first years of the Ottoman Empire by Jews from the small Macedonian town of Ichtip. Devastated by several fires, it was reconstructed for the last time in 1903. Facing it at numbers 63 and 67 on the same street are two beautiful homes notable for their corbelled wooden facades and finely carved decorations. They were once occupied by Jewish families of the area, who, even at that time, had already begun to occupy parts of the neighboring Greek enclave.

[Ichtipol Synagogue: Salma Tomruk sokak 62, Balat. Visits not permitted.]

■ The remains of several other synagogues can be found in Balat, sometimes reduced to a simple door, such as that of the Kastoria Synagogue, at 132 Hoca Cakir Street. Along Demir Hisar Street, one can make out the ruined walls of the Eliahuh (at number 231) and Sigri Synagogues. The former Egri Kapi cemetery, which closed in 1839, is now completely abandoned and being devoured by neighboring construction projects. The tombstones bearing inscriptions have been transported to the cemetery in Hasköy on the other side of the Golden Horn.

THE GOLDEN HORN: HASKÖY

Hasköy is the other Jewish suburb of Istanbul located on the northern bank of the Golden Horn. When the Ottoman Empire was at its height in the sixteenth and seventeenth centuries, Hasköy was slightly more populous than Balat and contained a greater concentration of elite Jews. One of the most famous inhabitants of the quarter, the prestigious physician from Granada Moshe Hamon, was an adviser to Sultan Mehmet II the Conqueror. Also in this quarter the first Jewish printing presses were set up. The most renowned educational and cultural institution of the period, the Gvira Yeshiva, established in the sixteenth century by Joseph Nasi is also located here. "There are more than a thousand homes surrounded by gardens in Hasköy, a beautiful spot with good air," recalled Evliya Tchelebi, the famous Ottoman traveler and diarist of the seventeenth century who wrote about the 17,000-strong Jewish population—at the time the overwhelming majority in the quarter. Soon after, the quarter began a period of decay, although the old traditions persisted. In 1858, Abraham de Camondo founded the institute that bears his name, the first Jewish school in the capital to teach according to western principles. The large school building of the Universal Israelite Alliance was opened in the same neighborhood in 1899. In 1955, the building became the administrative offices for the rabbinical seminary (which were later moved to Galata). Today it houses the main Jewish hospice for the elderly in Istanbul (at Köy Mektep Street). Urban reconstruction and the rerouting of major thoroughfares have devastated this neighborhood even more than that of Balat. Only two of the more than thirty synagogues in Hasköy remain.

■ The Maalem Synagogue was built in 1754. Recently restored after years of abandonment, this elegant building stands in a courtyard protected by a high wall. Two marble columns flank the porch, which opens onto a large, almost square hall with six pillars. The *tevah* stands in the middle of the room and has the form of a ship, like that of the Ahrida Synagogue. Beneath a small dome with floral decorations, is the *aron,* whose wooden doors have richly gilt moldings. Simpler and more restrained in the past with its light plastered walls contrasting with the darkness of the wooden pews, the hall interior today alternates between sky blue and white. The restorations have brought to life a part of the mural decorations.

[Maalem Synagogue: Harap Cesme sokak 20, Hasköy. ✆ 02122938794. Visits by appointment.]

■ Hasköy also is home today to Istanbul's main Karaite population. Their *kenassa* (synagogue), Bene Mikra, is a small wooden building behind a large brick wall. According to local tradition, a Karaite temple already existed on this spot in the Byzantine period. The current building, with its lovely portico flanked by two columns and a sculpted triangular pediment, was reconstructed in the eighteenth century after being devastated by fire. Access to the building is by way of a small staircase. Illan Karmi notes that "As with all Karaite synagogues, this one is constructed below the ground level in order to respect the biblical passage that states, 'From the depths

Karaite Synagogue, Istanbul.

I call to You, my God.'"[20] Inside, prayer carpets replace the conventional pews for worshippers. The wooden houses surrounding the temple were formerly inhabited by Karaite families.

[Karaite Synagogue: Mahlul sokak 3, Hasköy. ℘ 02122435166.

Visits by appointment.]

■ Going back up the hill to the north, you will arrive at Hasköy's large Jewish cemetery, the largest in the city along with that of Kuzgunçuk, on the Asiatic side of the Bosporus.

Half abandoned, the cemetery is today bisected by an urban thoroughfare. The road passes just at the foot of Abraham de Camondo's tomb, a neo-Gothic mausoleum meant to recall for posterity the grandeur of this enterprising financier, who, although living in Paris, asked to be buried in Istanbul.

THE KARAITES

This dissident sect of Judaism is characterized essentially by its rejection of the oral law represented by the **Talmud.** Karaite Jews were living in Byzantium even before the Ottoman invasion, as the writings of the twelfth-century traveler Benjamin of Tudela attest. Of interest is his reference to a community of 500 Karaites in Galata, close to the Bosporus in the present-day Karaköy quarter. More than eighty Karaite communities existed in the territory of the Ottoman Empire, as well as in Syria, Egypt, the Balkans, and especially Crimea.

THE EUROPEAN SIDE OF THE BOSPORUS AND THE SISLI AND NISANTAS RESIDENTIAL AREAS

In the nineteenth century, the villages along the Bosporus sheltered numerous "minorities"—Greeks, Armenians, and Jews. Swallowed up today by the great metropolis, Ortaköy, Arnavutköy, Bebek, Yeniköy, and others have become sought-after residential areas with interesting traces of this Jewish past, most noticeably in Ortaköy. On the hills and beyond extend the elegant new neighborhoods of Istanbul. This is where many wealthy Jewish families have settled since the interwar period, and especially in the last few decades, preferring its beautiful spacious avenues to Pera's cramped streets. With the large Beth Israel Synagogue and the administrative offices of most Jewish clubs and associations, today the heartbeat of the Jewish community in Istanbul is felt most strongly in Nişantaşi and Şişli. The weekly journal *Shalom* is also located here, with a small bookstore

where one can find books on Turkish Judaism.

[Shalom: Tesvikiye, Atiyesok, Polar apt. 12–6, Istanbul.
✆ 02122473082.]

■ The Etz Ahayim Synagogue stands near the Bosporus in Ortaköy along the edge of the isthmus where the great ships cross between the Black Sea and Sea of Marmara. The site is one of striking beauty, even if a rather plain and uninteresting modern building has replaced the former structure, which was destroyed by fire in 1941. The original synagogue, which was one of the oldest in Istanbul, was reconstructed in the eighteenth century. In the last few decades, a small Jewish community has formed in Ortaköy. Many of its members came from the great bazaar quarter, where their homes were destroyed by a fire. The synagogue's magnificent marble *aron,* featuring two finely carved neoclassical columns and carved wood doors, dates from the early period. Nearby stands the small building housing the **Midrash,** saved from the 1941 fire and which for more than a century had served the quarter's **Ashkenazic** synagogue.

[Etz Ahayim Synagogue:
Muallim Naci Caddesi 40–41, Ortaköy.
✆ 02122938794. Visits by appointment.]

■ As you walk around Ortaköy, notice the row of eighteen Jewish corbelled wood houses *(los diziogos)* on Bulguruc Street. At the top of the hill is a small Jewish cemetery established in the nineteenth century and later abandoned. Unfortunately, many of the beautiful tombstones have been destroyed.

■ As you walk north along the Bosporus, you will come to Yeniköy, where a small reconstructed eighteenth-century synagogue is still in use.

[Synagogue: Köybasi Caddesi: 242 Yeniköy
✆ 02122938794. Visits by appointment.]

■ The Beth Israel Synagogue is currently the most active and most frequented synagogue in Istanbul. Modern and functional, the building was enlarged in 1952 according to plans by the architect Aran Deragobyan. Especially noteworthy is the lovely stained glass above the large 500-seat rectangular prayer hall.

[Beth Israel Synagogue:
Buyukhavet Caddesi 61, Osmanbey.
✆ 02122936223. Open 9 A.M.–5 P.M.
Visits by appointment.]

THE ASIAN BANK

Today two large bridges cross the Bosporus, completely integrating the Anatolian part of the city with Istanbul proper. Formerly crossing was by ferry only. Consequently, the Asian districts of Istanbul and its neighboring villages lived according to another rhythm, somewhat at the margins of the pulsing heart of the city. In Kuzgunçuk, a little to the north of Üsküdar, is a significant Jewish quarter nicknamed Little Jerusalem. Today it is home to two beautiful synagogues. The lovely Hemdat Israel Synagogue is also located on the Asian side, near the Haydarpasa train station. The big city looms nearby, but Kuzgunçuk has managed to preserve the atmosphere of a village, a tranquil oasis with views of the Bosporus to the west. Icadiye Street is the heart of the quarter, inhabited by Greeks, Armenians, and, above all, by Jews for more than 400 years. Today not much more than a few Hebrew inscriptions on stone or wood facades remain to recall the Jewish past.

■ The elegant Beth Yaacov Synagogue was built in 1878 to take the place of an earlier synagogue on the same site. Restored at the end of the nineteenth century, the synagogue opens onto a beautiful garden. Notice the original landscapes on the ceiling.

[Beth Yaacov Synagogue:
Icadiye Caddesi 8, Kuzgunçuk.
✆ 02122435166. Visits by appointment.]

■ A Greek church and an Armenian church stand nearby. Higher up the hillside, the Beth Nissim Synagogue serves as a place of worship during the winter months. Constructed in

Giveret Synagogue, İzmir.

458

SYNAGOGUES OUTSIDE ISTANBUL

There are synagogues in several Turkish cities beyond Istanbul. Although in ruin, some retain their original splendor, as for example the synagogue at Edirne, a large city on the Bulgarian border where the Jewish community was particularly influential.

In southwestern Anatolia, in the impressive remains of the Lydian city of Sardes (fifty-six miles from İzmir), you can explore the ruins of an ancient synagogue dating from the third century. Sardes was the former capital of King Croesus, who was defeated by the Romans in 133 B.C.E.

The wealthy port of İzmir (formerly Smyrna), a bustling center of Jewish life during the Ottoman Empire, still has a half dozen interesting synagogues, of which the beautiful Giveret (Senoria) is one. Constructed in the sixteenth century under the sponsorship, it is said, of Dona Gracia Nassi, the aunt of the famous Joseph Nassi, it was remodeled following a fire in 1841. The Shalom Synagogue and the richly decorated Bikour Holim Synagogue are also noteworthy. In the latter, be sure to admire the niche ornamented with magnificent paintings above the *tevah*.

Jewish market street, Smyrna.

1840, it is noteworthy for its richly painted hall. The *aron* dates from the end of the eighteenth century.

[Beth Nissim Synagogue:
Yakup sokak 8, Kuzgunçuk.
✆ 02122435166. Visits by appointment.]

■ A slight distance from the center of Kuzgunçuk, the Nakas Tepe Jewish cemetery is a worthwhile destination during your visit. Many Jews had themselves buried here, even if they lived in the city, because the Asian soil was considered closer to the Holy Land. One can see a few beautiful gravestones from the sixteenth and seventeenth centuries. As with other Jewish cemeteries in the city, it has been thoroughly pillaged in the last decades. Its stones have served as construction material for the shanties built by the immigrants from Anatolia.

■ Descending along the banks of the Bosporus toward the south and after passing Üsküdar, you will arrive at Haydarpasa, a superb train station. Dating from the beginning of the twentieth century, it was the terminus of trains linking the capital to its Ottoman possessions of the Middle East, Jerusalem, Mecca, and Medina. Many Jews arriving in Kuzgunçuk settled in this quarter, whose development was in full swing at the time and where the beautiful new Hemdat Israel Synagogue had just opened in 1899 with the attendance of a number of Ottoman and western dignitaries. The building is surrounded by a garden that, although not apparent from the outside, contains a large rectangular prayer hall with a painted ceiling and beautiful wall decorations. The *aron* is installed in the middle of one of the broad walls across from the *tevah,* an arrangement typical of certain Italian synagogues. Not far from here one can visit a small, well-preserved Jewish cemetery.

[Hemdat Israel Synagogue:
Izzetin sokak 63, Haydarpasa.
✆ 02122435166. Visits by appointment.]

Greece

B ELOW THE ACROPOLIS IN ATHENS, a marble plaque engraved with a **menorah** has been uncovered amid the clutter of the Agora, near a statue of Emperor Hadrian. Perhaps it used to rest on one of the ancient synagogues visited by Saint Paul, who had as little success with the Athenian Jews as the Greek philosophers had with the Areopagus.

How far back does the Jewish presence in Greece date? This question remains unanswered to this day. An even earlier question is, When did the Greeks themselves come in contact with the Jewish people for the very first time? Legend has it that the first meeting between the two communities was peaceful and courteous. Alexander the Great, on his way to conquer Persia, is supposed to have bowed down before the high priest Jaddua in Jerusalem. That Jews and Greeks rubbed shoulders before the Macedonian conquest is certain, including as mercenaries in the Egyptian armies. The Hellenization of Judaea following Alexander's victory, however, was a source of extreme tension. A nationalistic and religious revolt was unleashed after a statue of Zeus was brought into the Temple of Jerusalem. For the Jews, such a sacrilege was, as the Bible describes it, the "abomination of desolation."

Jewish merchant, Thessaloniki.

Yet the unstoppable spread of Greek culture, along with the "scattering" of the Jewish people long before the Temple's destruction by Titus in 70 C.E., quickly led to the translation of the **Torah** into Greek. This was the book of the Septuagint, translated by seventy-two scribes in Alexandria, Egypt's great Hellenistic port where Jews numbered one million, or a third of the city's population. The book became, in the second century, the "official version" of that sacred text, the only intelligible one for Hellenized Jews and the sole means by which the earliest Christians received the Old Testament. Domination and coexistence, cultural and intellectual exchange and schisms (such as the one between the major Jewish philosophers Maimonides and Philo) thus wove the singular relationship between the two peoples.

Jewish communities first settled in present-day Greece most certainly around the third century B.C.E. However, according to Joseph Nehama in his monumental *Histoire des Israélites de Salonique* (History of the Jews of Thessaloníki), "more than immigration and the buying back of captives, it was the extreme force of proselytization animating the Jewish religion at the time that assured the recruitment and vitality of the colonies of the Diaspora."[21] It would be among such converts, the "God-fearers," that Christian preaching would encounter its earliest successes.

Though most often city dwellers, Jews also lived in the countryside. In the Kalamariá region of Macedonia, a tombstone reveals that Abraham and Theodote, a Jewish couple, worked the fields there around the year 200.

Beginning with Constantine's 312 C.E. conversion to Christianity, Roman emperors were from then on Christian, and the status of Jews within the realm began to erode. After the empire was split, moreover, the Jews abandoned the nation's Byzantine section; accusations of being *christoktonoi* or *theoktonoi* ("murderers of Christ" or "murderers of God") abound in religious literature of the era. Judaism was defined as the "death-bringing religion," and Jewish proselytizing and mixed marriages were fiercely prohibited under Theodosian Code. Justinian's *Corpus Juris Civilis* further reinforced in the sixth century restrictive laws against Jews. While synagogues remained protected religious sites, building new ones was strictly forbidden.

Life for the Greek-speaking, or "Romaniote," Jews during the Middle Ages is not well-known. It is certain that they endured invasions by the Slavs, Bulgars, and Normans both before and after the year 1000. Merchant and traveler Benjamin of Tudela, a Jew from Navarre, visited the Medieval diasporas in the twelfth century. In his *Massaoth Schel* (Itinerary), he mentioned the major Greek cities inhabited by Jews, including Corinth, Thebes, Návpaktos, Patras, Kastoria, and Thessaloníki in particular, where they numbered half a million and held a quasi-monopoly over the dye and silkworm industries.

After the fall of Constantinople in 1453, a nearly uninterrupted inflow of Jews found refuge in the Ottoman Empire's new possessions. After the edict signed by Ferdinand and Isabella on 31 March 1492 expelling all Jews from Spain, they were welcomed there en masse. At the east-west crossroads, "Byzantine Thessaloníki" became "Jewish Thessaloníki." The first group supposedly arrived from Majorca: they were called Baal Teshuva, signifying the return to Judaism of the *Marranos,* Jews who, on the surface, converted to Catholicism to escape the Inquisition. As the years passed, Castilians flooded in and imposed their linguistic dominance; they were followed by Aragonians, Catalonians, and Navarrans, and later by the Portuguese, Apulians, Venetians, Moroccans, and Livornians. They gathered together by synagogue: *kal Castilia, kal Aragon, kal Mayor,* or simply *Gueroush-Sepharad* (Expulsion from Spain).

Censuses show that the Ottoman metropolis of Thessaloníki contained only around 2,200 Islamic and Christian households in 1478; in 1519, less than twenty years after the Alhambra Decree, the city possessed 4,000 households, 56 percent of which were Jewish. A century later, there were 7,500 households here, the Jewish proportion reaching 68 percent. Thessaloníki, whose Jewish residents spoke a hybrid of Castilian and Hebrew called *Judezmo,* was called "Mother in Israel" and the "Jerusalem of the Balkans" for more than four centuries. The *responsa,* opinions by Jewish jurists in Thessaloníki on liturgical or practical questions, have become famous. Samuel Moise of Medina del Campo, who ordered the city's various congregations to adopt uniform **Sephardic** rituals, delivered around 1,000 such opinions.

Spanish exiles settling in Thessaloníki shook up Romaniote Jewish communities and their traditions, as they did as well in Serres, Kavála, Patras, Drama, Larissa, Tríkala, and Rhodes. (This was not the case in Ioannina, however.) In the seventeenth century, the major centers of Jewish life were drawn into a religious storm by a false Messiah named Sabbataï Zevi. The crisis subsided with Zevi's conversion to Islam, as rabbis smothered the faithful in suffocating rituals. Two centuries later, the fall of the Ottoman Empire plunged the Jewish communities of the Balkans, who had until then enjoyed official tolerance, into disarray and uncertainty.

One episode, or rather a legend with dramatic consequences, illustrates the difficult situation endured by the Jews during Greece's long war for independence. This war began with a revolt, in 1821, throughout the southern part of the country. In retaliation, the Greek ecumenical patriarch of Constantinople, Gregory V, was hanged from the gate of the Phanar. Greeks claimed that his body had been thrown into the Bosporus by three Jews on the order of the grand vizier. In any case, this was the excuse used by Greek insurgents for massacring thousands of Jews during the capture of the large city of Tripolis, in central Peloponnese. A flare-up of anti-Semitism punctuated every major liberation of "Greek lands" over the years to follow: Ioannina (1872), Corfu (1891), Larissa (1898), Tríkala (1898), Crete (1898), and Thessaloníki (1912 and 1931). Accusations of ritualistic crimes—the murder of Christian children by Jews— degenerated into pogroms. These events provoked the massive emigration of Jews to Marseille at the turn of the twentieth century, including the family of famous novelist Albert Cohen.

A reading of reports on this subject published by the Universal Israelite Alliance in the late nineteenth century is edifying. It is clear that such scheming was the work of a small minority in Greece, driven to extremes by a nationalist press and fringe of the lower Orthodox clergy. In contrast to these outbursts of anti-Semitism, which remained strong in Greece, liberal measures were also taken, beginning in 1832, by the Greek state in favor of equality of civil rights and religious tolerance.

With Thessaloníki's integration within Greece's borders after the Balkan wars in 1912, Greek-Jewish relations grew tenser. Greek soldiers had taken de facto the largest part in the Balkans and a cosmopolitan city with a Jewish majority. Coveted by the Serbs, Bulgarians, and, of course, the Greeks, Thessaloníki was once a political center under the Ottoman Empire. David ben Gurion, the founding father of Israel, came to study Turkish here in 1910 to plead the Zionist case before the Sublime Porte. The Young Turk Revolution broke out, pushing the last of the Sultans, Abdul Hamid, into the background. Their right to Thessaloníki having been solidified after the First World War, the Greeks made it their objective to assimilate into the nation-state an especially stubborn Jewish population. Hellenization progressed bit by bit, accelerated by the great fire of 1917 that reduced to ashes the historic Jewish city along with its thirty-two synagogues. Well versed in the French language and culture thanks to efforts by the Universal Israelite Alliance, a large number of Jewish families emigrated—to Paris, in particular.

The demographic balance was permanently upset by an influx of 150,000 Greeks from Asia Minor as part of the dramatic population transfer required by the 1923 Treaty of Lausanne. "Furthermore, after the massive refugee influx, tensions mounted between Greeks and Jews in the city and in Northern Greece generally, as a result of exacerbated competition for the control of local economic life," historian George Mavrogordatos stressed in *Stillborn Republic*.[22] A pogrom erupted in 1931 in the popular Campbell suburb, followed by other fits of violence. Dockworkers from the port of Thessaloníki left en masse for Haifa. Ironically, calm returned only after the establishment of General Jean Metaxas's Fascist regime in 1936, which publicly manifested kindness toward the Jewish community.

Such appeasement was to be short-lived. Describing the disappearance of entire communities, their uprooting by the Nazis from soil they had inhabited for centuries, the most ancient for 2,000 years, has never been properly accomplished—and cannot be done here. Before the despair that still grips the rare survivors and their descendants, the numbers poorly reflect the immensity of the drama that struck Greece's 80,000 Jews, 80 percent of whom were victims of the *Shoah*. Of Thessaloníki's 60,000 Jews, no more than 1,950 remained by the end of the war.

Beginning in 1941, the Germans began taking anti-Jewish steps in Greece. In 1942, the great Jewish necropolis, the oldest and largest of all the **Sephardic** east, was razed through the active participation of the local authorities and part of the population.

Marble from the Agora, Athens. Jewish Museum, Athens.

Under the iron rule of Eichmann lieutenant Dieter Wisliceny's SS and Alois Brunner, himself in exile in Damascus, the Final Solution was set in motion in 1943. After their temporary confinement within ghettos, the Jews of Thessaloníki were deported in sixteen convoys to Auschwitz-Birkenau. The Italians and, to a lesser degree, the Spanish made heroic efforts to save Jewish lives.

Beyond Thessaloníki, where indifference or hostility were manifest, Jews found courageous allies in a large part of the population, among the

Resistance and even the authorities. The Orthodox archbishop of Athens, Monsignor Damaskinos, constantly intervened on their behalf and took the initiative of transmitting to the Germans letters of protest signed by around thirty celebrities and community leaders. In Thessaly and "Old Greece," including Athens, hundreds of Jews were saved. The Athenian Parliament passed no anti-Semitic laws during the war, while the capital's chief of police, Anghelos Evert, provided Jews false papers.

Yitzhak Persky, British army volunteer and father of Shimon Peres, parachuted into the mountains of Attica in 1942. Captured by the Germans, he managed to escape, finding shelter for months in a monastery in Hassia. The 300 Jews of Zákinthos were all protected by the mayor and the archbishop, but the other communities in Epirus and the islands could not escape destruction. Of Corfu's 2,000 Jews, only 120 avoided the death camps. In Thrace, 2,700 of the region's 2,800 Jews were handed over to the Germans by the Bulgarian occupiers.

A half century has passed since the *Shoah*. The majority of those who survived have emigrated to Israel or the United States. Those who remained have settled mainly in Athens. Of the 5,000 Jews in Greece today, 4,000 inhabit the capital, while 1,000 are divided between Thessaloníki and a handful of smaller towns. An official monument in memory of the victims of the *Shoah* was recently unveiled in Thessaloníki.

→ **To call Greece from the United States, dial 011 302** followed by the number of the person you are calling minus the initial 0 (used only for domestic calls).

Continental Greece

Athens

A Jewish presence has been proven in Athens during the Hellenistic period, just as in Alexandria. It is certain that Paul of Tarsus came here, as elsewhere in Greece, to preach in Athenian synagogues. One of them, dating from the third century c.e., appears to have been identified at the Agora, at the foot of the Acropolis. However, for several centuries afterward there was no sign of a Jewish presence in the city. This ancient city was nothing more than a modest village of 4,500 in 1833, the year it was declared the country's capital.

Jews returned here in the wake of the first Bavarian monarchy. After his enthronement, King Otto I confided to a group of notable Jews "that he considered his realm blessed and honored to contain within its borders the biblical race of Israel." This laudable declaration of principle, however, could not prevent outbursts of anti-Semitism by the populace. After seeking to put an end to a traditional anti-Jewish ceremony, the "hunt for Judas," Jewish businessman and British citizen David Pacifico saw his warehouses looted in the mid-nineteenth century. England intervened on his behalf, and went so far as imposing a brief blockade of Greece's shores as a means of obtaining heavy compensation.

Far less sizable than the one in Thessaloníki, the Jewish community of Athens nevertheless proved to have better relations with both the government and general population. The city's seizure by the Germans in 1943 marked the beginning of the terror. Active resistance by the authorities, in particular by chief of police Anghelos Evert and Orthodox archbishop Monsignor Damaskinos, was exemplary.

THE ANCIENT SYNAGOGUE

At the foot of the Acropolis, within the Agora's vast field of ruins, archaeologists believe they have identified a synagogue dating to the third century C.E. The foundations of this ancient synagogue have been unearthed near the statue of Hadrian and the apse of an old basilica. A marble surface has been discovered on which a **menorah** and a palm branch are engraved.

[Ancient Synagogue: Enter the Agora from Adrianou Street on the Plaka next to the Monasteraki flea market.
Open Tue–Sun 8:30 A.M.–3 P.M.
The site of the ancient synagogue is freely accessible during open hours.
🚇 Monasteraki.]

THE MODERN SYNAGOGUES

Around 500 yards northwest of the Agora, at the end of Ermou Street near the ruins of the ancient Keramiko cemetery, are Athens's two modern synagogues. Located in a trendy neighborhood full of bars, the synagogues lie on opposite sides of Melidoni Street.

■ Built at the turn of the century, the older of the two, Etz Hayyim, has also been nicknamed Ioanniotiki due to its popularity among Jews from Ioannina. It is open only during the high holidays.

[Etz Hayyim Synagogue:
Odos Melidoni 8, 10553 Athens.
☎ 013252823 or 0102352875.]

■ The other synagogue, Beth Shalom, is a Neoclassical-style marble edifice, dating to the 1930s.

[Beth Shalom Synagogue: Odos Melidoni 5, 10553 Athens. Contact the Athens Jewish Community: ✆ 013252823 or 0102352875. Open 9 A.M.–1 P.M.]

THE JEWISH MUSEUM

After spending twenty years facing the former royal garden, the Jewish Museum of Athens has recently been transferred to a newly renovated neoclassical house on the Plaka. A large collection of documents, clothing, and religious artifacts from the Romaniote and **Sephardic** communities is displayed here by theme and by floor.

The former Romaniote synagogue of Patras has been rebuilt here on the first floor. With the new name of Alka Betz, it was dedicated in 1984 by the grand rabbi of France, Samuel Sirat. The cycle of Jewish holidays is observed on the second floor; the third floor contains historical documents about the Jewish communities of Greece, traditional costumes, and cultural and domestic objects, as well as an exhibit dedicated to the *Shoah*. The museum also features exhibit space, a library, and a souvenir shop on the first floor.

[Jewish Museum:
Odos Nikis 39, 10558 Athens.
✆ 0103225582. ❶ jmg@otenet.gr.
Open Mon–Fri 9 A.M.–2:30 P.M.,
Sun 10 A.M.–2 P.M. 🚇 Syntagma.]

"Ioanniotiki" Synagogue, Athens.

Thessaloníki

When David ben Gurion moved to Thessaloníki to learn Turkish in 1910, he was surprised to discover a city like none found in "Eretz Israel": The **Shabbat** marked the day of rest here, and even the dockworkers were Jewish. He was advised not to admit he was **Ashkenazic** (all the procurers were).

Jewish and **Sephardic**, Thessaloníki had been called "Mother in Israel" for over three centuries. A haven for Jews expelled from Spain, it resembled both a lost canton of Judaea and a neighborhood in Castile or Navarre. The language of the street was Judeo-Spanish (*Iudezmo* and *Ladino*), while the elites here spoke French.

Not far from here, nestled at the far end of the Thermaic Gulf (Gulf of Salonika), Hellenized Jews had already converged beginning in antiquity. Saint Paul, after preaching three consecutive **Shabbatim** in local synagogues, had to flee under cover of night. The Romaniotes, as Jews of the Eastern Roman Empire were commonly called, suffered countless invasions here.

Sold to the Venetians, the city was conquered before Constantinople by Ottoman armies in 1430. **Sephardic** refugees were welcomed with tolerance in Thessaloníki by the thousands, and then by the tens of thousands. The sixteenth century was the golden age of the city's Diaspora. Samuel Moise of Medina, the century's most preeminent rabbi and author of a thousand *responsa*, summed up in a sentence the intellectual splendor of the era: "We abound in the learned and libraries; knowledge is widespread among us."

Such blossoming was commercial as well, thanks to Thessaloníki's position as a stopping point between Venice and the Ottoman Empire. In 1556, a boycott of the port of Ancona was launched by Levantine Jews at the instigation of those in Thessaloníki, in protest against an auto-da-fé of twenty-five Portuguese Marranos on the order of Pope Paul IV. Moreover, the woolen garments worn by the powerful and fearful Janissaries were woven in the Jewish workshops of Thessaloníki.

In the late nineteenth century and encouraged by the Universal Jewish Alliance in Paris, philanthropic organizations, clubs of freethinkers, and political committees began to appear here. The entrance of Greek troops in 1912 was greeted with apprehension by the Jews, due to the fierce economic rivalry between the two populations. Rightly or wrongly, the Jews suspected that the great fire of 1917, which ravaged the Jewish quarter and devastated its thirty-two ancestral synagogues, had been an intentional act.

Thus began the emigration of tens of thousands of Jews to France and the United States in particular. Two events sped this exodus: the transfer of Greco-Turkish populations here as decreed by the 1923 Treaty of Lausanne, which shifted the demographic balance between Greeks and Jews, and a pogrom in the Jewish quarter of Campbell in 1931.

Ten years later, in April 1941, the first German columns marched into Thessaloníki. By the summer of 1942, all Jewish men were ordered to appear at the large Elefterias Square: for hours, they were subjected to humiliation by the Nazis before crowds of onlookers. The expropriation of the great Jewish necropolis was implemented—much to the satisfaction of the Greek authorities, according to Joseph Nehama. From March to August 1943, 46,000 Jews from Thessaloníki, or 96 percent of the Jewish community here, were deported and exterminated in Auschwitz-Birkenau. Fewer than 1,500 deportees survived. Jewish Thessaloníki had seen its final days. More than a half century later, in 1999, a monument commemorating the *Shoah* was put up here. At first glance, nothing recalls the "Jerusalem of the Balkans" in modern Thessaloníki, with its cold, crumbling concrete architecture. So thoroughly have their traces been erased, one might wonder if Jews had ever been present here, when they had in fact been the majority here until the 1920s.

[Community Center: Odos Tsimiski 24, 54624 Thessaloníki. ✆ 0310275701.]

VESTIGES OF PRIOR JEWISH LIFE

■ Several beautiful villas once belonging to the most prominent Jewish families were miraculously spared

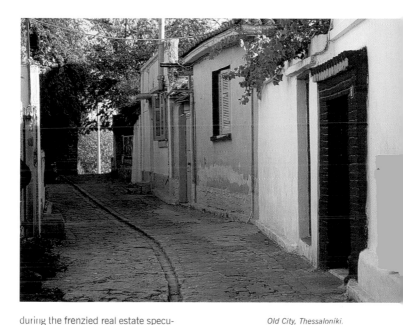

Old City, Thessaloníki.

during the frenzied real estate speculation that struck Thessaloníki during the 1950s. They were built in middle-class Belle Epoque style on a boulevard once named Hamadié, now called Vassilissis Olgas (Queen Olga). Two Italian architects fought for the favors of the rich merchants who chose to settle here.

At 182 Vassilissis Olgas Boulvard sits the eclectic "Casa Biança," built for the Fernandez family and designed by the architect Piero Arrigoni. It is today abandoned behind its garden, seemingly doomed to destruction.

More classic and luxurious, the villa once owned by Charles Allatini, Thessaloníki's most important Jewish miller, was built based on plans by Viteliano Poselli, at number 198 of the same boulevard. From 1909 to 1912, Ottoman sultan Abdul Hamid II was forced to reside here after the Young Turk Revolution.

Housing the Macedonian Folklore Museum, the former Modiano family mansion is located at 65 Megas Alexandros Avenue.

■ Across the street from the Archaeological Museum on Stratou Avenue, a mosque was constructed in 1902 for the *deunmé* community, Jewish converts to Islam following the heresy of Sabbataï Zevi. The work of Poselli, the new mosque, Yeni Djami, combines turn-of-the-century Ottoman architecture with Renaissance, Baroque, and Moorish elements.

SYNAGOGUES AND MUSEUMS

■ Monastirioton is the most important synagogue still active in Thessaloníki. Built in the 1920s by Jews originating from Monastir, a city located in current Macedonia, it was used by the Red Cross during the Second World War. The structure was copied exactly from classical **Sephardic** design, the *aron kodesh* to the east, and the chest of the **bimah** to the west.

[Monastirioton Synagogue: Odos Syngrou 35, 54630 Thessaloníki. ✆ 0310275701.
The synagogue is perpendicular to Egnatia Street, one of the main arteries through the city center. Open for services Fri evenings and Sat mornings, or by appointment.]

■ Another synagogue, Yad Lezikaron was reconstructed in 1984 inside a modern building on the Herakleios Street. The arch comes from the former Kal Sarfati, the French synagogue, while the **bimah** originates from the Baron Hirsch Synagogue, which bears the name of the famous Jewish philanthropist.

[Yad Lezikaron Synagogue: Vassilis Herakleios 24–26, 54624 Thessaloníki. ✆ 0310275701. Open mornings and holidays for services around 8 A.M. or by appointment.]

■ A small Museum of History of the Jews of Thessaloníki is currently located on Herakleion Street, beside Yad Lezikaron. Another, much larger museum with a conference room is expected to open in a building that once housed a Jewish bank, at the corner of the Aghia Mena and Venizelos streets.

[Museum of History of the Jews of Thessaloníki: Stratou Avenue 2, 54013 Thessaloníki. ✆ 0310868570. Open Tue–Sun 8:30 A.M.–3 P.M., Mon 10:30 A.M.–7 P.M.]

■ The Yad Lezikaron Synagogue and the Museum of History of the Jews of Thessaloníki are located in the district around the Modiano market, named after the large Jewish family that originated in Livorno. All sorts of trades were practiced by Jews here, as much in the metal and glass-roofed market as in the surrounding neighborhood. Thessaloníki's oldest and largest bookstore, Molho Solomon, is located on a street parallel to Herakleios Street. A meeting place for the cultural elite, this bookstore belonged to the Molho family, who were saved during the war by a Greek Orthodox family.

[Molho Solomon Bookstore: Odos Tsimiski 10, 54624 Thessaloníki. ✆ 0310275271. Open Mon, Wed, Fri 8:30 A.M.–3 P.M., Tue, Thu, Sat 5:30–9 P.M.]

THE NECROPOLIS AND CEMETERY

■ In the exact spot of the ancient Jewish necropolis now stands Aristotelous University. The huge cemetery, where the remains of twenty generations once lay, was destroyed by the Nazis to the great satisfaction of the local Greek authorities; crowds of pillagers then descended on the site, convinced that the Jews, already packed into ghettos, had hidden their treasures here. The tombstones were later used in the construction of school playgrounds, university stairwells, sidewalk gutters, and even barrack latrines; at times, the funerary inscriptions were not even removed and can still be read today.

■ The modern cemetery, where a few ancient gravestones have been gathered, is located on Karaoli Demetriou Street, across the street from the AGNO factory.

[Cemetery: Odos Karaoli Demetriou 31, 54624 Thessaloníki. ✆ 0310655855. Open 9 A.M.–2 P.M.]

Epirus and the Ionian Islands ■

Ioánnina

Ioánnina still bears the deep imprint of the long Ottoman presence in Greece. At the heart of the mountainous Epirus region, Ioánnina (280 miles from Athens near the Albanian border, the two cities connected by a difficult road) still harbors a small Jewish community.

In the ninth century, and perhaps even earlier, Hellenized Romaniote Jews were already present here; they were later joined by a large contingent of **Sephardim** a few centuries later. Shut away with their traditions, indifferent to other cultures, according to a seventeenth century Turkish traveler, the Jewish community maintained a poor relationship with the Greek Orthodox majority, a situation the Turkish government did all it could to exploit. In the late eighteenth

century, Ioánnina fell into the hands of a tyrant, Ali of Tebelen, an Albanian pasha of the Sublime Porte who, during a forty-year reign, carved for himself his very own fiefdom, with borders stretching as far as Albania and Macedonia. A former Napoleonic officer and Strasbourg Jew, Samson Cerf Berr converted to Islam and moved to the court of Ali the Rebel; he was the nephew of Cerf Berr de Mendelsheim, a military supplier to Louis XV and overseer of the Alsatian Jewish community.

Several anti-Jewish riots broke out in Ioánnina in the late nineteenth century on the occasion of the Orthodox Easter, under pretext of accusations of ritualistic crimes. Hundreds of Jews were forced to leave the city, emigrating mostly to Jerusalem or New York. In the early twentieth century, they founded synagogues

476

dedicated to Ioánnina in Jerusalem's Mahane Yehuda and New York's Lower East Side that still stand today.

On the eve of the Second World War, Jews in Ioánnina numbered just under 2,000; they were all rounded up by the Nazis in March 1944. The community consists of only around fifty people today, many of whom live in a building constructed on the site of the former "new" synagogue at the border of the Kastro district and the Jewish Alliance school. Several Albanian Jews, smuggled out of that country by the Jewish Agency before the fall of the Communist regime, passed through Ioánnina in transit.

■ In the Kastro citadel, where Jews settled in the early seventeenth century, the old Yashan synagogue can still be visited, the sole remnant of the faded importance of Ioánnina's Jewish community. An inscription dates the structure back to 1829, but it was most likely built on the site of a much earlier synagogue. In the temple's courtyard, an ablution fountain reserved for **kohanim** is located to the right, beside a well used in the **tashlik** ceremony; to the left, a frame used during the **sukkah** leans against the synagogue wall. The main door was reserved for men; a side entrance allowed women access to an upper gallery. The interior architecture, with its arches circling a central dome, reflects Ottoman influence. The synagogue, for a while used as a library, was spared during the war.

[The Old Synagogue is located near the western wall of the citadel, on Ioustinianou alley 16, to the left of the Kastro main gate. To visit, contact the Jewish Community Center: [phone] 0651025195.]

■ In the Its Kale (southeastern) citadel of the Castle of Ioánnina is the Byzantine Museum. Here, several relics are on display: a synagogal wall hanging, a Jewish dress, and a **ketubah**—a calligraphic and illustrated marriage contract.

[Byzantine Museum: ✆ 0561025989. Open Mon–Sat 8:30 A.M.–5 P.M.]

■ Outside the citadel, a segment of the Jewish community has regrouped in the neighboring Leonida district, bordering the lake. Stars of David are still visible on the facades of houses and wrought iron gates. On Joseph Elia Street (Elia was a Ioánnina-born Jewish poet who died in 1931 at the age of thirty) once stood the Hadash Synagogue, the new synagogue. Jewish families live here today in a building put up on the site of the former temple, in the middle of a street that, parallel to the citadel's southwestern wall, leads to the lake.

Corfu

In the late twelfth century, Jewish traveler Benjamin of Tudela encountered a lone Jew on Corfu. Three centuries later, however, Jews had become so numerous here that the Venetians, then in control of this much-coveted, strategically important

EPIRUS AND THE IONIAN ISLANDS

Adriatic island, had them confined to ghettos. A local Christian legend, which, strangely, spoke of Judas as a native of Corfu, made Jewish life here even more unpleasant. The expulsion of Jews from Spain, however, led **Sephardic** colonies to settle on Corfu or on the six other Ionian Islands. Thanks to prevailing revolutionary ideals, French domination from 1807 to 1815 offered Corfu's Jews equal rights, which did not please the Orthodox Christian and Catholic majority. When Corfu and the Ionian Islands were placed under England's protection following the Congress of Vienna, the fate of the 4,000 Jews here rapidly worsened, due to a series of discriminatory measures including the suppression of their right to vote. The islands' reattachment to Greece in 1864 meant a return to civil equality for the Jews, but also recurrent flare-ups of anti-Semitism. In 1891, a pogrom broke out after accusations of ritualistic crimes. An exodus of Jewish families ensued, including that of Albert Cohen, one of the most important **Sephardic** writers of the twentieth century.

On the eve of the Second World War, the Jewish community of Corfu consisted of only 2,000 members. According to historian Mark Mazower, however, the Wehrmacht territorial commander made several attempts to stop their deportation, an extremely rare occurrence. On 9 June 1944, the order was finally given to deport them, to the overt satisfaction of the collaborationist authorities. The attitude of prominent civic and religious citizens was quite the opposite on the neighboring island of Zákinthos, where Jews were both protected and permitted to hide on the mountainside. Only about sixty Jews remain in Corfu, today.

■ Of the four synagogues in Corfu's old ghetto, only the Scuola Greca (Greek Temple) survived the Second World War. In Venetian style, it dates back to the seventeenth century. The prayer room is located on the second floor, with a section for women on the mezzanine. Made out of wood with a Corinthian colonnade, the *tevah* and *aron kodesh* face each other to the west and east.

[Scuola Greca Synagogue: Odos Velissariou 4, 49100 Corfu. For visiting times, contact the Jewish Community: ✆ 0661030591.]

■ The Jewish quarter, the old Venetian "ghetto" that is still called Evraiki in Greek today, stretched across the southeast section of the city, near the Venetian fortifications. It was crisscrossed with alleyways lined with faded, multistoried houses, as in Venice. The ghetto lost its urban unity due to bombardments during the Second World War.

It can be walked through starting from the Porta Réale, heading toward Solomou, Palaiologou, and Velissariou streets. Columns from a synagogue destroyed during the war were rediscovered in the early 1990s at 74 Palaiologou Street.

The Cyclades and Rhodes ■

Delos

Visiting the site in Delos is quite easy throughout the summer, the island being accessible by boat from nearby Mykonos.

If one place attests to the presence of a Jewish community in Ancient Greece, it is certainly that of Delos, an arid island of the Cyclades. The existence of Jews here is referred to in the Book of Maccabees, while Flavius Josephus mentions them as well. Too tiny to flex any real political muscle, the island was an important religious center and cosmopolitan trade city, however, comparable in

Throne of Moses, synagogue, Delos.

the Hellenistic period to Pompeii. During that era, Delos had as many as 30,000 inhabitants, hailing from all parts. Merchant guilds were established here, including ones from Alexandria, where Jews were numerous. Such prosperity, which lasted until the dawn of the Christian era, certainly drew Jews here, such as Samaritans. Nevertheless, their history remains unknown to us.

■ At the end of the nineteenth century, digs were undertaken here by French archaeologists from the Athens School. Southwest of the former stadium, just beside the Aegean Sea, a synagogue dating from the first century B.C.E. has been uncovered. Considered as the oldest one of the Diaspora, this synagogue was a two-room house designed for religious use. Sitting against a stone wall, a remarkable, finely worked marble armchair goes by the name of Throne of Moses. Among these ruins, an arch leads to a cistern that might have served as a mikvah.

■ About fifty yards or so northwest of here, right against the outer wall of the stadium, French archaeologists have uncovered another house once used as a place of worship. It was a Samaritan synagogue, sometimes referred to as the House of Agathocles

THE CYCLADES AND RHODES

and Lysimachus. This attribution comes from the discovery of a funerary stele dedicated to Serapion, a Samaritan from Knossos, found near this house. A cistern flanks this building as well.

In this area around the site, several Jewish inscriptions in Greek have been deciphered. On one of them the words "Theos Hypsistos" are engraved, the equivalent of *Shaddai* ("The All-Powerful" in Hebrew). In the early 1990s, another Jewish inscription was deciphered on a block of stone reused as part of a pasture wall, not far from the shore.

[The synagogues are located on the northwest section of the island. A small museum houses as well several pieces unearthed during the digs.]

Rhodes

In the fourteenth century, a Jewish community settled behind the ramparts of Rhodes erected by the knights of Saint John after their flight from the Holy Land. These Jews had the strange destiny of finding common ground with the Crusaders in their war against the Ottomans, only to be forced by Grand Master Pierre d'Aubusson to convert to Christianity or flee. The waves of expulsion from the Iberian peninsula brought many **Sephardic** Jews to the shores of Rhodes. Glimmers of rabbinical quarrels between these new arrivals and the Romaniote Jews settled here much

earlier were recorded in numerous *responsa.* In the first half of the twentieth century, the Jews of Rhodes emigrated, in particular to Rhodesia. The vast majority of the 2,500 Jews who remained on the island were deported by the Nazis in July 1944.

LA *JUDERÍA*

In the eastern section of the old medieval city, the former Jewish quarter, *la judería,* begins at the square called Evreon Martyron (Of Jewish Martyrs). In the 1920s, the district contained six synagogues, and 4,000 Jews lived here.

■ Walk along Pindarou Street, then turn left down Dosiadou Street, where you will find the Kal Kadosh Shalom Synagogue.

■ If you head back up Pindarou Street, you will find a Hebrew plaque at 4 Byzantinou Street that blesses all those who pass beneath its arch. It is dated Nisan 5637 (1837).

■ The tour continues up to the old Puerta de la Mar, then right along the ramparts on Kisthiniou Street, where the Grand Synagogue of Rhodes and the Universal Jewish Alliance School once stood. A plaque recalls the existence of this institution, founded at the turn of the century thanks to a gift from Baron Edmond de Rothschild, who visited Rhodes in 1903. This was the first mixed school here, with teaching conducted entirely in French. It was destroyed by bombardments during the war.

THE KAL KADOSH
SHALOM SYNAGOGUE

A single synagogue, Kal Kadosh Shalom, remains in Rhodes. Well restored under the care of the significant Diaspora community, it was first built at the end of the sixteenth century. On the fountain in the courtyard, the date Kislev 5338 (1577) gives a sense of its age. The main door leads to the synagogue; on the left, a small entrance leads to the upper, women's section built in the middle of the 1930s. Before then, women were confined to the rooms adjacent to the temple's southern wall. The interior layout, with the *tevah* in the center, is typically **Sephardic.** The western wall peculiarly possesses a door to the courtyard with two *aronot kodesh* with neoclassical capitals for the Scrolls of the Law on either side of the door. The little courtyard once led to the **yeshiva,** which was destroyed during the war. The floor is covered with a black-and-white stone mosaic, as found in other buildings of old Rhodes. Decorated during the nineteenth century, this synagogue exudes real charm with its Ottoman architectural influence. Numerous plaques celebrating donors, including the Adlaheff family, are written in Judeo-Spanish, **Ladino** or *Judezmo.*

[Kal Kadosh Shalom Synagogue:
Odos Simiou-Dossiadou 8, 85100 Rhodes.
✆ 0241022364. Open Apr 1–Nov 1,
10 A.M.–4 P.M.]

Kal Kadosh Shalom Synagogue, Rhodes.

[Rhodes Jewish Community Center: Odos Polydorou 5, 85100 Rhodes. ✆ 0241022364.]

THE CEMETERY

In the 1930s, the Italian occupying authorities moved the ancestral Jewish cemetery beyond the ramparts; it is now located in the modern city. Important restoration work in 1997 has revealed some 200 graves, several of which date back to the sixteenth century. The names figuring on the tombstones are those of **Sephardic** families from the Ottoman Empire, with dedications in *Judezmo* and abbreviations in Hebrew, like those of Moshe Sidi (1593), Dona de Carmona (1671), and the "humble, honorable, pure" Reina Hasson, who died on the seventeenth day of Tishri in the year 5623 (1863).

[Cemetery: Along the road to Kalitheas in the new city. Open 9 A.M.–noon.]

Crete ■

The Jews have a unique and turbulent history on Crete, one of the most important islands in the Mediterranean. Under the Byzantine Empire, Cretan Jews believed the hour of the final redemption had rung: in 430 C.E., a false messiah, the rabbi Moses, promised to lead them all to Jerusalem; they then threw themselves en masse into the raging sea and drowned. Several centuries later, the hand of Venice reached the island, and the Jewish community was forced to live in ghettos. Under Ottoman domination, they were treated more peacefully. In the mid-nineteenth century, the Greeks themselves protested against granting them a seat in the local chamber of deputies. After a major uprising, punctuated by anti-Semitic incidents, Crete's autonomy was decreed, a prelude to its reattachment to Greece in 1913. On 6 June 1944, on the very day the Allied army landed in Normandy, 269 Jews from Canea were deported by the Nazis. They all perished at sea in a ship sunk by German planes or, more likely, by an English submarine.

Canea

■ The oldest synagogue in Canea, Etz Hayyim, lives again after a half century of neglect. Raised from its ruins by Nicholas Stavroulakis, former director and founder of the Jewish Museum of Athens, it was rededicated in October 1999. (It should be noted that its reopening was violently protested by the island's prefect.)

Ancient Roman historian Tacitus did not hesitate, in the second century C.E., to voice such a hypothesis. These "Judaei," he wrote in Book V of the *Histories,* "might once have been, judging by their name, Idaei"—that is, "neighbors of Mount Ida," the Cretan mountain towering 8,200 feet above the island.

Etz Hayyim appears to have been the former Venetian oratory of Santa Caterina, yielded to the Jewish community in Canea in the seventeenth century by the Ottomans. It is designed after Venetian-inspired Romaniote synagogues: the main entrance faces north, while the *aron kodesh* and the **bimah** face each other on an east-west axis. Both were rebuilt with exotic wood, made possible by donations. From the southern wall, a door provides access to an upper floor where women were permitted. The *mehizah* is also accessible by way of the courtyard. The roof of the ritual bath, the **mikvah,** located on the first floor, has also been redone. Numerous inscriptions have been uncovered as well.

[Etz Hayyim Synagogue: At the end of a small impasse on Kondylakis Street; it has no street number, but is clearly marked. P.O. Box 251, 73110 Canea. ✆ 0821086286. Open Mon–Thu 9 A.M.–11 A.M. and 6–8 P.M. The synagogue is located near the Venetian port. From the port, take Kondylaki Street, head down the second alley to the right, then turn right again.]

■ A second temple, the "New," or Shalom Synagogue, once stood in this district, still called Evraiki today ("Jew" in Greek). It was completely destroyed by bombardments during the 1941 Battle of Crete.

■ The Archaeological Museum, located on Halidon Street, an artery parallel to Kondylaki Street, contains evidence of Jewish life in Canea. In an outdoor courtyard, six medieval epitaphs in Hebrew are on display. Inside, three other, more recent ones can be viewed as well.

[Archaeological Museum: Odos Halidon 25, 73131 Canea. ✆ 0821091875. Open Tue–Sun 8:30 A.M.–3 P.M.]

Iráklion

■ Within the Venetian outer walls of ancient Candia, the old Jewish quarter is found right beside the seafront. Four synagogues once stood in this district, its perimeter today delimited by Venizelou, Makariou, and Giamalki streets. The last, still active at the start of the Second World War, was bombed. The Hotel Xenia has been built upon its ruins.

■ Several neighboring Venetian houses were inhabited by Jews, as was the building housing the Historical Museum. Two sculptures in its heraldic collection depict two crowned lions brandishing sabers.

אִילוּ שָׁקַע צָרֵינוּ בְּתוֹכוּ וְלֹא
סִפֵּק צְרָכֵינוּ בַּמִּדְבָּר אַרְבָּעִים
שָׁנָה דַּיֵּנוּ

אִילוּ סִפֵּק צְרָכֵינוּ בַּמִּדְבָּר
אַרְבָּעִים שָׁנָה וְלֹא
הֶאֱכִילָנוּ אֶת הַמָּן דַּיֵּנוּ

אִילוּ הֶאֱכִילָנוּ אֶת הַמָּן וְלֹא
נָתַן לָנוּ אֶת הַשַּׁבָּת דַּיֵּנוּ

אִילוּ נָתַן לָנוּ אֶת הַשַּׁבָּת וְלֹא
קֵרְבָנוּ לִפְנֵי הַר סִינַי דַּיֵּנוּ

אִילוּ קֵרְבָנוּ לִפְנֵי הַר סִינַי וְלֹא
נָתַן לָנוּ אֶת הַתּוֹרָה דַּיֵּנוּ

אִילוּ נָתַן לָנוּ אֶת הַתּוֹרָה וְלֹא

They once belonged to the powerful
Sephardic Saltiel and Franco families.
[Historical Museum of Crete:
Lysimahou Kalokairinou 7, 71 202 Iráklion.
✆ 0821083219 or 0821088708.]

Haggadah, Crete, 1583.
Bibliothèque Nationale de France, Paris.

Belgrade.
la nouvelle synagogue.

Београд.
Нова јеврејска синагога.

Serbia and Montenegro

 SERBIA AND VOIVODINA FORM, along with Montenegro, a nation that had been called the Federal Republic of Yugoslavia until 4 February 2003, when it was renamed Serbia and Montenegro. The Serbian and Voivodinan regions witnessed one of the first implementations of the Final Solution, its Jewish population as brutally martyred by German troops as were Jews in Poland or the Soviet Union. In fact, the extermination project began in the former Yugoslavia the moment the country was invaded in April 1941—several weeks before Hitler's attack upon the Soviet Union.

In the zones directly administered by the German army, it took the Einsatzgruppen SS less than four months to arrest the 4,000 Jews of Banat (the region north of Belgrade), with the help of gangs of local *Volksdeutschen* (ethnic Germans), and deport them to Belgrade. The men of Banat were placed in a concentration camp, while the women and children were held in the city's Jewish community housing. The men were gunned down in groups of 50 to 200 beginning in September 1941; the women and children were gassed several months later in trucks designed to asphyxiate human cargo using exhaust fumes.

Synagogue, Belgrade.

Jews throughout the rest of Serbia met a similar fate, beginning in late 1941. During the summer of 1942, an SS officer reported to his superiors that Serbia and Banat were from that moment on *judenreinen* (cleansed of all Jewish presence). This was, alas, in large part true. Of the 17,000 Jews inhabiting the region before the war, barely 10 percent survived. In Bačka and Baranya, largely Hungarian-speaking regions in Voivodina that were reattached to Yugoslavia after the First World War but annexed in 1941 by German-allied Hungary, Hungarian troops "were content with" implementing an array of exclusionary measures against the Jewish minority: approximately 16,000 strong before the war, Voivodina's Jews endured seizure of property, forced labor, and kidnappings. Properly speaking, systematic extermination did not occur here, beyond reprisals following acts by the Resistance. In early 1944, however, Germany invaded Hungary and deported en masse the Jewish population. Only 3,000 would return from the camps.

[Jewish Community of Yugoslavia: ulica Kralja Petra 71A/III, 11000 Belgrade. ✆ 11624359, fax 11622449. ✆ jcb@drenik.net. Open 8 A.M.–3 P.M.]

→ **To call Serbia and Montenegro from the United States, dial 011 381** followed by the number of the person you are calling.

Serbia

Belgrade

After the conquest of Belgrade by the Turks in 1521, **Sephardic** Jews quickly supplanted in number the **Ashkenazic** community that had arrived before them, from Hungary in particular. Loyal Turkish subjects, Belgrade's Jews enjoyed an initial phase of relative prosperity, transforming the city into one of the premier **Sephardic** centers in the Balkans. The Belgrade **yeshiva** was known throughout Europe, thanks to the reputation of rabbis like Meir Andel, Yehuda Lerma, and Simha ha-Kohen, who had to publish their books abroad, lacking a suitable printing press at home.

The Jews suffered, however, at regular intervals during the Austro-Turkish wars, repeated assaults on the city in the seventeenth and eighteenth centuries. When the Austrians seized Belgrade in 1688, they sacked the Jewish quarter of Dorçol and captured a portion of its residents,

forcing their fellow believers to buy them back. The city's great **Sephardic** rabbi, Joseph Almoslino, counted among the victims. This did not prevent the Turks, in their turn, from reproaching the Jews for failing to retreat with them, unleashing a new wave of persecutions.

The Jews later tied their fate in large part to that of Serbia's movement for national emancipation, supplying the insurgents with arms and munitions during the anti-Turkish revolt of 1815. Thus, in 1830, when the sultan agreed to a statute providing autonomy to Prince Milos Obrenovic's Serbia, they were granted civil rights equal to those of other citizens. Many Jews joined the ranks of the new Serbian state, most notably the army, where they formed the prince's personal guard, while one of them, Joseph Slezinger, directed the military orchestra. The prince authorized as well the printing of books in Hebrew and *Judezmo*.

The community's status noticeably began to erode under the reign of Prince Mihajlo Obrenovic, who succeeded his father in 1839. A scandal involving ritualistic crimes contrived by anti-Semitic circles exploded in 1841. A pogrom took place in the fortress city of Šabac in 1865. It was only after the Congress of Berlin in 1878, which required all the Balkan states to grant complete equality to all ethnic and national minorities, that the Jewish community began to grow and prosper here, especially in Belgrade.

The historic districts of Jalija and Dorçol, on the banks of the Danube, soon became too cramped: while the **Ashkenazic** community began settling the banks of the Sava River, the **Sephardic** population climbed the hill up to Prince Mihajlova Street and Terazje Square, where they opened some of the city's most beautiful shops at the turn of the century. Religious institutions and buildings remained in Dorçol, however, a quarter which, before the *Shoah* itself, would be largely destroyed during the terrible bombardment of Belgrade by the Luftwaffe in April 1941. This is why there remains little trace of Jewish life in Belgrade, with Jews numbering around 2,000 before the war in Kosovo in 1999. In Dorçol, a monument to the memory of the Jewish community was recently put up on the bank of the Danube by Jewish sculptor Nandor Glid.

■ The Jewish Historical Museum presents a history of Jewish life throughout the former Yugoslavia, with a collection of religious objects, clothing typical of the country's Jewish communities, and photographs.

[Jewish Historical Museum: Second floor, ulica Kralja Petra 71A/I, 11000 Belgrade. ✆ 11622634, fax 11626674. Open Mon–Fri 10 A.M.–2 P.M.]

■ Of the three synagogues in Belgrade before the war, only one still serves as a house of worship. Built in 1926, it was transformed into a military brothel by the Nazis and rehabilitated after the war with German reparation money. The city's largest synagogue, erected in 1908, was destroyed by the Germans in

A NATIONAL HERO

It was in splendid Kalemegdan Park, between the Sava and the Danube, that Moshe Pijade, the most famous Jewish Communist poet of the Tito era, was buried in 1957. Yugoslavian Communist Party pioneer in the 1920s, Pijade was one of the principal collaborators with the future Marshal Tito during the Resistance. After the war, Pijade in particular arranged the departure to Palestine of 6,000 of the 14,000 Yugoslavian Jews who had survived the genocide, before obtaining the post of National Assembly president.

1944. A commemorative plaque has been placed at the site (Cara Urosa 20), where a museum with no particular relationship to Judaism now sits.

■ The Jewish cemetery contains most notably an impressive monument to the victims of the *Shoah* and the Jewish combatants during the Balkan Wars (1912–13) and the First World War.

[Cemetery: ulica Mijo Kovacevica 1, 11000 Belgrade. It is located east of the city.]

Niš

■ A monument dedicated to the victims of the *Shoah* has been put up on Bubanj Hill. The former synagogue today serves as an art gallery.

[Jewish Community: ulica Cairska 28/II, 18000 Niš. ✆ 18352164.]

Voivodina ■

Novi Sad

The Jewish community of Voivodina's capital was, until World War II, one of the most prosperous in all Yugoslavia. Present since the city was founded in the late seventeenth century and 4,000 members strong before its extermination, the community was keen on building structures to rival those of other ethnic groups in this majority-Hungarian Catholic city (it belonged to the Austro-Hungarian Empire until 1918).

[Jewish Community: ulica Jevrejska 11, Novi Sad. ✆ and fax 21615750.]

■ The Municipal Museum of Novi Sad, set up in the former Petrovaradin fortress, has a collection of relics gathered from the Celarevo archaeological site, located around eighteen miles west of the city on the shores of the Danube. Hundreds of brick fragments bearing various symbols (**menorot**, shields of David, Hebrew markings) are on display here; they date to the late eighth and early ninth centuries, when the region was under domination by the Avars. Researchers have advanced the hypothesis that this people of Mongolian origin had been influenced by the Khazars of Crimea, a tribe that had itself converted to Judaism during the eighth century.

[Municipal Museum: The Municipal Museum is located in the Petrovaradin fortress, above the river. Dunavska 35 ✆ 21420566.]

■ Built in 1909 in the so-called "Neolog" style (modernist **Ashkenazic**,

Synagogue, Subotica.

as opposed to Orthodox), the synagogue is the work of Hungarian architect Lipot Baumhorn, to whom we owe forty-some synagogues in eastern Europe. It remains one of the largest synagogues in Central Europe, with a dome 130 feet high and 40 feet wide, a three-nave basilica, and a seating capacity of 900. Along with the adjacent buildings that housed Jewish community activities (**mikvah,** slaughterhouse, school, retirement home, orphanage, cultural center) built several years later, it was spared during the war by its Hungarian and German occupants. This was not the case for its people, however: the synagogue was used as a temporary concentration camp for Jews of the region before their deportation to various death camps.

After the war, when Novi Sad contained no more than 300 Jews, community leaders negotiated with Yugoslavian authorities for the donation of the synagogue, whose excellent acoustics were underscored by **cantor** Mauricius Bernstein. The temple has served as a concert hall ever since. Services held here are of only secondary concern. Renovation projects on the site from 1985 to 1991 have uncovered the stone Decalogue of a previous synagogue built here in the late eighteenth century.

[Synagogue: Sloboda Trg, Novi Sad.]

■ Beside the Danube, a monument honors the memory of the city's thousands of inhabitants, both Jewish and Serbian, shot down or thrown in the river by Hungarian militias on 23 January 1942, in revenge for an assassination committed by the Resistance.

Subotica

■ Subotica's synagogue, built in 1903, was converted into a theater after the war. In 1999, the neglected building was still awaiting its eventual restoration. It is located in the city center a few steps from city hall.

[Jewish Community:

Dimitrija Tucovica 13, 24000 Subotica.

✆ 24554491, fax 24455526.]

■ In the Jewish cemetery, a monument commemorates the victims of the *Shoah*.

Bosnia-Herzegovina

♛ SARAJEVO AND SURROUNDING AREAS

♛ MOSTAR AND SURROUNDING AREAS

IN SARAJEVO, WHERE MOST OF BOSNIA'S JEWS LIVED, the earliest refugees from the Iberian Peninsula began arriving around 1565, having first stopped in Italy, Greece, Bulgaria, and other regions under Turkish domination. Belonging to the *rayah* (the term used by the Turks to designate non-Muslim populations under their control), as such they had a status equivalent to that of other non-Muslims. A certain autonomy to manage religious and community affairs was accompanied by various requirements and constraints, as well as repeated exactions by local pashas. For example, Jews had to step aside for any Muslim they encountered in the street, and they were forbidden to ride horses and bear arms, except when traveling; any Jew over the age of nine was required to pay a residence tax. During the final decades of Turkish rule, until 1878, Jews had to pay a special tax, the *bedelija,* to avoid being drafted into the military. Jews were expected, moreover, to provide horses for maintenance work on roads and to the Turkish army when it launched campaigns.

Bosnian rabbi holding a tipsh in his right hand.

The Turks imposed restrictions on clothing as well. In Bosnia, which had been conquered in 1463, Jews had the right to wear turbans provided they were not too large and, most important, that they were yellow, to the exclusion of any other color. If a Jewish man wore a fez, as his ancestors did in Arabian Spain and descendants would continue to do long after the Turks were gone, it had to be dark blue. Similarly, wearing green was strictly prohibited to all non-Muslims, while shoes could only be black.

Such constraints led **Sephardic** women of the region to develop a very specific code of dress, the memory of which has been preserved by Jewish museums in the former Yugoslavia. Until the early twentieth century, for example, Jewish women in Bosnia continued to wear long, embroidered dresses called *anteriyas,* as well as *tokados,* small hats decorated with a row of ducats called the *frontera* in Judeo-Spanish. Hair remained hidden, though the back of the *tokado* was extended by long cloth fringes, named the *purçul.* And if widows dispensed with the *frontera,* young girls were content with displaying only a single ducat on their foreheads.

Beyond that, life for Bosnian Jews under Ottoman rule was more or less similar to that of other inhabitants of this poor and mountainous corner of the empire, far from the main roads and commercial centers of the era. Although the Jewish community here included numerous doctors and scientists, like the mid-nineteenth-century proto-Zionist rabbi Judah ben Soloman Hai Alkalai, it was composed mostly of people of modest means, who were no better off than other ethnicities in the province. A charitable association, the Benevolencija, was thus established to aid the most impoverished;

it was still active during the recent interethnic war from 1992–95, to the benefit of country's entire population.

♆ FAR FROM HOME

Winner of the Nobel Prize for literature, Ivo Andric set the scene for his Bosnian Chronicle *in his native town of Travnik, a small city in western Bosnia that temporarily served as capital to this Turkish province in the early nineteenth century.*

On a hot morning in May 1814, Salomon Atijas, the patriarch of the town's small Jewish community, reeking of garlic and untanned sheepskin, came to offer twenty-five ducats to the French consul. The latter had been ordered to close down the consulate in Travnik but did not have the means to finance his trip home. Atijas brought him the money because the diplomat, over the seven years he has spent in the town, showed kindness and care toward the Jews "in ways neither the Turks nor any other stranger had ever done."

"No matter what part of this earth beyond Spain we might be in, we would always suffer, for we would always have two homelands. This much I know. But here in this place, life has been particularly harsh and degrading for us. . . . We are wedged between the Turks and the Christian peasants, the poor downtrodden peasants and the terrible Turks. Utterly cut off from our own kind, we try to preserve everything that reminds us of Spain, the songs and the food and the customs, but the changes within us goes on relentlessly; we can feel the erosion, the fading of memory," old Atijas exclaimed to the western-bound voyager. In fact, whereas they were most grateful to Turkey for welcoming them after their

*expulsion from Spain, the Jews who landed in Bosnia suffered, more than other **Sephardim**, from their uprooting, cultivating nostalgia as the centuries passed for their "incomparable Andalusia."*

IVO ANDRIĆ, *BOSNIAN CHRONICLE,* TRANS. JOSEPH HITREC (NEW YORK: ALFRED A. KNOPF, 1963).

Austria-Hungary occupied Bosnia-Herzegovina in 1878 and annexed it in 1908. The region experienced rapid economic development during this period, notably under the impetus of **Ashkenazic** arrivals, who invested in industry and the intellectual and liberal professions. The **Sephardic** Jews here remained working as tradespeople and artisans, but

their cultural level began to rise considerably. They say here that at the turn of the century, all the doctors in Sarajevo were Jewish.

After World War I, when Bosnia-Herzegovina found itself integrated with the new realm of Yugoslavia, the Jewish youth of Sarajevo and the provinces became known for their political activism. While the Zionist movement was gaining influence throughout Yugoslavia, in Sarajevo it was a radical Marxist organization, the Matatja, that attracted local Jewish youth. Established in 1923, this cultural and political organization soon boasted 1,000 members.

On the eve of the Second World War, Bosnia-Herzegovina contained 14,000 Jews, 8,000 of whom lived in Sarajevo. When Germany invaded Yugoslavia in April 1941, it handed Bosnia-Herzegovina over to the puppet state installed in Zagreb. As in Croatia, the Jews of Bosnia-Herzegovina were pursued by Ustashis with the support of Muslim gangs formed by the mufti of Jerusalem, the Palestinian Haj Amine el Husseini. This admirer of Hitler pushed for the formation of an SS division composed of Muslims called the Ansar,

Mantle of the Law, Bosnia-Herzegovina, late nineteenth century. Musée d'Art et d'Histoire du Judaïsme, Paris.

whose ferocity toward the Serbs and Jews rivaled that of the Ustashis.

A thousand Bosnian Jews managed to join the ranks of the Resistance, a third of whom died in combat. In the years following the liberation, half of the 2,200 survivors in the region made their **aliyah** to Israel. This is why, even before the 1992–95 war, the Jewish community in Bosnia-Herzegovina consisted of only around 500 members. This number has dropped even further due to the fighting and the transfer of refugees.

→ **To call Bosnia-Herzegovina from the United States, dial 011 387**
followed by the number of the person you are calling.

Sarajevo
and Surrounding Areas ■

Sarajevo

When the grand vizier Syavush Pasha came to Sarajevo in 1581, the local representatives of the Sublime Porte asked him to separate the Jews from the rest of the population, for they lit too many fires and made too much noise. Syavush Pasha ordered the construction of communitarian housing for the Jews, with a courtyard and synagogue. The Velika Avlija (Old Temple Synagogue) offered forty-six bedrooms to the city's poorest Jews, while the rest of the community lived in the other *mahallahs* (districts) of the city. Enjoying freedom of movement from that point on, Jews in Sarajevo never lived in ghettos, strictly speaking.

■ Destroyed by a fire in 1879, the Velika Avlija has never been rebuilt,

Synagogue, Sarajevo.

Jewish cemetery, Sarajevo.

with the exception of its synagogue. It houses today the small Jewish Museum of Sarajevo, which features various collections of clothing and religious objects, some of which originated in Spain.

[Jewish Museum: Velika avlija bb,
71000, Sarajevo.
Ø 33535589 or 33535688.]

■ The *Haggadah of Sarajevo,* a famous fourteenth-century illumination, recounts the parting of the Red Sea. It was brought to Bosnia by Catalonian Jews. After many trials and tribulations, it has ended its journey in Sarajevo, where it is preserved at the National Museum of the Republic.

[National Museum of the Republic:
Zmaja od Bosne 3, 71000 Sarajevo.
Ø 33668027. Open Tue–Fri and
Sun 10 A.M.–2 P.M.]

■ The modern synagogue was built in Moorish style in 1902 by **Ashkenazic** Jews; it is decorated with superb arabesques, and today serves as the Jewish Community Center.

[Synagogue: Hamdije Kresevljakovica 83,
71000 Sarajevo.]
[La Benevolencija: same address.
Ø 33663472. ❶ oa_bene@open.net.ba.]

Kovacici

■ The old Jewish cemetery of Sarajevo is located in Kovacici, on Mount Trebevi overlooking the city. Founded in 1630, it shelters a large number of graves with inscriptions in *Judezmo* that are still legible. The cemetery unfortunately served as a strategic position during the civil war of 1992–95: the Bosnian Serbs set up their artillery here to bomb the city from above, at the same time drawing gunfire from those under siege below. The Bosnian Serbs also mined the site before their withdrawal. A private Norwegian organization has since then been hired to clear the area of mines.

Vrace

■ In Vrace, not far from the Sarajevo cemetery, a monument honors the memory of the city's 9,000 residents massacred during the Second World War, including more than 7,000 Jews. Their names and ages have been inscribed on the inner walls of the old fortress, which has since been turned into a memorial.

Mostar
and Surrounding Areas ■

Mostar

■ The city's Jewish cemetery, which dates back to the eighteenth century, was severely damaged during the 1992–95 war, though it has been partly rebuilt since. The city still houses a tiny Jewish community.

[Community Center: ✆ 36314389.]

Stolac

For nearly two centuries, Stolac was the destination for a pilgrimage to the grave of rabbi Moshe Danon. In 1820, Grand Rabbi of Sarajevo Moshe Danon and ten other prominent members of the Jewish community were accused of assassinating a local dervish, a Jewish convert to Islam named Ahmed. The pasha of Sarajevo threatened the death penalty unless they handed over a ransom of 500,000 groschen, an impossible sum to raise. Sarajevo's Jews then requested the help of the city's Muslim residents, who in turn stormed the prison, freed the captives, and obtained the contemptible pasha's removal by the sultan. Ten years later, on his way to Palestine, Moshe Danon fell ill at a stopping point in Stolac, where he died. Soon after, the practice of a pilgrimage to the site came into being, every first Sunday in July.

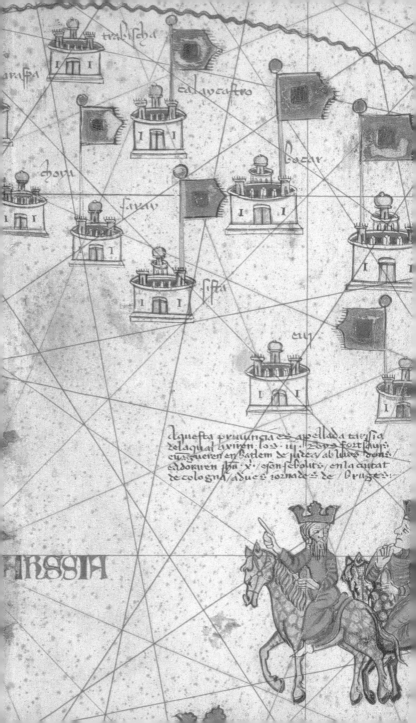

tralischa

calanrastro

Bocar

chora

faxav

fista

euy

Aquesta pruuincia es apellada tursia
delaqual hixen los iij zors fortums
cnaqueren en Bariem de jndea ab laus dons
cadoruen fha x / eson sebolts / enla ciutat
decologna / adues romades de / Bruges :

ARSSIA

Eastern Europe

Yiddishland:
Ruins of a Civilization Destroyed

T HE VISITOR TO EASTERN EUROPE hoping to discover a rich Jewish architectural heritage must remember that what was once the center of Judaic cultural and religious life in Europe—principally in Lithuania between the eighteenth century and the *Shoah*—has disappeared beyond ruins and cemeteries. The complete eradication of a Jewish presence, the sworn objective of the Nazis, was conducted with the complicity of a segment of the local population. This was followed by the antireligious policies of the Soviet Union and its series of population transfers and persecutions, reducing to nothingness an incomparable culture and the unique language of Yiddishland. Any Jewish-themed journey into the Baltic countries is therefore first and foremost a matter of archaeology and genealogical research. That said, there is still much to gain by visiting the small communities that have tried, courageously, to bear witness to the past and reveal their Jewish roots to younger generations.

The term *Yiddishland* is a neologism denoting after the fact a country that never existed as such and which might be described, rather, as a linguistic and cultural space, the place where the **Yiddish** language was used. The term can thus be understood in its broader sense, with both a historical and geographical meaning: it covers the evolution of the **Yiddish** language from its formation by **Ashkenazic** communities from Germany (the Valley of the Rhine, Moselle) in the tenth and eleventh centuries, its migration across Bohemia through Poland and Eastern Europe, and finally its transfer in the late nineteenth century to cities like New

York, Antwerp, Paris (around Rue des Rosiers), Buenos Aires, and others.

In its most common usage, however, Yiddish-land refers to the extension of **Yiddish** across eastern Europe, as much in space as in time, as it actually evolved and was spoken by nearly all the members of the Jewish communities here. This was the case in Poland, Lithuania, Belarus, Ukraine, Bessarabia, Moldavia, and in sections of Hungary and Romania from the seventeenth and eighteenth centuries to the mid-twentieth century.

A map of the Polish Union before 1772 (the date Poland was first divided), which stretched northward to the gates of Riga, eastward as far as Vitebsk, southeastward to the gates of Kiev, and southward to Lvov and Podolia, roughly described the historical boundaries of Yiddishland, for this was where speakers of **Yiddish** were concentrated. Formed upon a Germanic background (it evolved from Middle High German) and coupled with many Hebrew words (around 10 percent of the vocabulary), **Yiddish** also absorbed over the course of its history a fair number of slavisms (another 10 to 15 percent of its vocabulary) of Polish or Russian origin.

After the division of Poland led to that country's disappearance between 1795 and 1918, Yiddishland was almost completely integrated within the Russian Empire (with the exception of Galicia, Bukovina, sub-Carpathian Ukraine and Transylvania, which all fell within Austria-Hungary) and hemmed inside the *tcherta osiedlosti* (residential zone), after a ukase issued by Catherine II imposed significant restrictions on movement, notably a ban on entering central Russia, Saint Petersburg, and Moscow. This state of affairs remained unchanged until the First World War.

The centers of Yiddishland were Vilnius (the "Jerusalem of Lithuania"), Warsaw (the Muranów district), Kraków (the Kazimierz suburb), Łódź (northern and central neighborhoods), Minsk, Lvov, Iaşi, Kishinev, Czernowitz, and Odessa. This "nation" was characterized most of all by the **shtetlach,** small rural towns where Jews were a majority within clearly defined neighborhoods centered around the synagogue and the marketplace, where the community gathered and traded with the non-Jewish world as well. There existed countless **shtetlach,** whose names still vividly evoke Jewish life in the region: Lubartów, Chełm, Szczebrzeszyn, Włodawa, Zamość, Raziechów, Sambor, Drohobycz, Brody, Belz, Bursztyn, Brzezany, Kremenets, Sadgora, Kossov, Wyznitz, Czortków, Iaşi, Bershad, Berdichev, Pinsk, Borboujsk, Baranovichi, Slonim, Vitebsk, Dvinsk, Tykocin. . . . In each of these towns can still be found traces of times past: synagogues, cemeteries, marketplaces, old *mikva'ot,* typical houses with galleries and rectangular courtyards—a certain spirit of the place that endures even after the extinction of its residents. Architecturally, one of the best preserved examples is found in Tykocin, near Białystok, with its two Christian and Jewish districts clearly demarcated, the synagogue and church at the center of each neighborhood, the marketplace between the two, and the two cemeteries at the far ends.

The **shtetl** was the birthplace of a rich culture that, beyond folklore, achieved veritable nobility and formed a common heritage: **Yiddish** literature through nineteenth-century founders Sholem Aleichem, Itzhak Leybush Peretz, and Mendele Moykher Sforim and twentieth-century poets such as Glatstein, Gebirtig, and Katzenelson, as well as the work of Nobel Prize winner Isaac Bashevis Singer; painting depicting life in the **shtetl,** culminating in the masterpieces of Chagall; photography by

Vishniac or even Alter Kacyzne; music through **Yiddish** songs (like "Mayn Shtetele Belz," "Di Yiddishe Mame," "Kinderyorn," "Az der Rebbe Tanzt," and "Rabbi Elimelech") but especially through musical comedies like *Fiddler on the Roof* (or *Anatevka*) by Jerry Bock or, more generally, the **klezmer** tradition, which is experiencing a strong revival today. All these artistic expressions have idealized the **shtetl** in present-day consciousness as a place of well-being, a warm atmosphere with its joys and sorrows, an idealization all the stronger now that this world is forever lost, swallowed up for eternity by the *Shoah*.

Life in the **shtetl** was far from idyllic: Jews suffered unemployment, insecurity, pogroms, and ignorance, resulting in heavy emigration, from the late nineteenth century through the 1930s.

In northern Yiddishland (Lithuania, Belarus, northeast Poland), the Gaon of Vilna (now called Vilnius) had a determining influence on Jewish life, in the form of an orthodoxy respectful of the letter of the law and the commandments, but open to a certain form of rationalism (the **Haskalah**). In southern Yiddishland (southeast Poland, Ukraine, Bessarabia), **Hasidism** began to develop in the mid-eighteenth century, a mystical, anti-Enlightenment movement seeking to revive Judaism's original fervor by sending its practitioners into trances and promising immediate contact with God. It was centered around the charismatic **tsadikim,** who in turn built around themselves veritable courts and a new form of orthodoxy.

Today, Yiddishland exists only in memory, in its intellectual creations and artistic and cultural expressions, and in the hearts and songs of those who strive to breathe life back into both its spirit and letter. Revisiting this bygone world resembles an archaeological dig through both real terrain and memory itself.

Belarus

♆ CENTRAL BELARUS ♆ POLISH BORDER
♆ UKRAINIAN-RUSSIAN BORDER

THE REPUBLIC OF BELARUS is a state formed of the disintegration of the Soviet Union. It has retained, however, close ties to Moscow. Historically, Belarus belonged to Lithuania in the four teenth century, Poland in the fifteenth century, and later the Russian Empire in the late eighteenth century. From 1920 to 1939, its western regions (including Grodno and Brest-Litovsk) were integrated within Poland, while the rest of the country fell within the Soviet Union. The history of the Jewish communities in Belarus is thus related to that of neighboring countries Lithuania, Poland, and Russia. Jewish communities were first mentioned in Brest-Litovsk in 1388, in Novogrudok in 1445, in Minsk and Smolensk in 1489, in Pinsk in 1506, and later still in Vitebsk, Mogilev, and Orsha. After Poland's division, Belarus was surrounded by the "Pale of Settlement" of the Russian Empire and thus subject to the restrictive policies of those areas. In 1847, 225,000 Jews lived in Belarus; in 1897, the number had reached 725,000 (or 13.6 percent of the total population).

From an intellectual and spiritual point of view, Belarusian Judaism resembled Lithuanian Judaism,

Marc Chagall, The Synagogue, *1917. Private collection.*

marked by the **Haskalah** (Enlightenment movement). The majority of Jewish communities here, in particular those to the north and west, were composed of **Mitnaggedim**, Orthodox rationalists opposed to **Hasidism**. Imported from Ukraine, **Hasidism** nevertheless took root in Vitebsk, thanks to Menahem Mendel. In the nineteenth century, the Socialist movement became popular in Belarus, which had become the homeland of the Bund, the Jewish Socialist party that would later be repressed by the Bolsheviks. In the 1920s and under German occupation in World War II, the Communist movement had a strong following among Belarusian Jews, who in large part joined the ranks of the partisans or became soldiers in the Red Army. The occupation was especially violent in Belarus, where the Jews were exterminated inside their ghettos, and where one in four inhabitants were killed. In 1970, there remained 148,000 Jews here, but emigration has significantly reduced this number, today estimated at approximately 30,000.

→ **To call Belarus from the United States, dial 011 375** followed by the number of the person you are calling minus the initial 0 (used only for domestic calls).

Central Belarus

Minsk

Minsk, the capital of Belarus, first welcomed Jews in the fifteenth century. They settled here to engage in the trade between Poland and Russia. After Poland was divided, the Jewish community began to grow: it consisted of 47,560 members at the time of the 1897 census, or 52 percent of the population.

The Germans arrived in Minsk on 28 June 1941, only six days after launching their offensive, and the occupation was particularly violent. The ghetto was created on 15 July and extended across Khlebnaya and Nemiga streets, the Street of the

Train station in Minsk, with inscriptions in Russian, Belarusian, Polish, and Yiddish, 1920.

Republic, Ostrovsky Street and Jubilee Square, and streets including Obuvnaya, Chornaya, Sukhaya, and Kollektornaya. The Germans committed abuses, crimes, and mass executions, notably those of 7 November 1941, 2 March 1942, and 18 July 1942: thousands of people were beaten, murdered, or gassed in trucks used as gas chambers and tossed into mass graves in either Toulchinka or the "hole" *(lama)* on Zaslavskaya Street. German Jews were also deported to the Minsk ghetto. On 14 September 1943, they were all loaded onto trucks and gassed.

■ The neighborhood of the former ghetto still exists but is unrecognizable today. Destroyed by the Germans, it was reconstructed in Soviet style, like much of the rest of the city.

The most important remnant of the Minsk ghetto is the site of the "hole" *(lama),* at the intersection of Melnika and Zaslavskaya streets, where many Jews were executed. On 10 July 2000, a large sculptural ensemble by sculptor Leonid Levine depicting women, old men, and children descending into the grave was unveiled before a large crowd that included President Lukashenko and other prominent figures.

■ There is a synagogue at 13b Daumann Street, in the northern section of the city. The building itself is large, but the interior room is surprisingly small.

[Community Center:
22 Kropotkina ulitsa, 220000 Minsk.
✆ 01722342273.]

Minsk.

Bobruysk

The city of Bobruysk was once a typical Belarusian **shtetl**. In 1897, 20,759 Jews lived here (60.5 percent of the population), while in 1926, the Jewish community had a population of 21,558 (42 percent).

■ To form an image of what a Jewish city once looked like, explore the downtown area of Dzerjinsky Street and its marketplace. Stroll down Karl-Marx Street and Komsomolskaya Street with their typical balconies, then take Socialistitcheskaya Street, which had a synagogue at numbers 34–35, now the site of a clothing workshop. Finally, be sure to explore the crowded Tchongarskaya Street, on which another synagogue once stood at number 31, in ruins today. Downtown as a whole resembles certain old photos of Jewish villages—without their inhabitants, however, as the majority have either died or moved away.

■ The Jewish cemetery is located outside the city along the route to

Jewish cemetery, Bobruysk.

Minsk (Minskaya Street), on the right just upon leaving town. It is huge for such a small city, and well maintained and still much visited.

[Community Center: ulitsa Pushkin, 213826 Bobruysk. ✆ 0225176064. Open Mon–Fri 9 A.M.–5 P.M.]

Polish Border ■

Brest (Brest-Litovsk)

The first city across the Polish border, Brest is located on the right bank of the Bug River. Its name evokes the famous Brest-Litovsk Treaty of April 1918, whereby Trotsky's Red Army put an end to the war with Germany by ceding to the latter large amounts of Russian territory (the treaty was annulled in November of that same year by the Soviet government). On 22 June 1941, in Brest, Hitler's columns began their violent march across the Soviet Union.

Brest-Litovsk had for many years a Jewish majority. According to the 1936 Polish census, the city contained 51,170 inhabitants, of whom 21,134 were Catholic (the Poles), 8,228 were Orthodox Christian (Russians and Belarusians), and 21,518 were Jewish (or more than 40 percent of the total).

In 1941, the Germans created a ghetto around Sovietskaya and Dzerzhinsky streets, and from 17 September Street up to Macherova Street. In April 1942, all of the ghetto's 19,000 residents were deported, taken in cattle cars to the village of Bronnaya Gora, thirty miles to the east, and murdered and thrown into eight huge mass graves. Among them was the mother of the future Israeli prime minister Menachem Begin. A unique case in the history of the *Shoah*, the exact identity of every victim was recorded before their deportation, including both a photo and fingerprint; these files are preserved in the Brest archives, as documented in Ilya Altmann's 1995 film *The Brest Ghetto*.

■ The entire downtown (around the present-day Karl-Marx, Dzerzhinsky, 17 September, Macherova, Sovietskaya streets, and Liberty Square) was Jewish and contained many synagogues. The main one was located on what is now called Sovietskaya Street; it has been converted today into a movie theater, the Belarus. Another synagogue stood at the intersection of Dzerjinsky and 17 September; it is now residential housing. Notice as well the housing block at the corner of Macherova and 17 September, with its stores and courtyards of typical Jewish architecture. The Jewish hospital, today a regional medical clinic, was located at 24 Sovietskikh Pogranitchnikov (Soviet Border Guard) Street, while the adjacent synagogue has been turned into office space.

■ On Macherova Street, near the Tets tram stop, the ramp used for the loading and departure of the trains can still be seen. At 43 Dzerjinsky Street, a monument has been erected in memory of the victims of the ghetto.

[A small Jewish community center has been active here since 1996: 23–30 Sovetskoy, Konstitutzi ulitsa, 224032 Brest. ✆ 0162263366.]

Ruzhany

■ It is worth exiting the highway midway between Brest and Minsk and heading toward Slonim: in the middle of the village of Ruzhany, a beautiful synagogue still stands today. Its roof is in imminent danger of collapsing, however.

Slonim

In the nineteenth century, more than 70 percent of Slonim's population was Jewish. The ratio was 53 percent before the war.

■ The ghetto was burned down between 29 June and 15 July 1942. At the city's edge, at the site of a former cemetery, a monument commemorates the city's 35,000 Jews exterminated during the war.

■ In the city center, set back in relation to the marketplace, the ruins of a magnificent Baroque synagogue can be seen. Built in 1642, it is still standing, but in deplorable shape inside, though certain bas-reliefs (two lions presenting the Ark of the Law) and frescoes depicting musical instruments and biblical landscapes have been preserved—a unique event in Belarus. The market is located around the synagogue. Urinals, moreover, have been installed right up against the walls of this historical monument.

Grodno

Grodno, seat of a Catholic bishopric, was once a major city within the Polish-Lithuanian Union, as evidenced by Farny, the beautiful Baroque Jesuit church that towers over Sovietskaya Square. Jews began settling here in the fourteenth century: they were permitted to live in the town by Grand Duke Witold in 1389. In the nineteenth century, over 60 percent of the population was Jewish; at 42 percent in 1931. The city contained many synagogues, *yeshivoth,* and study groups presided over by the **Mitnaggedim.** Grodno was a hub for both the Bund and Zionism.

■ The Grand Synagogue was located downtown on Witoldowa Street (now called Sotsalistichnaya). The building, though neglected, still stands at number 35. The Jewish quarter, properly speaking, was located a little farther away from the central square, between Zamkowa Street and the fish market *(rybi rynek),* around Pereca and Nochima streets. The majority of these streets no longer exist. In their place runs a thoroughfare named Velikaya Troitskaya; you will need to refer to an old map of the city to get a sense of the former Jewish district.

■ On Zamkowa Street, at its intersection of what used to be Ciasna Street, a door crowned with a Star of David marks the entrance to the former ghetto; a plaque recalls the murder of its 29,000 residents. Several houses in ruin can still be seen, as well as the old synagogue on Velikaya Troitskaya Street, almost at the edge of a ravine. A plaque reading "Jewish Community of Grodno" is the only sign that it is still active. A little farther away, at Velikaya Troitskaya Street 13, there is a smaller synagogue that now functions as a school. Nothing remains of the old cemetery, which was located on nearby Krzywa Street.

[Community Center:
ulitsa Velikaya Troitskaya 59a,
230023 Grodno.]

Ukrainian-Russian Border ■

Gomel

In 1897, 20,385 Jews lived in Gomel (54.8 percent of the population), as compared with 37,475 (43.7 percent) in 1926. Today, little remains of their life here. The Jewish quarter was located on the right bank of the river.

■ A beautiful synagogue with colonnades once occupied the slight bend that forms on the main road (Lenin Street). In its place stands the Mir cinema, whose columns—those of the former synagogue—give the theater a temple-like presence. The streets in front of and surrounding the cinema appear to have once been Jewish.

■ The cemetery, now in ruins, is located to the left just beyond the southern edge of the city.

[Community Center:
ulitsa Pobedi 21a–27, 246000 Gomel.
✆ 0232534405.]

Mogilev

Mogilev, on the Dnieper, was for many years a Jewish majority (21,539 Jews in 1897, or 50 percent of the population). As elsewhere, the ghetto was annihilated during the occupation. Traces of the former Jewish quarter are easily spotted in the center of the old town.

■ Turn right on Karl-Liebknecht Street to find, at number 21, the building that housed the former synagogue, transformed today into a fitness center. If you walk around it to the adjoining building and pass under the porch, you will enter a Jewish-style courtyard facing 27 Lenin Street. The entire residential block is remarkable.

[Community Center:
ulitsa Let Pobedi, 281130 Mogilev.
✆ 0222221156.]

Vitebsk

In northeast Belarus, on the road to Moscow and Saint Petersburg, Vitebsk symbolizes all the Jewish shtetlach of Russia immortalized in the work of Marc Chagall, who was born here in 1887 and lived here until 1907, and again from 1917 to 1919. In the era of Chagall's childhood, Vitebsk had a Jewish majority (there were 34,420 Jews here, or 52 percent of the population), as depicted in the images he bequeathed to us: they describe, in a playful and fantastical way, the shtetl with its various rabbis, synagogues, livestock traders, tavern keepers, rooftop violinists, and ancient cemeteries. His best-known evocations of Vitebsk are *Red Gate, Blue House, The Synagogue, Cemetery Gates,* and *Above the City.*

Vitebsk was also home to the **Hasidic** master Menahem Mendel, a student of the Great Maggid of Mezritch. Numerous churches, both Catholic and Orthodox, dotted the city center. The center has lost much of its charm, however, as many of these buildings have since been destroyed. Vitebsk nevertheless remains the most artistic and visited city in Belarus. The City Museum of Fine Arts welcomed in 1997 the first Chagall exhibit ever to be held on the painter's native soil, thus marking a milestone in the cultural life of the nation. On Souvorov Street, the palace can still be seen where Napoleon, on the road to Moscow, stopped for a few days after capturing the city.

■ To locate the former ghetto and visit Chagall's childhood home, cross the Dvina River, take Kirov Boulevard, turn right on Dimitroff Street, and finally left to Pokrovskaya and Revolutionnaya streets. At this intersection, a sculpture of the painter can be seen. Continue along Pokrovskaya Street down to number 29, the house where Chagall spent his childhood years. You will find several Jewish religious artifacts, photographs, and furniture that perhaps belonged to the artist's family. In the courtyard stands another statue of Chagall.

Next take Revolutionnaya Street, which provides a glimpse of what the ghetto once looked like. At number 14 lie the ruins of the former synagogue, of which only the facade remains.

[Chagall House: ulitsa Pokrovskaya 29.]
[Chagall Museum: ulitsa Putna 2, 210026 Vitebsk. ✆ 0212363468. Open Tue–Sun 11 A.M.–6:30 P.M.]

Lithuania

THE JEWISH COMMUNITY IN LITHUANIA numbers only some 6,000 people. It is no more than a shadow of what it once was: until the *Shoah*, it was a center of the **Yiddish**-speaking lands. In a sense, everything began here from the fifteenth and sixteenth centuries when European Judaism's center of gravity shifted from Germany and France to Poland and Belarus. As a reaction to the pietistic practices of the Hasidism then in fashion among common Jews in the middle of the eighteenth century, the rigorous and elitist intellectual current of the **Mitnaggedim** emerged, personified by the Gaon of Vilna (1720–97). Lithuania, which alternated repeatedly between periods of independence as a regional power, submission to Teutonic lords, and Polish domination, was finally divided between the historic center around the capital under Russian domination, and the region around Klaipėda (Memel), controlled by Prussia. Despite the politics of the forced Russianization in the middle of the nineteenth century, a national renaissance began with the revitalization of the national language, Europe's oldest. Submerged in a profoundly Catholic country, the Jewish communities nevertheless

Choral Synagogue, Vilnius.

established a number of thriving *yeshivoth.* This fashioned the cultural landscape of Orthodox Judaism, especially in communities such as those of Panevėžys and Kaunas (Kovno).

Lithuania was not only a religious center, but also the cradle of Jewish secularism and the **Yiddish** language. The Socialist movement Bund was established in Vilnius in October 1897. At the time of the 1924 census Jews numbered 155,000, or 7.65 percent of the population, a number that would be larger if one included the thousands of Karaites. Subjected to anti-Semitism, Lithuanian Judaism was totally annihilated by the *Shoah*, with the help of many from the local population.

→ To call Lithuania from the
United States, dial 011 370
followed by the number of the person
you are calling.

The Belarusian Border

Vilnius

The capital of Vilnius, once known as the "Jerusalem of the east," has few Jewish monuments today.

■ The Shulhof, the large 3,000-seat synagogue built in 1630, was partly destroyed by the Nazis in 1941. The remains of the synagogue were razed after the war by the Soviets, who constructed a building complex on its former location. The current synagogue, located at 39 Pylimo Street, is a modern building of no particular interest. The Jewish community of Lithuania today numbers around 5,000 members and publishes a newsletter entitled *Jerusalem of Lithuania,* with articles in English. The community's institutional buildings are concentrated on Pylimo Street: the administrative offices at number 4 also house the Israeli Center for Art and Culture and, on the second floor, the State Jewish Museum. You can also explore a

matzoh factory at number 39 of the same street.

[Administrative Offices of the Jewish Lithuania Community: 4 Pylimo Street, 2001 Vilnius. ✆ 2613003. Open Mon–Thu 10 A.M.–6 P.M., Fri 10 A.M.–4:30 P.M.]
[Israeli Center for Art and Culture: same as above.]
[State Jewish Museum: same address as above. ✆ 52620730. ❶ jmuseum@delfi.lt. Closes at 4 P.M. on Fri.]

■ Apart from the renovated remains of the former ghetto, the major monument of interest is the Gaon of Vilna's tomb. In the recent past, the gaon's tomb was located in the Jewish cemetery of Shnipishok (a district in the city, also called Snipiskis), to the north of the Neris (Viliya) River. It is now to the northwest of the former ghetto in the Dembovka cemetery, known by the name Saltonishkiu and close to Virshulishkes and Sheshkines. The exact site of the gaon's tomb is uncertain, since, under the Communist regime, the gaon's corpse was

exhumed and reburied with others, including that of Count Potocki, a Polish nobleman who converted to Judaism. The remains of another cemetery on Zaretchna Street still exist.

■ The University of Vilnius now houses an interesting research center on stateless cultures that includes a

Gaon of Vilna Synagogue, Vilnius.

department of Jewish and **Yiddish** studies.

[Department of Jewish and Yiddish Studies: 7 University Street, 2734 Vilnius. ✆ 2687187. ❶ institute@yiddishvilnius.com. Open Mon–Fri 9 A.M.–5 P.M.]

Central Lithuania ■

Kaunas (Kovno)

Nothing of the Jewish presence in Kaunas remains but the synagogue, whereas before the war there was a yeshiva, a kosher slaughterhouse, and a prison. The birthplace of Emmanuel Levinas, Kaunas was before the *Shoah* a major center of European Judaism, with a population of 40,000 Jews. The large yeshiva of Slobodka was located in a suburban district today called Vilijampole.

■ The synagogue features a blue, two-story classical facade and is located at 11 Ozheshkienes Street. The Jewish orphanage and the former Jewish school were closed in 1951.

[Jewish Community:
26b Gedemino Street, 3000 Kaunas.
Contact: Gertsas Zhakas,
Gedemino 26b, 3000 Kaunas.
✆ 7203717, fax 7201135.]

Coastal Lithuania ■

Klaipėda

Klaipėda is the former German city of Memel, a place where Judaism came under the influence of the modern nineteenth-century Orthodoxy originating in Germany. The city is still home to some 300 Jews.

[To visit, contact N. Shustertanas:
3 Zhiedu Street, 5808 Klaipėda.]

Panevėžys

Panevėžys is Lithuanian for Ponevezh, famous for its yeshiva that its prewar leader, Rav Yosef Kahaneman,

reestablished following the war in Bnei Brak, the Orthodox quarter of Tel Aviv. The Ponevezh yeshiva in Israel is today the principal center for the Mitnagdim sect and has given birth to the Israeli political party Degel Hatorah. Rav Eliezer Schach, Degel Hatorah's leader, was, until his death in November of 2001, one of the last survivors of the religious world from before the *Shoah*, nothing of which now remains. The current community contains only a hundred or so people.

[Seat of the Jewish Community:
6–22 Sody Street, 5300 Panevėžys.
✆ 5468848.]

Latvia

RIGA · LATVIA'S JEWISH CEMETERIES

THE JEWISH COMMUNITY OF LATVIA traces its
origins to the middle of the fourteenth century.
Numbering today some 15,000 persons, it developed in the principalities of Kurland and Livonia,
territories that have often changed hands. The presence here of Baltic barons contributed to the Germanization of the country and placed the Jews
themselves under this cultural influence. The gradual annexation of the country by the Russian Empire
weakened the Jewish presence, since only Jews
who could prove to have lived there before it was
absorbed into the Russian Empire were authorized
to stay. However Germanized or Russianized the
Jews became (even if for 85 percent of them the
everyday spoken language was **Yiddish**), their position was always uncertain in relation to the national
movement in Latvia, which saw them as foreigners.
The large majority of Jews now established in Latvia
came from the former Soviet Union, and are thus
Russian speaking. As in the other Baltic states, Latvians conceive of citizenship as rooted in ethnicity,
which means, in effect, Jews are not citizens of the
new republics, and yet are no longer Russian citizens either. In the 1970s, Riga was an important
center of refusenik activity.

Synagogue, Riga.

Outside the big cities, Jews obeyed strict religious observances. Latvia gave us two remarkable figures of Orthodoxy: Rav Joseph Rosen (1858–1936), known by the name "Gaon of Rogatchov," after his birthplace, or "Rogatchover," who officiated in Daugavpils (Dvinsk); and Rav Meir Simha ha-Kohen (1843–1926), known as Or Sameah, who also lived in Daugavpils. In addition, the Zionist revisionist movement was powerful among the country's 85,000 Jews (4 percent of the population), who before 1940 were concentrated in Riga and Liepāja. Indeed, Riga was the cradle of Betar, the right-wing Zionist youth movement. Before the *Shoah*, Betar had even organized a nautical club, whose members later helped establish Israel's first navy.

The *Shoah* destroyed 90 percent of Latvia's Jewish community, and the work of remembrance has not been accomplished as it should have been. The Latvian Waffen SS are still perceived by Latvians as "patriots" who fought against the Soviet Union; neo-Nazis are free to parade in the streets under the gaze of the authorities. As a result, only a single monument to the genocide exists, in the Bierkerniecki forest, where 46,000 Jews were killed.

→ To call Latvia from the
United States, dial 011 371
followed by the number of the person
you are calling.

Riga ■

Around 9,000 Jews live in Riga. Riga is also home to the only Jewish hospital in the former Soviet Union. The Latvian Society for Jewish Culture is the principal organization of the Jewish community, which is in large part secular, although according to certain sources a **matzoh** factory still exists.

[Latvian Society for Jewish Culture:
Skolas 6, Riga LV-1050. ✆ 7289602,
fax 7289601.]

[Administrative Headquarters for the Jewish
Community of Latvia: 141 Lacplesa Street,
Riga LV-1003. ✆ 7204022.]

■ Few of Riga's religious edifices remain. The Kar Schul Synagogue, which opened in 1871 and was located at 25 Gogol Street, burned down in 1941. Several hundred people trapped inside perished in the blaze. Some ruins of the synagogue can still be seen, as well as a gray stone monument engraved with a Star of David. Constructed in 1905, the synagogue on Peitavas Street was able to be restored because it was used by the Nazis as a warehouse and so escaped destruction. It is currently used for worship.

[Synagogue: 6–8 Peitavas Street,
Riga LV-1050. ✆ 7210827, fax 7224549.]

■ The Jewish Museum features exhibits devoted to the history of Latvian Jews and a video that retraces the history of the *Shoah* in Latvia. There is also an exhibit related to famous Jews of Riga. Among them are the Israeli philosopher Yeshayahu Leibowitz, an original and controversial thinker whose strict Jewish Orthodoxy nonetheless makes room for modernity and a left-leaning pacifism; the political philosopher Isaiah Berlin (1909–97), who became a British citizen and a professor at Oxford; and the great rabbi Avraham Kook (1865–1935), the mentor of the religious Zionist movement and the first Chief Rabbi of Palestine under the British mandate.

[Jewish Museum: Skolas 6, Riga LV-1322.
✆ 7289580.]

There is a plaque on the building where Isaiah Berlin lived on Alberta Street. (The building is next to the only building on the street with a yellow facade.) The former home of Isaiah Berlin, like all those on the street, was designed by the famous Russian architect Eisenstein, father of the celebrated film director. The former Jewish cemetery, with its thousands of gravestones, was transformed into a park in 1920. Registers of the deceased dating from 1951 to the present are available for examination.

The Center for Judaic Studies at the University of Latvia was set up in 1998 and is directed by Professor Aina Antane. It includes a library.

[Center for Judaic Studies: Latvia University, 19 Rainis Boulevard, Riga LV-1586. ✆ 7034421, fax 7225039. ❶ It is possible to contact Professor Ferber via e-mail: Ferber@latnet.lv. Open 10 A.M.–4 P.M.]

Visitors doing genealogical research can go to the State Historic Archives, which possesses documents regarding most of the cities and villages with a Jewish presence before the *Shoah*.

[State Historic Archives: Skolas 16, Riga LV-1007. In most cases, it is useful to know place names in German, Russian, and Latvian.]

One should also note that the Shefayim kibbutz in Israel is the site of the Association of Jews of Estonian and Latvian Origins, which has a library and important archives relating to life in the **shtetlach** before the *Shoah*.

Latvia's Jewish Cemeteries ■

The number of active Jewish communities in Latvia is much smaller since the *Shoah*. All information concerning them is likely to quickly prove obsolete, since demographic trends in the communities leave little doubt about their dying out in the near future. The **aliyah** toward Israel is likewise becoming increasingly significant. Inquiries can be made at the offices of the Jewish community in Riga. Despite present circumstances, a trip to Latvia must above all include visiting cemeteries. The best way to find the remains of a Jewish cemetery is to solicit the aid of a local elderly person (financial compensation being the rule in the case of a visit). The main difficulty visitors encounter in finding ancestral graves is that the tombstones generally bear only the Hebrew name of the deceased (i.e.

LATVIA'S JEWISH CEMETERIES

the first name and the name of the person's father), without any indication of the family name. Although not exhaustive, following is a list of cemeteries and their state of preservation. For each city of the country, we give a brief description of its cemeteries.

[Aleksandr Feigmanis, a Jewish genealogist living in Riga, has a significant collection of photographs of Jewish cemeteries in all three Baltic countries. Visits can be arranged for a fee. P.O. Box 19, Riga LV-1021. ✆ 6416972. ❶ aleksgen@mailcity.com.]

■ Aizpute: Some hundred or so gravestones still remain, dating for the most part from the beginning of the nineteenth century.

■ Auce: There are some ten stone grave markers, located on a piece of land adjacent to a Christian cemetery.

■ Dagda: Approximately seventy gravestones remain.

■ Daugavpils: In the old cemetery of the Alte Vorstadt, only one broken gravestone remains (from the 1830s). The new cemetery has close to 200 tombs. The registers of the

Cemetery, Jaunjelgava (Friedrichstadt).

local Hevra Kadisha, going back seventy years or so, are available for examination at the nearby community center.

■ Gostini: The cemetery, with 160 tombs, is located about three miles from the city, on the route to Madona.

■ Jaunjelgava (Friedrichstadt): The large cemetery possesses a number of stone tombs decorated with engraved motifs, including carved lions and birds.

■ Jekabpils (Jakobstadt): Situated close to the Duiha River, the cemetery is still in use by the remaining twenty Jewish families, although it is not in good condition.

■ Jelgava (Mitau): This cemetery, created in the sixteenth century, was almost entirely destroyed by the Nazis and later by the Soviets. Located at the corner of Zalites and Bauskas Streets, it now retains no more than thirty tombs.

■ Kraslava: This seventeenth-century cemetery is in an excellent state of preservation and has a hundred or so gravestones, some belonging to Russian soldiers of the Red Army.

■ Kuldiga (Goldigen): Located to the west of the city (Vecie kapi) between Liepajas and Parka streets, this cemetery has been transformed into a municipal park. It has a Jewish section (on the Parka side) with approximately twenty-five gravestones. Damaged gravestones have been transferred to the neighboring city of Skrunda. *Note:* With a few exceptions in the capital cities (and even

there. . .), these exhumations have taken place without any respect for Jewish religious laws.

■ Liepaja (Libau): This cemetery, which is both Jewish and Christian, contains around 500 graves in relatively good condition. The funerary registers (up to 1941) are available for examination by request from the caretaker.

[Contact Mr. Agris Furmanis: 25–36 Dzerves, Liepaja LV-3400.]

■ Piltene: This well-preserved cemetery dates from the seventeenth century.

■ Prejli: The cemetery has around twenty graves, overgrown with vegetation; it also includes a memorial to the victims of the *Shoah*.

■ Rezekne: Situated at the top of a hill in the suburbs of the city, this well-preserved cemetery contains some 300 graves.

■ Sabile: The small cemetery here is home to some twenty untended graves and is located at the end of an unmarked path.

[Mr. Vitolds Masnovskis can serve as guide: 37–36 Strelnieku, Tukums LV-3106.
⌀ 3123436 or 3129351.]

■ Saldus (Frauenburg): The cemetery is located just at the exit of the city in an unmarked location of the forest. Sixty graves remain in a site that is completely unmaintained and unguarded.

■ Skaistkalne: Bordering the Christian cemetery, this cemetery has forty graves.

LATVIA'S JEWISH CEMETERIES

■ Subate: The town curate, who would bear contacting, is interested in preserving this site, which is approximately 200 years old.

■ Talsi: The cemetery is situated on the other side of the path leading to the Christian cemetery; it is overgrown with vegetation and has been vandalized.

■ Tukums: The cemetery is in good condition and contains around 200 graves, including a significant mausoleum (belonging to the last rabbi of the town).

■ Valdemarpils (Sasmachen): This cemetery is situated to the east of the city between Dzirnavu and Ezera Streets at the top of a wooded hill above Lake Sasmaka. Destroyed by the Soviets in the 1960s, almost nothing of this cemetery remains. A number of gravestones were used for paving the walkways.

■ Varakljany: This cemetery has 250 graves in good condition, the oldest dating from 1820.

■ There are other, less important cemeteries in Ventspils (Windau), Viljani, and Viski (on a small island in a lake).

Estonia

♔ TALLINN AND SURROUNDING AREAS |

THE ESTONIAN JEWISH COMMUNITY is the smallest of the Baltic states, and historically, the one that played the least important role in Yiddishland before the *Shoah*. Indeed, the community never counted more than 4,500 members. Although present in Estonia since the fourteenth century, the Jews did not assume a permanent residence in Estonian territory until after 1865, when the czar abolished the decree forbidding them to live there. The cantonists, Jewish soldiers serving in the imperial army, established the community in Tallinn in 1830; that of Tartu was begun in 1866. Synagogues were built in the two cities in 1883 and 1900, respectively; both burned down during the *Shoah*. Nothing remains of the small Jewish communities of Narva, Valga, Pärnu, and Viljandi, which were destroyed during the war. Jews in Estonia today are in very large part Russian-speaking Jews who arrived after 1945.

During the interwar period, independent Estonia treated its Jewish minority fairly. Jews enjoyed all the civil liberties granted to other Estonian citizens, and beginning in 1925, cultural autonomy as well. A minority chose to settle in Palestine, where

Former synagogue, Tallinn.

they contributed to the foundation of two famous kibbutzim: Kfar Blum and Ein Gev.

The 1940 Soviet occupation of Estonia put an end to all Jewish communal life: 400 Jews were sent to work camps. The Nazi invasion in July 1941 succeeded in exterminating the community, whose members were killed by the *Einsatzgruppen* with the active complicity of local collaborators, most notably militants from the Omakaitse Fascist movement. After 1945, the Soviet state outlawed all forms of Jewish cultural activity: all that remained was a small community that maintained the cemetery of Tallinn (which still exists). In contrast, one of the effects of anti-Jewish Soviet policy in terms of higher education was that a number of Jewish students from Moscow, Leningrad (Saint Petersburg), and Kiev went for their studies to the University of Tartu or the Polytechnic Institute of Tallinn, which were considerably more open. Also, during its Soviet occupation, Estonia was a relatively accessible exit door for the refuseniks heading toward the United States or Israel. The Jewish community in nearby Finland has helped and continues to aid many Estonian Jews.

Jewish life in Estonia began again in 1988 with the creation of a Jewish Cultural Society and later a school in one of the locations of a former Jewish gymnasium. Since Estonia's independence in 1991, the Jewish community has become openly active. It scarcely numbers 1,000 people (mostly of retirement age) according to official Estonian sources—3,000 according to Jewish sources. In October 1993, a law granting autonomy was passed. Unlike the tendencies today in Latvia and, to a lesser degree in Lithuania, the former Estonian Waffen SS receive absolutely no official or public support and the extreme right is hardly visible.

→ **To call Estonia from the
United States, dial 011 372**
followed by the number of the person
you are calling.

Tallinn
and Surrounding Areas ■

Tallinn

■ The modern synagogue is a low
building, resembling a large majority
of synagogues before the *Shoah*.

[Synagogue: 9, Magdalena Street,
11312 Tallinn.]
[Cemetery: 5, Rahumäe Street,
11316 Tallinn.]
[Administrative Offices of the Estonian
Jewish Community and Jewish Cultural
Society: 16A, Karu Street, P.O. Box 3576,
10507 Tallinn. ✆ and fax 6623034.
❶ Estonia@fjc.ru.]

Klooga

■ Of interest in Klooga is the *Shoah*
Victims' Memorial. A concentration
camp occupied the site and another
was in Vaivara.

Traces of the Jewish past are rare and include the Jewish cemeteries in Tartu
and Rakvere in the northern part of the country. The University of Tartu, an
intellectual center since before the war, offers classes on Jewish topics. There
are Jewish cultural clubs in Tartu, Narva, and Kohtla-Järve.

Russia

Until the early twentieth century, the history of Russia's Jews unfolded primarily in territories that no longer belong to the present-day Russian Federation (Ukraine, Belarus, Bessarabia, and Lithuania). With a few rare exceptions, Jews were forbidden to settle in Moscow, Saint Petersburg, and the cities of central Russia. Of course, Jewish colonies have existed since antiquity on the shores of the Black Sea and in Crimea, and a bit later in the Khazar kingdom, which took Judaism as its main religion in the late eighth and ninth centuries. The Khazar realm soon crumbled, however, eventually replaced by the principality of Kiev, the birthplace of the Russian nation, between the tenth and thirteenth centuries. After the decline of Kievan Russia and its absorption by Lithuania and Poland, Russia's center shifted northward to Moscow, Pskov, and Novgorod, where Jews had no right to reside. It was only after conquering Polish territories that Russia inherited its Jewish communities and, consequently, a "Jewish problem" it had never grappled with before.

In 1654, after annexing Ukraine up to the right bank of the Dnieper, Russia appropriated territories

Russian Jew, circa 1907.

inhabited by many Jews, though the latter had in large part already been massacred in Khmelnitski. In 1721, moreover, Peter I issued a ukase expelling the Jews from "Little Russia." This decree was reconfirmed by Empress Elizabeth Petrovna in 1742, who then forced the Jews beyond the borders of the Russian Empire.

It was therefore principally only during the three divisions of Poland (in 1772, 1793, and 1795) that Russia truly gained lands occupied by large Jewish communities—"Russia's enigmatic acquisition," according to the phrase coined by historian John Klier.[23] In the span of several decades, a country previously devoid of Jews found itself governing a Jewish population 700,000 to 800,000 members strong, the largest community in the world. In 1791, Catherine the Great took measures aimed at restricting the Jews' freedom of movement and preventing them from settling in other regions of the empire. These measures, reaffirmed by successive monarchs between 1804 and 1825, gave birth to

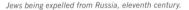

Jews being expelled from Russia, eleventh century.

Catherine the Great.

what was called the "residential zone" inside which Jews were forced to live; it stretched across the entire western edge of the empire, from the Baltic Sea to the Black Sea, in what is present-day Lithuania, Poland, Belarus, and Ukraine. Forbidden from working the land, moreover, Jews survived as merchants and artisans concentrated in small rural towns, or **shtetlach**. In addition, certain large cities, like Kiev, were off limits to Jews.

In the mid-nineteenth century, these restrictions began to soften: permission to live beyond the "residential zone" was granted in 1859 to "merchants of the first guild," in 1860 to tenured professors at major universities, in 1865 to certain tradespeople, in 1867 to military veterans, and in 1879 to those with a higher education. Because leniency was offered only to the most affluent Jews, who were in turn attracted to the nation's two capitals, by the late nineteenth century the highest circles of Jewish intelligentsia had left the **shtetlach** and moved to Saint Petersburg and Moscow.

♆ THE "RESIDENTIAL ZONE"

"But in order to live in Petersburg, one needs not only money, but also a special permit. I am a Jew. And the Tzar has set aside a special zone of residence for the Jews, which they are not allowed to leave."
MARC CHAGALL, *MY LIFE*, TRANS. DOROTHY WILLIAMS (LONDON: PETER OWEN, 1965).

It was not until 1917, however, when the "residential zone" was abolished, that this became a mass movement. Large communities of Jewish

RUSSIAN JEWISH THEATER

The origins of **Yiddish**-language theater in Russia dates to the nineteenth century and evolved primarily out of *Purimspiele,* plays retelling the story of Esther. The father of **Yiddish** theater was Abraham Goldfaden (1840–1908). This basically traveling form of theater began to take off after the Revolution of 1905, thanks to Peretz Hirschbein, who established in Odessa the Jewish Artistic Theater, where "classics" by Itzhak Leybush Peretz, Sholem Aleichem, and Shalom Asch were performed, along with plays of his own. With the Revolution of 1917 and during the 1920s, **Yiddish** theater moved through a second phase: Alexander Granovsky (1890–1937) founded the Jewish Studio in Petrograd, where he discovered Solomon Mikhoels, a cult figure in the world of Jewish and Soviet theater. In 1920, Granovsky's troupe moved to Moscow and became GOSET (the Jewish State Theater), which garnered fame with the help of set designers such as Chagall, Altman, Rabinovitch, and Faltz.

intellectuals and artists began settling in Petrograd (St. Petersburg) and Moscow, raising cultural life in those cities to new heights during the 1920s. A major catalyst was the Jewish State Theater (GOSET) founded by Alexander Granovsky and Solomon Mikhoels. The Bolsheviks of the era supported **Yiddish** as an expression of the popular Jewish classes and encouraged the theater's development in Minsk, Kiev, and Odessa. Jewish schools teaching in **Yiddish** began to appear (there were 1,100 of them in Russia by the early 1930s), while Jewish sections started opening at the universities.

The Soviet regime viewed the "Jewish question" largely in socioeconomic terms, and sought to gain the support of the Jewish masses by offering them land, previously forbidden to them under the czar. It also offered them a secular, Soviet Yiddish culture but repressed Hebrew culture. In the 1920s, Jewish *kolkhozes* began concentrating in southern Ukraine and Crimea, within national Jewish districts. In 1928, the Far East region of Birobidzhan was declared an autonomous Jewish region with **Yiddish** as its official language and open to all Jews willing to colonize it. At the same time, however, Zionist activities were prohibited, including the He-Halutz, Makkabi, Ha-Shomer ha-Tsair organizations, the Poalei Tsion Party and, in the name of atheism, anything else pertaining to religion, including synagogues, *yeshivoth,* **hadarim,** and *mikva'ot.*

In the mid-1930s, the government's antireligious policies worsened: from 1937 to 1939, at the height of Stalinist oppression, practically every Jewish institution and organization was prohibited, with a large number of Jews falling victim to purges, deportations, and execution. In 1939, more than 3 million Jews lived in the Soviet Union, a number that climbed to 5 million after the annexation of eastern Poland following the German-Soviet nonaggression pact.

On 22 June 1941, Nazi Germany surged across the Soviet Union and exterminated the Jewish population in the occupied territories, which corresponded approximately to the former "Pale of Settlement." Between the summers of 1941 and 1942, Jews were executed by the hundreds of thousands, city by city and town by town, then tossed into mass graves—all this before the "clean" death in the gas chambers had been invented in Poland.

In 1942, the Jewish Anti-Fascist Committee was founded under the leadership of actor Solomon Mikhoels, designed to sensitize and alert international opinion to the Nazi massacre of the Jews. Most members of this committee were arrested and executed in 1952.

Beginning in 1948, anti-Semitism became official government policy, in the guise of the struggle against "cosmopolitanism." All remaining active synagogues, Jewish theaters, libraries, and **Yiddish** presses were shut down. Jews who held high positions were dismissed, such as the famous photographer Evgueni Khaldei, who snapped the famous photo of the Soviet flag flying over the Reichstag. Great **Yiddish** writers were murdered—Peretz Markish, Der Nister, David Bergelson, and others.

After Stalin's death and a slight thaw under the Khrushchev regime, Jews accused of the so-called "doctor's plot" were pardoned, and a **Yiddish**-language review, *Sovetish Heymland,* was allowed to appear beginning in 1961. After the Six Day War of 1967, official anti-Semitism reappeared in the form of anti-Zionism and hostility toward the state of Israel. Soviet Jews who asked to emigrate were flatly denied, such as Anatoly (Natan) Shcharansky, who later became the Israeli Minister of Housing.

It was only in the late 1980s, under Mikhail Gorbachev's perestroika, that the situation improved for Russia's Jews, who were finally permitted to practice their religion and cultural activities and given the right to emigrate. Many synagogues and Jewish schools reopened across Russia and the other former Soviet republics, and a hundred or so Jewish Russian-language newspapers and periodicals were founded besides a host of other Jewish organizations, congresses, and communities. In Moscow and Saint Petersburg, "Jewish universities" were established, along with the Judaic Institute in Kiev, near the Mohyla Academy. The massive emigration of Russian and Soviet Jews that began in the 1990s has abated somewhat today. **Yiddish** is no longer much spoken, and the *Sovetish Heymland* shut down operation in 1992.

→ **To call Russia from the United States, dial 011 7**
followed by the number of the person you are calling minus the initial 0 (used only for domestic calls).

From Moscow to Saint Petersburg ■

Moscow

Due to the expulsion of Jews from Russia and their strict confinement within the "residential zone," there were few Jews in Moscow prior to 1900, which explains the absence of a Jewish quarter in the capital. The 1902 census lists 9,048 Jews in Moscow, or well below 1 percent of the city's population.

THE SYNAGOGUES

■ With columns worthy of a Roman temple, the Grand Choral Synagogue was built in 1891 in neoclassical style following a design by the architect Simon Eibushitz. Procrastination by the government and various restrictions imposed by the czarist regime delayed its official opening until 1906. It had hardly been completed, in fact, when a ukase issued by Moscow's new chief of police expelled Jewish tradespeople from the

city and forced the community to either sell the synagogue or convert it into a "charity organization" before 1 January 1893. The government at first hoped to install a trade school in the building but changed its mind and allowed the Jewish community to open a **Talmud Torah** school here instead. Authorization was finally granted in June 1906 for the completion of interior work necessary for the building's use as a synagogue, a task entrusted to an architect by the name of Klein.

It has been continuously active ever since, on a quiet street behind Kitay Gorod.

[Choral Synagogue:
pereulok Bolshoy Spasoglinishchevsky 10,
101000 Moscow. Contact the rabbinate:
✆ 2312777. Open daily 10 A.M.–5 P.M.
🚇 Kitay Gorod.]

■ What is now a Chabad Lubavitch Synagogue was founded in 1883. It was presided over by Rabbi Moshe ben Itshak-Ayzik, who was gunned

THE HIDDEN SYNAGOGUE

During the Soviet era, the address of Moscow's Grand Synagogue was kept secret. A 1988 guidebook thus presented the site in the following terms: "The building, with its ceremonial colonnade (at number 10) was built in the mid-1890s by Eibushitz (interior by Klein, 1906)."[24]

In 1948, the synagogue welcomed the first Israeli ambassador, Golda Meir.

down in 1938. Reopened fifty years later, today it serves the Orthodox Jewish community. An interesting Jewish bookstore is located inside.

[Chabad Lubavitch Synagogue: ulitsa Bolshaya-Bronnaya 6, 103104 Moscow. ✆ 0952027370. 🚇 Pushkinskaya or Tverskaya.]

[The bookstore is usually open Sun–Thu 11:30 A.M.–6 P.M., Fri 11:30 A.M.–2 P.M., but it is advisable to call beforehand.]

■ The synagogue located in the remote neighborhood of Marina Roshcha, currently under renovation, also serves as a neighborhood community center.

[Marina Roshcha Synagogue: pereulok Vycheslavtsev 5, 111250 Moscow. ✆ 0952180001. 🚇 Saviolovskaya.]

■ Another synagogue in an even more remote neighborhood belongs to the Shamir of Perovo Community Center.

[Shamir of Perovo Community Center: prospekt Svobodnyi 37–18, 111396 Moscow. ✆ 0953700051. 🚇 Novogireevo.]

■ A contemporary Jewish Community Center is located in the American-style Reform temple Memorialnaya Synagogue on Poklonnaya Gora, next to Pobiedy Park.

[Memorialnaya Synagoga: ploshad Pobiedy 3, 121170 Moscow. ✆ 0951480887 or 0951481907.

🚌 157 or 91 starting from the Kievskaya or Koutourovskaya subway stations.]

MUSCOVITE JEWISH LIFE

In the years following the First World War and the October Revolution, Jews left the former "Pale of Settlement" and began pouring into the new capital. In 1917, 60,000 Jews lived here, or 3.5 percent of the population; by 1932, they had reached 86,000, or 5.6 percent, and by 1939 they numbered 250,000, or more than 6 percent. This included many intellectuals and innovative artists, writers like Ehrenburg, Grossmann, and Peretz Markish; filmmakers like Sergey Eisenstein; theater personalities such as Alexander Granovsky and Solomon Mikhoels; and painters like El Lissitzky and Marc Chagall. One of Moscow's major Jewish intellectual haunts in the 1920s was the GOSET, the Jewish State Theater founded by Alexander Granovsky; Marc Chagall worked as a set designer there, soon followed by Faltz and Altman. Among actor Solomon Mikhoels's greatest successes was the production of Mendele Moykher

Sforim's *The Travels of Benjamin III* in 1927. The theater was located in Malaya Bronnaya, near Tverskoy Boulevard, at the site of the present-day Na Maloy Bronnoy Theater. Such intellectual ferment was smothered in the late 1920s and completely extinguished in the 1930s with the closure of **Yiddish** schools in 1935 and the later prohibition of all Jewish cultural life. Jewish life would have to wander fifty years in the desert before its rebirth in Moscow.

■ Fans of more or less **kosher** cuisine may want to try the U Yusefa (Chez

Sergey Eisenstein's Battleship Potemkin, *1925.*

Josef) Restaurant. It is difficult to find and, with its somewhat cafeteria-like atmosphere, is definitely not much to look at. Located on the first floor of what resembles low-income housing, business here is hardly thriving. After deciphering the menu, meanwhile, you may discover that only one or two of the proposed dishes is actually available. The service is friendly and the check reasonable, however.

[U Yusefa: ulitsa Dubinskaya 1–12, 113054 Moscow. Located behind the Paveletsky station. ✆ 0952384646. 🚇 Paveletskaya.]

■ An important Jewish cultural hub is the new Jewish University in Moscow, in reality a mere institute of Jewish studies within the university and linked to the Department of Journalism. The institute publishes the review *Vestnik* and features a small bookstore.

[Jewish University of Moscow: ulitsa Mokhovaya 11, room 329, 103009 Moscow. ✆ 0952033441 (after 4 P.M.). 🚇 Okhotny Riad or Biblioteka im. Lenina.]

■ Finally, it should be noted the weekly newspaper *Mezhdunarodnaya Evreiskaya Gazeta,* in circulation since 1989, offers additional information on Jewish life in Moscow.

[*Mezhdunarodnaya Evreiskaya Gazeta:* ulitsa Pleteshkovsky 3, building 1, entrance 3, 105005 Moscow. ✆ 0952650869.]

Saint Petersburg

Despite the prohibition against Jews living in Russia beyond a clearly defined zone, there were a few remarkable exceptions in the eighteenth century, particularly in the capital, Saint Petersburg, where the Russian-Jewish intelligentsia was concentrated.

In 1900, Jews in Saint Petersburg already numbered 20,385, or 1.4 percent of the population. This figure would climb to 50,000 by 1917 (2 percent), 95,000 by 1929 (5.3 percent), and 201,500 in 1939 (6.3 percent). Official sources estimate Saint Petersburg's Jewish community today at somewhere between 80,000 and 100,000 members.

Jews in Saint Petersburg (Leningrad during the Soviet era) came from a higher social class than those living in the **shtetlach** in Ukraine or Belarus, for it was the community's more affluent segments that managed to leave the ghettos for the big city. These were often tradespeople, but also white-collar workers, civil servants, members of the liberal professions (doctors and lawyers), and artists, the majority of whom were assimilated. Although, in 1869, 98 percent of Jews in Saint Petersburg claimed **Yiddish** as their native language, that number had fallen to 55 percent by 1910, 30 percent by 1926, 20 percent by 1939, and to microscopic levels today.[25] This progressive loss of interest in the mother

Numerous Jewish luminaries in Saint Petersburg made their mark on the social and political life of Russia. To name a few:

Piotr Shafirov (1669–1739): Son of a merchant from Smolensk, preeminent statesman, diplomat, and businessman, he was an adviser to Peter I. An ennobled master of Russian foreign policy, he was also an ancestor of the poet Viazemsky and the writer Aleksey Tolstoy.

Simon Dubnov (1860–1941): The great historian of the Jewish world, author of numerous books, including his ten-volume *History of the Jews,* he died in the Riga ghetto.

Abram Peretz (1771–1833): Son of a rabbi from Lubartów (Poland), he came to Saint Petersburg under Potemkin's protection and became a government economic adviser.

David Feinberg (1840–1916): Hailing from Germany, he moved to Saint Petersburg in the late 1860s. He became the patron to the Choral Synagogue.

Jacob Halperin (1840–1914): A civil servant in the Ministry of Justice.

Samuel Palakors (1837–88): Financier, founder of banks and builder of railroads, he contributed 16 percent of the construction of the Choral Synagogue of Saint Petersburg.

Anton Rubinstein (1829–94): Born in Podolia (Ukraine), this famous pianist, composer, and conductor founded the Russian Musical Society in 1859 and the Saint Petersburg Conservatory in 1862, which bore his name.

Maxim Vinaver (1863–1926): Jurist and politician, Kadet Party member and deputy, he was elected member of the Constituent Assembly in 1917 and later became a minister.

tongue, fairly logical for those living in a world-class capital where everyone vied for social advancement, also contributed to the poor success of Jewish Theater Studio: founded by Granovsky in 1919 on Vasilievsky Island, the studio was forced to relocate to Moscow in 1920, where the public was more working class.

Properly speaking, there was no Jewish quarter in Saint Petersburg, as Jews were spread out across the city. However, they were more concentrated in and more partial to some areas than others.

DEKABRISTOV (DECEMBRIST) STREET

■ On what was formerly Offizier-skaya Street near the synagogue and Teatralnaya Square, the building of the Eisenbeth Jewish secondary school still stands at number 18, behind the Marinsky Theater (it serves today as the Marinsky box office).

■ The neighborhood continues around the Griboiedov canal, where at number 140 a society dedicated to helping the city's impoverished Jews provided a soup kitchen and **mikvah.**

VASILIEVSKY ISLAND

This very popular neighborhood, with its market on Bougskaya Street, looks as if it were taken right out of Podolia, Chortkow, or Zhmerinka. On the adjacent streets called Tenth Line and Fifth Line, there was a Jewish school (Fourteenth National Jewish School at 37 Tenth Line Street) and the Ethnographic-Historical Society Museum (at 50 Fifth Line Street). Simon Dubnov once worked at this museum, which was opened in 1916 by An-Ski, pseudonym of Shlomo Zanvil Rapoport, but it closed in 1929 along with the majority of other Jewish institutions in Saint Petersburg.

THE CHORAL SYNAGOGUE

■ The Choral Synagogue is the nerve center of Jewish life in Saint Petersburg. This imposing, high-domed building was constructed in 1899 with financial support from many patrons. The main room has been restored and was reopened in 2001. In contrast to Moscow, this is the city's only synagogue; it thus serves the entire Jewish community. The chief rabbi, Menahem Mendl Pevsner, stresses that although he is a follower of Chabad, the community itself is not explicitly Chabad. The site today houses all Jewish community institutions, including a **yeshiva,** a **kosher** kitchen, a shop, and a library. A **kosher** restaurant, Shalom, is located nearby.

[Choral Synagogue:
prospekt Lermontovsky 2,
190121 Saint Petersburg. ✆ 08121136209.]
[Shalom: ulitsa Koli-Tomtchakta 8,
196084 Saint Petersburg. ✆ 08123275470.
Open Sun–Fri 11 A.M.–11 P.M.]

■ The memory of Saint Petersburg's Jewish community and, more generally, that of all Russian Jews is preserved in the Jewish Community Center's well-stocked library. It contains in particular a unique collection of Jewish samizdat publications of the Soviet era and Jewish periodicals dating back to the days of perestroika.

[Jewish Community Center:
ulitsa Rubinstein 3, apt. 50,
191025 Saint Petersburg. To visit, contact
✆ 08121133889 or 081211311540.]

■ Saint Petersburg boasts two major Jewish publications: *Ami,* a bimonthly newspaper in circulation since 1990, and *Lekhaim,* a review in circulation since 1992.

THE PREOBRAZHENSKY
JEWISH CEMETERY

Choral Synagogue, Saint Petersburg.

Unlike Moscow, Saint Petersburg has a Jewish cemetery, Preobrazhensky, located far from downtown near the southeast edge of the city. It is truly immense. A prayer-house built in 1908–12 and designed by the architect Gewirtz stands at the cemetery's entrance and includes a sort of columned atrium. Of course, the cemetery attests to the vibrancy of Saint Petersburg's Jewish community.

[Preobrazhensky Jewish Cemetery: Prospekt Alexandrovskoy-Fermy, Saint Petersburg. ▢ Proletarskaya.]

Ukraine

☙ FROM KIEV TO THE BLACK SEA
☙ EASTERN GALICIA, PODOLIA, AND BUKOVINA

Ukraine, THE LARGEST OF THE FORMER SOVIET REPUBLICS, is, along with Belarus and Lithuania, heir to the former "Pale of Settlement," the buffer zone designed to contain the Jews within the westernmost margins of the Russian Empire. Despite considerable losses due to the *Shoah* and resulting emigration, Ukraine still contains a large Jewish community (around 500,000 members, or 1 percent of the population), concentrated primarily in the major cities (Kiev, Odessa, Dnepropetrovsk, Kharkov, and Donetsk) and in certain old **shtetlach** to the south. Jewish cultural life, in full blossom here ever since the country's independence in 1991, nevertheless remains limited due to both the weight of seventy years of assimilation and per-secution by the Soviet regime and fresh waves of emigration.

The history of the Jewish communities in the Ukraine needs to be retold in the context of the complex historical reality of Ukraine itself, which never before held the status of an independent state, except in the era of the powerful eleventh to thirteenth century Kiev principality (Kievskaya

Amulet, Ukraine, nineteenth century. Jüdisches Museum der Schweiz, Basel.

Rus'), shared birthplace of both the Russian and Ukrainian nations.

For centuries, the history of Ukraine's Jews was conflated with that of the Jews of Poland. From the time Poland was divided until the First World War, it was associated with that of Russia's Jews, with the exception of Galicia, which fell within the Austro-Hungarian Empire. Since the 1917 Revolution, Ukrainian Jewish history has been tied to that of the Soviet Jews (again, except for Galicia, and Volhynia, which belonged to Poland until 1939).

When the Jews were expelled from France in 1394, and later from Spain and Portugal in 1492, they were taken in by Poland. In full economic and military expansion at the time, Poland represented a host country where religious tolerance reigned for all who willfully submitted to the authority and primacy of Catholicism.

The kings of Poland, in particular Sigismund I and Sigismund II in the sixteenth century, engaged in a policy of tolerance toward Jews. They offered them certain tariff exemptions and encouraged their communities to establish institutions responsible for collecting taxes. The growth of the Jewish community throughout the fifteenth century was apparent in nearly every city of the Polish realm, especially in the central and eastern regions (such as Galicia, Volhynia, Podolia, Lithuania, and the Ukraine), where Jewish craftspeople and merchants had been immigrating for years.

This period of growth was brutally interrupted in 1648 and 1649 by the first great catastrophe to strike these communities: revolts by Khmelnitsky Cossacks against the Polish nobility. The Cossacks massacred the Jewish population of every town they captured, pogroms of an incredible cruelty that left 100,000 Jews dead throughout Ukraine. The

Jewish communities of certain cities, such as Ostrog, Sokal, Vladimir-Volynski, Uman, and Proskurov, were completely wiped out. They only regenerated many years later, but only in areas that enjoyed the protection of a nobleman or the king himself.

It would take an entire century after these massacres for Jewish communities in Ukraine to begin growing again, sparked by an upsurge in religious fervor marked in particular by **Hasidism,** a movement founded in Podolia by Israel ben Eliezer (1700–60), also known as the Baal Shem Tov of

Hanukkah lamp, Odessa, nineteenth century. Musée d'Art et d'Histoire du Judaïsme, Paris.

Medzihbozh. The movement had considerable suc-
cess in Lithuania, Poland, and throughout Ukraine.
This revival was fueled as well by the many *magidim,*
or itinerant preachers, including the *maggid* of
Dubno Jacob Kranz (allied with the anti-**Hasidic
Mitnaggedim**), Dov Ber of Mezritch, Nahman of
Bratslav, and other **tsadikim.**

Yiddish theater artists, circa 1920.

In the late eighteenth century, with the repeated division of Poland in 1772, 1793, and 1795 and Ukraine's absorption by Russia, the situation changed starkly for the Jews. Russia, which had forbidden Jews the right to reside in its territory, suddenly found itself in charge of the largest Jewish population in the world. The czarist government thus established the boundaries of a "Pale of Settlement" within which Jews were forced to settle, an area coinciding approximately with the regions taken from Poland (Lithuania, Belarus, Ukraine west to the Dnieper, the kingdom of Poland); added to these were virgin lands in the New Russia (Kherson, Nikolayev, Odessa, Crimea), as well as the left bank of the Dnieper (Poltava, Kremenchug, Ekaterinoslav—renamed Dnepropetrovsk).

The Russian Empire's repressive policies persisted throughout the nineteenth century. In 1827, Jews were officially expelled from Kiev. After a period of liberal reforms under Alexander II, oppression of the Jews picked up again with Alexander III, during whose reign a number of pogroms took place against the Jewish population, driving the latter to emigrate in ever larger numbers to Europe and the United States. At the same time, classic **Yiddish**-language literature began to develop, most notably by the writers Sholem Aleichem and Mendele Moykher Sforim.

At the end of the First World War, from 1917 to 1921, revolution and civil war tore through Ukraine. Nationalist gangs led by Simon Petliura perpetrated atrocious pogroms, massacring 100,000 Jews across the country in cities such as Zhitomir, Proskurov, Rovno, Belaya Tserkov, Kiev, and Vinnitsa. The Soviet powers, in contrast, abolished the "Pale of Settlement" and other restrictions against the Jewish community, and even supported early

Yiddish theater in Kiev and Odessa. However, they simultaneously began antireligious campaign that led to the closure of many synagogues.

By far the most traumatic event for the Ukrainian Jewish community was the Second World War and the *Shoah*. The Germans invaded the Soviet Union on 21 June 1941 and immediately arranged for the community's extermination. After forcing the Jews to reside in ghettos, the Nazis liquidated these districts one by one, most often in mass, public executions, and tossed the bodies of the victims in common graves dug by the victims themselves.

The locations of these executions can still be found in the woods neighboring almost every Ukranian city; they are usually marked with a stele reading "to the victims of Fascism." An inventory of these sites would require an entire book in itself.

After the war, certain Jewish communities regenerated following the return of those who managed to escape into central Russia in time, but the official antireligious and anti-Semitic policies continued; after the so-called "doctor's plot" in the early 1950s, many synagogues and community institutions across the country were closed. It was not until perestroika in 1985 and Ukraine's independence in 1991 that a Jewish cultural renaissance began. Increasing emigration by younger generations, however, has ultimately aged, impoverished, and weakened the community.

→ **To call Ukraine from the United States, dial 011 380** followed by the number of the person you are calling minus the initial 0 (used only for domestic calls).

From Kiev to the Black Sea ▪

Kiev

From the outset, the history of Kiev has been tied to that of its Jewish community. One of the earliest references to the city is in a tenth-century document discovered in the *genizah* in a Cairo synagogue: a letter sent to Kiev by Jacob bar Hanuker. A synagogue in Kiev proper is mentioned in a document dating to 1113. A *zhydovskie vorota* (Jewish gate) is mentioned in a text from 1146, near present-day Lvov Square.

Decimated by the Tatars and then the Cossacks, the Jewish community never truly regained its footing here until the late nineteenth century. The city's two major temples, Tailors' Synagogue and Brodsky Synagogue, date back to this era and are both still active today.

THE SYNAGOGUES

▪ Built in 1894–95 and designed by the architect Nikolai Gordenin along the Dnieper in the Podol district, the Kravtsev (tailors') Synagogue bears no apparent Judaic marking on its facade. It nevertheless contains eastern and neo-Roman architectural features typical of nineteenth-century synagogues. Despite its luxurious interior, it was never shut down during the Soviet era.

[Kravtsev Synagogue: Chtchekavitska Street 29, 04071 Kiev. ✆ 0444161383.]

▪ The Central Synagogue has long been referred to by the name Brodsky in honor of Lazare Brodsky, the wealthy Kiev industrialist and patron who financed its construction. Built according to plans by the architect Georg Schleifer, it dates to 1898.

Kravtsev Synagogue, Kiev.

"He's important, that Brodsky! When he rides by in his carriage, everyone on Kreshchatik Street and all the Jews tip their hats, myself included. Ah, if only one day I might become a Brodsky!" So wrote Sholem Aleichem.

The Central Synagogue functioned as a puppet theater until 1997. It has since been returned to the Jewish community; it is overseen by the Chabad (Lubavitch) community. It was completely restored in March 2000 and has regained its former splendor.

[Central Synagogue: Shota-Rustaveli Street 13, 0123 Kiev. ✆ 0442350069. A small bookstore is located in the basement.]

■ There were other synagogues in Kiev, though their structures have not all survived.

The Merchants' Synagogue, a few steps away from the Central Synagogue on Shota-Rustaveli Street, has been converted into the Kinopanorama cinema. The film *Shoah* was shown here in September 1998 with director Claude Lanzmann in attendance. The Galicia Synagogue once stood at Jilanska Street 97, not far from the station, while the Karaite Synagogue stood on Yaroslavov-Val Street; it was later turned into the "Actors' House." The **Hasidic** oratory once sat in the courtyard at Nijny-Val Street 37, in the Podol district.

"YEHUPETS"

■ A tour of Jewish Kiev is linked to the personalities who lived here, such as Sholem Aleichem, who referred to the town by the rather silly name of Yehupets. "Everyone is laughing at me. I cannot even go out for a walk. They point at me and say, 'That's the wife of Menahem Mendel of Yehupets.' Not such a bad name, actually," Aleichem claims in *Menahem Mendel*.

The houses where Aleichem lived are easily located: 5 Bolshaya-Vassilikovska Street from 1897 to 1903, and 27 Saxaganski Street from 1903 to 1905. A monument dedicated to Sholem Aleichem was erected on Basseinaya Street near the Bessarbia Market in 1997, not far from 5 Basseinaya Street, where Golda Meir was born and lived from 1898 to 1906.

Karaite Synagogue, Kiev.

■ Other well-known figures of this Jewish world include Isaac Babel, who studied here, pianist Vladimir Horowitz, who was born here in 1903 and lived here until 1925 (when he emigrated to the United States), musicologist and **Yiddish** folklorist Moses Beregovski, writer Ilya Ehrenburg, actor Solomon Mikhoels, and writer Peretz Markish, later arrested and gunned down by the Soviets along with other members of the Jewish Antifascist Committee.

BABI YAR

The most tragic event in the history of Jewish Kiev was the Babi Yar massacre, committed by the SS and the *Einsatzgruppen* on 28 and 29 September 1941, several days after they captured the city. All of Kiev's Jews were rounded up and led to the Lukianovka Jewish Cemetery, and from there to the Babi Yar ravine. They were all shot to death in the two days that followed.

Two monuments now commemorate this tragic episode:

■ The first, on Dorogojitska Street, was put up in 1976 after the poet Evgenii Evtushenko, composer Vladimir Shostakovitch, and other members of the Soviet intelligentsia protested the government's efforts to erase the memory of the event. It is an official monument in grand Soviet statuary style. The plaque is inscribed in three languages, Russian, Ukrainian, and **Yiddish**, yet fails to mention menorah but makes no additional clarification. "In memory of the tragedy at Babi Yar," it reads in Ukrainian. Each year, on 29 September, memorials are held, bringing together the Jewish community and other prominent figures from the city.

Berdichev

Founded in 1546, the illustrious city of Berdichev (which was Polish until 1793) is towered over by the dome of the large Baroque church here, a former Carmelite cloister dating from 1627.

Jews began settling in Berdichev in the seventeenth century, drawn by the fairs regularly held here. In the late eighteenth century, the city had become a major **Hasidic** hub centered around the **tsadik** Yitshak Levi of Berdichev (who died in 1808), a disciple of the Great Maggid of Mezritch. A century later, Berdichev had become an almost entirely Jewish city, with a community of 41,600 members of a total 53,300 residents, or 80 percent of the population. In Russian jokes or "anecdotes," Berdichev was the epitome of a Jewish city.

French novelist Honoré de Balzac, who married Mme Hanska in a church in Berdichev, described the city as "a Jewish encampment."

Statue of Sholem Aleichem, Kiev.

the Jewish identity of the victims, reading only: "In this place, German Fascists executed nearly 100,000 citizens of Kiev and prisoners of war."
■ The second monument, erected on Melnikova Street in 1991 and located at the Babi Yar ravine only yards away from where the actual executions took place, depicts a large

FROM KIEV TO THE BLACK SEA

♔ A REAL DUMP!

A well-dressed stranger once came to Berdichev. A Jewish tailor asked him:

"Where did you have your clothes made?"

"In Paris."

"Is it far from Berdichev?"

"Over a thousand miles."

"It must be a dump. But they sure know how to sew."

Because of its symbolic name, the Germans attacked Berdichev with particular ferocity when they occupied the city on 6 July 1941. They liquidated the ghetto within three months. Vassili Grossman, a native of Berdichev, described the details of this annihilation in his books *Life and Fate* (New York: Harper & Row, 1986) and *The Black Book* (New York: Holocaust Publications, 1981).

The ghetto, properly speaking, where the Jews all had to gather in July 1941, was referred to as Yatki. It stretched west of Žitomirskoye Road (today Lenin Street) and encompassed the streets Staragorodskaya, Bielopolskaya (current 9-May), Glinka, Bolshaya-Žitomirskaya, and Malaya-Žitomirskaya (now Sholem-Aleichem). These streets have hardly changed since then and appear just as Grossmann describes them: unpaved dirt roads full of puddles and mud. At the center of the Yatki ghetto there was a market and the old Berdichev synagogue. In September 1941, young men and women in the

Former synagogue, Berdichev.

ghetto were ordered to come "dig up potatoes." On 15 September, 18,600 people, practically the entire ghetto, were murdered near the village of Khajino. A commemorative gravestone marks the site, indicating merely that the victims were "peaceful Soviet citizens."

☙ DIGGING FOR POTATOES

"And we learned today, from a peasant friend who was passing by the barbed wire, that the Jews who had been taken to dig up potatoes were actually digging deep trenches, two miles from the city near the aerodrome on the road to Romanovka. Remember that name, Vitia, for that is where you will find the mass grave where your mother will be buried. "

VASSILI GROSSMAN, *VIE ET DESTNI,* (LAUSANNE: L'ÂGE D'HOMME, 1995). SEE ALSO: *LIFE AND FATE.* (NEW YORK: HARPER & ROW, 1986).

■ Berdichev once featured a number of synagogues, prayer houses, and even a Hebrew printing shop. Only one synagogue remains today, at the top of Sverdlov Street, where the city's last 700 Jews, most of them elderly, strive to keep their traditions alive.

[Synagogue: Sverdlov Street 8, 13300 Berdichev. ✆ 0414320222.]

■ The large Jewish cemetery in Berdichev is impressive, with beautiful old graves often overgrown with vegetation. A path between the graves

leads to a mausoleum built above the grave of Rabbi Levi Yitshak, the "great master who knew how to read between the lines of the **Torah.**"

[Great Jewish Cemetery: To the left of the city's entrance heading away from Žitomir on Žitormiskoye Road. Contact the synagogue at the address above for the key.]

Pereyaslav-Khmelnytsky

The city of Pereyaslav, to which the name Khmelnytsky was added in honor of that Cossack leader, was also the birthplace of Sholem Aleichem. To lovers of musical comedy, the city is better known as Anatevka, the name it bears in *Fiddler on the Roof.* Aleichem found inspiration for his novels' many characters here: the ones who seek their fortune, the boy who joins the revolution and is sent to Siberia, the girl who betrays her faith by marrying a Ukrainian, the mother who remains in the **shtetl** with her children while the father plays the market in Odessa and Yehupets, etc. Today, Pereyaslav has retained a certain charm, even if the city has lost its Jewish community. The former Jewish quarter was located right downtown.

■ The Grand Synagogue of Pereyaslav, which dates to the nineteenth century, is located across the main square behind city hall in a large, rectangular building named the House of Culture today. No plaque indicates

SHOLEM ALEICHEM

His real name Sholem Rabinovitz, founder of classic **Yiddish** literature, Sholem Aleichem was born in Pereyaslav in 1853 and died in New York in 1916. The world of the **shtetl** and the everyday people who lived there are immortalized in his writings. His most famous work, *Tevie the Milkman,* was magnificently set to music as *Fiddler on the Roof,* or *Anatevka,* by Jerry Bock and featured the song "If I Was a Rich Man." His other well-known works include the 1892 *Menahem Mendel.*

the building's previous purpose. On Saturday and Sunday afternoons, locals pack the stifling main room to sing Ukrainian folk songs. To the side, a section of the building has been converted into a café-disco.

■ To find Sholem Aleichem's birth house, take Lenin Street to the intersection and turn right; a commemorative plaque to the left marks the site.

Uman

The city of Uman is most famous for the Sophievka, a park built by Count Potocki in the grand style typical of eighteenth-century landscape architecture. It is also where Rabbi Nahman of Bratslav (Braşov), a great-grandson of Baal Shem Tov and continuer of his doctrine, settled and later died in 1810.

■ Only one grave remains from the old Jewish cemetery: that of Rabbi Nahman, a holy shrine today. A synagogue has been built beside the gravesite itself, allowing for reflection both indoors and out.

A number of pews have been installed, as well as a railed footbridge designed to keep the faithful in line before they enter the prayer room. The cemetery entrance is protected by a guard, where an inscription in French, English, Russian, and Hebrew reminds visitors that they are in a holy place.

Behind Rabbi Nahman's tomb stretches what used to be the cemetery, now merely a snow-covered field (in winter) surrounded by housing projects.

[Jewish Cemetery: From the bus station, take Shevchenko Street and continue straight approximately one mile on Pushkin Street; when you reach number 41, turn right.]

[Visitors, usually from Israel, come to pray in the synagogue every day of the week. The guard is permanently on duty.]

Odessa

Established in 1794, Odessa was captured by Admiral de Ribas from the Turks for Empress Catherine II of Russia. The city developed rapidly

564

during the nineteenth century, largely due to the arrival of colonists from "New Russia." It soon became a melting pot of Russians, French, Armenians, Poles, Greeks, Moldavians, and Jews. Forbidden to reside in Saint Petersburg, Moscow, or Kiev, Jews poured into the southern Russian cities of Odessa and Nikolayev, eventually constituting a third of their population before the Second World War. Even today, Odessa still bears their mark.

A JEWISH CITY

An Odessan was asked one day:
"How many people live in
Odessa?"

"One million."

"And how many of them are
Jews?"

"I just told you. One million."
You see, in people's minds,
"Odessan" and "Jew" are often
confused.

Jewish Odessa began at the Greek Square ("Gretsk, that's what they call the street where the Jews do business," Sholem Aleichem wrote),

Alexandrovski Prospect, the old marketplace, and the streets named Evreiskya, Bazamaya, and Malaya-Arnautskaya. It continued on the other side of Preobrajenska Street, down Tiraspolskaya to Staroportofrankovskaya streets, and beyond that to the neighborhood by the train station. It covered the entire Moldavanka suburb, where the famous Privoz market is found, and ended at the Slobodka district, where the deportation convoys waited during the German-Romanian occupation. The Jewish quarter encompassed a tremendous area, in other words, stretching from downtown all the way to the western and northern suburbs. Before the war, 350,000 Jews lived here. They number no more than 50,000 today.

Touring Jewish Odessa involves a great deal of footwork. You need to pace up and down the streets, stroll through the neighborhoods, enter and exit courtyards . . . At Privoz market, breathe in the smell of fresh vegetables, bitter herbs, almonds and raisins, and soak up the atmosphere of the Moldavanka, the children

FROM KIEV TO THE BLACK SEA

Battleship Potemkin,
Sergey Eisenstein, 1925.

playing in the streets. As fancy suits you, stop by one or more of the few remaining synagogues, examine the various monuments and plaques, and pay a visit to the Slobodka cemetery.

THE SYNAGOGUES

Before the First World War, Odessa contained seven synagogues and forty-nine prayer houses. The oldest was the Brodskaya (Brody), or Choral, Synagogue, built in 1840. With its four domes, it still towers over the intersection of Pushkin and Jukovsky streets, an archival warehouse today.

Only two synagogues are still in service: the Glavnaya (Main) Synagogue and the Hasidic Synagogue. There was also a Dockworkers' Synagogue (near the port, now in ruins) and even a synagogue for kosher poultry sellers.

■ The Glavnaya Synagogue was returned to the Jewish community a few years ago after being converted

ODESSA, BIRTHPLACE OF KLEZMER MUSIC

Odessa was also the birthplace of klezmer music. Blending clarinet, cello, and balalaika with Middle Eastern rhythms, klezmer is making a comeback in Europe after crossing the Atlantic. In Odessa, the klezmer group Migdalor improvises from scores by Alexander Tcherner.

into a gymnasium. Until recently, the markings of a basketball court could still be seen on the floor. The women's galleries have been removed, while a wall has been built on the first floor that divides the main room into two sections. The fairly new community manages a school and dormitory and publishes *Or Sameakh,* a daily newspaper. On holidays like **Purim** or **Passover,** the synagogue reverberates with the hubbub of the faithful.

[Glavnaya Synagogue:

Evreiskaya Street 25, 65001 Odessa.

✆ 0482240087.]

■ The smaller **Hasidic** Synagogue, which has a beautiful interior, was recently renovated.

[Hasidic Synagogue:

Remeslennaya Street 21 (formerly

Ossipova) 65011 Odessa.

✆ 0482243640.]

■ Located on Malaya-Arnautskaya Street, the Jewish Cultural Center offers Hebrew instruction and organizes various events. At number 9 of this street lived the writers Hayyim Nahman Bialik and Ilya Ilf (from his real name Fainzylberg). Ilf was born in Odessa right near the train station, where a plaque in his memory has been mounted.

[Jewish Cultural Center:

Malaya-Arnautskaya Street 46a,

65023 Odessa. ✆ 0482226590 or

0482218376.]

IN THE FOOTSTEPS OF ISAAC BABEL

The most famous character set in Jewish Odessa was the bandit Benia Krik, gangster king and hero from Isaac Babel's *Odessa Tales.* The writer painted a portrait of the Jewish life of the suburb of Moldavanka: ". . . Our generous mother, a life filled with suckling children, rags out to dry and wedding nights full of suburban chic and the indefatigable vigor of a trooper."

■ Getting your bearings in Odessa is rather difficult, for no map yet exists showing the new street names, while the residents only know the old ones. To find the places depicted by Isaac Babel in Moldavanka, who lived at 23 Dalnitskaya Street, arm yourself with a map, get a sense of the street layout, and compare what you see to Babel's descriptions.

■ The shop owned by Liubka Shneeweiss, or Liubka the Cossack, was located at the intersection of Dalniskaya and Bankovskya streets, near the present-day Isaac Babel Street (formerly Vinogradnaya). Gluchaya Street, where the gangsters took refuge in Yoska Samuelson's house of tolerance, today bears the name Bougaevskaya, after many years as Instrumentalnaya. Prokhorovskaya Street, where Piatirubel the blacksmith lived, after years as Chvorostin has taken back its previous name.

FROM KIEV TO THE BLACK SEA

ISAAC BABEL

Isaac Babel (1894–1941), born in Odessa in the Moldavanka suburb and author of the *Odessa Tales,* admired Flaubert and Maupassant and made an impression on Gorki. He joined Semion Budenny's Red Cavalry during the civil war and, though in favor of the Revolution, was nevertheless arrested in 1939 and executed in 1941. His work, now among classic of twentieth-century fiction, was rediscovered in the 1950s.

■ At the triangular public square formed by Prokhorovskaya's intersection with Staroportofrankovskaya (Old Free Port) Street, a monument was recently erected commemorating the deportation of ghetto residents to Bogdanovka, Domanievka, Berinzovka, and other Trans-Dniestrian extermination camps between 1941 and 1943. Tens of thousands of Odessa's Jews died in the camps.

■ Not far from the square, a picturesque street bore the name of Sholem Aleichem during the Soviet era; it now bears its previous name, Miasoedovskaya (meat eaters). The Jewish Hospital was found at this street's intersection with Bogdan-Khmelnitsky Street.

■ Odessa, whose famous steps were immortalized by Eisenstein in *Battleship Potemkin,* was also the home of the writers Ilf and Petrov (authors of the very funny *Twelve Chairs*), Arkady Lvov, Sholem Aleichem; the musicians Jascha Heifetz, Emile Gilels; and other famous figures.

THE CEMETERIES

■ The first Jewish cemetery in Odessa (the oldest grave dates to 1793) was razed and turned into Illitch Park, just behind Privoz. Only the layout of the paths here hints at the former purpose of this place.

■ The second Jewish cemetery, near a retirement home, was located on Lustdorfskaya Street, in front of the Orthodox cemetery. Only the entrance arcade remains. The grave of the **Yiddish** writer Mendele Mokher Sefarim was supposedly moved into another cemetery.

■ The only Jewish cemetery left to visit is found at the very end of the long Razumovskaya Street, at the intersection of Khimicheskaya Street and Leningradskoya Road. It is very large, well kept, and constantly visited; it does not have that neglectful aspect common to most Jewish cemeteries in Ukraine.

[Jewish Cemetery: Khimicheskaya (intersection with Leningradskoya Road), 65010 Odessa. Open 9 A.M.–5 P.M. There are many florists at the entrance.]

Eastern Galicia, Podolia, and Bukovina ■

Chernivtsi (Czernowitz)

The former capital of Bukovina, the large German-influenced city of Chernivtsi (Czernowitz) once belonged to the Austrian Empire. It then became part of Romania during the wars, was annexed by the Soviet Union in 1940, and occupied by Germany and Romania from 1941 to 1944, only to become part of Ukraine after the war.

This once major Jewish hub (Jews made up around 40 percent of the population before the war) hosted the World Conference on the **Yiddish** Language in 1908. It is also the birthplace of the **Yiddish** poet Itzik Manger, the fabulist Eliezer Steinbarg (who adapted into **Yiddish** the fables of La Fontaine, Aesop, and Krylov), the singer Sidi Tal, and the German-language poets Paul Celan and Rose Ausländer.

The magnificent city is well worth a visit. It retains its nineteenth- and twentieth-century Austrian feel, especially around its central square (formerly Ringplatz) and city hall, along Olga-Kobylianska Street (formerly Herrengasse), Ivan-Franko Street (formerly Rathausgasse), and Soborna Square (formerly Austria Platz).

■ A tour of the Jewish city begins at the former Grand Synagogue (or "Tempel") located on Tempelgasse, today Universitetska Street. Though the Germans dynamited it, they failed to completely destroy it. The building functions today as a movie theater, Kinoteatr Chernivtsi, which the Jews of Chernivtsi ironically refer to as "Kinagoga."

■ At Teatralna Square, to the right of the theater, stands the old House of Jewish Culture, transformed as of late into the Eliezer Steinbarg Cultural Association headquarters. The Association is presided over by **Yiddish**-language writer Josef Burg, who also publishes the newspaper *Czernowitzer Bleter.* Notice the monumental staircase and its Stars of David, their points sawn off since the Soviet era.

[Eliezer Steinbarg Cultural Association: Sheptitskogo Street 13–9, 58001 Chernivtsi. ✆ 0372220601.]

■ Steinbarg himself once lived on a neighboring street recently renamed in his honor, as pointed out by the plaque there. A door adorned with a Star of David can be seen just across the street.

■ Not far from here, at 16 Clara-Zetkin Street stands the home of Mrs. Zuckermann, the ninety-two-year-old star of the film *Mr. Zwilling and Mrs. Zuckermann* (Volker Koepp: 1998). A victim of the *Shoah*, deported to

Trans-Dniestria from 1941 to 1944, yet also an expert in the history of Chernivtsi, she once proudly declared: "I have remained Austrian; I love Czernowitz alone."

■ Paul Celan was born at 5 Saxaganski Street (formerly Wassilkogasse). A plaque in Ukrainian and German marks the site.

♛ PAUL CELAN

Paul Celan was born in Chernivtsi in 1920 and died in Paris in 1970. His parents perished after being deported to Trans-Dniestria. He moved to Paris after the war but continued to write in German, the "language of executioners." His work, which grew more and more hermetic over time, deeply revitalized contemporary poetry. His most famous poem is

Todesfuge (Fugue of Death):

"Black milk of daybreak we drink it at sundown
we drink it at noon in the morning we drink it at night
we drink and we drink it
we dig a grave in the breezes there one lies unconfined . . ."

FROM *POEMS OF PAUL CELAN*, TRANS. MICHAEL HAMBURGER (NEW YORK: PERSEA BOOKS, 2002).

■ The active synagogue in town, located on Lukian-Kobylitsa Street, is very small, but the interior is beautiful, with murals depicting biblical themes.

[Synagogue: Lukian-Kobylitsa Street 54, 58003 Chernivsti. ✆ 0372554878.]

Former Grand Synagogue (or "Tempel"), Chernivtsi.

On the road to the market, Chernivtsi, 1899.

■ Properly speaking, the Jewish quarter was located a bit further down, on the other side of Ruska Street. Transformed into a ghetto between 1941 and 1944, its entire Jewish population was deported to Trans-Dniestria. Take Turecka Street ("Turk," after the former Turkish Fountain), and cross the bridge leading to the ghetto's main street, Morariugasse, today Sagaidachny Street. The architecture of the block where Rose Ausländer was born has remained typically Jewish over the years. A wide street, it is bordered by a triangular public square formerly called Springbrunnenplatz where the markets were held.

■ A right turn after the square leads to Henri-Barbusse Street, formerly Synagogengasse, one of the poorest and most crowded streets of the ghetto. The former Grosse Schul (Big Synagogue) can be still be seen in the center at number 31; a very large building with a Greek pediment, it serves today as a "repair and production complex." Further down, at number 18, a former prayer house features two Stars of David struck with the letter *shin* on the door. There was an inscription that read in Romanian and Hebrew "makhsike sabatul" (those respectful of the **Shabbat**), but it was painted over in 1998. Chernivtsi's oldest synagogue is located a little further up; it dates from the eighteenth century. A Hebrew inscription once read "Hevra Tehilim" (brotherhood of Psalms), but this also disappeared in 1998. Donated to the Protestant community, the synagogue has been renovated, its main room divided into two levels and facade (where the inscription was located) repainted.

Further still, at the spot where Henri-Barbusse Street converges with Sagaidatchny Street, the Jewish hospital, now neglected, can still be seen through a locked gate. A commemorative plaque mounted on a house off the square points out, in Ukrainian and **Yiddish**, that the ghetto was once located on this street until its 40,000 residents were deported.

■ The Jewish cemetery is both impressive and fairly well maintained. The inscriptions on the tombstones are mostly in German, though a few are in Hebrew or Russian.

[Jewish Cemetery: To get there, take Ruska Street to the end, then turn left: It is about a twenty-minute walk from the city center. You may also take a taxi. Open daily 9 A.M.–6 P.M.]

Medzhibozh

Medzhibozh, in Podolia, has been a mythic city for Jewish communities ever since Israel ben Eliezer, better known today as Baal Shem Tov, settled here in 1740.

☰ ISRAEL BEN ELIEZER, THE BAAL SHEM TOV

*Israel ben Eliezer (1700–60), also known as Baal Shem Tov (Master of the Good Name) or Besht, was the founder of the **Hasidic** movement, which had a great influence in the eighteenth and nineteenth centuries throughout the Jewish world of Ukraine and Poland. Eliezer's preaching added a spiritual, popular, as well as festive dimension to Judaism. "One Simhat Torah evening, the Baal*

Shem himself danced together with his congregation. He took the scroll of the Torah in his hand and danced with it. Then he laid the scroll aside and danced without it. At this moment, one of his disciples who was intimately acquainted with his gestures, said to his companions: 'Now our master has laid aside the visible, dimensional teachings, and has taken the spiritual teachings unto himself.'"

MARTIN BUBER, *TALES OF THE HASIDIM: THE EARLY MASTERS*, TRANS. OLGA MARX (NEW YORK: SCHOCKEN BOOKS, 1947).

Medzhibozh, which means "between the Bugs," is magnificently situated between two rivers bearing practically the same name: the southern Bug, a long river crossing all of Podolia to the Black Sea, and its tributary the Boujok (Little Bug). Beside the river at the town's entrance stands a large medieval fortress built between the fourteenth and seventeenth centuries but largely still intact. Before the war, more than 6,000 residents, two-thirds of whom were Jewish, lived at the foot of this fortress. There remains, it is said, only one Jew today: the man who guards the cemetery.

■ The Baal Shem Tov cemetery is very old. The master's grave is enclosed and protected in a small concrete structure containing prayer books and candles.

[Baal Shem Tov Cemetery: To get there, cross the village, turn right after the House of Culture, and continue to the end of the dirt road named Karl-Marx Street. To see the site, request information at the tourist and pilgrims' synagogue located next to the cemetery.]

■ Walking along the cemetery for about a half mile further, you will reach the new Jewish cemetery of Medzhibozh, whose graves date from the late nineteenth century to 1941. This cemetery, much larger but less well-known than the old one, is quite beautiful as well. The graves are relatively well preserved, but the tombstones have already begun to sink, and a neighboring farmer has turned part of the cemetery into a farmyard.

■ Further still, in a difficult spot to reach in the forest, is located the place where the Jews of Medzhibozh were executed. The mass grave has been covered with a huge concrete slab and a stele bearing the inscription: "Here, in these ravines, on 22 September 1941, the German Fascist barbarians cruelly gunned down more than 3,000 women, children, and the elderly, prisoners of the Medzhibozh ghetto. In eternal memory of our dear compatriots."

Lvov

Lvov—Lviv in Ukrainian, Lwów in Polish, Lemberg in German, Léopol in French—a city long Polish, then Austro-Hungarian, was again Polish between the wars. Annexed in 1939 by the Soviet Union after the German-Soviet nonaggression pact, it was occupied from 1941 to 1944 by Nazi Germany, taken back by the Soviets after the Second World War, and later reattached to the Ukraine.

The Jewish community of Lvov was mentioned as far back as the thirteenth century, since, that is, the founding of the city. In the latter half of the fourteenth century, the city featured two Jewish quarters, distinguishing Lvov from most other large European cities. The first, dating from 1352, was located "beyond the walls" around the Stary Rynek (Old Market) Square in the Kraków suburb (Krakowskie Przedmiejsce); the other, which dates from 1387, was located inside the city.

THE OLD GHETTO WITHIN THE WALLS

The former ghetto stretched across the present-day Ruska, Straroevreiska, and Federova streets, near the Arsenal, southeast of the center of town. Today, you can see the remains of the Fedorovaolotaya Roza Gildene Roiz (Grand Synagogue of the Golden Rose) at the intersection of Straroevreiska and Fedorova streets. Built in 1582, the synagogue was a late Gothic masterpiece with high lancet arches that towered over the entire quarter. It was one of the most beautiful and oldest buildings in Lvov—until the Second World War. It owed its name to Rabbi Nahman's wife,

Rosa Jakubovna. Destroyed in 1941 by the Nazis, today there remains only the empty square, a few vestiges of the arches, and a commemorative plaque in English and Ukrainian.

THE FORMER GHETTO BEYOND THE WALLS

■ The former ghetto "beyond the walls" covered a much larger area. This is where, north of the city center, Jews from Lvov settled throughout the nineteenth and twentieth centuries. The quarter became, during the German occupation, a "ghetto" in that special sense the Nazis gave the term.

■ Behind the opera was located the Żydowska Brama (Jewish Gate), a few steps away from the Krakowska Brama (Kraków Gate), referred to as Vor der Shul (in front of the Synagogue) by the Jews of Lvov.

■ The present-day Bogdan-Khmelnitsky Street turns into Zamarstynowksa Street, the central street of the ghetto. Here, all the houses before the war were Jewish. On little Santa Street, formerly Bożnicza (Synagogue Street) stood the suburb's great synagogue and, a bit further down, the Hasidim Schul. The two sites are today empty lots. A plaque in English and Ukrainian was recently mounted on the wall of the former **Hasidic** synagogue; built in the seventeenth century it was reconstructed in the nineteenth century and destroyed in 1941.

■ Only one temple can still be visited in this quarter, which once contained so many: the former Synagogue of Hasidic Innovators. Used for many years as a gymnasium, it was recently returned to the Jewish community and now contains the offices of the Sholem Aleichem Cultural Association. The association organizes meetings for the elderly and publishes the review *Shofar*.

[Former Synagogue of the Hasidic Innovators/Sholem Aleichem Cultural Association: Ugolnaya (Vugilna) Street 3, 79019 Lvov. ✆ 0322729843.]

■ To penetrate Lvov's old Jewish quarter, stroll along the streets named Zamarsynowska, Muliarska, Balabana, Kulisha, and along the northern perimeter of the city. Beyond the railroad bridge on Chernovola Street (previously 700 Years of Lvov) stands a 1991 monument in memory of the massacre of 136,800 Jews in Lvov, either exterminated in the ghetto or deported between 1941 and 1943.

■ Another possible exploration of the ghetto begins on the other side of Gorodecka Street, in the shadow of the opera. A stroll down Szpitalna Street is like being slowly transported into the world of the former **shtetlach.** Although the street is no longer Jewish, it has preserved its look of yesteryear, with its market crisscrossed by merchants carrying clothes and other objects in their arms.

At the intersection the street forms with Kotliarska Street, a plaque indicates the house where the writer

Sholem Aleichem lived in 1906. Further down, the street opens onto a lively square where the streets named Rappaport, Sholem Aleichem, and Bazama converge: this was one of the nerve centers of the ghetto near the former Kraków market (Krakowski Rynek), today the "bazaar." On Rappaport Street stands the former Jewish hospital, a large, Moorish building with an eastern-style dome. Traces of Polish lettering can still be made out, "Izraelicki Szpital," while Hebrew characters covered over with a Cyrillic inscription still read "Maternity Ward number 3." The maternity ward's garden is bordered by a plot that was in fact Lvov's old Jewish cemetery. Dating back to the fourteenth century, its richness can be glimpsed in old photos. It has been totally razed and replaced by an extension of the bazaar.

■ A beautiful building on Sholem Aleichem Street features a monumental entrance resembling Paris's Gare d'Orsay: formerly the Jewish consistory, with the rabbinical tribunal, this structure now houses the B'nai Brith "Leopolis" and the Lvov Center for Jewish Studies.

[B'nai Brith "Leopolis" and Lvov Center for Jewish Studies: Sholem Aleichem Street 12, 79019 Lvov. ✆ 0322979584.]

■ You will next arrive at Shevchenko Street, better known by historians of the *Shoah* by its former name of Janowska. A veritable concentration camp within the ghetto, the sinister Janowska camp was located on this street. It stood on the spot where currently there are barracks. At the end of the street is the Janowski cemetery, a section of which is Jewish. Almost all the graves date from after 1945, and thus are inscribed in Russian.

[Janowski Cemetery: Eroshenko Street, 79010 Lvov. Open 9 A.M.–5 P.M.]

■ The only active synagogue in Lvov is located even further away, in the area of the train station on Brativ Mikhnovskikh Street, formerly Moskovskaya.

[Synagogue: Brativ Mikhnovskikh Street 4, 79018 Lvov. ✆ 0322330524. Open 9 A.M.–6 P.M.]

■ Lvov's Jewish quarter also stretched south of Gorodecka Street and west of the Svoboda Prospect. A synagogue once stood on the streets called Nalivaiko and Grebinka, but it has since been razed. Across the street, Grebinka Street puppet theater (Teatr Ialok) was once the Jewish theater of Lvov. A little further down Bankovska Street, an empty space between two houses was the site of yet another synagogue.

♕ A TESTIMONIAL

In 1929, Albert Londres visited the eastern European Jewish communities and gave the following account of the Lvov ghetto: "The market lies at the heart of the ghetto. A pile of shacks like those built after an earthquake or a city burns down—a market? A field of manure, rather. You can choose from any garbage can in the Polish city!"

ALBERT LONDRES, *LE JUIF ERRANT EST ARRIVÉ* (THE WANDERING JEW HAS ARRIVED). (PARIS: LE SERPENT À PLUMES, 2000). SEE ALSO, *THE JEW HAS COME HOME*, TRANS. WILLIAM STAPLES (NEW YORK: R. R. SMITH, 1931).

Brody

The city of Brody, founded in 1584 by Stanislaw Żołkiewski, started expanding in 1629 when the waywode Stanislaw Koniecpolski called on engineer and artillery captain Guillaume Levasseur de Beauplan to built fortifications and establish a zoning plan for the new city. After Polish Galicia's annexation by Austria in 1772, for a hundred years (1779–1880) Brody was granted the status of "duty-free city"—exoneration from taxes. This benefit served to draw Jewish merchants and craftspeople here. By the nineteenth century, Jews made up 80 percent of Brody's population.

■ The former Jewish quarter was demarcated by the streets named Sholem Aleichem, Evreiskaya, and Armianskaya, and today contains destroyed houses, Jewish-style courtyards, a defunct shop with the sign "Lustiger," and other remnants of a bygone Jewish life.

■ The walls of the former seventeenth-century synagogue still stand on Szkolna Street, or Shulgas. It was one of the most beautiful in the region, comparable to that in Żołkiew. It is a fortified synagogue, its levels marked by small columns and adjacent structures on both sides.

■ The former Israelitische Realschule, located outside the central square, was a German-language school until the First World War; Joseph Roth once studied here. It is now a Ukrainian school.

■ The immense, magnificent, and nearly intact Jewish cemetery is located at the northern edge of the city, just before the forest. It is a veritable open-air museum of graves bearing carefully carved designs, lions, stags, hands, candelabras. The inscriptions

BRODY IN LITERATURE

Balzac stopped here in September 1847 on his way to meet Mme Hanska in Ukraine. He was supposed to spend a day and a night here before catching his coach, for no one worked in Brody on **Rosh Hashanah.** "The Jews of Brody, despite the millions they could earn, wouldn't leave their ceremonies behind" (Balzac, in a letter about Kiev).

Other writers have also mentioned Brody: Joseph Roth was born here in 1894 and evokes it in *The Radetzky March* (1932); Isaac Babel described the city in *Red Cavalry* (1933) and in his *1920 Diary.*

are almost always in Hebrew, but occasionally in German. No grave dates before 1941. At the edge of the cemetery, in the forest, a monument commemorates the extermination of the Jews of Brody, either executed and buried in a common grave in July 1941 or deported to Bełżec. Of the 12,000 Jews in Brody before the war, only one remains today.

[The cemetery is located at the end of the street heading north away from the city center. Open 24 hours.]

Rivne (Rovno)

On the road from Lvov to Kiev, the most important city is Rivne, formerly a Polish city called Rovno, that was over 40 percent Jewish before the war.

■ It is worth a stop to see what remains of its Jewish quarter on Zamkowa Street; the spacious Wielka (Ancient) Synagogue at the street's intersection with Skolna Street towered over the whole neighborhood (it has since been converted into a gymnasium). Beside it stands the even older Mala (Small) Synagogue, which is again active.

[Wielka Synagogue: Skolna Street 6, 26600 Rivne.]

[Mala Synagogue: Skolna Street 4, 26600 Rivne.]

■ On the road to Kiev, around two miles from Rivne, stands the impressive Sosonki memorial. It occupies the spot where, on 6 November 1941, the 17,500 inhabitants of Rovno's ghetto were executed in a single day and left to rot in a huge, circular mass grave. Until 1998, this memorial with its tall marker could be easily seen from the road; the inscription read "Sosonki" in Hebrew and Cyrillic letters. The inscription was defaced in 1998, and the monument also lost its most original feature: a line of metal characters seeming to sink into the earth. All that remains today are stelae surrounding the mass grave bearing the names of the dead in **Yiddish**.

Żółkiew (Zhovkva)

Established in 1594 by the waywode Stanislaw Żołkiewski, Żółkiew was built, like other Polish cities, according to the Renaissance notion of the "ideal city" imported from Italy by theorist Pietro Cattanneo. The city is laid out in orderly fashion around the vast *rynek* (central square), from where are visible the castle (in the seventeenth century the royal residence of the Polish king John Sobieski), the majestic Catholic cathedral, and the uniate church. Only slightly hidden from view are the Żydowska Brama gate and the town's magnificent seventeenth-century synagogue: financed by King John II Sobieski himself, it was designed by the royal architect Piotr Bebra and constructed between 1692 and 1700.

■ The Żółkiew synagogue, which escaped destruction by the Nazis despite their attempts to dynamite it, appears relatively well preserved from the outside, even if the stained-glass windows are broken and the roof damaged. The building's future looks grim, however: in ruins in the middle of the city, it is not open to the public. This Renaissance masterpiece was one of the most beautiful and largest synagogues in Poland and today is undeniably the most beautiful in all Ukraine. Its pink, painted facade, now somewhat discolored, is adorned with three gates in bas-relief delimiting three naves, while the roof is sculpted like a cathedral. Inside, only the heavy columns supporting the roof remain: the walls are bare and the floor is strewn with rubble. Though officially protected as a city landmark, since 1993 nothing has been done to preserve this magnificent yet endangered building.

Synagogue, Żółkiew.

Northern Europe

קמה בראשם שלשים ונשאים עבות מעובד ר הכונה היה בזה המאמר
לבאר מה שיש עתיד לעתיד ואז פינחס נזה בשאור הנ ומתשנ ממלכה
עשיר וקצר ובשכל זה המאמר ונבאר בשברו עליע הנשבני עד
קה שקר כלל שקר שהשתלשבהבהוגוןע ואם ט קועמות גמתתו
זל כות עולה ונפש אנוכס ונ ל בנ ומכל דיולם של וחקק תעה
מכרואף רבא נשר שריש נטוין עמה קתאהאודאימעת ואוזקף
נשבר רי קם את חות שבל לאקמה ראשי ע זני המותהעה
ונקה בראתם רקה קמן קי ישראל נשראת נשורהשאה שבשל
להה בראתם ל הן שש של שבנושים הבן שעמבהאנחשעל
אבשה שםם בחר עדתה ובארבשדבה גלז וק מתטה מקביר
ותתה נשוך שיבתוגאמ בם ובלמ שמאת מקושיך מלמני
סב מנים שלשמב שם שבתעה ותבם בק עלב מעלשב

Scandinavia

♥ DENMARK ♥ FINLAND ♥ SWEDEN ♥ NORWAY |

SCANDINAVIA HAS NOT ALWAYS BEEN DIVIDED along its current national borders. When King Christian IV (1588–1648) opened Denmark to the Jews, the country included not only southern Sweden and several cities in northern Germany (Schleswig-Holstein), where the majority of Danish Jews lived, but also a part of the Virgin Islands in the Antilles, where Danish Jews had a central role. In contrast, Jews remained excluded from Danish possessions: Norway, Iceland, the Faeroe Islands and Greenland. In 1814 Norway came under Swedish domination, becoming independent only in 1905. In 1851, after years of debate, the Storting (Denmark's Parliament) authorized Jewish immigration, which, however, remained marginal (only 200 people in 1890) until the twentieth century. Sweden authorized Jewish immigration as early as the eighteenth century in a territory that included Finland until 1809, as well as German cities such as Altona and some cities of the Baltic with a Jewish population such as Riga, Memel (Klaipèda), and Reval (Tallinn). In Iceland, the Althing (Iceland's Parliament) defeated in 1850 a law proposed by

Illustrated copy of Moses Maïmonides' A Guide for the Perplexed, *1938. Royal Library, Copenhagen.*

the king of Denmark that would have authorized Jewish immigration. The Althing reversed its position in 1855, but, despite the rapid voyage of celebrated Zionist journalist Max Nordau in 1874, no Jews settled in Iceland until the early years of the twentieth century, when the expansion of fisheries led the Jews of Copenhagen, active in maritime armament, to settle in Reykjavík. After 1933, Iceland adopted a very restrictive immigration policy regarding Jews demanding asylum. Even today there is no organized Jewish community in Iceland. The history of Scandinavian Judaism is that of communities learning to live among religious societies (Lutheranism is the state religion) that, from a linguistic or ethnic point of view, were quite homogenous. These traditional destinations for immigrants were opened to Jews only toward the end of the nineteenth century, and manifest even today strong xenophobic and populist undercurrents.

A certain ambiguity characterizes the relations between the Scandinavian countries, the nation of Israel, and the Jews. Humanism is an integral part of the Protestant message. For that reason, the attitude of the Nordic countries toward the *Shoah* was more active and humane than that in many other countries. Denmark, for example, adopted a courageous attitude toward their Nazi invaders. In 1943, just before a massive German raid and arrest of Jews was to take place, the Danish authorities succeeded in sending 5,191 Jews and close to 2,000 individuals classified as "partially" Jewish or Christian spouses of Jews to Sweden. In Finland, Himmler's request that the Finnish government deport the Jewish community there met with a categorical refusal of the government. Finally, in Norway the populace was largely resistant to its Nazi invaders, despite being governed by a puppet regime set in

place by the Nazis. Led by the Fascist Vidkun Quis-
ling, who enacted anti-Semitic legislation, 767
Jews were deported from Norway, the majority sent
to Auschwitz. Sweden, which remained neutral,
continued to maintain commercial relations with
the Reich and demonstrated a policy on asylum
that did not match the needs of the moment.

Humanism drove the Scandinavians to take a
sustained interest in the Third World and in the
Middle East, where they have always assumed
the role of mediator. It was a Swede, Count Folke
Bernadotte, who was the mediator for the United
Nations in the War of Independence; he was assassinated on 20 November 1948. The first Israeli-
Palestinian accords were signed in Oslo in 1993.
The quasi-messianic significance attached to the
creation of a Nation of Israel from the perspective of
fundamentalist Protestants drove certain groups to
involve themselves in supporting the rights of Israel.
However, aside from public demonstrations of opinion, the radical foreignness of Jews since the beginning of the century has provoked hostile reactions.
In Sweden Nazi sympathies were widespread, and
Norway opened its doors to the immigration of
Jews persecuted by Hitler only too late. Finally, the
Scandinavian tradition of freedom of expression,
closer in its conception to that of the Anglo-Saxon
model than that of the French or German, tolerates
public demonstrations of Neo-Nazism with sometimes dramatic consequences. In 1999, a Neo-Nazi
splinter group committed a series of attempted
murders in Sweden.

→ **To call Denmark from the United States, dial 011 45** followed by the number of the person you are calling.

Denmark ■

Of the approximately 8,000 Jews living in the country of Denmark, the great majority of them are **Ashkenazim** who make Copenhagen their home. In 1968, 2,500 Polish Jews fled the anti-Semitic purges led by the Communist government there and settled in the capital and in Århus.

Copenhagen

■ Copenhagen has a Grand Synagogue constructed in 1833. All information about the synagogue is available at the Mosaiske Troessamfund, which houses a variety of Jewish associations. A strictly Orthodox community prays at the Makhzikei ha-Das Synagogue.

[Grand Synagogue: Krystalgade 12,
1172 Copenhagen K.]

[Mosaiske Troessamfund:
Ny Kongensgade 6, P.O. Box 2015,
1014 Copenhagen K. ✆ 33128868.]
[Synagogue: Makhzikei ha-das,
Ole Shurs Gade 12, 1354 Copenhagen K.]
[Lubavitch Community Center:
Makhzikei ha-das, Ole Shurs Gade 12,
1354 Copenhagen K. ✆ 33161850 for
more information.]

■ The Royal Library contains the Simonsen Library, which possesses an interesting **Judaica** section. The Freedom Museum (Friheedsmuseet) contains a section devoted to the history of Nazi resistance and the *Shoah*.

[Royal Library: Christians Brygge 6,
1219 Copenhagen K.]
[Friheedsmuseet: Churchillparken,
1263 Copenhagen K. ✆ 33137714.
Open May 1–Sep 15, Mon–Sat 10 A.M.–4 P.M.,
Sun 10 A.M.–5 P.M.; Sep 16–Apr 30, Mon–Sat
11 A.M.–3 P.M., Sun 11 A.M.–4 P.M.]

Synagogue, Copenhagen.

Hornbaek

The only *glatt* **kosher** hotel in Scandinavia, the Strand Hotel is located in the well-known spa town of Hornbaek.

It operates between **Passover** and **Rosh Hashanah** and has a synagogue on the premises.

[Strand Hotel: Kystvej 12, 3100 Hornbaek. ✆ and fax 49700088. Open Mar 1–Sep 1.]

THE JEWS OF THE DANISH ANTILLES

What are today the U.S. Virgin Islands were a Danish possession from 1672 to 1916. The Danish influence remains in the architecture (notably on Saint Thomas), and in the names of places (Christiansted) and people—or in the Jewish community of the island. The synagogue of Saint Thomas, still active, was built in 1796 (reconstructed after a fire in 1833). Denmark named Jewish governors, and in 1850, half the European inhabitants there were Jewish, coming for the most part from the Dutch Antilles.

→ **To call Finland from the United States, dial 011 358** followed by the number of the person you are calling.

Finland ◼

The first Jews who settled in Finland were of Russian origin and were soldiers of the czar's army, called cantonists. With its independence in 1917, the country promptly granted civil rights to Jews. In 1939, when Finland became an ally of the Third Reich against the Soviet Union, Finnish Jews found themselves in the uneasy position of serving in an army allied with the Nazis: a prayer tent was even set up on the Russian front a stone's throw from the Germans, and the community helped Soviet Jews who were prisoners of war observe dietary requirements. After 1945, the Jewish community reconstructed itself and gave, at the time of the Israeli War for Independence in 1948, the largest number of volunteers of all the Diaspora communities. Ben Zyskowicz, the Jewish premier of Finland who was elected deputy in 1979, is one of the best-known politicians of the capital. In 1999, the government caused a lively controversy by agreeing to help support financially the maintenance of the tombs of the Finnish Waffen SS who died in the Ukraine.

The number of Jews living in Finland today is 1,500, of which 1,200 live in Helsinki, while 200 live in Turku and 50 in Tampere.

Helsinki

◼ Helsinki's synagogue was constructed in 1906 on a piece of land donated by the municipality near the market where the Jews practiced the only profession open to them: trade in used clothing. Morning prayer services following the **Ashkenazic** liturgy are offered daily.

◼ The Jewish community center, built in 1961, includes a Jewish library of 5,000 volumes, a children's playground, and a school founded in 1918. One can view a **Sepher Torah** made of copper from the first

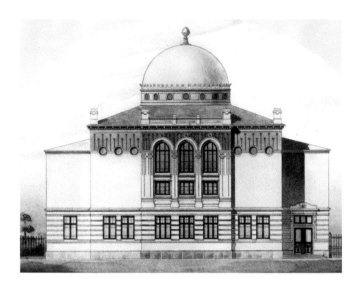

Synagogue, Helsinki.

synagogue in the city constructed of wood in 1840. The center is also home to the Hazamir Choir (founded in 1917), which has given concerts at the Finnish Cultural Center in Paris, the bi-monthly magazine *Ha-Kehila,* and all the Jewish organizations in Finland.

[Synagogue and Community Center: Malminkatu 26, 00100 Helsinki. ✆ 958603121.]

■ The **kosher** store Avi's Deli (Avi Hovav) is adjacent to the community center. **Kosher** meals can be ordered at the center.

[Avi Hovav: ✆ 96854548.]

SWEDEN

→ **To call Sweden from the United States, dial 011 46** followed by the number of the person you are calling minus the initial 0 (used only for domestic calls).

Sweden

Sweden's Jewish community is the most important one in Scandinavia, as much in terms of the number of practicing faithful (18,000–20,000) as culturally. In February 2000, the Swedish capital hosted the International Conference on the *Shoah*, dedicated to drawing attention to the process of the restitution process of Jewish stolen goods and to the teaching of the genocide.

Stockholm

■ Established in 1775, the Jewish community of Stockholm numbers 5,200 members. Its community center is situated near Raoul Wallenberg Square. The square was named after the Swedish diplomat who, after saving a number of Hungarian Jews, was arrested and then most likely assassinated by the Soviets. A sculpture by Willy Gordon representing a Jew fleeing with a **Sepher Torah** stands in front of the building.

[Community Center: Nybrogatan 19, 10242 Stockholm. ✆ 0858785800.
🚇 Östermalmstorg.]

■ In the same building as the community center, there is a **kosher** deli, Kosherian & Co., a cafeteria, and a restaurant.

[Shop: ✆ 086636580.
Open Mon–Fri 9 A.M.–6 P.M.; light meals available throughout the day.]

■ The Jewish Museum was founded in 1987 by a patron of the arts named Aron Neuman. It consists of three rooms and houses, with, in one area, a collection of cultural objects (including an important collection of **Judaica**), and in another area, temporary exhibitions dedicated mostly to works of Scandinavian Jewish artists.

[Jewish Museum: Hälsingegatan 2, 10234 Stockholm. ✆ 083100143.
Open Apr–Sep, Wed–Fri and Sun noon–4 P.M.,

Tue noon–8 P.M.; Oct–Mar, Tue–Fri and Sun noon–2 P.M.; 🚇 Odenplan.]

■ The most interesting feature of the community center's library is its excellent collection of the community's publication *Judisk Kronika* and the volumes on the history of Sweden's Jewish community.

[Library: Wahrendorffsgatan 3, 11147 Stockholm. ℘ 0858785835. Open Mon–Thu. 1 P.M.–5 P.M. 🚇 Kungsträdgarden or Östrmalmstorg.]

■ There are three synagogues in Stockholm. Built in an oriental style and completed in 1870, the Grand Synagogue in the city center follows the Liberal liturgy and can hold 1,000 worshippers. The Orthodox synagogue Adat Yeshurun contains furnishings that came from a synagogue in Hamburg vandalized during Kristallnacht. The other Orthodox synagogue, the Polish-rite Adat Yisrael, is situated in the Södermalm quarter in a seventeenth-century building.

[Grand Synagogue: Wahrendorffsgatan 3a, 11147 Stockholm. ℘ 0858785800. Open Jun–mid-Sep. Free guided tours every day at 10 A.M. and 2 P.M. Call for winter times. 🚇 Kungsträdgarden or Östermalmstorg.]

[Synagogue Adat Yeshurun: Riddargatan 5, 11435 Stockholm. ℘ 086119161. Services on Fri at 6:30 P.M. and Sat at 9:15 A.M. Visits by appointment at other times. 🚇 Östermalmstorg.]

[Synagogue Adat Yisrael: St Paulsgatan 13, 11846 Stockholm. ℘ 086441995. Services on Fri at 6:30 P.M. and Sat at 9:15 A.M. Visits by appointment at other times. 🚇 Mariatorget.]

■ In the cultural arena, the Swedish community has its own FM radio station, Radio Shalom.

[Radio Shalom (95.3 MHz): Box 7427, 10391 Stockholm. ℘ 086117979.]

Uppsala

The large university city of Uppsala does not have a Jewish community but it does have a Jewish student club.

[Jewish Students' Club: Dalgatan 15, 75105 Uppsala. ✆ 8125453.
❶ sjp_up@hotmail.com.]

Synagogue, Malmö.

Malmö

Danish Jews evacuated during the Nazi occupation arrived by boat in Malmö thanks to Count Folke Bernadotte. Some Jews died after their arrival and are buried in the city cemetery, where a monument honors their memory.

■ A Jewish community (originally made up of German Jews) was established in this city on the Baltic coast facing Copenhagen in 1871, shortly after the emancipation. It now numbers 1,200 members. Its community

center, partially financed from German reparations, was built in 1962. An Orthodox synagogue continues to function on the Föreningsgatan at the corner of the Betaniaplan. Built in 1903 in an eastern style, the synagogue is crowned by an onion dome reminiscent of Orthodox churches.

[Community Center: P.O. Box 4198, Kamrergatan 11, 20313 Malmö. ✆ 406118460 or 6118860, fax 40234469. Kosher meals can be served here.]
[Synagogue: Betaniaplan, Föreningsgatan, 20313 Malmö.]

■ Malmö's Jewish community carries out its activities in two suburban centers: the community center in Lund, which houses the Institute for Jewish Culture, is used only for holidays, while Helsingborg's community center is always open. The Jewish community centers of Landskrona and Kristianstad, on the other hand, have been closed since the early 1990s. The interior decorations and furniture of Kristianstad's synagogue are now being used by a Scandinavian community living in Raanana, Israel.

[Community Center and Institute for Jewish Culture: contact by e-mail only: ❶ ijk@ijk-s.se.]
[Helsingborg Community Center: Springpostgränden 4, 25112 Helsingborg.]

Göteborg

Jews have lived in Göteborg since 1782. The Conservative *(masorti)* rite synagogue is located at the same address as the community center. There is also an Orthodox minyan in Göteborg.

[Community Center: Östra Larmgatan 12, 41107 Göteborg. ✆ 31177245.]
[Minyan: Storgatan 5, 41107 Göteborg.]

NORWAY

→ **To call Norway from the United States, dial 011 47** followed by the number of the person you are calling.

Norway ■

Visitors walking on the street named after Norway's national poet Henrik Wergeland (1808–45) will be reminded that it was Wergeland who was behind the law that allowed Jews to immigrate to this country. Most of Norway's Jews live in Oslo (950 people), with about 100 living in Trondheim. The Norwegian community can pride itself on having given Israel a minister: the great rabbi Michael Melchior, who became a deputy in 1999 and later a member of the Barak government in charge of relations with Diaspora Jews. Although strictly Orthodox, Rabbi Melchior (son of the former grand rabbi of Denmark, Bent Melchior) belongs to the center-left party Meimad.

Oslo

■ Oslo's Jewish community centers around the Mosaiske Trossamfund. This Orthodox **Ashkenazic** synagogue offers daily services.

[Mosaiske Trossamfund and Synagogue: Bergstien 15, 0172 Oslo. P.O. Box 2722, 0131 Oslo. ✆ 22696570, fax 22466604. Open Mon–Thu 9 A.M.–4 P.M. Synagogue open by appointment only.
[Community Center: P.O. Box 2722, St. Hanshaugen, 0131 Oslo. ✆ 22696570. Visits by appointment.]

■ There is a **kosher** store, Colonial, at the corner of the Bergstien and Waldemar Thranes streets. Because Norway forbids ritual slaughter, **kosher** meat is imported from Canada.

[Colonial: ✆ 22609166.]

■ A monument to the Jewish victims of the *Shoah* is located in the Ostre Gravlund cemetery.

[Ostre Gravlund Cemetery: Tvetenveien 7, 0172 Oslo.]

Trondheim

Synagogue, Trondheim.

■ Trondheim's synagogue is doubly unusual: it is the northernmost synagogue in the world and the only one that, for a time, served as a train station! The Jewish community in Trondheim has never really recovered from the mass deportation of its members in March 1942. The city's Jews were arrested by the Norwegian police and were detained at the Falstad camp, near Trondheim.

[Synagogue: Ark. Christiesgatan 1, 7001 Trondheim.]

AR · ARAMAIC; GER.: GERMAN;
H.: HEBREW; L.: LATIN; Y.: YIDDISH

aliyah (H., pl. **aliyahs**), "ascent."
This term has two primary meanings: 1. The immigration of Diaspora Jews to the land of Israel, or 2. Being called to pronounce the blessing before and after the reading of the **Torah** during religious services.

aron (H., pl. *aronot*), "Ark."
The Ark of the Law. An enclosed structure in the wall of the synagogue that protects the **Sepher Torah** (the scroll of the Law). Also called the *aron kodesh* (holy ark) or *heikhal* (shrine).

Ashkenazi (H., pl. **Ashkenazim**)
(adj. **Ashkenazic**)
In Genesis 10:1–3, this term designates the great-grandson of Noah and the territory of an ethnic group. The term was adopted in the Middle Ages by rabbis to designate the Jews of northern France and the Holy Roman Empire. By extension, Ashkenaz designates a civilization characterized by particular customs, religious practices, juridical standards, and social institutions. The Ashkenazim are Jews originally from Western, Central, and Eastern Europe, as distinguished from the **Sephardim**, Mediterranean communities, especially those in Spain and Portugal before the expulsion of 1492.

beth hamidrash (H.), "house of study."
The house of prayer and study often connected to the synagogue itself.

bimah (H., pl. *bimot*), "platform."
See also **tevah**.
Elevated platform bearing a lectern from which the **Torah** is read and prayers recited. The platform where the reading takes place sometimes has an overhead structure supported by four pillars.

cantor (L.).
The cantor, or Hazan, who leads the prayer service at the synagogue.

cholent (Y., from Old French for "warm spring").
A **Shabbat** dish of potatoes, meat, groats, or barley, beans, and other legumes prepared the day before and kept warm in the oven from Friday afternoon until the afternoon meal of **Shabbat**.

Haggadah (H., pl. **Haggadoth**), "narrative."
Narrative read during the Seder meal at **Passover** that relates the story of Jewish enslavement and escape from Egypt.

Hanukkah (H.), "dedication."
The festival of lights, it commemorates the victory of the Maccabeans

over Antiochus IV, Epiphanes. According to the Talmudic tradition, after the battle there remained nothing in the Sanctuary for celebrating the service except a vial of oil consecrated for illuminating the **menorah**. Miraculously, the **menorah** burned for eight days instead of one. Hanukah is thus celebrated for eight days beginning on the twenty-fifth of Kislev (November–December).

Haskalah (H.), "intelligence, discernment."

Jewish Enlightenment movement related to the emancipation of the Jews beginning around the end of the eighteenth century. Essentially, **Haskalah** is an expression of the more open attitude towards secular values and lifestyles of Jews in relation to the surrounding society.

Hasid (H., pl. **hasidim**, adj. **hasidic**), "pious."

Designates a pious Jew and a member of a **Hasidic** movement.

Hasidism

Movement of mystical Jewish piety that emphasizes the joy and the fervor of prayer over Talmudic erudition. It was founded around 1740 in Podolia by Rabbi Israel ben Eliezer, called Baal Shem Tov. It eventually spread throughout Central and eastern Europe.

heder (H., pl. **hadarim**), "room."

Jewish elementary school for boys ages 5–13. The schoolmaster *(melamed)* teaches reading, writing, and interpretation of the primary sacred texts (Bible, prayers, the commentaries of Rashi and the Mishnah). The **hadarim** were widespread among Eastern European Jewish communities until the Second World War. They continue to thrive in ultra-Orthodox communities.

herem (H.), "excommunication."

Punishment imposed by a court of rabbinical justice on those who seriously violate the commandments or who fail to conform to the decrees of the Jewish religious authorities.

Judaica.

All things (books, ritual and religious objects) having to do with the practice and traditions of Judaism.

Judezmo. See **Ladino.**

kabbalah (H., pl. kabbalists), "tradition."

Term designating the esoteric and theosophical doctrines of Judaism and Jewish mysticism, notably as they developed from the twelfth and thirteenth centuries in the Zohar.

kaddish (Ar., pl. **kaddishim**), "saint." Prayer in Aramaic language that one recites at the end of important passages of the service and at the occasion of a funeral. It is also recited by orphans who thus express their trust and submission to divine will.

ketubah (H., pl. **ketuboth**) "legal writ."

Jewish marriage contract outlining spousal obligations. Ancient illuminated **ketubah** reflect the art of the countries in which they were created. The decorative elements— swags of drapery, architectural frames, flora and fauna—are often the same as those of other sacred works.

kiddush (H.), "sanctification."

A prayer recited during the **Shabbat** and feast days, and usually accompanied by a wine toast that serves to sanctify the holy day.

klezmer (H., pl. **klezmorim**), "musical instrument."

By extension this term designates a style of music and the musicians who play it in the **Ashkenazic** tradition. This musical genre spread throughout Eastern Europe from celebration to celebration, particularly at marriage feasts. It draws inspiration as much from secular songs and popular dances as from prayers and *nigunim* (melodies through which the Hasidim attempted to approach God in a sort of mystical ecstasy). As a result of its Slavic, Gypsy, Greek, and Ottoman influences, and the later influence of jazz, **klezmer** music is highly diverse.

kohen (H., pl. **kohanim**).

Priest in charge of service in the Temple of Jerusalem whose primary function was to lead religious ceremonies. The **Kohanim** constitute a distinct class dedicated to holy service. They are subject to specific purity laws.

kosher (H.), "fit to eat."

Designates foods that conform to Biblical and Talmudic law. Determination depends on strict adherence to the Jewish food laws.

Ladino, *Judezmo* (Judeo-Spanish).

Ladino is the written language of Biblical translations. *Judezmo* is the vernacular language, both written and spoken, used by **Sephardic** Jews in Spain, Portugal, Turkey, the Balkans, and the Maghreb. Also called Judeo-Spanish, it derives from Castilian Spanish with borrowed Hebrew or Talmudic words and expressions, as well as terms from Arabic, Turkish, and Greek.

Levites.

Tribe of the descendants of Aaron, its High Priest. The priests (**kohanim**) constituted a subcategory of the **Levites** in charge of maintaining the Sanctuary and later the Temple of Jerusalem.

matzoh (H., pl. **matzoth**). "unleavened bread."

Bread made without yeast or other leavening agents *(hamets)*. Matzohs, symbolizing the time of slavery in Egypt, are ritually consumed during **Passover**. The **Haggadah** declares, "this is the bread of misery that our fathers ate in Egypt." Matzoh simultaneously recalls servitude and deliverance.

mehizah (H., pl. *mehizoth*), "separation."

A partition of wood, metal, or fabric separating the men's space from the women's area in a synagogue.

menorah (H., pl. *menorot*). "lamp, candelabrum."

Candelabra, most often with seven branches that became the principal symbol of the exile and salvation of the Jews. With the passage of the centuries the **menorah** has become the central motif in Jewish consciousness. The symbol can be seen on the floors, walls, lintels, interiors, and ceiling beams of synagogues and on grave monuments. It was chosen as the national symbol of modern Israel.

mezuzah (H., pl. **mezuzoth**), "door jamb."

The **mezuzah** is a small roll of parchment containing biblical passages traditionally attached to the door jamb of a Jewish home as protection.

Midrash (H., pl. **Midrashim**). *See* **beth hamidrash.**

mikvah (H., pl. *mikva'ot*), "pool of water."

Ritual purification bath. The fundamental ritual of Jewish communal life. In Judaism, physical and spiritual purity are intrinsically linked.

minyan (H., pl. **minyanim**) "number."

Quorum of ten adult Jewish men needed for prayer. Since the synagogue has no value in and of itself, a **minyan** can officiate in any place. This institution testifies to the importance of community in Judaism.

Mitnagged (H., pl. **Mitnaggedim**), "opposition."

Those opposed to **Hasidism** and the spiritual direction taken by the Baal Shem Tov's movement. This term designates, above all, a way of life and study belonging to Lithuanian-Belarussian Orthodox communities centered around the Gaon of Vilna.

parnas (H., pl. **parnassim**), "leader, administrator."

Title given to the leaders and administrators of communities and synagogues.

Passover (H., Pesah), "to pass over."

Springtime festival, celebrated over eight days in the Diaspora and seven in the Holy Land, commemorates the Exodus and the end of slavery in Egypt. Leavened foods are prohibited during the period and, before it starts, homes are given a thorough cleaning.

Purim (H.), "lots."

Holiday commemorating the salvation of the Jews of the Persian Empire who escaped the threat of King Assuerus and his grand vizier Haman. Celebrated around March–April, **Purim** is a sort of Jewish carnival. It is marked by readings from the Book of Esther in the synagogue and festivities such as presentations of so-called *Purimshpiln,* plays or parodies associated with **Purim.**

rimmonim (H.), "pomegranates."

Designates the decorative metal flower motifs ornamenting the sleeves or the wooden supports (*atse hayyim,* "trees of life") of the scrolls of the **Torah.**

Rosh Hashanah (H.), "head (beginning) of the year."

Jewish New Year. Today, in Diaspora countries as in Israel, this feast is celebrated the first and second days of Tishri (September). This solemn feast marks the beginning of the ten days of penitence whose culmination is **Yom Kippur** (the day of forgiveness).

Sepher Torah (H., pl. **Siphrei Torah**) "Scroll of the Law."

A manuscript copy on parchment of the five books of the *Penta-*

teuch, preserved in the Holy Ark in the synagogue. The **Sepher Torah** is removed from its location during services for the reading of the Law.

Sephardi (H., pl. **Sephardim,** adj. **Sephardic**).

Jews who lived in Spain and Portugal before the expulsion of 1492 and their descendants. The name came to include the Jews of North Africa and the Middle East and was used to differentiate them from the **Ashkenazim,** mainly Eastern European Jews and their descendants.

Shabbat (H., pl. **Shabbatim**), "day of rest."

Seventh day of the week (from Friday night to Saturday night). The **Shabbat** is a basic element of Judaism that corresponds to the culmination of the creation of the world as told in the Bible. It is a day of rest for the entire household, a testimony to the Covenant between God and his people. In practice it translates into a formal prohibition of performing any work on this day.

shofar (H., pl. **shofroth**), "ram's horn."

A musical instrument made from a ram's horn that one blows on feast days dedicated to penitence, repentance, and forgiveness (e.g., **Rosh Hashanah, Yom Kippur**).

schnorrer (Y., *schnorer*), "beggar."

Wandering beggar or vagabond, all Jewish communities had at least one **schnorrer,** who was considered a marginal member of the community.

shul (Y., from Latin *scola*), "school."

Designates the synagogue in the **Ashkenazic** world. The **shul** was the center of both religious life

(i.e. study and prayer) and the community. It is the meeting place of the community *(kahal)* and the rabbinic tribunal *(beth din)*.

shtetl (Y., pl. **shtetlach**), "Jewish townlet."

Jewish village or town that typified the traditional Jewish life in Central and Eastern Europe before the Second World War.

sukkah (H., pl. **sukkoth**), "tabernacle, tent."

Sukkoth, or the Feast of Tabernacles, commemorates the forty years that the Jews spent wandering in the desert and living without permanent shelter. During this festival, all meals are eaten in the **sukkah,** a tent or hut constructed for this religious celebration.

tallit (H., pl. **tallitim**), "cover."

Rectangular shawl with fringes *(tsitsit)* worn for morning prayers. The garment is often called *tallit gadol* (large **tallit**), as opposed to the *tallit katan* (small **tallit**), which is regularly worn during daytime hours under the clothes.

Talmud (Ar., from the roots LMD, adj. Talmudic), "teaching."

Oral codification of the Law *(Torah she-be-al pe)* preserved in the Talmud of Babylon *(Bavli)* and the Talmud of Jerusalem *(Yerushalmi)*. Made up of opinions, discussions, and decisions of the masters of the Law accumulated during seven centuries (200 B.C.E.–500 C.E.). It includes the Mishnah (from the Hebrew root meaning "to repeat") its commentaries and explanations, and the Gemarah (from the Aramaic *gemar,* "what one learns from tradition"). The **Talmud** is made up of essentially two parts, the legislative Halakah and the narrative **Haggadah,** which includes stories and homiletic interpretations.

tashlik (H.), "you will throw."

Ceremony performed the first afternoon of **Rosh Hashanah.** One goes to the edge of a stream and, while reciting prayers, casts bread crumbs taken from one's pockets. This ritual symbolizes the casting away of sins through repentance.

tevah (H., pl. *tevot*), "chest."

This term has two meanings: 1. Elevated platform bearing a lectern from which the **Torah** is read and prayers recited, or 2. Chest or armoire containing the Tablets of the Law.

Torah (H.), "teaching, law."

The **Torah** is the codification of Jewish Law written by God's prophet, Moses. By extension, it designates the complete written Bible, the Jewish canon of twenty-four holy books.

tsaddik (H., pl. **tsaddikim**), "just."

Referring to an exceptionally pious and faithful man, the term also designates a rebbe (rabbi) or leader of a group or of a **Hasidic** community. It is generally applied to those who imitate God by incarnating the ideal of moral religious practice.

yeshiva (Ar. and H., pl. *yeshivoth*), "made to be seated."

Talmudic academy, the **yeshiva** is the institution of higher learning dedicated to the discussion and interpretation of the **Torah** and the **Talmud.**

Yiddish.

Vernacular language of mainly Eastern European Jews, or **Ashkenazim.** Developing in the Jewish communities of the Rhine valley in the Middle Ages, **Yiddish** derives from Middle High German and was diffused in Eastern Europe and spread throughout the **Ashkenazic** world during approximately 1,000 years. At the dawn of the Second World War, there were several million **Yiddish**-speaking Jews in Europe, the United States, and in South America. The *Shoah* marked a brutal end to **Yiddish** life and culture in Europe. **Yiddish** continues to be spoken above all in the ultra-Orthodox communities **(Hasidim)** in the United States and Israel.

Yom Kippur (H.), "day of forgiveness."

Also called the Great Forgiveness, this is the most solemn and holy day of the Jewish calendar. Fixed on the tenth day of Tishri (September), it constitutes the culmination of the ten days of penitence beginning with **Rosh Hashanah.** A strict fast is observed for twenty-five hours, from sunset on the first day until the following dusk.

Northwestern Europe

1. Nahum Goldmann, Translated from the French *Autobiographie: une vie au service d'une cause* (Paris: Fayard, 1971). See also *The Autobiography of Nahum Goldmann: Sixty Years of Jewish Life.* Trans. Helen Sebba (New York: Rinehart and Winston, 1969).

Southwest Europe

2. Attilio Milano, *Storia degli Ebrei in Italia* (Turin: Einaudi, 1992).

3. Cecil Roth, *The History of the Jews of Italy* (Philadelphia: The Jewish Publication Society of America, 1946).

4. Annie Sacerdoti and Luca Fiorentino, *Guida all'Italia Ebraica* (Casale Monferrato: Marietti, 1986).

5. Ibid.

Central Europe

6. Bertandon de La Brocquière in G. Komoroczi, ed., *Jewish Budapest* (Budapest: Central European University Press, 1999).

7. Hungarian for "soldier."

8. Many Jewish families lived in this district until the Second World War.

9. "He's still moving."

10. Isaac Bashevis Singer, *In My Father's Court* (New York: Farrar, Straus, and Giroux, 1966).

11. Foundation: ulica Jelink 48, 01-646 Varsovie. Telephone: 0228330021.

Southeast Europe

12. Arthur Koestler, *The Thirteenth Tribe: The Khazar Empire and Its Heritage* (London: Hutchinson, 1976).

13. Curzio Malaparte, *Kaputt* (New York: E. P. Dutton & Co., 1946).

14. Vicki Tamir, *Bulgaria and Her Jews: The History of a Dubious Symbiosis* (New York: Sepher-Hermon Press, 1979).

15. Esther Benbassa and Aron Rodrigue, *The Jews of the Balkans: the Judeo-Spanish Community, 15th to 20th centuries* (Oxford: Blackwell, 1995).

16. Stanford J. Shaw, *The Jews of the Ottoman Empire and the Turkish Republic* (New York: New York University Press, 1991).

17. Benbassa and Rodrigue, *The Jews of the Balkans.*

18. Ilan Karmi, *Jewish Sites of Istanbul: A Guide Book* (Istanbul: Isis Press, 1992).

19. Marie-Christine Varol, *Balat, faubourg juif d'Istanbul* (Istabul: Isis Editions, 1993).

20. Karmi, *Jewish Sites of Istanbul: A Guide Book.*

21. Joseph Nehama, *Histoire des Israélites de Salonique* (Thessaloníki: Librairie Molho, vols. 1 and 2: 1935; vols. 3 and 4: 1936; vol. 5: 1959; vols. 6 and 7: 1978).

22. George Mavrogordatos, *Stillborn Republic: Social Coalitions and Party Strategies in Greece, 1922–1936* (Berkeley: University of California Press, 1983).

Eastern Europe

23. John Klier, *Russia Gathers Her Jews: The Origins of the "Jewish Question" in Russia* (1772–1825) (Dekalb, Il.: Northern Illinois University Press, 1986).

24. S. Romaniok, *Iz istorii moskovskikh pereulkov,* 1988, cited by M. and N. Chatine, "Stroenie pod literoï A," in *Vestnik evreiskogo universiteta v Moskve,* 2 (6) (Moscow: 1994).

25. Cf. Mikhael Beiser, *Evreï Leningrada* (Moscow-Jerusalem: Gesharim, 1999).

Contents by City

Southwest Europe   147

Farabola: 350; A. Jemolo: 216, 217, 225, 236, 338; L. de Selva: 298, 299. – Magnum/E. Lessing: 261, 444. – J. Manuel/ICEP, Lisbon: 195. – Mary Evans Picture Library: 58. – Musée d'art et d'histoire du judaïsme, Paris: N. Feuillie: 80–81, 134, 426; M. Goldman: 19, 63, 84, 414, 419, 434, 496; M. Laserson: 594. – Jewish Museum of Greece, Athens: 467, 478, 480. – W. Neumeister, Munich: 95, 339. – Z. Radovan, Jerusalem: 289, 377, 457, 499. – RMN: J. G. Berizzi: 25, 74, 77, 79, 90, 150, 163, 190, 200, 205, 295, 553. – G. Blot: 86. – R. G. Ojeda: 22. – M. Sagnol: 371, 375, 410, 513, 561, 577. – J. St. Leger/The Irish Times: 68. – Scala: 215, 219, 223. – Sipa: Nordfoto: 584; Pitamitz: 302; Scanpix Sweden: 591. – V. Terebenin: 549. – Thévennart: 28, 30. – Timepix: 96. – J. Vasseur: 23, 27. – World Monument Fund: 490. – Wostok Press: 539; D. Chouquet: 383, 387, 392, 394; S. Levigoureux: 558, 560; Osztapovics: 292; P. Zupnik: 344. – Zapa/R. Zeboulon: 54, 55.

ILLUSTRATIONS COLLECTED BY KHADIGA AGLAN AND FRÉDÉRIC MAZUY

Acknowledgments

To Jean Baumgarten, Garance Giraud, Florence Illouz,
and the Fondation du Judaïsme Français.

To Jacques Binsztok and Bulle Helardot for throwing
themselves so enthusiastically into this editorial adventure.

And to everyone who helped make this guide possible.

Originally published in France by Éditions du Seuil / Fondation Jacques et Jacqueline Lévy-Willard in 2002 under the title *Le Guide culturel des Juifs d'Europe*.

Copyright © 2002 by Éditions du Seuil / Fondation Jacques et Jacqueline Lévy-Willard.

Original ISBN: 2-02-035971-5

English translation copyright © 2004 by Éditions du Seuil / Fondation Jacques et Jacqueline Lévy-Willard.

Library of Congress Cataloging-in-Publication Data:

Guide culturel des juifs d'Europe. English. The cultural guide to Jewish Europe.

p. cm.

English translation by Peter DeDomenico, Noël Schiller, and Charles Penwarden—CIP t.p.

Originally published in 2002 in France by Éditions du Seuil and Fondation Jacques et Jaqueline Lévy-Willard under the title: *Le Guide culturel des Juifs d'Europe*.

ISBN 2-02-061211-9

1. Jews—Europe—History—Guidebooks. 2.Judaism Europe History—Guidebooks.
3. Europe—Guidebooks.
I. Fondation Jacques et Jacqueline Lévy-Willard. II. Title.

DS135.E8G8513 2004

940'.04924—dc21

Book Design by Valérie Gautier
English cover design by Flux, SF
Type design by Janis Reed
Manufactured in France

Distributed in Canada by Raincoast Books
9050 Shaughnessy Street,
Vancouver, British Columbia V6P 6E5

10 9 8 7 6 5 4 3 2 1

Chronicle Books LLC
85 Second Street,
San Francisco, California 94105

www.chroniclebooks.com

Achevé d'imprimer en france
par MAME Imprimeurs à Tours (03102119)